Sebastian Bach Smith

Elements of Ecclesiastical Law

Sebastian Bach Smith

Elements of Ecclesiastical Law

ISBN/EAN: 9783741194672

Manufactured in Europe, USA, Canada, Australia, Japa

Cover: Foto ©Lupo / pixelio.de

Manufactured and distributed by brebook publishing software (www.brebook.com)

Sebastian Bach Smith

Elements of Ecclesiastical Law

ELEMENTS
— OF —
ECCLESIASTICAL LAW.

COMPILED WITH REFERENCE TO

THE "CONST. APOSTOLICAE SEDIS" OF POPE PIUS IX., THE COUNCIL OF THE VATICAN, AND THE LATEST DECISIONS OF THE ROMAN CONGREGATIONS.

ADAPTED ESPECIALLY TO THE DISCIPLINE OF THE CHURCH IN THE UNITED STATES, ACCORDING TO THE RECENT INSTRUCTION "CUM MAGNOPERE," AND THE THIRD PLENARY COUNCIL OF BALTIMORE.

BY

REV. S. B. SMITH, D.D.,

FORMERLY PROFESSOR OF CANON LAW, AUTHOR OF " NOTES ON THE SECOND PLENARY COUNCIL OF BALTIMORE;" OF " COUNTER-POINTS IN CANON LAW ; " " THE NEW PROCEDURE IN CRIMINAL AND DISCIPLINARY CAUSES OF ECCLESIASTICS," ETC., ETC.

VOL. III.
ECCLESIASTICAL PUNISHMENTS.

THIRD EDITION.

NEW YORK, CINCINNATI, AND CHICAGO :
BENZIGER BROTHERS,
PRINTERS TO THE HOLY APOSTOLIC SEE.

Nihil Obstat.

H. GABRIELS, S.T.D.,
Censor Deputatus.

Imprimatur,

✠ MICHAEL AUGUSTINUS,

Archiepiscopus Neo-Eboracensis.

DATUM NEO-EBORACI,
DIE 12 APRILIS, 1888.

PREFACE.

After fifteen years of ceaseless toil and unwearied study, we have at last finished these *Elements of Ecclesiastical Law*. The first volume was published in 1877; the second in 1882; the third and last is now given to the public.

This third volume deals with a subject which grates harshly on the ear of the reader. Punishments are never agreeable, either to the superior imposing, or to the subject receiving them. Yet they are coëval with fallen man, and will exist as long as man. Hence the necessity of a full and clear knowledge of them. By this knowledge, the superior will be enabled to impose them wisely, justly, moderately; the inferior, to safeguard and protect the rights given him by the law of the Church.

The law of the Church has determined the various kinds of punishments which can be inflicted. They are of two kinds: preventive and repressive. The latter are subdivided into punitive and reformative. The chief repressive punitive remedies are: Penal transfers, removals from office, disqualifications for offices and orders, and infamy. The principal repressive reformative penalties are: Suspensions, excommunications, and interdicts.

The law of the Church has also defined (*a*), what actions are punishable; (*b*), what specific penalty is annexed to a punishable action; (*c*), how the superior proceeds in imposing the remedy; (*d*), how the inferior can protect himself against unmerited punishment.

All these points are fully and accurately explained in the present volume. They are treated with special reference to our own times, and to this country, to England, Ireland, and to other English-speaking countries. Hence we have taken into full account the latest Instruction of the S. C. de Prop. Fide, *Cum Magnopere*, issued in 1884, and the *Third Plenary Council of Baltimore*. For the same reason, we explain the law as it is *now*, not as it existed *formerly*.

We have spared no pains to make the book perfectly accurate and reliable. Consequently we have taken nearly all our quotations from the originals, not at second hand.

We avail ourselves of this occasion to express our heartfelt gratitude for the kind, indulgent, and generous patronage bestowed upon our works by the clergy of this and other English-speaking countries.

PATERSON,
Feast of St. Monica,
May 4, 1888.

PREFACE TO THE SECOND EDITION.

The present volume, like the first and second, met with a welcome reception. The *Dublin Review* and other foremost journals bestowed upon it the most flattering encomiums. The present edition has been greatly improved. A large number of printers' typographical mistakes have been corrected. Many other changes have been made. Some of them are intended to make expressions which were somewhat obscure clear and unmistakable. Others affect the matter itself. In this manner we have sought to make the present edition as accurate and satisfactory as possible.

PATERSON, April 22, 1889.

BOOK III.

ECCLESIASTICAL PUNISHMENTS.

1656. We shall divide this book into four Parts: the first will treat of punishments in general; the second, of preventive or paternal remedies; the third, of repressive punishments which are called vindicatory; the fourth, of repressive punishments which are termed correctional.

PART I.

ECCLESIASTICAL PUNISHMENTS IN GENERAL.

1657. In this part we shall explain the true nature of punishments; what actions are deserving of them; their aim; by whom they can be imposed, etc.

CHAPTER I.

TRUE IDEA OF ECCLESIASTICAL PUNISHMENTS.

ART. I.

Has the Church a Right to Inflict Punishments?

1658. As we have already shown, the Church is a Sovereign State, that is, a perfect and supreme society, established by our Lord for the purpose of leading men to heaven.[1] We say, *a society;* now what is a society? Speaking in general, it is a number of persons associated together,

---

[1] Supra, vol. ii., n. 702 sq.; Tarqu., n. 4, 41.

in order to attain, by united efforts, some common end. We say, *perfect;* because she is complete of herself, and therefore has within her own bosom all the means sufficient to enable her to attain her end.[1] We say, *supreme,* because she is subject to no other society on earth. Like every society, the Church is an external organization. For she is composed of human beings, who have a body as well as a soul. She is, in fact, by the will of her divine Founder, a community, an association of men, governed by men.[2]

1659. Like every external organization, the Church must be governed by laws and regulations that will enable her to fulfil her mission and attain her end. The aim and end of the Church is the worship of God and the salvation of souls. Any action or omission, therefore, on the part of her members, which hinders her from carrying out her mission or reaching her end, and, consequently, whatever contravenes the regulations made by her concerning the worship of God and the sanctification of her children, is punishable by her. For God, having given her a mission, also gave her the means or the power to fulfil it. Hence she can establish, in fact has established, laws, and regulations, obligatory on her members. If the members violate those laws, they not only sin against God, but they offend also against the order, discipline, laws, or regulations established by the Church.

1660. That the Church can punish her members for such infractions of her laws, is evident from her very character as a society, and is, moreover, apparent from divine revelation, as we have already shown.[3] St. Paul the Apostle writes to the Corinthians: "And having in readiness to avenge all disobedience."[4] We have also seen that the Church can inflict temporal and physical as well as spiritual punishments.

[1] Tarqu., n. 6.
[2] Soglia, vol. i., p. 137.
[3] Supra, n. 705-710.
[4] II. Cor., x. 6.

ART. II.

What is a Punishment?

1661. *What then is meant by a punishment?* Speaking in general, a punishment (*pœna*) is an evil, a pain or a suffering, whether of the body or the soul, inflicted for crime.[1] When a person transgresses a law, he always does so in order to satisfy his disorderly passion, and procure for himself some unlawful enjoyment. The lawgiver punishes him for his disobedience, by depriving him of some lawful gratification, or by making him suffer some pain, either in his soul, or in his body, and thus the illicit pleasure is atoned for and expiated by the privation and suffering.[2] From this it will be seen that punishment and guilt are correlatives. There can be no punishment where there is no crime; otherwise the punishment would be unjust and barbarous.[3] "Sine culpa" says the law of the Church "non est aliquis puniendus."[4] Now there is no guilt, no crime, where there is no premeditated, intentional violation of the law. Hence there must be, not simply a material, but also a formal crime.

1662. Punishments are either secular or ecclesiastical, according as they are established by the civil or ecclesiastical power. Ecclesiastical or canonical punishments, of which alone we here speak, are the pains, sufferings, or privations, inflicted by ecclesiastical authority, in the manner prescribed by the sacred canons, upon Christians who have transgressed the laws of the Church, and have thus committed a crime, in order that the offender may be made to feel the gravity of the wrong done by him, be brought

---

[1] München, l. c., vol. ii., p. 8.   [2] Stremler, l. c., p. 3.   [3] Ib., p. 4.
[4] Reg. jur. 23. in 6⁰; Reiff., l. c., l. 5., t. 37., n. 2. Natural law itself teaches, that, as those who observe the law should be *rewarded*, so those who break it should be punished.

back to the path of duty, prevented from repeating the crime, and also that others may be deterred from following his bad example.¹ The chief object of the ecclesiastical punishments, in the strict sense, is to cause the laws of the Church to be respected and observed.² Hence canonists very properly say that canonical punishments are established for the purpose of maintaining the external order or public discipline of the Church.

ART. III.

What are Crimes?

1663. *What is meant by a crime in the canonical sense of the term?* We have just said that ecclesiastical punishments are inflicted for *crimes*, not *sins*. Let us explain the difference between the two. By a crime (*crimen, delictum*), in its legal or canonical acceptation, is not meant every sin, but only certain grave sins, to which the law of the Church has attached a punishment. Thus St. Augustine says: " Apostolus Paulus, quando elegit ordinandos ... non ait: ' Si quis sine *peccato* est' (hoc enim si diceret, omnis homo reprobaretur, nullus ordinaretur), sed ait: ' Si quis sine *crimine* est,' sicut est homicidium, adulterium ... *Crimen autem est peccatum grave, accusatione et damnatione dignissimum.*"³ St. Thomas likewise writes: " Aliud est *crimen*, et aliud *peccatum*. Peccatum dicitur quodcumque sive magnum, sive parvum, sive occultum, *crimen* autem magnum et infame."⁴

1664. A crime, therefore, is an unlawful act or omission punishable in the external forum of the Church.⁵ Now, as we have seen, the Church, in her external forum, punishes only those unlawful acts or sins, which not merely offend God, but also violate the rules, regulations, and laws en-

---

¹ Phillips, Lehrb., § 180., p. 375.   ² Cavagnis, vol. i., pp. 85, 93, 97.
³ Can. *Apost.* 1., dist. 80.   ⁴ Lect. 2. Com. Ep. ad Tim.
⁵ Pellegr., P. 4, Sect. vii., n. 1.

acted by her, and which, therefore, are not only offensive to God, but also detrimental to the public discipline of the Church.[1] A sin, on the other hand, is any action or omission, which is contrary to law, divine or natural, but which does not redound directly to the detriment of the Church.[2] Consequently a sin simply disturbs the *moral* order, while a crime also violates the *social* order, that is, the external regime or public discipline of the Church.[3] Whether there are actions that may be punished as crimes, not because they are transgressions of an ecclesiastical law and disturb the social or external order of the Church, that is, ecclesiastical discipline, but purely as sins or offences against God and as violating the moral order, we shall not here undertake to show. The Church can, it is true, treat grave sins as crimes; but even she does so only when the sin takes the form of an action which is also injurious to others, and thus dangerous to the common good of the faithful.[4]

[1] Soglia, vol. ii., p. 531.   [2] Stremler, l. c., p. 65.
[3] Cavagnis, vol. i., p. 90; Tarqu., n. 25, p. 17.   [4] München, l. c., vol. ii., p. 24.

CHAPTER II.

THE VARIOUS KINDS OF ECCLESIASTICAL PUNISHMENTS.

ART. I.

Penances.

1665. Taken in their broadest sense, ecclesiastical punishments are divided into punishments of the *forum internum* and punishments of the *forum externum*. The former are imposed in the internal forum, or in the tribunal of penance, and are called penances (*pœnitentiæ*) rather than punishments (*pœnæ*).[1] The latter are inflicted in the external or judicial tribunal of the Church. Penances are *voluntarily* received and performed, while punishments are inflicted upon those *who may be unwilling* to accept them. For a person who commits a crime can be punished therefor, whether he consents or not to the punishment.[2] Again, penances are imposed, not only for *crimes*, but also for *mere sins*, and that even though purely internal; punishments only for crimes which are external, and which violate, not merely a divine law, but also an ecclesiastical, that is, not only the moral order, but also the social or disciplinary order of the Church. In the present volume, we speak of punishments only, not of penances.

ART. II.

Punishments.

1666. The punishments of the external forum are divided (*a*) into preventive and repressive; (*b*) reforming and vin-

---
[1] Reiff., l. 5, t. 37, n. 17.
[2] Cavagnis, Insti. Jur. Publ. Eccl., vol. i, p. 99. Romæ, 1882.

Various kinds of Ecclesiastical Punishments. 13

dictatory; (c) ordinary and extraordinary; (d) *ferendæ* and *latæ sententiæ*; (e) temporal and spiritual. We shall now briefly explain each of these divisions.

§. 1. *Preventive and Repressive Punishments.*

1667. All ecclesiastical punishments are either preventive or repressive. Thus the instruction *Cum Magnopere* of the S. Congr. de Prop. Fide, speaking of canonical punishments, says: " Hæc vero remedia, alia *præventiva* sunt, alia *repressiva*." The *preventive* punishments or remedies are those which aim chiefly at *preventing* the fall of those persons who are already on the inclined plane of evil. Thus the above instruction (*ib*) says: "Illa (præventiva remedia) quidem ad præpedienda mala, scandalorum stimulos amovendos, voluntarias occasiones et causas ad delinquendum prox imas vitandas ordinantur." The chief preventive remedies are spiritual retreats, canonical warnings, and precepts. *Repressive* punishments are those which aim at bringing back the offender who has fallen into crime to the path of duty, and at wiping out the consequences of his guilt. Thus the Instruction *Cum Magnopere*, Art. II., decrees: "Hæc vero (remedia repressiva) cum in finem constituta sunt, ut delinquentes ad bonam frugem revocentur, ac culparum consectaria de medio tollantur."

§. 2. *Reforming and Vindicative Punishments.*

1668. Repressive punishments are subdivided into those which primarily have in view the good of the offender, and, therefore, aim principally at reforming him or bringing him back to the path of duty; and those which have for their chief object the common good of the faithful, and therefore aim directly at making the guilty party suffer and atone for his guilt, in order that others may be deterred from following his bad example, and that thus the social order of the

Church, that is her discipline and law, may be upheld. The first are called correctional punishments (*pœnæ medicinales, censuræ*); the second, punitive, or punishments proper and in the strict sense of the term (*pœnæ, pœnæ vindicativæ*).

1669. This distinction is also clearly indicated in the answer of the S. C. de Prop. Fide to questions of our American Bishops relative to the Instruction of July 20, 1878, on Commissions of Investigation. Here are the words of the Propaganda: "Instructio diei 20 Julii, 1878, lata est de casibus, in quibus ecclesiastica *pœna* seu *censura* sit infligenda." Here the words *pœna* and *censura* are carefully distinguished from one another. By *pœna* the Sacred Congregation means vindicatory punishments: by *censura*, correctional.

1670. In drawing the distinction between the end and aim of these two classes of punishments, we must guard against an erroneous impression. It would be a mistake to suppose, that, in inflicting punishments proper or vindicatory, the Church excludes altogether the reformation of the delinquent; or that, *vice versa*, in imposing correctional punishments, she does not aim at terrifying others from crime and maintaining respect for her laws and discipline. In all her punishments, whether medicinal or punitory, the Church always has a twofold object in view: first, to cause the offender to repent and amend; second, to deter others from crimes.

1671. In other words, she always aims both at the good of the offending individual and at the common good of the Church. All ecclesiastical punishments therefore, both punitive and correctional, have a twofold object, viz., (*a*) the amendment of the offender, (*b*) and the atonement or retribution for, and consequent repression of, the crime, and an example or warning to others.[1] The difference, then, in the aim of these two kinds of punishment is this: In correctional punishments, the amendment of the culprit is the *preponder-*

---

[1] Arg. Cap. Novit ille 13 (II. 1); Salz., vol. 4, p. 81.

Various kinds of Ecclesiastical Punishments. 15

ating motive, and the atonement for the crime the secondary; whereas in vindicative punishments the reformation of the offender is but the *secondary consideration*, and the retribution or atonement for the crime the chief and primary object.[1] This distinction between medicinal and vindicatory punishments is made by all canonists, and is of the utmost importance and must be carefully borne in mind.[2]

1672. Against this division it may perhaps be objected that the Instruction June 11, 1880, of the S. C. EE. et RR., as also the Instruction *Cum Magnopere*, issued by the S. C. de Prop. Fide, in 1884, for the United States, has modified the discipline of the Church, and made the above division untenable, at the present day at least, in those countries where the above Instructions obtain. For according to these Instructions all repressive punishments whatever, and consequently not only those which are usually termed *medicinal*, but also those which are *punitive*, appear to aim equally, nay primarily, at the reformation or correction of the offender, and only secondarily at the atonement for the crime. Thus article II. of these Instructions says: "Hæc vero (remedia repressiva) eum in finem constituta sunt, *ut delinquentes ad bonam frugem revocentur*, ac culparum consectaria de medio tollantur."

1673. We answer: We do not think the objection will hold. The article quoted from the Instruction does not appear to warrant the inference that all repressive punishments are primarily correctional. Unless we are mistaken, it means simply that all repressive punishments—whether called vindicatory or correctional—have more or less both ends in view: namely (*a*) to cause the delinquent to amend;

---

[1] Schulte, K. K., vol. 2., p. 387.
[2] See Reiff., l. 5., t. 39., n. 5; Schmalzg., l. 5, t. 37, n. 4, 5; idem, l. 5, t. 39, n. 1, 2, 5; Leuren, For. Eccl., l. 5, t. 37, q. 492, n. 4; idem, l. 5, t. 39, q. 550, n. 11; Santi, Præl., l. 5, t. 37, n. 1, 2; idem, l. 5, t. 39, n. 1; München, vol. 2, pp. 119, 176; Præl. S. Sulp. vol. 3, pp. 224, 247; Sanguineti, Inst., p. 459.

(*b*) to deter others from crime, (*c*) and thus to preserve social order, and cause the law to be observed and respected. It is true that the end of the Church is to save souls, to go after and reclaim the lost sheep. She never loses sight of this, even when she inflicts what are called vindicatory punishments. But from this it does not follow that in some of her punishments she cannot aim principally at the atonement for the crime and the maintenance of her laws.[1]

1674. Correctional punishments are inflicted upon those who are guilty of crime and are contumacious or incorrigible at the time, but of whose amendment there is yet some hope. They are to be preceded not only by a trial, but also by the canonical admonitions and the precept, as we shall see. For their chief aim is to amend the delinquent. Hence, when the superior finds that a subject has committed an offence which is deserving of a reforming or medicinal punishment, he shall first warn him; and should the canonical admonitions prove of no avail, he shall give him the precept. When even the precept fails to recall the delinquent to the path of duty, he can proceed with the trial, preparatory to inflicting censure.

1675. Vindicative punishments are imposed upon those offenders, of whose conversion scarcely any hope is left, or who are convicted of atrocious or heinous crimes, which it is necessary to punish in order to deter others from similar crimes, or to avert or to repair scandal.[2] Yet even these punishments aim also at the reformation of the offender, though only secondarily. The Church never excludes this aim altogether from any of her punishments.[3] For her mission or end is *to save souls*. Hence, when the Superior finds

---

[1] Sanguineti, Inst., p. 459, says: "Cum igitur Ecclesiæ finis sit salus animarum, etiam in pœnis materialibus, quibus plectit delinquentes, id potissimum curat, ut eorum salutem obtineat. Hinc pœnæ ecclesiasticæ, etiam materiales, sunt medicinales, saltem quoad fieri potest."

[2] Præl. S. Sulp., vol. 3, p. 224.   [3] Sanguineti, Inst., p. 459.

that one of his ecclesiastics is guilty of an offence which is deserving of a vindicative punishment—v. g., dismissal from parish or office—he will, even then, as a rule, laudably give the delinquent repeated admonitions and the precept; and only when these prove ineffectual will he proceed to the trial, preparatory to inflicting punishment.

1676. We say, *laudably;* for he is not *obliged*, as in the case of correctional punishments, to give the warnings and the precept, but may, absolutely speaking, proceed at once to a trial and, upon conviction, impose the penalty. We say also, *as a rule;* for sometimes—v. g., where the offence is very heinous and notorious—the Superior may find it necessary or opportune to dispense with the admonitions and the precept.

This whole teaching is beautifully laid down by the *Third Plenary Council of Baltimore*, n. 300, 309, to which we refer the reader.

ART. III.

Is the procedure for inflicting reformative punishments different from that for imposing vindicative? Meaning of causa criminalis and causa disciplinaris.

1677. From the division of ecclesiastical punishments into punitive and correctional, some canonists take occasion to divide ecclesiastical proceedings and causes into disciplinary (*causa disciplinaris*), and criminal (*causa criminalis*), according as the punishment to be inflicted is correctional or punitive. Here we may be allowed to digress somewhat from our subject, in order to explain these terms —*causa disciplinaris* and *causa criminalis*—especially as these two phrases occur in the titles or headings of all the recent Instructions of the Holy See which treat of ecclesiastical trials. For proof of this, see the Instruction of the Propaganda, July 20, 1878, on Commissions of Investigation; the

18 *Various kinds of Ecclesiastical Punishments.*

Instruction of the S. C. EE. et RR. of June 11, 1880; the Instruction *Cum Magnopere*, 1884. The heading of the latter *Instruction* is: "Instructio S. C. de Prop. Fide de modo servando in cognoscendis et definiendis *causis criminalibus et disciplinaribus clericorum* in Fœderatis Statibus Americæ Septentrionalis."

1678. What then is the meaning of these two phrases? According to some canonists, who divide ecclesiastical punishments into correctional and vindicatory, a *disciplinary proceeding, trial, or cause* (*causa disciplinaris*) is that where *medicinal* punishments are imposed. By medicinal remedies, they mean not merely censures, but also other remedies having the amendment of the offender in view, v. g., assignment to a religious house for a time.[1] A *criminal trial or cause* (*causa criminalis*), according to them, is one where vindicatory punishments are imposed.[2] This division of trials is based on the fact that the proceedings which take place prior to the infliction of vindicatory punishments differ, so far as the canonical warnings and the precept are concerned, from those which precede the imposing of correctional punishments. Thus, in the infliction of the latter, not only a previous trial is required, but moreover a previous canonical warning and the precept; while in the imposing of punitive remedies the trial alone is, absolutely speaking, requisite. The trial proper is the same in both cases. The difference lies in this, that for vindicatory punishments the trial is, strictly speaking, sufficient; for correctional, the previous canonical warning and the precept are necessary besides the trial.

1679. We say, *absolutely speaking*. For the authors in question observe that the line must not be too strictly drawn between *causæ disciplinares* and *causæ criminales*. In fact, they say, and justly, that all ecclesiastical punishments

---

[1] München, l. c., vol. 2, p. 7, n. 8; p. 8, n. 9.   [2] Droste, l. c., pp. 2, 3.

Various kinds of Ecclesiastical Punishments. 19

have always more or less the amendment of the delinquent in view; that, consequently, it is, as a rule, laudable, though perhaps not strictly obligatory, to give not merely the trial, but also the canonical warnings and the precept, prior to imposing even vindicatory punishments. Hence, they say, practically speaking, the proceedings by which vindicative punishments are inflicted are, in most cases, the same as those by which reformative or medicinal ones are imposed. Thus Droste, as edited by Messmer, writes: " Ecclesiastical punishments are by custom divided into corrective and vindicative... According to this, we may distinguish between disciplinary and criminal proceedings... However, the terms disciplinary punishment and strictly called punishment, as well as disciplinary and criminal procedure, are often interchanged; the more, as the boundary line between them cannot be easily drawn in practice."[1]

1680. These writers say again: " We have already remarked above (n. 3) that the division of punishments into corrective ones, whose direct object is the amendment and reformation of the delinquent, and vindicative ones, whose direct object is mainly the restoration of the disturbed order and retribution, *is in most cases rather logical than real.* For all punishments effect more or less in the offender a change for the better... From this it will be seen that a strict division of the procedure into disciplinary, *i. e.*, such as applies to corrective or reformative means, and criminal, *i. e.*, such as imposes a penalty for the committed offence, is not practicable."[2]

1681. The above explanation of *causæ criminales and causæ disciplinares* appears to be also in harmony with the following authentic declaration given by the S. C. de P. F. in answer to questions proposed by Bishops of the United States in regard to the Instruction *Quamvis* of July 20, 1878: " In-

---

[1] Droste—Messmer, p. 17.   [2] Ib , pp. 78–79.

structio diei 20 Julii 1878 lata est de casibus, in quibus ecclesiastica pœna seu censura sit infligenda, aut gravi disciplinari coercitioni sit locus."[1] Here then the Holy See declares that the trial prescribed in the Instruction *Quamvis* shall take place in all cases where (*a*) a vindicatory (pœna) or (*b*) correctional punishment (censura) is to be inflicted, or (*c*) where there is room for a grave disciplinary correction. Now the above Instruction *Quamvis*, as is expressly stated in its title, prescribed the trial or mode of procedure which had to be followed by the Bishops of the United States "in cognoscendis et definiendis *causis criminalibus et disciplinaribus clericorum.*" Consequently the Holy See would appear to mean by *causæ criminales*, causes where vindicatory punishment is to be inflicted, and by *causæ disciplinares* those where correctional or reformative measures are imposed.

1682. A second explanation of the above clauses is, that by the phrase *causæ criminales* are meant causes, proceedings, or trials where transgressions of the *moral law*, as punishable in the ecclesiastical *external* forum,—*v. g.*, drunkenness, concubinage—are punished; by the phrase *causæ disciplinares* those where an infraction of a purely disciplinary law of the Church—*v. g.*, the non-recital of the divine office—is chastised, whether the chastisement consist in a reformative or in a vindicatory punishment. Perhaps a better insight into this solution will be gained by recalling the division of the sacred canons into, (*a*) dogmatic, (*b*) moral, (*c*) and disciplinary.[2] The *dogmatic canons* relate to matters to be believed; the *moral* are those which define the rule of action in matters which are intrinsically good or bad, such as false oaths, adultery, theft. The *disciplinary canons* are those which refer directly to the external discipline of the Church, that is, to the order, rules, and regulations made by

---

[1] Our Elements, vol. ii., p. 422. *Second edition*, 1888.   [2] Supra, vol. i., n. 137.

her for her government as an external society. Such are the canons which determine the mode and time of fulfilling the divine and natural precepts, whenever this is not done by the divine or natural law itself; such are, moreover, the rules which regulate the observance of Sunday, or regard the Paschal Precept, the appointment to ecclesiastical offices, the administration of the sacraments or other acts of divine worship, the recitation of the divine office, the celibacy of the clergy, etc.

1683. Whatever may be said concerning this explanation, it should be observed here that the Church never inflicts punishments for acts which are mere sins,—*i. e.*, which offend God or the moral order, but do not at the same time redound to the detriment of her external polity; nor, *vice versa*, for acts which offend merely against her external social order, but do not in any sense contravene the moral order or law.

1684. A third opinion is that *causæ disciplinares* mean causes and proceedings where a *preventive* remedy is imposed; *causæ criminales* those where repressive punishments, vindicatory or correctional, are inflicted. Finally, a fourth opinion holds that by *causæ disciplinares* are understood causes and proceedings where the violation of the precept is punished; by *causæ criminales* those where *reatus communes* and the *violatio legum ecclesiæ* are chastised.[1] See our *New Procedure*, n. 29, 30.

Art. IV.

Ordinary and Extraordinary or Discretionary Punishments.

1685. Sometimes the law itself, that is, the Sacred Canons or lawful custom, determine the specific punishment for a certain crime. Thus the *can. Si quis suadente diabolo*, 29,

---

[1] Cf. Instr. *Cum Magnopere*, art. x.

Cans. 17, Q. 4, enacts, that, if any person maliciously maltreats an ecclesiastic, he shall incur excommunication. Here is a penal law having a determinate punishment or sanction annexed to its violation. Punishments of this kind are called ordinary (*pœna ordinaria*).[1]

1686. At other times the law or custom enacts, indeed, that a certain action or offence is punishable, and therefore it has a penal sanction annexed, though only a general one; yet it does not determine what particular punishment is to be inflicted, but, either implicitly or explicitly, leaves the ecclesiastical judge free to inflict that punishment which he may deem proper and just, considering the quality of the crime and the circumstances of the case. These punishments are named discretionary (*pœnæ arbitrariæ, pœnæ extraordinariæ*). It should be observed, however, that in inflicting extraordinary or discretionary punishments the judge cannot proceed from *arbitrary motives*, but must be guided by right reason. His will must be the will of *a good man* (*boni viri arbitrium*) and not of a despot.[2] In other words, he is obliged to impose such punishments as will seem equitable and just in the estimation of good and prudent persons, considering the quality of the crime and the circumstances of the case.

1687. However, while in such a case the judge is allowed a certain discretion, he can, in no case, as was seen, inflict punishment for actions or offences which are not expressly designated in law as punishable. Consequently the Instr. of the S. C. de P. F. *Cum Magnopere*, issued in 1884, for the United States, distinctly says, that, when the Ordinary or other ecclesiastical judge pronounces sentence of condemnation, he shall expressly mention the canonical sanction— *i. e.*, the law of the Church which authorizes him to inflict the punishment in the case. The words of the Instruction

---

[1] Reiff., l. 5, t. 37. n. 5.
[2] Arg. l. 6 et l. 76, ff Pro Socio (xvii. 2); Ferraris, v. Pœna, art. i., n. 46.

are: "Præstituta die... sententia pronuntiatur... *expressa mentione facta,* si damnationi sit locus, *sanctionis canonicæ,* quæ contra imputatum applicatur." (Art. XXXIV.)

ART. V.
Punishments "*ferendæ* and *latæ sententiæ.*"

1688. Ordinary punishments are enacted by the law, either (*a*) in such a manner as to be incurred *ipso jure* or *ipso facto,* that is by the very fact of the commission of the crime; (*b*) or only after the judge has pronounced condemnatory sentence in the manner prescribed by the Sacred Canons.[1] The former are styled punishments *latæ sententiæ;* the latter *ferendæ sententiæ.*

ART. VI.
Temporal and Spiritual Punishments.

1689. Finally, it should be observed that the punishments of the Church may produce not only spiritual, but also temporal effects, and accordingly they may be either temporal or spiritual. The *temporal punishments* of the Church are those which chiefly affect the temporal or worldly interests of the delinquent. They may be such as more directly affect (*a*) the soul, such as the loss of good name; or the (*b*) body, such as whipping, exile, detention in a monastery; (*c*) or also the property or possessions of the offender, as pecuniary fines. *Spiritual punishments* are those which deprive the culprit, either temporarily or permanently of a spiritual office or privilege, or of the exercise of sacred Orders, such as dismissal from benefice or office, privation of ecclesiastical burial, of active and passive vote in ecclesiastical elections, etc.[2] However, as Stremler[3] well

[1] Schmalzg., l. 5, t. 37, n. 11.   [2] Schmalzg., l.c , n. 14.   [3] L. c, p. 9.

remarks, this distinction between temporal and spiritual punishments must not be so strictly drawn as not to allow in one also some of the elements of the other. Thus dismissal from ecclesiastical benefice, office or dignity, (with us in the United States, dismissal of a rector) is a spiritual punishment; yet it brings also with it a temporal punishment, since it causes the loss of the salary or income, and dishonor. The distinction, therefore, is based simply on the *predominant* or principal effect of each of the two kinds of punishment.[1]

[1] Sanguineti, l. c., p. 461.

CHAPTER III.

WHEN AND BY WHOM ECCLESIASTICAL PUNISHMENTS CAN BE INFLICTED.

ART. I.

For what unlawful acts can a Person be Punished?

1690. *Q.* For what cause can ecclesiastical repressive punishments be inflicted?

A. First, Canonical Punishments, whether vindicatory or correctional, can be inflicted *only for crime*, and for no other cause, as we have already seen.[1] Hence no person can be punished, save when he has committed a crime. This truth is founded in the very law of nature, and is also repeatedly and solemnly inculcated by the law of the Church, as a fundamental and essential condition of all punishment. Thus the sacred canons say: " Rem, quæ culpa caret, in damnum vocari non convenit."[2] The Roman law expresses the same principle thus: " Sancimus ibi esse pœnam, ubi est noxa."[3]

1691. Now, as we have already shown, a crime, in the canonical sense of the term, is an act or omission contrary to the law of the Church, *and imputable to its author.*[4] We say *imputable;* now, where an act is not *wilful*, that is, where it is done without due knowledge or free will, it is not a human act, is not imputable to its author, and therefore not punishable. Hence a violation of a law which proceeds from a want of knowledge, from grave fear, or

---

[1] Supra, n. 1569. [2] Cap. 2, de Const. (I. 2.)
[3] L. 22 C. de pœnis. [4] Tarqu., l. c., n. 25.

from violence is but a material, not a formal, violation of the law, and therefore no crime. But of this later on.

1692. *Second*, The crime must be *external*. For it is manifest that internal acts or mere thoughts, and consequently offences which are committed merely in thought, cannot be proven externally and therefore lie beyond the pale of the Church's external tribunal. Hence the Roman law,[1] as adopted by the Church says: "*Cogitationis* pœnam nemo patitur."[2] And the *Glossa*, commenting on the canon *Erubescant* 11, dist. 32, writes: "Ex hoc patet, quod ecclesia non judicat de occultis."[3]

1693. *Third*, The crime must be *personally* committed. In other words, a person can be punished only for a crime which he has himself committed, and not for a crime which another person has perpetrated. Hence the rule: "Non debet aliquis alterius odio prægravari."[4] Our natural sense of justice tells us that the punishment should not extend beyond the criminal himself to a third party who is innocent. Thus Pope Boniface VIII. expressly enacts that excommunication should not be inflicted upon a whole body corporate or community, but only on such members of said body as have been duly convicted of crime, lest, as he adds, the innocent might suffer with the guilty. His words are: "In universitatem vel collegium proferri sententiam excommunicationis penitus prohibemus... Sed in illos dumtaxat de collegio vel universitate, quos culpabiles esse constiterit, promulgetur... volentes animarum periculum vitare, quod exinde sequi posset, cum nonnunquam contingeret innoxios hujusmodi sententia irretiri."[5] As to the sense in which an innocent person may sometimes be affected by or suffer (not punishments in the proper sense) through the crime of a third party, see Kober, *Suspensions*, p. 51.[6]

---

[1] L. 18 ff. de pœnis, (48, 19).   [2] Can. 14, dist. 1. de pœnit.
[3] Cf. München, l. c., vol. 2, p. 46; Kober, Kirchenbann, p. 130.
[4] Reg. 22 in 6º.   [5] Cap. 5, in 6º (V. 11.)   [6] Reiff., in reg. jur., reg. 22-23.

1694. *Fourth*, the crime must be *mortal* or *grievous*. Not only the law of the Church, but the very law of nature tells us that there should be a just proportion between the crime and its punishment, and that therefore, if the punishment be severe, the crime must also be grievous. Thus Pope Benedict XIV.,[1] speaking of censures, writes: " If, according to the opinion of all canonists, a grievous and heinous crime is required, in order to authorize the Superior to inflict a censure which is merely *ferendae sententiae*, it is manifest that a far greater and more execrable crime is necessary in order that a person may be punished with a censure *latae sententiae*." What the Pope here says of censures, applies equally to all the other ecclesiastical punishments. For all the punishments established by the sacred canons, whether they are punitive or correctional, are heavy and severe punishments, and therefore cannot be inflicted for light offences.[2] Besides, as we shall see, no ecclesiastical punishments, if we except sentences *ex inf. conscientia*, can be imposed save by a canonical trial. Now it were ridiculous to have recourse to judicial proceedings for offences which are not of a very grave character.[3]

1695. *Fifth*, the crime must be, moreover, *complete*. Hence, for instance, a person who strikes another person, with intent to kill him, does not incur the penalty of murder, if he merely wounded him, or broke his arm, but did not really kill him. Consequently also the *sole attempt* to commit a crime, or the mere co-operation, whether by advice, command, or otherwise, cannot be punished with the punishment decreed by the law for the crime itself, unless the law expressly states that not only those who commit the crime, but also all those who give aid, counsel, etc., or who attempt to commit the crime, shall incur the same penalty, as though they had perpetrated the crime itself. The rea-

[1] De Syn., L. x., c. 1, n. 5. [2] Pra-l. S. Sulpit., vol. 3, n. 758.
[3] Craisson, Man., n. 6325.

son of this principle is, that penal laws must be strictly construed.

1696. *Sixth, it must be proved juridically*, that is, by a trial, as prescribed by the sacred canons. This is founded in the very law of nature, and is repeatedly inculcated by the sacred canons in the most emphatic and solemn manner, as we have already shown.[1] In the United States no less than elsewhere, the crime must be *proven* and proved *juridically*, that is by trial as conducted either according to the latest Instruction *Cum Magnopere* of the Propaganda, issued in April 1884, or before the commission of Investigation, where it still exists by Papal dispensation, in the manner pointed out by article XII. of the Instruction *Cum Magnopere*. The only exception to this rule is that introduced by the Council of Trent, which in its 14th session, chapter I. on Reformation, authorizes Bishops, as we have already seen,[2] to inflict suspension in certain extraordinary cases, *ex informata conscientia, i. e.*, without any previous trial.[3]

1697. Besides, in the case of repressive punishments which are *correctional* or *reformative*, it is necessary that, before the trial is begun, the canonical warnings and the precept, as laid down in the Instruction *Cum Magnopere*, shall be given as we have shown. In the case of repressive punishments which are *vindicatory*, the trial alone is, absolutely speaking, sufficient. But even in their case, the admonitions and the precept will, as a rule, be laudably given before the trial is commenced, as we have stated already.

1698. Thus our divine Master, on the occasion of conferring upon His Church the power to inflict repressive punishments, whether vindicative or reformatory, at the same time pointed out in a manner unsurpassed and as a pattern for all times, the order and the course of the criminal and

---

Supra, n. 1279–1306. [2] Supra, vol ii., n. 1282 sq.
[3] See our *New Procedure*, n. 87–88.

disciplinary procedure, in these words: "*Si autem peccaverit in te frater tuus, vade, et corripe eum inter te et ipsum solum. Si te audierit, lucratus eris fratrem tuum. Si autem te non audierit adhibe tecum adhuc unum vel duos, ut in ore duorum vel trium testium stet omne verbum. Quodsi non audierit eos, dic ecclesiæ. Si autem ecclesiam non audierit, sit tibi sicut ethnicus et publicanus.*"[1] Here our Lord speaks first of a private reproof, and therefore of paternal warnings; then of a reproof before witnesses, and consequently of the warnings in a legal form and of the precept; and lastly, by inference, of the trial or criminal procedure.[2] See our *New Procedure*, nos. 85–88.

1699. *Finally*, the crime *must be designated by law as punishable*, as we have seen. Now there are two ways, in which the law designates a crime as punishable. *First*, the law expressly annexes a *specified penalty* to a certain unlawful act or omission; in other words, the law itself determines the particular punishment. *Second*, the law states that an act is punishable, but does not express what special penalty is attached to it, leaving the ecclesiastical judge free to inflict whatever punishment he may deem just. See our *New Procedure, or a full and clear Explanation of the Instr. Cum Magnopere*, n. 53 sq.

ART. II.

When are Persons Guilty of Unlawful Acts Free from Punishments?

1700. *Who are exempt from punishment.*—We have already seen that a violation of the law, in order to be punishable, must be *imputable* to the person guilty of the violation. Now it is admitted by all, that only *human acts* are imputable. A human act is one that proceeds from a *deliberate* and free *will*. Hence it must spring from man *as man*, that is, from

---

[1] Matth. xviii. 15 sq.   [2] Cf. Conc. Pl. Balt. iii., n. 300–309.

a human being as endowed with reason. The will is said to be deliberate when it determines itself freely to some act, with advertence to its malice or goodness. Hence the intellect or knowledge is the condition, free-will the efficient cause of a human act.

1701. Three things, therefore, are required to constitute a human act: 1. knowledge; 2. will; 3. liberty. The will necessarily presupposes knowledge; since a person cannot will something which is unknown to him. Freedom in its turn presupposes both knowledge and will; for liberty is the power of choosing between several things. Now a person cannot choose between two or more objects, unless he *wills* one or the other; and he cannot will unless he *knows*.[1] Opposed, therefore, to a human or imputable act are: 1. *ignorance* or the absence of due knowledge; 2. *grave fear*, or the apprehension of serious evil; for a person acting from grave fear acts against his will; 3. *violence or force*, that is, external or physical compulsion, actually inflicted upon a person by a third party.

§. 1. *Ignorance.*

1702. *When does ignorance exempt from ecclesiastical punishments?* Let us distinguish between the various ways in which a person may violate the law from ignorance. *First,* a person may be fully aware that his act is forbidden by the law, and yet be ignorant of the punishment annexed to his act. On the other hand, he may be unaware not merely of the punishment, but also of the law forbidding his act. *Second*, his ignorance may be conquerable (*ignorantia vincibilis*) or unconquerable (*ignorantia invincibilis*), according as he can overcome it or not by due or ordinary diligence. Invincible ignorance is twofold: physical and moral. Ignorance is physically unconquerable, when it can in no way

---

[1] Konings, n. 3.

be removed; morally, when it can be laid aside by due diligence.

1703. In like manner, vincible or conquerable ignorance is threefold: 1. *simply such* (*ignorantia vincibilis simpliciter*), namely when, to remove it, *some* diligence or exertion is used, though not enough; 2. *gross* (*ignorantia crassa*), when no pains at all, or scarcely any, are taken to overcome it; 3. *studied or intentional* (*ignorantia affectata*), when a person wilfully or designedly and intentionally shuns the means of removing his ignorance, in order that he may not be diverted from his purposes.[1]

1704. It is certain, that, so far as *correctional punishments* (commonly called censures) are concerned, ignorance, even though conquerable, provided, however, it be not studied, whether of the law or merely of the punishment, exempts from the punishment.[2] We say, *whether of the law;* this point requires no further explanation. We say, *or merely of the punishment;* this would seem rather incorrect at first sight.[3] For a person who knows that the action which he is performing is forbidden by the law certainly commits a sin, and seems therefore liable to the punishment annexed by the ecclesiastical authorities to his act, even though he is unaware of this punishment. Yet it must be borne in mind that the reforming punishments, of which we are now speaking, are inflicted not simply for a wilful violation of the law, but for a violation of the law of the Church, which, besides being wilful and malicious, *is also stubborn and obstinate*, or *joined with contumacy.* Now the law of the Church takes it for granted that a person who violates the law, with a knowledge, indeed, of such law, but not of the penalty annexed, would not persist stubbornly in his perverse conduct, if he knew the punishment he would incur thereby. Hence

---

[1] Konings, n. 10.   [2] Cap. 2. in 6° (I. 2); Konings, l. c., n. 1664, qu. 2-3.
[3] Supra, vol. i., n. 678, *sixth edition.* 1887.

such a person is not regarded as *contumacious*, and therefore does not become liable to medicinal punishments.

1705. We have said, moreover, *provided it be not studied;* for such ignorance springs from design and utter indifference to or contempt of the law, and is therefore justly placed on the same footing with full knowledge. Hence an act which *proceeds* from such ignorance is just as punishable as though it had been done with full knowledge and deliberation.

1706. *Practical inference.* From what has been said, Reiffenstuel and canonists in general infer that the faithful are very often exempt from correctional punishments or censures, even when imposed by their own Ordinary, *v. g.*, by episcopal statute; since they frequently do not know the penalty attached to an act which is forbidden, though they may be aware of the fact that the act is prohibited.[1]

1707. As to *vindicative punishments*, ignorance, even though invincible, merely of the *punishment*, does not, as a rule and absolutely speaking, exempt from such punishments. The reason is, that these punishments are inflicted directly and mainly for the purpose of making the offender suffer and atone for his crime, and only indirectly to cause him to amend. Hence they are incurred by any one guilty of crime, *i. e.*, of a wilful violation of the law. Now a person who knows the law, and yet violates it, is certainly guilty of a wilful and malicious violation of the law, though he is unaware of the punishment; and therefore he becomes liable to such punishments.

1708. We say, *as a rule;* for where it is expressly provided by the law that only those shall incur the penalty, who presumptuously (temere), or advisedly (consulto), or knowingly (scienter) violate the law, or commit a crime, there mere ignorance of the punishment, even though vincible, that is,

[1] Reiff., l. 5., t. 39, n. 32.

even though it could have been removed by ordinary diligence, exempts from the punishment.¹

1709. We have also said, *absolutely speaking;* for it should be ever remembered that in all her punishments, even in those which are called *vindicative*, the Church, like a good mother, seeks not merely to *vindicate* or uphold the law, but also to *reclaim* the delinquent. Consequently all ecclesiastical punishments, even those which are termed punitive, partake more or less of a reformative character. Hence while, strictly speaking, vindicatory punishments are incurred even by those who are ignorant of the punishment, yet practically the Church or ecclesiastical judge will not unfrequently in these cases either refrain altogether from inflicting the punishment, or at least consider the ignorance a mitigating circumstance, and impose a lighter punishment.

1710. *Q.* Does ignorance of the *law*, (not merely of the punishment), exempt from vindicative punishments?

A. 1. First of all, it is certain that intentional or studied ignorance (*ignorantia affectata*) does not exempt. It is, moreover, beyond controversy that invincible ignorance exempts from the punishment. For a person thus ignorant violates the law without knowledge, and therefore without will or malice; he is on that account excused from sin, and consequently also from all punishment.

1711. 2. But does conquerable or vincible ignorance of the law also exempt from punishment? Here canonists differ; the common opinion is that it does not exempt. The reasons on which this view is based are that such ignorance proceeds from culpable, imputable neglect to inquire into the existence of the law, and therefore does not excuse from sin nor from punishments that are punitive.² Those, however, who maintain the opposite contend that this reasoning holds indeed where a person is ignorant of the law owing to

---

¹ Cf. München, l. c., p. 45.   ² Reiff., l. 3, t. 5, n. 321, 322; ib., l. 5, t. 37, n. 5.

the fact that he takes no pains at all, or scarcely any, to find out the law, but not where a person uses some diligence, though not enough, to remove his ignorance. For, they say, the Church inflicts her punishments only for a *wilful, intentional*, and *malicious* violation of her laws. Now it cannot be said that a violation is wilful, in the full and penal sense, when it proceeds from ignorance as described. This view, they contend, seems also borne out by the sacred canons. Thus Pope Boniface VIII. says: " Ligari nolumus ignorantes; dum tamen eorum ignorantia crassa non fuerit aut supina."[1] Here, according to these canonists,[2] the Pontiff establishes the general rule that all ignorance of the law, save that which is gross or affected, exempts from punishment, whether punitive or correctional. Hence, they say, conquerable ignorance of the *law* (not merely of the *punishment*) exempts from punishment.[3]

1712. This opinion, they say, is also in perfect harmony with the aim of ecclesiastical punishments, and with the more recent legislation of the Church.[4] For all ecclesiastical punishments, even those called vindicative, aim more or less at the amendment of the delinquent; they are consequently imposed more or less for *stubborn* persistence in crime. Now a person cannot be said to be stubborn and incorrigible, when he does not know the law, even though his ignorance be conquerable and therefore sinful, provided, of course, it be not studied or affected.

1713. One exception, however, must be admitted to this rule; namely, where a person, by reason of the duties of his office or position, is bound to make himself acquainted with the laws and regulations bearing on his office or duties. For in this case it is plain that a person is under a special

---

[1] Cap. 2 de Const. in 6º (I. 2.)   [2] Cf. Reiff, l. c., l. v., t. 39, n. 30.
[3] Kober, Kirchenbann, p. 205-208; München. l. c., p. 45, n. 17.
[4] Cf. Instr. S. C. de P. F. *Cum Magnopere*, art. II; Conc. Pl. Balt. III., n. 72, 300, 309.

obligation of using ordinary diligence to overcome this ignorance, and to become acquainted with his duties. Hence conquerable ignorance will not excuse him from punishment. Thus a rector of a parish, in the United States, who neglects his duties as rector, cannot plead, in extenuation, ignorance of these duties. His very ignorance is of itself a crime. The law of the Church very justly says: "Nec ignorantia te excusat, si scire *debuisti*, et quam debueras, non curasti diligentiam adhibere."[1]

1714. Another remark in regard to ignorance must be borne in mind. In the *forum externum* of the Church, the ignorance of the law is not presumed, but must be proven. For, once the Church has properly promulgated a law, she justly takes it for granted that it has come to the knowledge of all whom it concerns, except those who are very illiterate. Hence, if a person pleads ignorance as an excuse for a criminal act, the burden of proof lies upon him, *i. e.*, he must show conclusively that he really labored under such ignorance as will exempt him from punishment, according to the principles above laid down.

§. 2. *Forgetfulness and Inadvertence.*

1715. What has been said concerning ignorance applies also to forgetfulness and inadvertence. For it is clear that when a person violates a law of the Church from forgetfulness or inadvertence, he does not wilfully violate it, unless his forgetfulness or inadvertence be culpable. Perfect forgetfulness and inadvertence are therefore placed on the same footing with invincible ignorance, and consequently exempt from ecclesiastical punishments, whether correctional or punitive. In like manner, imperfect forgetfulness or imperfect inadvertence is placed on an equal footing with conquerable ignorance.

[1] Cap. ult. de injur. (v. 36); München, l. c; Kober, l. c., p. 206.
 Konings, n. 10.

§. 3. *Violence and Fear.*

1716. As ignorance *juris et facti* exempts from ecclesiastical punishments, in the sense explained, so does violence (*vis, violentia*) or the application of physical force, and grave fear (*metus*) or the apprehension of grave evil, as of death, of loss of property, of mutilation, etc. Whoever violates a law of the Church, under these influences, does not act with that free will and malice which are necessary to render him liable to ecclesiastical punishments. Besides, no human or ecclesiastical law obliges under such serious inconveniences. It is only when the violence is inflicted, or the threats that produce the fear are made directly for the purpose of exposing the Church and her laws to open contempt, that the person who is thus threatened or coerced is bound to resist the pressure brought to bear upon him, and that on pain of incurring the ecclesiastical punishments.[1]

1717. It will be readily seen, from the above, that the great principle underlying all that has been said is this: that an action, even though otherwise criminal, done without a *bad will*, or an *evil intention*, is not a crime; that no person can have a wicked design, unless he acts with knowledge and free will. Hence a person commits a crime only when he violates the law *knowingly* and *wilfully*.[2] From this it also follows that infants, idiots, lunatics, and imbeciles are incapable of committing crimes, and therefore cannot be punished for acts which would otherwise be criminal; for they cannot harbor any criminal design or volition.

1718. Finally, we observe that in employing the term *law*, in the above places, we mean the ecclesiastical law, not the secular. Moreover, we use the term in its broadest acceptation; in other words, by the word *law*, we understand all enactments and regulations whatever, which emanate from any competent ecclesiastical authority, that is, decrees and

---

[1] Kober, l. c., pp. 208, 209.   [2] Cavagnis, l. c., p. 90.

When can Ecclesiastical Punishments be Inflicted?

statutes of Popes, Bishops, and others vested with jurisdiction *in foro externo;* of general, plenary, provincial and diocesan Synods.

Art. III.
Who can Punish?

1719. *Who can impose ecclesiastical punishments?* There is question (*a*) either of making penal laws, (*b*) or of *actually* inflicting punishments decreed by law. As to the former, it is evident that only those can enact punishments by law, who can make laws, namely the Pope, Bishops, and prelates having quasi-episcopal jurisdiction. As to Vicars capitular, (with us, administrators) see *supra*, n. 637. As to the latter case, those only can actually inflict ecclesiastical punishments, who are lawfully appointed ecclesiastical judges with ordinary or delegated power. The power to pronounce sentence inflicting punishment pertains, as we have repeatedly seen, to the *forum externum*.

§. 1. *Can the Bishop exercise contentious jurisdiction out of his own diocese?*

1720. The ecclesiastical judge must, as a rule, be in his own territory, when he inflicts punishment; for the law of the Church forbids the exercise of contentious jurisdiction out of one's own territory. Thus the Cap. Quamvis says: "Sacris canonibus (est) generaliter interdictum, ne quis Episcopus *jurisdictionem* in diœcesi exerceat aliena."[1]

[1] Clem. Cap. unic. de for. Comp. (II. 2.): cf. supra. n. 210.

This decretal or constitution was issued in the fifteenth general Council, held at Vienne in France, in the year 1311. by Pope Clement V. (1305-1314). The occasion of its promulgation was this: There was at the above Council a number of Bishops, especially from Italy, v. g., from Milan, Vicenza, etc., who had been expelled from their sees, by their enemies, barons and powerful noblemen and rulers. It was at the request of these exiled Prelates that the above constitution was promulgated.

Glossa in Clem., cap. *Quamvis* cit., v. *quamvis.*

1721. From this rule, however, the following two cases must be excepted: 1. Where the Bishop of the place consents to the exercise of such jurisdiction in his diocese, and the contending parties also agree to it. 2. Where the Prelate or Bishop is unjustly expelled or driven from his diocese; for in this case the expelled Bishop can remain in some neighboring diocese or other convenient place, and there, having asked, though not obtained permission from the ordinary of the place, erect his own judicial tribunal and exercise full contentious jurisdiction over all his subjects, provided, however, he cannot exercise this jurisdiction through a substitute in his own diocese, and provided that, in the case of his subjects who did not participate in his expulsion, they be not obliged to go more than a two days' journey to reach the Bishop.[1] Of course, as will be readily seen, what has been said applies only to cases where a Bishop is actually about to inflict punishment. For a Bishop may everywhere exercise voluntary jurisdiction, and consequently he may everywhere enact penal laws or statutes.[2]

§. 2. *Can a Bishop exercise voluntary jurisdiction outside his diocese?*

1722. We have just said, "A bishop may *everywhere* exercise *voluntary* jurisdiction." As this teaching is of great practical bearing, we shall dwell upon it at some greater length, though it is here but an incidental question. We have already explained what is meant by voluntary and contentious jurisdiction (n. 210). Nevertheless, we deem it useful to elucidate the matter still further. Voluntary jurisdiction differs from contentious both as to the subject matter, and the manner in which it is exercised.

1723. *Voluntary* jurisdiction is that which regards matters

---

[1] Cap. Quamvis, cit. [2] Præl. S. Sulp., vol. 3., p. 239.

or affairs which the Bishop or Superior can expedite according to his own prudent judgment, guided not by arbitrary motives, but by the rules of natural justice and equity; and which he can exercise without the formalities of judicial procedure. Such is (a) the *gracious* or *favorable* jurisdiction, by which the Superior grants favors, privileges, faculties, etc.; (b) the *legislative* and *administrative* jurisdiction, by which he enacts laws, even though penal, makes appointments to ecclesiastical offices; (c) the *correctional* jurisdiction, by which he corrects his subjects in a *fatherly manner*.[1]

1724. The *contentious* jurisdiction is that which has reference to matters which are the subject of controversy, and which must be decided according to the formalities laid down by the law of the Church for trials, and not by the mere will of the Superior. Causes of this kind are those where there is a dispute between two contending parties, namely, (a) matrimonial causes, (b) and those relating to ecclesiastical offices and benefices; (c) the punishments of the Church, (namely those which exceed the limits of paternal correction), such as excommunication, suspension, interdict, dismissal, penal transfer, etc. In the decision of these causes, the superior must observe the rules prescribed by the Church, *i. e.*, he must observe the juridical formalities of trials.

1725. Now it is certain, as we have seen above, that an Ecclesiastical Superior or Judge, whether he be an Ordinary or merely a delegated judge, must be *in his own territory or diocese* when he exercises contentious jurisdiction, and that he cannot, either licitly or validly, exercise it while he is outside of his own district or diocese, excepting in the case of his unjust expulsion.[2] For by an exercise of such jurisdiction in the territory of another he would evidently

---

[1] Prael. S. Sulp., n. 279.
[2] Cap. 7. de off. legat. (I. 30); L. 2 ff de off. proc. (I. 16); Kober, Excom., p. 125.

disturb the latter's jurisdiction. On the other hand, all canonists agree, and it is certain, that a Bishop may exercise voluntary jurisdiction, *wherever he may be, as well while he is outside of his diocese, as while he is actually in it.*[1] For he does not thereby infringe upon the rights of the Ordinary of the place, since no external apparatus or display of authority is needed in the exercise of voluntary jurisdiction.

1726. This is beyond controversy, so far as concerns the *ordinary* voluntary jurisdiction of the Bishop. Does it also apply to the *delegated* voluntary jurisdiction of the Bishop? In other words, and to make the question more practical: can the Bishops, *v. g.*, of the United States, exercise the faculties they receive from the Holy See—which, it is needless to say, are *delegated* faculties—when they are *out of their own diocese?* The reason of this question is, that the Holy See, in granting these faculties, has of course the right to prescribe that they cannot be used by the Bishop when he is out of his own diocese. In fact, it would seem at the first glance that the Holy See had in reality made this condition. For in some of the faculties usually communicated to our Bishops, the Holy See enjoins on our Bishops " Nec illis uti possit extra fines suæ diœcesis."[2]

1727. But as Father Konings well explains,[3] this restrictive clause applies *to those in whose favor* the above delegated faculties are exercised, but not to the Bishop himself or the one exercising these faculties. The former must indeed be (*a*) a *subject* of the Bishop, *i. e.*, have a domicile or quasi-domicile in the diocese, or be there as a *vagus*, (*b*) and also be actually in the diocese at the time the dispensation or favor is conferred upon him. For it is certain at present, from an answer of the S. C. Inq., given May 2, 1877, to the Synod of Maynooth, held in 1875, that the Bishop need not be in his diocese when he exercises the faculties granted him by

---

[1] Trael. S. Sulp., n. 756.   [2] Fac., form I. and C.   [3] Com. in. Fac. Ap. n. 118.

Rome.[1] The decision is as follows: "Ad postulatum tertium," (Syn. of Mayn.) "de sensu clausulæ Facultatum: *extra fines diœcesis*, responsum fuit: Verba relatæ formulæ ita esse intelligenda, ut Episcopus uti possit facultatibus erga subditos, qui actu quo dispensandi sunt in propria diœcesi commorantur: *quamvis ipse Episcopus extra suam diœcesim degat.*"[2]

1728. Of course, where the above phrase *extra fines*, etc., is not appended to the faculties, the Bishop can exercise them in favor of those who are his subjects, even when they are at the time out of the diocese, just as in the case of his *ordinary* voluntary jurisdiction, which a Bishop or Superior can exercise over his subjects, even though neither he nor they are in the diocese at the time.[3] There is but one case where a Bishop cannot exercise his ordinary voluntary jurisdiction when he is outside his own diocese, namely, where it would involve the exercise of Pontifical functions (*Pontificalia*), *v. g.*, when a Bishop confers the Sacrament of Confirmation, or of Holy Orders.[4] For, as was seen above (n. 575), a Bishop cannot exercise Pontifical functions in the diocese of another Bishop without the consent of the Ordinary of the place.

§. 3. *Rules which guide the Judge, when he inflicts Punishment.*

1729. We subjoin a few of the general rules to be followed by judges: 1. Only the Supreme lawgiver—namely, the Sovereign Pontiff—can establish or introduce any new ecclesiastical punishment. Consequently the inferior Ordinary or delegated judge can impose only such punishments as are provided by the sacred canons. This is also stated in the Instruction *Cum Magnopere* of 1884, article I., as follows:

---

[1] Konings, in Fac., cit., n. 120.
[2] Ib. Comp., t. 2., p. 412.
[3] Ib., in fac., n. 124.
[4] Craisson, n. 281.

When can Ecclesiastical Punishments be Inflicted?

"Ordinarius pro suo pastorali munere tenetur disciplinam correptionemque clericorum ita diligenter curare, ut . . . remedia *a canonibus statuta* . . . provide adhibeat."

1730.—2. The remedies or punishments established by the sacred canons are divided into two classes: Preventive and repressive.[1] The *Preventive* remedies are imposed on Ecclesiastics who give scandal, or remain in the proximate voluntary occasion of sin: they are intended to remove the cause of the scandal, and the occasion of crime, and thus to *prevent* the Ecclesiastic from falling into crime.[2] The *repressive* punishments are inflicted upon Ecclesiastics who are not merely in the occasion of sin, but have already fallen into grievous offences. They are imposed for a twofold purpose: (*a*) to bring the delinquent back to the path of duty; (*b*) to deter others from breaking the law.[3] While all repressive punishments have these two ends, nevertheless some of them tend more directly to *reform* the delinquent, others to vindicate the law, and cause it to be respected and observed. The latter are called *vindicative* punishments, the former *reformative*, as we have seen.

1731.—3. In inflicting ecclesiastical punishments, the judge should naturally bear in mind their end or aim. Punishments are a means to an end. The means should be such as are adapted to the end. Now, as we have seen, in all her punishments, the Church acts more like a good mother than a severe judge. The Church's mission is the salvation or sanctification of souls.[4] Hence, in all her punishments, even in those which are called punitive and vindicatory, she aims, not merely at vindicating the law, but also reforming and reclaiming the delinquent. She never excludes this latter aim altogether.[5]

---

[1] Instr. *Cum Magnopere*, Art. II. [2] Ib.
[3] Ib. [4] Sanguineti, l. c., p. 459.
[5] Cf. Stremler, p. 154; Droste—Messmer, pp. 66, 167; Schulte, K. K. R., vol. ii., p. 387.

When can Ecclesiastical Punishments be Inflicted? 43

1732.—4. From this, it follows, that, when an ecclesiastic falls into crime, nothing should, as a rule, be done, if he amends and repairs his offence. But if he persists in his criminal course, he should, as a rule, be first warned repeatedly ; if the admonitions prove of no avail, he should be given the precept; if even the latter produces no effect, he should be put on trial, and, if convicted, be visited with *medicinal* punishments, namely censures ; and if even these fail to reform him, vindicatory punishments should follow, *servatis servandis*.[1]

1733. We have just said, *as a rule:* for where the offence committed is of great enormity and therefore shows that the delinquent acted with exceeding great malice prepense, and is, so to say, hardened in crime, or where the greatness of the scandal given requires it, the vindicative punishments may be inflicted at once, that is, without the previous admonitions or precept, though not without a previous trial.[2]

1734.—5. In general, it may be said that it belongs to the conscientious discretion of the Ordinary to determine what particular punishment he is to inflict in a given case whether he is to impose a preventive or a repressive remedy ; whether the repressive measure is to be a reformative or vindicatory one ; what particular preventive medicinal or punitive measure is to be imposed. Thus Article III. of the Instruction *Cum Magnopere* enacts: "Conscientiæ ordinarii remittitur cujusque remedii (præventivi vel repressivi) applicatio, canonicis præscriptionibus servatis pro casuum ac circumstantiarum gravitate."

1735.—6. Where the law itself clearly states what punishment shall be incurred for a certain offence, the judge should, as a rule, inflict this punishment and no other. Where the law leaves the judge free to inflict whatever punishment seems fair and equitable, he should be guided in

[1] Sanguineti, l. c., p. 460.   [2] Conc. Plen. Balt. III., n. 300.

his action by good and conscientious motives, and always incline to clemency rather than to severity. Thus Pope Honorius III. (A. D. 1220) speaking to the Ecclesiastical Judge, says: " In his vero, super quibus jus non invenitur expressum, procedas æquitate servata, semper in humaniorem partem declinando, secundum quod personas et causas, loca et tempora videris postulare."[1] For other excellent rules for the guidance of the Judge, see Rota, Enchir., n. 752-761. See also, in regard to the discretionary power of the Ordinary, our *New Procedure, or a clear and full explanation of the Instr. Cum Magnopere*, p. 25, sq.

ART. IV.

Upon Whom can Punishments be Inflicted?

1736. *Upon whom can punishments be inflicted?* Upon all subjects who are juridically convicted of crime.[2] We say, *subjects;* here the question arises: In how many ways may a person become subject to an Ecclesiastical Judge so as to be punishable by him? The answer has been given above, Vol. II., Nos. 781-813.

---

[1] Cap. 11. de transact. (I. 36).   [2] Craiss., Man., n., 6317.

PART II.

ECCLESIASTICAL PREVENTIVE PUNISHMENTS.

(*Remedia Præventiva*).

General Remarks.

1737. Having thus far shown what is meant by canonical or ecclesiastical punishments, for what cause, by whom and in what manner they are inflicted, we shall now speak of each of these punishments in particular. As we have seen, the canonical punishments of the external forum of the Church are divided into two classes,—*preventive* and *repressive*. The chief preventive punishments are (*a*) spiritual exercises, (*b*) admonitions, (*c*) and precepts. All the other canonical punishments, whether punitive or correctional, are called repressive punishments.[1] Under the present heading we shall treat of preventive punishments; in the succeeding, of repressive.

1738. What is meant by *preventive remedies?* They are those which have for their object not so much the punishment for a crime *already committed*, as the *preventing or hindering it from being committed*. Hence they are thus described in the Instruction *Cum Magnopere*, Art. II.: "Illa (remedia præventiva) ad præpedienda mala, scandalorum stimulos amovendos, voluntarias occasiones et causas ad delinquendum proximas vitandas ordinantur."

1739. While, however, these remedies are intended to act as *preventives* of crime, and are therefore imposed, generally speaking, upon Ecclesiastics who are in culpable danger of

---

[1] S. C. EE. et RR., 1880., Instr. *Ordinario*, art. ii. et ix.; S. C. de P. F., 1884, Instr. *Cum Magnopere*, art. iv. et ix.; Rota, Enchir., p. 408.

falling into crime, and who, by these remedies—namely, timely warnings, spiritual retreats, precepts—are to be brought to a realizing sense of their danger and approaching spiritual shipwreck, and thus snatched from their near spiritual ruin, it does not follow that these remedies cannot be imposed in cases where grave offences have been already committed.

1740. For, as we have seen, the law of the Church gives the Ordinary a great deal of discretionary power. It allows him, even where grave offences have been already perpetrated, either to refrain altogether from inflicting repressive measures, or to remit them, if he judges it best, and if the enormity of the crime or the greatness of the scandal does not demand otherwise. Hence it permits him *a fortiori* to apply preventive remedies, even where repressive ones could be justly imposed. All this is clearly implied in Article III. of the Instruction *Cum Magnopere*, and also in the *Third Plenary Council of Baltimore*, n. 309.

1741. How many kinds of preventive punishments are there? As we have seen, chiefly these three: spiritual exercises, admonitions, and precepts. We shall now briefly discuss each of them.

CHAPTER I.

SPIRITUAL EXERCISES.

(*Spiritualia Exercitia.*)

ART. I.

How are Spiritual Exercises Preventive Remedies?

1742. We have shown (n. 1661.) that a punishment is an evil, a pain or suffering, whether of the body or the mind, inflicted for crime. Now a spiritual retreat may be imposed in two ways, first, as a general means of sanctification; second, as a punishment for censurable conduct.

1743. *Spiritual exercises as a means of sanctification.* The ministers of the Church should, above all, strive to be holy and perfect. Hence they should frequently follow the example of our divine Master, and retire for a few days into solitude, in order to gain new strength in the service of God. It is for this reason that the Roman Pontiffs, especially Pope Innocent XII., by encyclical letter of the S. C. EE. et RR., Feb. 1. 1700, and Pope Pius IX., in the encyclical *Qui Pluribus*, exhort Bishops to urge the entire clergy of their respective dioceses, especially Rectors of parishes and confessors, to make a spiritual retreat once a year. The words of Pope Innocent XII. are: "Sanctitas sua eosdem Ordinarios admonet et hortatur ut... universos ex clero sibi subjecto, sed præcipue animarum rectores, confessarios ... diligenter excitent ad eadem exercitia spiritualia saltem semel in anno peragenda."[1]

1744. Hence also the *schema* 3, de vita et hon. cleric., cap.

[1] Cf. Lucidi, de V. SS. LL., vol. 3., p. 295.

ii. of the *Vatican Council,* proposed this enactment: " Et quoniam in medio corrupti sæculi facile evenit, ut de mundano pulvere etiam religiosa corda sordescant, ad ecclesiastici vero ordinis dignitatem et sanctimoniam retinendam ac fovendam, pium spiritualium exercitiorum institutum vel maxime conducat; omni studio curent episcopi ut clerici, præsertim parochi et confessarii, *singulis saltem triennis vel quadriennis* certo dierum spatio in opportunum aliquem locum iisdem peragendis exercitiis secedant." [1]

In accordance with these directions, the Fathers of the Third Plenary Council of Baltimore, n. 75., enact: " Statuimus itaque ut Episcopi clerum suarum diœcesium *quotannis vel saltem singulis bienniis* in sacrum istum secessum ducant ut omnes mente cordeque renovati . . . ad munus sacri ministerii fructuosius peragendum redeant." For similar reasons Pope Alexander VII., in his *Const. Apostolica Sollicitudo,* Innocent XI., by encyclical letters of the S. C. EE. et RR., Oct. 3, 1682, and Benedict XIV., in his encyclical *Ubi primum,* ordained that all who were promoted to sacred orders should be obliged to make a retreat of ten days, prior to their ordination. [2]

1745. *Spiritual exercises as punishments.*—Now it is plain that this sort of retreat has nothing about it which savors of punishment; for it does not contain anything that could humiliate or debase a person, or lower him in the eyes of others. On the other hand, when the Superior commands an inferior, out of the above cases, to make a retreat, it is evident that such a retreat is humiliating and painful to human feelings, since it implies some wrong-doing and therefore lowers a person in the estimation of others. Hence it is a punishment. Consequently this sort of retreat, which is the one of which the Instructions *Sacra hæc* and *Cum Mag-*

---

[1] See Martin, Doc. Conc. Vatic., p. 132.

[2] Cf. Bened. XIV., Inst. eccl. 104; De Syn., l. 11, c. 2., n. 16; Rota, Enchir., p. 417.

nopere speak and of which we here treat, cannot be imposed save for an offence or some action which is proximate to an offence and partakes of its nature. Such are voluntary occasions and causes leading proximately to crime. Such are also other acts which, though not of themselves sinful, yet appear sinful in the eyes of others and thus produce scandal. These acts, moreover, must be not occult, but external and known to others.[1]

1746. All this is clearly indicated by the Instruction *Cum Magnopere*, when it says that the preventive remedies, and consequently also the spiritual exercises in the case, are ordained for the purpose of removing the occasion of scandals and the voluntary proximate occasions of sin. A Bishop, therefore, has the right to impose a special spiritual retreat upon an Ecclesiastic who is the occasion of scandal, or who remains voluntarily in the proximate occasion of sin, and who consequently, though not yet guilty of crime, follows a slippery road leading to spiritual ruin. Such conduct is indeed already in itself an offence, though incipient, if we may use the word.

ART. II.

How are they imposed?

1747. Censurable conduct is not enough. The Bishop, before imposing any of the preventive remedies and consequently also spiritual retreats, is moreover obliged to verify in a summary or informal, though not superficial manner, by due inquiry and examination of witnesses and other evidence, the existence of the above acts calling for a preventive punishment. This is expressly enjoined by the Instruction *Cum Magnopere*, art. v., in these words: " Antequam vero ea (remedia præventiva) adhibeantur, *summaria factorum recognitio præcedat oportet.*"

[1] Acta S.S., vol. 15, p. 377.

1748. The object of this inquiry is chiefly twofold; 1. In order to prevent the punishment in question from being inflicted upon a person who may not be guilty of any of the above acts; 2. to prove the existence of these acts before the higher judge, in case the person who is commanded to make the retreat or undergo any other preventive punishment appeals against this command.[1] For this purpose, also, the Instruction *Cum Magnopere* expressly enacts that a written record shall be preserved by the Bishop or Ordinary of this inquiry.[2]

1749. Finally, *in what manner is this preliminary inquiry to be conducted?* 1. The object of this inquiry is to authorize the Bishop to impose a *preventive*, i. e., a *paternal* remedy, and not a repressive punishment, vindicatory or correctional. Hence this whole investigation should partake of *a fatherly character* and *be conducted in a paternal spirit*. Consequently it should be made by the *Ordinary in person*, since the Bishop is pre-eminently the father of his clergy.[3] If the Bishop, for good reasons, is hindered from conducting it himself, he may depute another Ecclesiastic to do it for him. This Ecclesiastic should be a man of great prudence and integrity, who will not be swayed by feelings of hatred or dislike, and who is therefore wholly free from any prejudice against the person whose conduct is being investigated.[4]

1750.—2. It should be made in an *informal manner*, i. e., in a plain, simple manner, and without any juridical formality. For, as has just been said, the whole proceeding is conducted by the Bishop *as a father rather than as a judge*.[5] This is also indicated by the words of the Instruction *Cum Magnopere*, art. v.,—*summaria factorum recognitio*. In order to verify the facts in the case, it will nearly always be necessary either to examine witnesses, or experts, or other evidence. But this examination of witnesses, etc., should be

---

[1] Instr. *Cum Magnopere*, art. v.   [2] Ib.   [3] Acta S. S., vol. 15, p. 380.
[4] Rota, Ench., p. 414.   [5] Droste, l. c., p. 76.

conducted, as was seen, without any judicial formality. Therefore neither the diocesan prosecutor nor the notary should take any part in it, or be present at it. The office of these officials begins only after the Bishop, having in vain applied the preventive measures, makes up his mind to order the trial prior to imposing a repressive remedy.

1751.—3. It is conducted *non citato nec constituto reo*, that is, the accused person has no right to be called to or to be present at the examination of witnesses or any other part of this investigation.[1] For it is made merely for the information of the Bishop. Besides, the accused cannot be invited or called upon to defend himself, unless there exists already at least a half proof of his guilt, which is not supposed to be the case at this stage of the proceedings. Then again, the witnesses, or other evidence in the case, are not examined for the direct purpose of obtaining juridical proof and of inflicting repressive punishments, but merely for the sake of gaining extrajuridical information and of imposing fatherly remedies. However, *after* this investigation is concluded, it is advisable for the Bishop, before he imposes the preventive measure, to call the accused to himself and inform him of the information and evidence obtained in the inquiry, as we shall presently see.[2]

1752.—4. The whole inquiry, *v. g.*, the examination of the witnesses, etc., should be made *as secretly as possible*, so that it may not become known in public: because otherwise the good name of the person inquired into would suffer.[3] Nay, it should be conducted in so prudent a manner that it will not become known even to the accused himself, lest otherwise his feelings be unnecessarily hurt.[4]

1753. We have seen that the preventive punishment cannot be imposed upon an Ecclesiastic, save when he is guilty

---

[1] Rota, Enchir., pp. 413, 414.
[3] Rota., l. c., p. 414.
[2] Pierantonelli, Praxis etc., p. 74 sq.
[4] Droste, l. c., p. 77.

of actions which are the proximate occasions of sin or which give scandal. The question now arises: Is the Bishop obliged, before proceeding to inflict a preventive remedy, to have full proof (*probatio plena*) of the existence of the above actions, or is half-proof (*probatio semi-plena*) sufficient?[1] All the commentators of the Instruction *Sacra Hæc* of June 11, 1880, agree that half proof is at least required for the preventive remedies properly so-called. We say, *properly so-called;* for some distinguish between the *monitio paterna* and the *monitio canonica*, and maintain that to give the *monitio paterna*, it is sufficient for the Bishop to have proofs or indications of guilt or of the above sinful actions, which are somewhat grave and strong, though they need not attain to the grade of half proof.[2] The other commentators who, as we shall see, teach that the canonical warnings, of which the Instruction *Cum Magnopere*, Art. IV., VI., speaks, mean both the paternal and the legal or canonical warning, say that half proof at least is always required.[3]

1754. Whatever may be said on this head, all the above canonists agree that, if after the above inquiry or *summaria factorum recognitio*, it is found that the evidence or proof of the faulty conduct of the person against whom the investigation was made, though not amounting to an imperfect or half-proof, is yet of a grave character and not to be despised, it is advisable for the Bishop, before going any further, to call the Ecclesiastic in question to himself and to inform him of the charges which have been made against him. As to whether he should also tell him who the witnesses or accusers are, or where and how he obtained the information, must be left to the discretion of the Bishop. Droste[4] says that, though the law does not require it, yet in most cases it

---

[1] We speak, of course, of *extrajudicial* proofs. For the inquiry which is to precede preventive remedies is extrajudicial. See our *New Procedure*, n. 46.
[2] Pierantonelli, l. c., p. 77 ; Droste, l. c., p. 78. [3] Acta. S. S. l. c., p. 37.
[4] P. 78.

will be found advisable for the Bishop to let the accused know who his accusers are and also who the witnesses are, so that he may not think that his Superior places more confidence in others than in him. Next the Bishop should ask him for his statement of the case and allow him to say what he thinks proper in his own defence. If he succeeds in refuting the charges, nothing further should be done. But if he does not succeed in breaking the force of the evidence, the Bishop should then, in a paternal manner, *reprove, entreat, and rebuke* him *in all kindness and doctrine* without making any threat whatever of punishment.¹ If he then promises to desist from his evil course and repair the scandal he has given, and in reality keeps his promise, nothing further should be done. If the Bishop does not think it proper to invite the Ecclesiastic to come to him, he may appoint another worthy and prudent Ecclesiastic to perform this office for him, or he may send the fatherly warning by letter—which must be private and not official.²

1755. If the accused disobeys the fatherly admonition, and the Bishop finds that there is at least a half proof of culpability, he may forthwith impose one of the preventive remedies, namely either the canonical admonition, or spiritual exercises, or the precept. However, before imposing the *præceptum*, he is obliged first to give the canonical warnings. For the Instruction *Cum Magnopere* clearly states that the precept is to be given only when the canonical warnings produce no effect.³ The precept not unfrequently contains a command to make a spiritual retreat.

1756. We say, *and if the Bishop finds that there is at least half-proof;* for, as was seen, the Bishop cannot impose the preventive remedies, unless there exists at least half-proof of culpability. This half-proof may arise not merely from

---

¹ Conc. Trid., Sess. xiii.,C. I, de Ref. ² Conc. Pl. Balt. III., n. 344.
³ Art. VII.; cf. Acta S. S., vol. 15, p. 381.

the testimony of one trustworthy witness, as was seen above, n. 1753, but under certain circumstances also from the refusal of the party to come to the Bishop, when asked to do so, or from the admissions which he makes to the Bishop, in case he does come, or in general, from his extrajudicial confession,[1] or other sources of information. On the manner of imposing preventive remedies, see also our *New Procedure*, n. 60–64.

[1] Acta S. S., l. c., p. 381; Pierantonelli, p. 7.

CHAPTER II.

CANONICAL ADMONITIONS.

(*Monitio Canonica.*)

ART. I.

What are the Canonical Warnings?

1757. As has been already noted, admonitions are classed by the Instruction *Cum Magnopere*, Art. IV., VI., among the preventive punishments or remedies. What then is meant by a canonical warning? It is the legitimate act of the Superior calling upon a subject to amend and correct his reprehensible conduct and to make due satisfaction therefor.[1] We say, *legitimate act, etc.*, because the canonical warning, in order to be competent, must be made in the manner prescribed by the Sacred Canons: hence its name *canonical* warning. That there are admonitions which are in no sense punishments, all will admit. Thus a general exhortation to perfection is an admonition; every sermon is a series of admonitions. Yet they are not regarded as punishments in any sense of the word; for they inflict no pain or humiliation upon the hearer, especially as they are addressed to all and not to any one in particular.

1758. But the case is different when we speak of a reproof, or rebuke addressed by the Bishop to one of his Ecclesiastics because of blame-worthy conduct. Such a warning is, of its very nature, painful to the feelings of the person warned; it is addressed to him individually and is based upon the belief that he is guilty of wrong doing at least in-

---

[1] De Brabandere, vol. 2, n. 1397.

cipient, and therefore it lowers him in the eyes of others. It is, therefore, a punishment, whose object is to prevent further and greater evil than that which has been already perpetrated. And in reality, it is plain that, when a Bishop informs one of his Ecclesiastics that his conduct is reprehensible and irregular, and indicates to him a different line of conduct to be followed, such a warning is naturally humiliating to the person thus addressed and grates harshly on his feelings,[1] no matter how delicately and prudently it may be given. Hence any such warning, even though made in a kind, fatherly, and informal manner (*monitio paterna*), is a punishment.

1759. This holds *a fortiori* of the warning which is given *in a legal manner* (*in forma legali*), *i. e.*, with all the formalities prescribed by the sacred canons. For in this case the admonition, given as it is, in an official and formal manner, becomes evidently far more painful and humiliating than that which is given in a fatherly and informal way, and with all possible prudence and delicacy.

Art. II.

When Can the Warning be Given?

1760. Consequently the first condition of imposing the canonical warning is *culpable conduct*. In other words, the Bishop cannot reprehend an Ecclesiastic, even though it be merely in a fatherly way,[2] except when the latter is guilty of censurable acts or reprehensible conduct, as explained above in the case of spiritual exercises. For the very law of nature dictates that, as a rule, there shall be no punishment where there is no offence.[3]

1761. The second condition is, that this censurable conduct *shall be verified by a "summaria facti recognitio,"* as we

---

[1] München, l. c., vol. 2, pp. 239-241.   [2] Rota, Enchir., p. 421.   [3] Rota, l. c.

Canonical Admonitions.

have shown in the case of spiritual exercises. It is not necessary to explain again in what manner this inquiry is to be made, since we have fully unfolded this point above, in speaking of the retreat. Now, it is requisite to state here again what we have already affirmed, namely, that at least half-proof, though extrajudicial, of the guilt of irregular conduct must be obtained in the above preliminary inquiry, before a canonical warning can be given. Any inferior grade of proof, though sufficient for the canonical warning given paternally, would make it incompetent and void, when given in a legal manner. Canonists, moreover, teach that, even where the degree of proof of guilt would justify the Superior in giving the canonical warning proper, it is always advisable to let the paternal warning precede the canonical.

1762. Finally, the old adage should be borne in mind that there shall be a just proportion between the guilt and the punishment. As the warning in question, especially when conveyed in a formal and official manner, is very humiliating, especially to Ecclesiastics, and is, therefore, a serious punishment, it follows that it cannot be given, except when the offence or reprehensible conduct is of a grave character. Slight offences should not be noticed by the Superior—*De minimis non curat Prætor.*

Art. III.

Is it Necessary that the Canonical Admonitions shall be Given in a Legal Manner?

1763. *Q.* Is it optional with the Bishop to make the canonical warnings either in a paternal or in a legal manner?

A. We premise: The reason why we ask this question lies in Art. VI. of the Instruction *Cum Magnopere*, which reads thus: "Canonicæ monitiones *vel* secreto fiunt (etiam per epistolam vel per interpositam personam) ad modum paternæ correctionis, *vel* servata forma legali adhibentur, ita tamen ut illarum executio ex aliquo actu pateat."

1764. We now answer: There are two opinions; one affirms,[1] the other denies. The *affirmative* teaches that the above article enacts that the canonical warning can be made either in a paternal, *i. e.*, informal manner, or in a legal *i. e.*, formal way, namely with the formalities prescribed by the Sacred Canons; that the Bishop is therefore free to give the canonical warning in either of these two ways, as he may judge proper and opportune. According to this view it is immaterial and makes no difference whether the canonical admonitions are given in a fatherly or legal manner; either mode is sufficient and both are not necessary. The Bishop is at liberty to choose the one or the other, as circumstances may demand. All that is necessary is that their execution or their having been really given be proved.[2]

1765. On the other hand, this view would appear to be in open and direct contradiction with the prescriptions of the Sacred Canons. The latter require in the clearest, most emphatic, and peremptory terms, and under severe penalties, that the canonical warning shall be made only in a legal manner *i. e.*, with all formalities prescribed by the Sacred Canons,[3] as laid down in our *New Procedure*, n. 70.

1766. To avoid this difficulty, some commentators of the above Instruction, *v. g.*, Droste,[4] interpret the above Article VI. of the Instruction as having reference only to the paternal warning, which *is made* obligatory prior to the giving of the *præceptum*, and hold that the canonical admonition, in the strict sense of the term, consists in the *præceptum*,

---

[1] Cf. Acta S. S., vol. 15, p. 381; Rota, Enchir., p. 422.
[2] Rota, l. c., n. 632; Acta S. S., vol. 15, p. 381.
[3] Cap. 48 de sent. exc. (v. 39); Kober, excom., p. 157 sq.   [4] L. c., pp. 102, 103.

of which Articles VII. and VIII. speak. In fact, they say the *præceptum*, both as to its intrinsic form or matter and its external form, *i. e.*, the formalities with which it is to be made, corresponds exactly to the canonical warning proper, as defined in the Sacred Canons and explained by canonists. Hence, they continue, although Article VI. of the above Instructions uses the words *canonicæ monitiones*, it would, nevertheless, seem to speak rather of the paternal, or, if we may use the word, semi-canonical or semi-official, than of the strict canonical warning, and to insinuate that, even where this warning is made in a legal manner, it nevertheless should, practically speaking, take the place of the fatherly admonition, which, however, is made obligatory prior to the imposing of the *præceptum* or the canonical warning proper.

1767. But it may be asked, if this be so, why should the above Article VI. employ the words *monitiones canonicæ*, and expressly allow the Bishop to make them in a legal manner? They answer thus: 1. As to the words *canonicæ monitiones*, the informal or fatherly admonition may and is in a wide sense justly called a canonical warning. For the Sacred Canons, and especially the Council of Trent, urgently exhort Prelates always first to make use of repeated fatherly warnings before coming to more official ones.[1]

1768.—2. As to the second objection, the above Article VI. seems to insinuate that there are some cases where the Bishop may find it more opportune to give the warning in a paternal and informal manner; and that there are others where he may deem it better to give it in a legal and formal way. Thus the Bishop may know that, with regard to certain persons, a paternal warning, given in a most prudent and delicate manner possible, will produce the desired effect. In other cases, he may be morally certain, *v. g.*, where he

[1] Conc. Trid., sess. xiii., c. 1. de Ref.

has already given repeated fatherly warnings in vain, that a formal admonition is necessary in order to impress the delinquent with a salutary fear and cause him to amend. The Instruction, therefore, would seem to have had these contingencies in view, and accordingly to have left the Bishop free to choose either mode of giving the required warnings, according to circumstances.

1769.—3. It might perhaps also be said that, as the Council of Trent[1] prescribes that at least *two warnings* shall precede the infliction of correctional punishments,[2] the *monitiones canonicæ* of article VI. of the above Instruction might be regarded as the *first* canonical warning, and the *præceptum* as the second and last.

1770. Here we remark, in passing, that, even though it be said that the *præceptum* constitutes the strict canonical warning, and that the *monitiones canonicæ* of article VI. of the Instruction, no matter whether they are made in a fatherly or legal manner, practically take the place of the fatherly warnings, it is certain that they also partake somewhat of the nature of the strict canonical warning. For they must be given prior to, and serve as a basis for imposing the *præceptum* and for beginning the judicial proceedings. Thus, they constitute the *first* canonical warning—the *præceptum* being the second. Now the mere fatherly warning, as commonly understood by canonists, possesses neither of these qualities, since it can never serve as the basis of juridical proceedings, or be considered as the *first* of the two or three canonical warnings. Consequently, as we have said, the canonical warnings mentioned in article VI. of the Instruction are *semi-official* or *semi-canonical* warnings, partaking partly and chiefly of the nature of the fatherly and partly of the strict canonical warning.

[1] Sess. 25., c. 3. de Ref.

[2] The Sacred Canons enacted prior to the Council of Trent require *three warnings*, as was seen.

1771. The *negative* or second opinion interprets the above Article VI. of the Instruction *Cum Magnopere* as speaking disjunctively of two kinds of admonitions—the paternal and the canonical proper,--and as imposing a strict obligation of making the canonical admonition in a legal manner and, therefore, as not leaving the Bishop free to make it either legally or paternally, as he may see fit.

1772. This appears to be the view taken by the *Third Plenary Council of Baltimore*. The *Council* enacts that, in accordance with the Instruction *Cum Magnopere*, Art. VI., the paternal warning should be given first; next, the canonical, which shall be made with all the formalities prescribed by the Sacred Canons; finally the *præceptum*.[1] The words of the Council are: "Modo paternæ correptionis (Matt. xviii., 15-17) eum (inquisitum) moneat, ut ad sensus meliores redeat . . . at si . . monitiones *paternas* sperant, Episcopus monitiones *canonicas* adhibebit, *servata omnino forma legali*. Tres numero fiant, sex dierum spatio explendæ. . . . . Quod si monitiones in irritum cedant, Ordinarius jubet per curiam delinquenti analogum *præceptum* intimari" . . . On this whole question, see our *New Procedure*, n. 65–69.

ART. IV.

How are the Admonitions given Paternally?

1773. *Q.* What formalities are to be observed by the Bishop in making the canonical warning?

A. We speak here of the *monitiones canonicæ* of article VI. of the Instruction *Cum Magnopere*. Having explained what these admonitions are, and what conditions are required prior to their being given, we now come to the formalities with which they are to be made. It is necessary to distinguish, at the outset, between the legal and the fatherly man-

[1] Conc. Pl. Balt. III., n. 309.

ner, in which the canonical admonitions are given. When given paternally, it should be made in as *informal a manner as possible*, so that the person warned may plainly see that it proceeds from the Bishop acting not as judge but wholly as father, who, in all kindness and paternal goodness, goes after the stray sheep in order to reclaim it, in imitation of our divine Master.[1] Hence this paternal admonition should be made *secretly, charitably*, and *prudently*.

1774. *First*, then, the canonical warning, when given paternally, should be *secret*, that is, nobody should be present at or made privy to it, except the Superior warning, and the Inferior warned. In other words, it should be made under four eyes. This mode of making the fatherly admonition is laid down by our Saviour Himself: "If," He says, "thy brother shall offend against thee, go and reprove *between thee and him alone*."[2] This is also clearly pointed out by the Instructions *Sacra hæc* of June 11, 1880, and *Cum Magnopere* of 1884, (Art. VI), when they say: "Canonicæ monitiones vel *secreto* fiunt (etiam per epistolam vel per interpositam personam)" etc. Consequently it should be made, if possible, (a) by the Bishop *in person*, (b) *orally*, (c) and as privately as possible, *i. e.*, without any witnesses and in so secret a manner that it will not become known to any one. The best way, therefore, to make it would seem to be the one traced out above, under the heading of spiritual retreats.

1775. It consists, as was shown, in the Bishop's calling the delinquent to himself, making known to him the accusations, hearing his explanations, and then, if the latter are not satisfactory, giving him the fatherly warning, *i. e.*, pointing out, in a kind and prudent manner, the wrong he has done, or the danger he is in, and suggesting the proper remedies, *v. g.*, the avoiding this or that place, such or such a person, or performing a retreat.

[1] Matth., xviii., 12. [2] Ib., 15.

1776. We have said above, *if possible*; for where the Bishop finds it inopportune or impossible to make the admonition in person, he can appoint some other worthy and prudent person to make it for him. But he should not select for this purpose either his Vicar-general, or any other official of his curia, lest it would seem to partake of a judicial character.[1] In like manner, if the Bishop deems it inopportune to give the admonition *orally*, and that either in person, or through some other discreet person, he may send it to the delinquent *by letter*, which, however, as seen, must be *private*, signed only by the Bishop, and not countersigned by his secretary, as official and juridical documents are. As in the admonition given orally, so also in the one given by letter, no threat whatever should be made of punishment.

1777. Although this kind of warning should be as secret as possible, yet a private record or memorandum of the whole affair, and of the inquiry that preceded it, should be made and preserved by the Bishop, so that, in case of appeal, he may forward a statement of the case to the judge of appeal, or else for the purpose of enabling himself to take ulterior steps, if need be.[2] We say, *a private record;* hence neither the warning, nor the proof of its execution, nor the inquiry, which preceded it, should be kept on file in the Episcopal chancery. These papers should be kept by the Bishop in a private place, and apart from his official papers.[3] He must likewise, while giving it as secretly as possible, nevertheless give it in such a manner that he will be able from some act or other, *v. g.*, from a letter of the person warned, to prove that the warning was really given to the delinquent. For if the person warned denies that he has been warned, the Bishop must prove it.[4]

1778. Secondly, this admonition (the same holds, in a

[1] Droste, l. c., p. 85; Rota, Enchir., p. 423. [2] Instr. *Cum Magnopere*, Art. V.
[3] S. C. EE. et RR., 7 Oct. 1801; Droste, l. c., p. 80.
[4] Instr. *Cum Magnopere*, Art. VI.

measure, also of the formal warning and the precept) should be made *charitably*, so that the person warned will see that it proceeds from compassion and kindness, and not from hatred or dislike. *Lastly*, it should be made with *tact and prudence*, *i. e.*, it should be made in such time, manner, and place as are likely to cause it to be received in good part.[1]

1779. *Practical observation.*—The Instruction *Cum Magnopere* of 1884 enacts, indeed, at least according to the opinion of some canonists, that it is optional to give the first canonical warning either in a fatherly or in a legal form; that if it be disregarded, the *præceptum*, or second and last canonical warning, can be at once imposed; that, if even this command be set at naught, the trial looking toward inflicting punishment can forthwith follow. Yet it is also plain that article VI. of the Instruction *Cum Magnopere*, by its way of designating both the paternal and the legal warning as canonical warnings, impliedly advises Bishops to proceed, as a rule, in the following order: first, to give repeated warnings in a fatherly manner; next, if they prove abortive, to give the warnings in a more formal, *i. e.*, in a legal manner; finally, if even the latter produce no effect, to impose the formal precept, or canonical warning in the strict sense.

1780. This is also the course traced out by our Lord Himself. First, the delinquent is to be admonished paternally, *i. e.*, privately. "If thy brother offend against thee," says our Divine Master, "go and reprove him *between thee and him alone*." Next, if the delinquent will not amend, he should be admonished in a more formal manner, *i. e.*, before witnesses: "If he will not hear thee, *take with thee one or two more*, that in the mouth of two or three witnesses every word may stand." Finally, if he still remains obdurate, he is to be handed over to the Church or judge, for trial and punishment.[2] It is true that this mode of procedure is pre-

---

[1] Corn. a Lapide, in Matth., xviii. 15. [2] Matth., xviii., 15–8.

scribed directly for private individuals. But it also applies, by implication, to Superiors. For our Lord explains the law of nature, which tells us that, before proceeding to inflict punishments, the Superior should do all in his power, by kindness and fatherly advice, to reclaim the offender, lest, by being visited with punishments before being warned in such a kind manner, the offender may become still more hardened in sin.[1]

1781. Hence, as was seen, the Council of Trent[2] most earnestly urges Bishops to strive, before inflicting any punishment, "by exhortation and admonition, to deter them (offenders) from what is unlawful: to reprove, entreat, rebuke, in all kindness and doctrine, those who should happen to sin in any manner through human frailty, seeing that *benevolence* towards those to be corrected often effects more than *austerity; exhortation* more than *menace; charity* more than *power*." The Council then gives, in these beautiful words, the reasons for this course: "Since it is the office of a pastor, at once vigilant and kind, to apply *first of all* gentle fomentations to the disorder of his sheep, and *afterwards* to have recourse to sharper and more violent remedies, when the grievousness of the distemper may require them."[3]

ART V.

Formalities of the Admonitions when given in a legal Manner.

1782. We now come to the formalities which are to be observed when the canonical warnings are made *in a legal* or formal manner. The general teaching of Canonists is that the legal mode of making the canonical warning is, as was seen, the following: The warning must (*a*) be repeated *three times*, except in case of urgent necessity; (*b*) given *in writing;* (*c*) state precisely *what is to be done or avoided;* (*d*)

[1] Corn. a Lap'de, Com. in Matth., xviii., 15.   [2] Sess. xiii., c. I. de Ref.   [3] Ib.

lay down a *suitable and fixed time* for compliance with the precept; (*e*) mention the *specific punishment* that will be inflicted, in case the warning is disregarded ; (*f*) be read or handed to the delinquent *in person ;* (*g*) in the presence of competent witnesses ; (*h*) be issued by authority of the judge. We shall now briefly explain each of these formalities.

1783. *First*, the warning must be repeated *three times*. This is expressly enacted by the Sacred Canons: "Sed quia modo multi inveniuntur decimas dare nolentes, statuimus, ut secundum Domini nostri præceptum admoneanter *semel*, et *secundo*, et *tertio*. Qui si non emendaverint, anathematis vinculo feriantur, usque ad satisfactionem et emendationem congruam."[1] Observe here that this canon states that the admonition is to be repeated three times, *according to the precept of Our Lord*.[2] Only in the case of urgent necessity, *v. g.*, when there is *periculum in mora*, is it allowed to give the warning but once.[3] When the Prelate gives only a single warning, he must expressly state in the warning that it is given peremptorily, or for the first and last time, and once for all.[4] As we shall see further on, *one* warning is absolutely necessary to the *validity* of the punishment, whether correctional or punitive ; *three* are required for its *liciturus*. These repeated warnings are prescribed in order that the stubborn disobedience of the delinquent may thus appear more clearly, and also that he may have sufficient time to comply with the warning, or to prepare for his deience.[5]

1784. The above law is substantially retained in the Instructions of June 11, 1880, and *Cum Magnopere* of 1884.[6] For they enact that the canonical warnings shall precede the formal precept. Wherefore, if with us a Prelate imposes the precept without having previously given the

---

[1] C. xvi., Q. vii., can. 5; Cap. 96 de sent. exc. in 6. (v. 11).
[2] Cf. Kober, Excom., p. 150.   [3] Arg. Cap. 9 de sent. excom. in 6° (v. 11).
[4] Kober, l. c., p 151.   [5] Reiff., l. v., t. 39, n. 24.   [6] Art. VII.

warning, either paternally or legally, the precept is of no force.

1785. *Second*, it should be *in writing*; this condition is required on pain of the illicitness, though not of the invalidity of the warning.[1] In case of necessity, it can be made *orally*. But if, out of the case of necessity, the judge inflicts a correctional punishment, after an *oral* admonition, he commits a mortal sin, and incurs severe penalties, as we shall see.[2] Bishops however do not incur these penalties, since they are not expressly mentioned in the law imposing them.[3]

1786. *Third*, it should state clearly and unequivocally the precept or injunction of the Superior, namely, what the person warned must do or avoid, in order to escape the threatened punishment.[4] *Fourth*, it should fix a suitable and peremptory time, within which the delinquent can obey this injunction, if he wishes. When but a single warning is given, a space of at least six days must be allowed him, within which he may comply with the warning. In case the triple warning is given, a space of at least two days must intervene between each, so that the time for compliance with the admonition is the same in both cases, namely, at least six days.[5] However, for special and urgent reasons, or *where* there is *periculum in mora*, this term may be reduced to a shorter time, *v. g.*, to one day or even less time.[6] The other formalities will be explained below, when we come to speak of the *præceptum*. See also our *New Procedure*, n. 75.

[1] Cap. *Cum Medicinalis*, de sent. excom. in 6º.   [2] Stremler, l. c., p. 20.
[3] Cap. 48 de sent. excom. (v. 39.); Cap. 5 de sent. excom. in 6º (v. 11); Cap. 4 de sent. excom. in 6º (v. 11.)
[4] Pierantonelli, p. 188.   [5] Cap. de sent. excom. in 6 (v. 11).
[6] Kober, l. c., p. 151.

CHAPTER III.

THE PRECEPT.

(*Præceptum.*)

ART. I.

What is the Precept?

1787. The third and severest kind of preventive remedies or punishments are precepts. We shall discuss three questions: 1. What is here meant by a precept? 2. What does it presuppose? 3. How is it given?—What then is meant by the *Præceptum*? The Instructions *Sacra hæc* of June 11, 1880, and *Cum Magnopere* of 1884, give the answer: "Quod si monitiones in irritum cedant, Ordinarius jubet per Curiam delinquenti analogum præceptum intimari, ita ut in hoc explicetur quid ipse vel facere vel vitare debeat, addita respectivæ pœnæ ecclesiasticæ comminatione, quam, si præceptum transgrediatur, incurret."[1] Hence the precept of which we here speak is the command of the Bishop or judge, formally directing a delinquent Ecclesiastic, *i. e.*, one who, upon the required previous informal inquiry, has been found guilty of reprehensible conduct and who has been duly warned, to do this or avoid that, on pain of being otherwise visited, *servatis servandis*, with such or such an ecclesiastical punishment.[2]

1788. As will be seen, the precept bears no small resemblance to the canonical warnings, when given in a legal manner, as above described. For this reason, as has been noted, some Canonists, and apparently not without good reasons,—regard the *præceptum* as the real canonical warning, in the strict sense of the term.[3] This analogy or, according to some, identity will appear more fully, when we

[1] Art. VIII.   [2] Cf. Rota, l. c., p. 430.   [3] Cf. Droste, p. 102.

When can the Precept be enjoined? 69

come to show how the precept is made. At present we merely observe that the canonical warnings, which are to precede the precept, should indeed, no less than the precept, state what the delinquent must do or avoid in order to escape punishment. But the precept, while imposing a command similar to that given in the warnings, imposes it in a more formal, precise, final, and penal manner, and with graver results, in case of disobedience. Hence the formal precept is designed to obtain by *compulsion* what the canonical warnings failed to effect by *suasion* or spontaneously, namely, the amendment of the delinquent.[1]

Art. II.
When can it be enjoined?

1789. Our second question is: What does the precept or command presuppose? First, it must be preceded by the canonical warnings mentioned in Article VI. of the Instruction *Cum Magnopere*. This is clearly pointed out in these words of the Instruction:[2] " *Quod si monitiones in irritum cedant*, Ordinarius jubet per Curiam delinquenti analogum praeceptum intimari." This order, consecutiveness, or gradation is obligatory, on pain of nullity of the procedure. Hence, if a Prelate, without first giving the canonical warnings, imposed the precept and subsequently ordered the trial for the violation of the precept, the whole procedure would be invalid.[3] In fact, if, as we have shown, the canonical warnings inflict pain and are therefore punishments, it is evident that the precept causes far greater humiliation and is therefore a severer punishment than the warnings, owing to the solemn and formal manner in which it is made. Now the Church, as a rule, does not make use of the severer punishment before she has tried the milder one.[4]

[1] Acta S. S., l. c., p. 382. [2] Instr. *Cum Magnopere*, Art. vii.
[3] Acta S. S., vol. xv., p. 383; Rota, l. c., p. 430. [4] Droste, l. c., p. 102.

1790. Consequently, as Rota[1] observes, if the precept were imposed by the Prelate without the previous warnings, it could be disregarded with impunity by the delinquent, since it would be notoriously invalid *ipso jure*, being against the express provision of the Instructions of June 11, 1880, and *Cum Magnopere* of 1884. See our *New Procedure*, n. 73.

We do not agree therefore with some authors, when they contend that the precept need not be preceded by the admonitions.[2]

1791. The order or gradation, therefore, to be observed by the Superior, when he inflicts preventive remedies, is as follows: First, the canonical admonitions are given, and that either in a paternal or in a legal form; next, when these admonitions are disregarded, the precept is enjoined. The reason is obvious: a precept, owing to its formal and mandatory character, coupled with the threat of specific punishment, is far more humiliating than mere admonitions. Now the law of nature dictates that the graver punishments shall not be imposed until the lighter ones have been tried in vain.

1792. We say, "when he inflicts *preventive* remedies;" for when, owing to the gravity and nature of the offence, the Superior is constrained to proceed to repressive measures, the following order or gradation is to be observed. When there is question of repressive punishments of a *reformative* character, *v. g*, censures, the above gradation or order obtains, except in certain specified cases, explained by us in this volume. In other words, the Superior first gives the admonition; next the precept, and finally the trial; and, upon conviction, he imposes the punishment. But when there is question of repressive remedies which are *vindicatory* in character, the above order need not, though it

---

[1] Enchir. p. 430.   [2] Cf. Droste—Messmer, pp. 81, 144, 148 sq.

may laudably, be observed. In other words, the Bishop may order the trial and, upon conviction, impose vindicative penalties, without having given the previous warnings and precept.

1793. It is owing, we think, to a want of adverting to this distinction, that some writers have fallen into the mistake of asserting, in *general* terms and without due restrictions, that the admonitions need not precede the precept, and that the latter can be given at once, if the Superior judges it expedient;[1] or, in general, that the Bishop may at once institute criminal proceedings, if he has sufficient proof of the crime, and that he is not bound first to make use of extrajudicial corrective means.

1794. Next, the precept presupposes an offence or culpable conduct, and summary verification of such conduct, as has been described above under the article on spiritual retreats. This follows from the fact that, as has just been remarked, the warnings should precede the precept. Now the warnings themselves must be preceded by guilt, ascertained by a summary inquiry or investigation. We observe, before giving the precept, the Bishop or judge should, if need be, continue and perfect the extrajudicial and informal inquiry (*summaria facti cognitio*) that preceded the giving of the warnings, so that he may have no reasonable doubt whatever of the culpability of the delinquent, and that he may be, if possible, even more certain of the guilt, than he was at the time he gave the canonical warnings. As has been seen, he cannot issue the precept, even validly, unless he has a moral certitude or at least a canonical probatio *semi-plena* of the guilt.[2]

---

[1] Droste—Messmer, pp. 81, 144, 148, note 2, 149, 152.

[2] Acta S.S., l. c., p. 378; Rota, l. c., p. 431; Pierantonelli, l. c., p. 84; Droste, l. c., p. 106.

Art. III.

How is it given?

1795. *Q.* What are the formalities with which the precept is to be given.

A. As in the case of the canonical warnings, given in a legal manner, so also in the case of the precept, some of the formalities refer to the precept itself, its contents and form; others to the serving of the precept upon the delinquent. The formalities which regard the precept itself are chiefly the following: 1. It is given, not by the Bishop in person, though at his order, but by the *curia episcopalis*, in the manner stated below. Herein the precept differs from the canonical warnings, which, as was seen, are made by the Bishop himself or some person authorized by him, but not by the *Curia*. The reason of this difference is that the canonical warnings, even though made in a legal manner, partake more of a fatherly than of a judicial character, while the precept, though also to some extent a paternal and extrajudicial act,[1] nevertheless partakes more of a judicial than of a paternal character.[2] Hence it is proper that it should emanate from the judicial tribunal of the Bishop.

1796. Consequently we cannot agree with those writers who maintain that the precept is *wholly* an extrajudicial act.[3] For, while it is true, as all know, that not every *formal* or *legal* or *official* act is a judicial act, it is also true that those formal or official acts which, like the precept, lead directly to a trial and to repressive punishment, are judicial acts, just as the *initiatory* steps are considered a part of the whole proceedings to which they lead.

1797.—2. It must, on pain of nullity, be *in writing*. We say, *on pain* of *nullity;* for the Instruction *Cum Magnopere*,

---

[1] Acta S. S., l. c., p. 382.   [2] Droste, l. c., p. 101; Cf. Sanguineti, p, 507.
[3] Droste—Messmer, p. 144.

Art. XIV., expressly enacts: "Intimationes et notificationes *semper in scriptis absolute fiant.*" 3. It must state clearly and unequivocally what is to be done or avoided, *v. g.*, what persons or places are to be shunned. This is obligatory, on pain of nullity, for it is evidently a substantial part of the precept.¹ 4. It must, on pain of nullity, mention the specific punishment, whether correctional or punitive, that will be imposed if the command is unheeded.²

1798. This threatened punishment should, of course, be in proportion to the offence. For the lighter offences, spiritual exercises are usually imposed;³ for the graver, suspension and similar punishments are generally inflicted.⁴ 5. It should fix a suitable time, within which the delinquent may comply with the injunction. But it need not, like the canonical warnings, given in a legal manner, be repeated three times; it is given but once. As will be seen, these formalities are substantially the same as those of the canonical warnings described above.

1799. We come now to the *extrinsic* formalities of the precept, namely those which refer to the manner in which it is to be communicated to the delinquent. How, then, is the precept to be executed, *i. e., served on the delinquent?* The Instruction *Cum Magnopere*, Art. VIII., answers thus: "Præceptum delinquenti a Curiæ Cancellario coram Vicario Generali injungitur, aut etiam coram duobus testibus ecclesiasticis vel laicis spectatæ probitatis. 1° Actus injunctionis præcepti signatur a partibus præsentibus, et a delinquente etiam, si velit. 2° Vicarius Generalis jusjurandum testibus imponere potest de secreto servando, si prudenter a natura rei, de qua agitur, id requiratur,"

1800. From this, then, it will be seen that the precept is (*a*) to be read or given to the delinquent *in person*, who is cited to appear in court, for that purpose; (*b*) by the chancellor or

---

¹ Acta S. S., l. c., p. 383.   ² Ib.   ³ Ib.   ⁴ Droste, p. 105.

secretary of the episcopal curia; (c) in the presence either of the Vicar General, or of two witnesses, who are either Ecclesiastics or laics of marked probity. (d) An official record is then written out by the chancellor, of the whole transaction, *i. e.*, of the serving of the precept in the above manner; this record should be signed by all present, namely by the chancellor, the Vicar General or the two witnesses, and also by the delinquent, if he wishes. Thus a complete juridical proof is obtained of the execution, *i. e.*, of the delivery of the precept to the delinquent.

1801. (e) Finally, the Vicar General can compel the witnesses to swear that they will not divulge the proceedings. The object of this enactment is to prevent scandal among the faithful, and also to shield the good name of the accused. In fact, as Rota[1] remarks, the ecclesiastical judge should have nothing so much at heart, as the honor and dignity of the ecclesiastical state. He should therefore do all in his power to prevent, as far as possible, the precept or other punishment imposed by him upon an Ecclesiastic from becoming public. For, says the law of the Church: " Nec enim debet sacerdos publice pœnitere, sicut laicus."[2] Hence, says the above canonist, a prelate should not impose, even for very grave crimes, which are not yet public, suspension from hearing confessions or saying mass, not only on week days, but also on Sundays or holy-days.[3]

1802. The above mode of serving the precept takes it for granted that the delinquent has been cited to appear before the curia in order to receive the precept, and that he has really appeared;[4] or that he has been accessible without any citation. But if he fails contumaciously to appear on due citation, or maliciously renders himself inaccessible to the curia, the precept may be sent to him (a) by a trustworthy person, who shall certify the serving of the precept,

---

[1] Enchir., p. 432.
[2] Can. Presbyter 5, Dist. 82.
[3] Rota, l. c.,p. 433.
[4] Droste, p. 104.

and whose testimony shall be full proof thereof ; or also (*b*) by registered mail, care being taken that the acknowledgment of the receipt or rejection of the registered letter containing the precept be kept. Such acknowledgment constitutes full proof of the delivery.[1] If even this is impossible, *v. g.*, if the delinquent conceals himself, so that neither the messenger nor the registered mail can reach him, it may be left at his house, or if he has none, posted on the doors of the church or other public place, where it may come to his knowledge.

[1] Instr. *Cum Magnopere*. Art. XIV.

PART III.

CANONICAL REPRESSIVE PUNISHMENTS WHICH ARE VINDICATORY.

(Pœnæ vindicativæ).

1803. Having discussed the *preventive* remedies, we come now to the *repressive*. As has been already noted, repressive ecclesiastical or canonical punishments are divided into two kinds: *vindicative* (*pœnæ, pœnæ vindicativæ*) and *reformative* (*pœnæ medicinales, censuræ*). The former are repressive punishments in the strict sense, the latter are also repressive punishments in every sense of the term, though their chief and direct aim is medicinal, that is, to heal the spiritual infirmity of the delinquent, and their secondary, punitive or vindicatory of the law. We shall treat of vindicatory punishments in this *Third Part*, and of correctional in the *Fourth Part* of this volume.

1804. The vindicatory punishments are divided into *spiritual* and *temporal*. The chief spiritual punishments are dismissal, penal transfer, deposition, degradation, disqualification for ecclesiastical offices, and incapacity for the ecclesiastical state.[1] The principal temporal punishments, still inflicted by the Church, are infamy, pecuniary fines, and assignment to a monastery or house of retreat.[2] Accordingly, we shall divide this *Third Part* into two sections, the first treating of the *spiritual*, the second, of the *temporal* vindicatory remedies of the Church.

---

[1] Reiff., l. 5, t. 37, n. 18.   [2] Stremler, l. c., p. 31.

SECTION I.

Spiritual Vindicatory Punishments.

CHAPTER I.

DISMISSAL OF RECTORS ALSO IN THE UNITED STATES.

(*Privatio*).

ART. I.

Correct Idea of Dismissal or Privatio Officii.

1805. Ecclesiastical offices, positions, and benefices, as we have seen,[1] may be lost, not only by the death of the incumbent, but also by resignation, by transfer, by the acquisition of another office or benefice which is incompatible with the first, and by privation or dismissal. Canonists, therefore, properly say that a person may lose an ecclesiastical office or position in two ways: either *voluntarily*, as by resignation, or *compulsorily*, as by dismissal or involuntary transfer. In the present chapter, we shall speak of dismissal; in the next, of penal transfers.

1806. Dismissal, or absolute removal, (*privatio definitiva, remotio a munere*) is a canonical punishment which consists in this, that an Ecclesiastic is deprived of his ecclesiastical office or position, without being at the same time appointed to another, but without being disqualified to hold other ecclesiastical offices or positions in the future.[2]

1807. We say, *canonical punishment;* for, to take away from an Ecclesiastic his office or benefice, and consequent-

---

[1] Supra, vol. i., n. 380.
[2] Supra, n. 402; Reiff, l. 5, t. 37, n. 21; De Brabandere, n. 1511.

ly all the emoluments, advantages, and honor or standing and position attached to it, will evidently inflict *great pain* and *suffering, bodily and mental,* upon him. Hence all canonists agree, as we shall presently see, that dismissal is one of the greatest penalties of the Church.[1]

1808. We say, also, *without being at the same time appointed to another;* since dismissal is a *total* removal from a particular office or position, for the time being. Consequently it differs, in this respect, from a *transfer,* made with or against the will of the incumbent. For by a transfer a person indeed loses or is deprived of his office, but yet is appointed at the same time to another.

1809. We add, *but without being disqualified,* etc. Herein dismissal differs from *deposition.* The latter not only deprives a person of his office, but also disqualifies him to be appointed to others in future. Dismissal, on the contrary, merely takes away the office which a person actually holds, and consequently does not incapacitate him from asking for, and obtaining other ecclesiastical offices, benefices, or dignities, in the future. Nay, it does not necessarily affect *all* the offices or benefices which a person possesses. Consequently, an Ecclesiastic who lawfully holds several positions at the same time, may be dismissed from one, without being deprived of the others.

1810. It may be observed here that, while dismissal does not legally incapacitate a person from being appointed to offices in future, yet morally and practically it produces, in most cases, the same result. For a dismissal casts such a slur and discredit upon the Ecclesiastic dismissed, that he will find it very difficult, if not well nigh impossible, to obtain any other ecclesiastical appointment, from his own Bishop, or from any other Bishop.

1811. We shall now proceed to discuss the dismissal, that

[1] Schmalzg. l. 5, t. 37, n. 128; Phillips, Comp., §. 87, p. 168, and §. 188, p. 377.

is, absolute removal, and not merely transfer, of Rectors of parishes or missions, also in the United States. According to the general law of the Church, as still in full force, the care of souls, or the office of Rector of a parish, is to be conferred upon the incumbent *for life*. Consequently, wherever this law obtains—and it obtains *per se* everywhere—Rectors of souls are irremovable. We say, *and it obtains " per se" everywhere ;* for, exceptionally, it is not in full force in certain countries. Thus, in some missionary countries, all Rectors are *amovibiles*. In other missionary countries, *v. g.*, in England, and at present, also in the United States, and also in France and Belgium, *some* Rectors are canonically irremovable, *others* are not.

1812. Accordingly, there are, at present, two kinds of Rectors, also in the United States—removable and irremovable.[1] We shall, therefore, first speak of the dismissal of Rectors who are irremovable; then, of the dismissal of those who are not irremovable.

ART II.

Dismissal of Irremovable Rectors.

For the sake of greater clearness, we shall discuss under separate heads, first, the dismissal of irremovable Rectors in countries where canon law fully obtains; secondly, the dismissal of irremovable Rectors in the United States, England, and Ireland.

§ 1. *Dismissal of Irremovable Rectors where the General Law of the Church fully Obtains.*

1813. *Q.* Why and how can Rectors who are canonically irremovable be deprived of their parishes, according to the general law of the Church, as still in force?

---

[1] Supra, vol. i., n. 402, 409, *sixth edition*, 1887.

A. 1. Only for *crimes;* 2. which are *very grave;* 3. and expressly stated in law; 4. and upon a canonical trial.[1] Hence the following rules must be observed in the dismissal of irremovable Rectors.

1814. *Rule I. The dismissal can be inflicted only for crimes.* In other words, the dismissal in the case can be inflicted, as a rule, only as a punishment for crimes committed by the incumbent. We say, *as a rule.* For the law of the Church has laid down certain cases where a Rector loses his parish or office *ipso jure,* even though he is not guilty of crime. Thus the Sacred Canons decree that an Ecclesiastic shall *ipso jure* lose or be deprived of his office or benefice, and consequently also of his parish, (*a*) when he obtains another benefice or office, which is incompatible with the first; (*b*) when he enters a religious order and has made his profession in it; (*c*) when a person who is not yet a priest obtains the appointment to a parish, and neglects to be ordained a priest, within a year after his appointment.

1815. These cases where an Ecclesiastic is deprived of his office or parish, even though he is not guilty of crime, are all expressly enumerated in law. For, as we shall presently see, an irremovable Rector can be deprived of his parish only for *canonical cause*; that is, only for causes which are expressly stated in law.

1816. Outside of the above cases, which are all expressly given in law, dismissal can be inflicted *only in punishment of crimes committed by the Rector.* In other words, *the only other cause,* besides the above, for which an irremovable Rector can be dismissed from his parish or office, is *crime.*[2] This is expressly enacted by the law of the Church, as still in full force.[3] The reason is, that dismissal is a *punishment,* nay a

---

[1] Supra vol. i., n. 408, *sixth edition.*

[2] Leur., For. Benef., P. iii., Q. 169, n. 2; Reiff., l. 5, t. 37, n. 5; München, l. c., vol. ii., p. 152.

[3] Can. 38., c. 16, Q. 7; Can. 7, Dist. 56; Supra., n. 418.

punishment of the gravest kind. Now there can be no punishment where there is no crime, as we show above, Vol. I., n. 418, *sixth edition*.

1817. That dismissal is a punishment, nay a punishment of the severest kind, is manifest from the very idea of punishment and from the unanimous teaching of canonists. For, as we have shown above, a punishment is a *pain, suffering*, or *evil*, inflicted for crime. Now, to take away from an Ecclesiastic his office or parish, and consequently all the *emoluments, advantages, honor, standing, and position* attached to it, is evidently to inflict *pain, suffering, humiliation, disgrace*, and pecuniary loss. It is, in fact, as canonists say, a *social* or *civil death*. For as the natural death deprives a person of all advantages in the natural or physical order, so dismissal deprives an Ecclesiastic of all that he values in the social or civil order of the Church.

1818. Accordingly canonists unanimously teach that dismissal is one of the severest punishments of the Church. The great canonist Cardinal De Luca, as quoted and approved by the learned Jesuit canonist Leurenius,[1] writes: " Privatio et amissio beneficii in materia beneficiali dicitur importare *pœnam gravissimam et ordinariam* . . . seu dicitur *pœna major*, quæ in jure ordinario dicitur assimilata *pœnæ mortis* in temporalibus, *cum sit mors civilis*."[2] Leurenius himself says that dismissal or *privatio* is a *pœna gravissima et ordinaria*. There can be no doubt therefore that dismissal is a *punishment*, nay one of the *severest or greatest of the regular or ordinary punishments of the Church*. Hence the law of the Church, as well as the law of nature, prescribes that it shall not be inflicted save for crime.

1819. It is, therefore, in consonance with this principle that the law of the Church expressly provides, that, when an

---

[1] For. Benef., P. iii., Q. 169, n. 2.
[2] Card. de Luca, l. 12, Benef., Disc. 35., n. 10; Disc. 75, n. 4.—Venetiis. 1734.

Ecclesiastic, by reason of inexperience, want of knowledge or of ability, or by reason of old age or infirmity, becomes unable to discharge the duties of his office, parish, or benefice, he cannot be deprived of it, [1] but simply that an assistant or coadjutor be assigned to him. [2]

1820. *Rule II. Dismissal can be inflicted only for crimes which are grave and atrocious.* The reason is, that, as we have seen, dismissal is one of the *severest punishments*. Now there must always be a due proportion between the offence and its punishment. [3]

1821. *Rule III. The crimes must be expressly stated in law.* In other words, dismissal can be inflicted, not for *any* and *every* crime, no matter how grievous, but only for those heinous crimes which are expressly designated by the law of the Church as being punishable, either *ipso facto* or *per sententiam*, with dismissal. The law gives the Ordinary a certain amount of discretionary power in the infliction of *minor* punishments, but does not allow him to impose those which are *severe*, except in cases expressly stated. [4] For the specific crimes which have dismissal annexed, [5] whether *ipso jure* or only *ferendæ sententiæ*, see above, Vol. I., n. 412–415, *sixth edition.*

1822. Here it should be observed, that, by the older canons of the Church, dismissal was imposed for less grievous crimes than are now required, the severity of the ancient discipline having been somewhat mitigated by the more recent legislation of the Church. [6]

1823. *Rule IV. The crime must be fully proved by a regular canonical trial.* [7] This is clearly and repeatedly laid down

---

[1] Cap. 5, de cleric. ægr. (iii. 6).
[2] Cap. 3, 4, de cleric. ægr. (iii. 6); Conc. Trid., sess. xxi., cap. 6; De Angelis, l. 3., t. 6, n. 2; Præl. S. Sulp., vol. iii., n. 836.
[3] Leur., l. c., Q. 169, n. 2.   [4] Supra. vol. i., n. 410, *sixth edition.*
[5] Leur., For. benef., P. iii., Q. 14. sq. ; Reiff., l. 3. t. 5, n. 343 sq.
[6] Leur., l. c., Q. 169, n. 1; Stremler, l. c., p. 33   [7] Permaneder, §§. 275, 443.

in the law of the Church. Pope Alexander III., in his decretal *Conquerente nobis* 7 (ii. 13), as we have shown elsewhere,[1] ordered an Ecclesiastic, who had been dismissed from his place without a trial, to be reinstated in his parish by his Archbishop, solely on the ground that the dismissal had been imposed without a previous trial. The *Glossa*, commenting on the above decretal *Conquerente*, says: "Nullus debet destitui vel spoliari etiam a prælato suo, *juris ordine non servato.*"

1824. The reason why a previous trial is required is, that dismissal, as we have seen, is one of the severest punishments of the Church. Now it is a maxim of canon law that no regular or ordinary punishment whatever can be inflicted upon a person, unless he has either *confessed* his crime, or been *legitimately, i. e., juridically, convicted of it.* Thus Leurenius teaches:[2] "Cum privatio sit pœna gravissima et ordinaria, ut dictum est, hinc intrat criminalistarum propositio, quod ad pœnam ordinariam procedi non potest, *nisi contra legitime confessum vel convictum.*"

1825. It should be observed that a previous trial is required, not only when dismissal is imposed *per sententiam*, but also when it is inflicted *ipso jure*. In other words, a previous trial is required, not only when there is question of inflicting dismissal for crimes which have dismissal annexed *post sententiam*, but also when there is question of inflicting it for offences for which the law imposes dismissal *ipso jure*. In both cases, the fact that a person has really committed the crime must be established by a trial.[3] But the sentence following such trial is different in the two cases. For, in the cases of crimes having dismissal annexed *ipso jure*, the sentence is merely *declaratory;* that is, simply de-

---

[1] Supra, vol. ii., n. 1105, *second edition*.   [2] For. Ienef., P. iii., Q. 172.

[3] Where the crime is *notorious* permanently, no trial is, strictly speaking, necessary. See our *New Procedure*, n. 107. But even in this case, it is safer to give a trial. See Conc. Pl. Balt. III., n. 310.

clares that the crime has been committed, and that therefore the dismissal inflicted by the law itself (*ipso jure*) has been incurred. In the other case, the sentence is *condemnatory*.

1826. We have said, *by regular canonical trial;* that is, by a *solemn* or *formal* canonical trial. For, as we have seen, the Sacred Canons ordain that, where *punishments* are to be inflicted, it can be done only by a *formal* or *solemn*, not by a *summary* canonical trial. In 1880, however, the Holy See partly modified the prescription of the Sacred Canons by the Instruction of the S. C. EE. et RR., dated June 11, 1880.[1] See above, Vol. I., No. 408, *sixth edition;* Vol. II., Nos. 1277, 1278, *second edition;* Our *New Procedure*, No. 581, sq.

§. 2. *Dismissal of Irremovable Rectors in the United States.*

1827. The *Third Plenary Council of Baltimore* has, in accordance with the *schema* agreed upon at the Conferences held in Rome, November, 1883, between the Cardinals of the Propaganda and our Archbishops, made the following enactments. 1. " In singulis diœcesibus, auctoritate Episcopi, de Consultorum suorum consilio seligantur certæ missiones, quæ magis aptæ videntur, ut parœciarum instar haberi possint, atque a rectoribus missionariis permanenter institutis seu inamovibilibus sicut in Anglia regantur.

" Ejusmodi missio, cui præficiendus erit rector inamovibilis, omnino instructa esse debet ecclesia congrua, schola pro utroque sexu, domo sacerdotis usui accommodata, et proventibus sufficientibus et satis certis ad sacerdotis, ecclesiæ, et scholæ necessariam sustentationem." [2]

1828—2. " Missio cujus rector semel inamovibilis est constitutus, in posterum semper habebit rectorem inamovibilem, licet aliqua territorii parte juxta normam in n. 20 descriptam minuatur. Novarum autem parœciarum ex dismem-

---

[1] This Instruction is given above, vol. ii., p. 424 sq.
[2] Conc. Pl. Balt. III., n. 33.

bratione efformatarum rectores non erunt inamovibiles, nisi Episcopi auctoritate tales constituti fuerint. Parœciæ eadem dismembratione efformatæ independentes tamen constituentur ab ecclesia matrice." [1]

1829—3. "*Pro nunc*[2] instituantur in singulis diœcesibus rectores missionarii inamovibiles tali numero, *ut inter omnes diœceseos rectores decimus quisque sit inamovibilis*, dummodo conditiones requisitæ adsint tum ex parte missionis, cum ex parte rectoris eligendi. Quæ proportio (unus inter decem) ne inconsulto excedatur intra viginti primos annos post concilium promulgatum."

1830—4. "Institutio autem rectorum inamovibilium, ut præscripta, *ultra triennium a promulgatione concilii computandum* non erit differenda.

"Inter rectores inamovibiles tamen *rector ecclesiæ cathedralis non est ponendus;* et quando nova diœcesis erigitur, rector ecclesiæ quam Episcopus in cathedralem eligit, ipso facto erit amovibilis."

1831—5. "Ad cônditiones quod spectat, quæ ex parte eligendorum ad missiones inamovibilitatis privilegio insignitas requiruntur, ut quis sacerdos ejusmodi missioni præfici valeat, opus erit: I. ut per decem saltem annos in diœcesi sacrum ministerium laudabiliter exercuerit; II. ut intra idem temporis spatium sese habilem probaverit ad parochiam administrandam et in temporalibus et in spiritualibus; III. ut concursum faciat juxta normam infra statuendam. Inter eos qui hisce conditionibus satisfecerint, electio dignioris relinquitur judicio et conscientiæ Episcopi, salva appellatione juxtà constitutionem S. M. Benedicti XIV. *Cum illud*, diei 14 Dec. 1742."

1832. According to this legislation, which now forms the law for this country, we have at present two classes of Rec-

---

[1] Ib., n. 34.

[2] In regard to the meaning of the words *pro nunc*, see note b, on p. 411 of vol. i. of the *sixth edition of our Elements of Eccl. Law*.

tors: some are irremovable, others are not irremovable, as we show in the *sixth* edition of the *first* volume of this work, n. 409, 416, and in our treatise entitled, " *The New Procedure*," or "clear and full explanation of the Instruction *Cum Magnopere*." We shall first speak of the removal (and by removal we here mean *dismissal*, not merely *transfer*) of our irremovable Rectors; next, of that of our Rectors who are not irremovable.

1833. *Q.* For what causes, and in what manner can our irremovable Rectors be deprived of (not merely *transferred* from) their missions?

A. The *Third Plenary Council of Baltimore* answers thus:[1] " Rector missionarius permanenter institutus seu inamovibilis, a sua missione definitive removeri non poterit, *nisi ob canonicam causam*, et tam in remediis præventivis quam repressivis servata forma procedendi juxta normam Instructionis S. Congregationis de Propaganda Fide de cognoscendis et definiendis causis criminalibus et disciplinaribus clericorum, quæ incipit *Cum Magnopere*, nuperrime ad Episcopos Fœderatorum Statuum Americæ Septentrionalis directæ."[2] In other words, our irremovable Rectors can be deprived of their missions or parishes: 1. only for *canonical cause*, that is, for cause expressly stated in law; 2. and in the manner outlined in the Instruction *Cum Magnopere*, both as regards preventive and repressive punishments.

1834. We say, *only for canonical cause*—" *nisi ob causam canonicam.*" By a *canonical cause* is meant a cause expressly stated in law. Now this law, as we have shown above, when speaking of the dismissal of irremovable Rectors in Catholic countries where canon law fully obtains, provides, 1. that an irremovable Rector can be dismissed in certain cases specifically enumerated by it, even though he is not guilty of

---

[1] Conc. Pl. Balt. III., n. 38.
[2] See this Instruction *Cum Magnopere*, together with an accurate and paraphrased English translation in our work entitled The *New Procedure*, p. 255 sq.

Dismissal of Irremovable Rectors.

crime;[1] 2. that, outside of these cases, the dismissal cannot be inflicted save (*a*) for *crime*, (*b*) which is *very grave*, (*c*) and *specifically mentioned in law*

This is also the teaching of the *Third Plenary Council of Baltimore*, when it says: " Causae ob quas rector inamovibilis deponi possit et debeat *in jure continentur*, et ad eas pertinent generatim *omnia delicta in grave discrimen* disciplinam ecclesiasticam vel jura sive spiritualia sive temporalia missionis adducentia, quorum reus convictus fuerit."[2]

1835. What are, in particular, the crimes expressly stated in law, for which dismissal is imposed *ipso facto*, or can be imposed *per sententiam?* For the answer, see Vol. I., Nos. 412, 413, *sixth edition.*

1836. To these canonical causes or offences, for which dismissal is or can be imposed, by the general law of the Church, upon irremovable Rectors here as elsewhere, the *Third Plenary Council of Baltimore* has added seven other causes or offences for which our irremovable Rectors can be dismissed. The words of the *Council* are : " Pro praesenti rerum nostrarum conditione ad has causas (canonicas) nominatim pertinere declarantur sequentes:

1. " Inobedientia pertinax in re magni momenti regulis ab Ordinario constitutis sive pro administratione ipsarum etiam rerum temporalium suae missionis, sive pro oneribus dioecesanis sublevandis." For the other six causes added by the *Council*, see Vol. I., No. 414, *sixth edition.*

1837. We say, secondly, *and in the manner outlined by the Instruction Cum Magnopere*, both as regards preventive and repressive punishments. Now the mode of proceeding prescribed in this *Instruction* is as follows : Before inflicting *punishments* proper or repressive measures, even those which are vindicative, the Superior should, as a rule, try *paternal* remedies, *v.g.*, admonitions, precepts, retreats. When these

---

[1] Supra, n. 1816. [2] Conc. Pl. Balt. III., n. 38.

remedies prove of no avail, he proceeds to inflict repressive measures, in such order, however, as to impose first *milder* punishments, *v.g.*, suspension, and afterwards the *severer* ones. The preventive remedies are to be preceded by an *extra-judicial* investigation; the repressive, by a *judicial*, that is, by a canonical trial.

1838. Consequently dismissal should, as a rule, be inflicted upon our irremovable Rectors[1] (*a*) only after the preventive remedies and the milder punishments have been applied to them, without effect, and they have thus shown themselves incorrigible; (*b*) by a canonical trial, as outlined in the Instruction *Cum Magnopere*. This is expressly ordained by the *Third Plenary Council of Baltimore* in these words of the above quoted passage: "Rector missionarius inamovibilis, a sua missione definitive removeri non poterit, nisi ob causam canonicam, *et tam in remediis præventivis quam repressivis servata forma procedendi juxta normam Instructionis Cum Magnopere.*"[2]

1839. In fact, as we have seen, dismissal from office being a privation of what is dearest to man—namely, of his position, standing, and of the honor and emoluments connected with it—is one of the *severest punishments* of the Church. Now it is a general principle of canon law and also of natural justice, that, as a rule, the heavier punishments should not be inflicted until the more moderate ones have been applied in vain.[3] Therefore canonists all agree that dismissal should be made use of only *as a last resort*, and consequently only when all the milder remedies have been tried, but produced no effect.

1840. From what has been said it will be seen, that our irremovable Rectors, though not Canonical Parish Priests proper,[4] yet enjoy the right of *inamovibilitas* in the same

---

[1] This applies, of course, also to irremovable Rectors in countries where canon law is in full force. (Prael. S. Sulp., vol. iii. n. 835.)
[2] Conc. Pl. Balt. III., n 38.   [3] Prael. S. Sulp., vol. iii. n. 835.
[4] See vol i., note b under n. 654, *sixth edition*.

Dismissal of Rectors who are not Irremovable.

manner as Canonical Parish Priests in the full sense of the term, with the exception that they can be dismissed for the additional seven causes given in the above decree of the *Third Plenary Council of Baltimore*.[1]

§. 3. *Dismissal of our Rectors who are not irremovable.*

1841. Having seen when and how irremovable Rectors, also with us, may be dismissed from their missions or parishes, we shall now examine when and how our Rectors who are not irremovable may be dismissed or absolutely removed from their missions.

1842. *Q*. For what cause and in what manner can our Rectors who are not irremovable be dismissed (not merely transferred) from their missions?

A. For the answer see above, Vol. i., Nos. 415, 416, 417, 418. See also the work recently published by us, entitled *The New Procedure, or a clear and full explanation of the Instr. " Cum Magnopere " of* 1884, chapter VIII., article XLV., Nos. 581-593.

1843. In these places we maintain that, as under the Instruction of July 20, 1878, so also under the Instruction *Cum Magnopere* of 1884, a removable Rector cannot, as a rule, be dismissed from his mission save (*a*) for *crimes*, (*b*) and by *trial*.[2]

1844. That this teaching is correct, is now beyond doubt, as appears from a very important decision recently given by the S. C. de Prop. Fide, and graciously communicated to us by His Eminence, the Cardinal Archbishop of Baltimore. This decision is as follows: " Jamvero Emi Patres S. Concilio Christiano nomini propagando præpositi in Comitiis Generalibus die 28 Martii 1887 habitis sequentia decreverunt: *In casibus remotionis peragendæ, seu privationis totalis ab officio Rectoris, (ubi de amovibilibus sermo sit) in pœnam criminis*

---

[1] Conc. Pl. Balt. III., n. 3 8; supra, vol. i, n. 414, *sixth edition*.
[2] Our *New Procedure*, n. 591.

vel reatus disciplinaris, canonicus processus juxta præfatæ Instructionis "*Cum Magnopere*" *et Concilii III. Plenarii decreta confici debet.*"

1845. This is in harmony with the letter and spirit of the common law of the Church as laid down in the Sacred Canons. For it is a general principle of canon law, enunciated by Pope Gregory, that an Ecclesiastic, even though he be *amovibilis*, shall not be deprived of his office, especially when the care of souls is annexed to it, *except when he has made himself unworthy of it by crime.* The words of the great Pope are: "Satis perversum et contra ecclesiasticam probatur esse censuram ut frustra pro quorumdam voluptatibus suis quis privetur officiis, quem *sua culpa vel facinus* ab officii quo fungitur gradu non dejicit."[1] The *Glossa*, commenting on this passage, says: "Non enim privandus est quis jure suo, *nisi pro gravissimo delicto.*" The same Pontiff decrees in another place: "Quam (ecclesiam) si juste adeptus fuerit, hanc nonnisi *gravi culpa* coram Episcopo canonica severitate amittat."[2] The *Glossa*, in explaining this passage, writes: "Et postquam ipsam (ecclesiam) juste fuerit (aliquis) adeptus, nonnisi *gravi culpa* interveniente coram Episcopo *ordine judiciario probato*, eam perdat."

1846. This legislation is founded upon natural justice. For the dismissal, also of a removable Rector, is a privation, or taking away from him, of office, and consequently also of the honor, position, and emoluments connected with the office. Hence it inflicts both *disgrace* and *pecuniary loss*, and is therefore a *punishment*, nay, a punishment of the severest kind. Now the very law of nature prescribes that, as a rule, there can be no punishment where there is no crime, and that the crime must be established by a trial.

1847. Here it may be asked: What, then, is the difference between our removable and irremovable Rectors, if neither

[1] Can. Satis 7, D. 56; Corpus Juris Can. cum Glossa. Lugd. 1555.
[2] Can. Inventum 38, causa 16, Q. 7.

can be dismissed without a trial? For the answer, see above, Vol. I., No. 418, *sixth edition.*[1]

§. 4. *Dismissal of Rectors in Ireland, England, Scotland, and other English speaking Countries.*

I. Dismissal in England.

1848. *Q.* How are Rectors dismissed, that is, absolutely removed from their missions, in England?

A. We premise: First, there are, as yet, no *canonical parishes* in England. This appears from the following decree of the First Provincial Synod of Westminster, which is still in force: "Neque enim parœcias circumscribere *vel canonice instituere licet,* tum ob locorum ubi existunt ecclesiæ inter se distantiam, tum quod multis in casibus, ecclesiarum loco, missionibus inserviant oratoria virorum laicorum aedibus annexa, necnon alias ob causas, quas hic enumerare supervacaneum videtur. Quapropter Archiepiscopus et Episcopi supplicandum censuerunt SSmo Domino Nostro, ut dignaretur concedere ac sancire formam regiminis ab ipsis propositam, per quam. . .et *parochialis regiminis methodus paulatim introduceretur.* Quibus nostris precibus SSmus annuit, ut patet ex decreto a S. C. de Prop. Fide die 21 Apr. 1852 emisso.

1849.—1. Hujus igitur vigore, donec a S. Sede aliter provideatur, in singulis dioecesibus, auctoritate Episcopi, de consilio tamen Capituli, ecclesiae nonnullae seligantur, quae magis aptae videntur, ut *adinstar parœciarum haberi possint.*

1850.—2. Iis ordinarie praeficiatur sacerdos qui titulum habeat *Rectoris* Missionarii, qui ecclesiae et animarum curam gerat, quemadmodum caeteri ecclesiis in Anglia praepositi ; *sed permanenter institutus habeatur.* . . .

1851.—3. In caeteris ecclesiis seu missionibus, *simplices missionarii, ad nutum* Episcopi amovibiles, curam animarum

---

[1] See also the Acta S. S., v. l. iii., p. 506 sq; De Angel's. Prael., l. i., t. 28, n. 7.

habebunt, intra limites unicuique missioni ab Episcopo pro tempore assignatos."[1]

1852. We premise again: While there are no canonical parishes proper in England, there are, as is evident from the above passage, two classes of Rectors: some are appointed permanently (*parochi permanenter instituti, Rectores missionarii*); the others are *amovibiles ad nutum Episcopi*.

1853. We now answer: Rectors in England *who are permanently appointed* cannot be validly dismissed from their missions or quasi-parishes, (*a*) except for *grave crimes*; (*b*) and by *trial* before the Commission of Investigation, which is to be established in every diocese, and is composed of five priests, presided over by one of their own number, as chairman. The manner of proceeding or of conducting the trial is outlined in the acts of the above Synod of Westminster,[2] and is substantially the same as that given in the Instruction of July 20, 1878, for the United States.

1854. In regard to the dismissal of *removable Rectors* in England, the ecclesiastical legislation of that country is silent. It is, therefore, necessary to fall back on the general principles of canon law and canonical equity. These are set forth by us above, Vol. I., Nos. 415-420, *sixth edition*. They are, briefly stated, as follows: Dismissal, even of removable Rectors, is a privation or taking away of what is and should be as dear as life itself, namely of social standing and of the means of an honorable subsistence. Hence it entails not only dishonor and disgrace, but also the loss of support. Consequently it inflicts the greatest pain and humiliation. It is, therefore, a great punishment, and can, in consequence, be imposed, as a rule, only (*a*) for *crime*, (*b*) and by *trial*, in which the substantial rules of justice, as laid down by the very law of nature, are observed. What

[1] Conc. Prov. Westmin. I., 1852, Decretum xiii. See Coll. Lac., Vol. iii, pp. 925, 950, 960.

[2] Coll. Lac., vol. iii, pp. 925, 960.

II. Dismissal in Ireland.

are these substantial formalities or rules of justice? For the answer, see above, Vol. II., Nos. 692, 693, 694, second edition, 1888.

1855. *Q.* How are Parish Priests dismissed from their Parishes in Ireland?

A. Before answering we remark: The general law of the Church respecting canonical parishes and canonical parish priests is in full force in Ireland. In other words, the churches or congregations are canonical parishes, and the Rectors canonical Parish Priests, in the proper sense of the term. They are consequently irremovable.[1] This was their status prior to the Synod of Maynooth, held in 1875; and it was not changed by that Synod. Hence this status still exists in Ireland. His Grace, the Most Rev. Dr. Walsh, the present illustrious Archbishop of Dublin, wrote us, a short time since, in reply to our inquiry, that the ecclesiastical status and legislation in Ireland are about the same, at present, as they were under the Plenary Synod held in Maynooth, in 1875.

1856. We now answer: Parish Priests in Ireland can be deprived of their Parishes (*a*) only for causes or crimes expressly stated in the sacred canons; (*b*) and by a canonical trial. However, the Synod of Maynooth states that in Ireland, owing to the law of the land, the formalities of trials, laid down in the sacred canons, cannot be observed in every particular, and seems to leave the determination of the particular mode of conducting trials to the Provincial Councils of the respective provinces. The words of the Fathers of Maynooth are: "Cum vero in hac regione omnes formae in jure canonico praescriptae pro judiciis ecclesiasticis nequeant observari, habita legis civi-

---

[1] Cf. Syn. Pl. Mayn., pp. 109, 299, 300.

iis ratione, cavendum ut saltem ea omnia fiant quae ad veritatem inveniendam et ad justam rei defensionem necessaria sunt. Qua de re in Synodis Provincialibus sedulo agendum erit."[1]

1857. At the same time this Synod, in the decree just quoted, refers to, and embodies in its Acts,[2] the mode of proceeding adopted in England, and would therefore seem to recommend that the Parish Priests in Ireland be dismissed upon trial, to be conducted before Commissions of Investigation, as is the case in England and was also prescribed for the United States in the Instruction of July 20, 1878.

1858. The obstacle on the part of the *civil law* referred to in the above decree appears to be the prohibition to swear in witnesses.

For, as appears from the testimony in the famous trial of the Rev. Robert O'Keefe, P. P., *v.* His Eminence Cardinal Cullen, the swearing in of witnesses by the ecclesiastical judge, in Ireland and also in England, seems illegal and positively forbidden by the law of the land. Thus the Most Rev. Dr. Leahy, Archbishop of Cashel, being examined for the defence, and asked: " Now, in proceeding in canon law, must not witnesses be sworn?" answered thus: " Yes, that is one of the formalities, and it is because witnesses cannot be sworn in such a proceeding in this country that an ordinary judicial proceeding is impossible."[2] In the United States the swearing in of witnesses is not forbidden by the civil law, as we show above, Vol. II., Nos. 843, 1344.

[1] Syn. Pl. Mayn., n. 261.   [2] Ib., p. 248.   [3] See vol. ii., n. 843.

ART. III.

Support of Dismissed and Suspended Ecclesiastics.

§ 1. *Support of Dismissed Rectors.*

1859. *Q.* Is an Ecclesiastic who is dismissed from his parish, office, or benefice, to be left without any support whatever, even though moderate?

A. We premise: we say in the question, *even though moderate;* since there can be no question of giving Ecclesiastics who are discharged for unworthy conduct an *ample* or even *comfortable* living, such as they had when they were in good standing. The law of the Church, as laid down already by the great Apostle of the Gentiles, is: " They who work in the holy place, eat the things that are of the holy place: and they who serve the altar, partake with the altar... they who preach the gospel, should live of the gospel."[1] In other words, those Ecclesiastics only are entitled in justice to a *sustentatio congrua*,[2] that is, comfortable living, in keeping with the dignity of their state, who work in the ministry. Consequently those who, by their own criminal conduct, render themselves unworthy to work in the sacred ministry, and are therefore deprived of their office or suspended from it, have no right to this ample and honorable support, derived from the income of the office. The reason is plain. For, to give such Ecclesiastics the same ample support which they received while they

---

[1] I. Cor., ix., 13-14.

[2] By *congrua sustentatio* is here meant not a *scanty*, but a *comfortable* and honorable support; that is, a living which supplies, not merely the *necessaries*, but also the *comforts* of life, in keeping with the ecclesiastical state. When a person is ordained *ad titulum beneficii* or *missionis*, this support is derived from the income of his office, benefice, or mission. When he is ordained *ad titulum Patrimonii*, it comes from his private property. Dismissal or suspension, as is evident, only entails the loss of the income of the office or mission, but not of the Patrimony.

were in good standing, would be putting a premium on crime.[1]

1860. We now answer: While unworthy Ecclesiastics who have unfitted themselves for work, and are in consequence deprived of their office, cannot claim an ample support, they are nevertheless given as much as is necessary to supply their actual wants. In other words, they receive, not, the *comforts*, but merely the *necessaries* of life, in order that they may not be obliged to go begging or to engage in secular pursuits, to the disgrace of the entire ecclesiastical state.

1861. This appears to be also the teaching of the *Third Plenary Council of Baltimore*, which says: " Quamvis itaque sacerdotes, qui ob suam culpam a sacris arcentur functionibus, non possint titulo justitiæ ab Episcopo exigere, ut eorum temporali necessitati provideat (Conc. Plen. Balt. ii., n. 77); qui enim titulo missionis ordinantur ex missione sustententur, ita ut ii solum qui in sacrario operantur, quæ de sacrario sunt, edant (I. Cor. ix. 13, 14). . . . attamen, quo efficacius aberrantes in semitam rectam reducantur, enixe commendamus ex S. Congregationis de Propaganda Fide consulto, ut domus quædam a religiosis viris regendæ instituantur, ubi sacerdotes lapsi, qui spem fundatam conversionis exhibent, pro tempore ab Episcopo statuendo, vitam degant."[2]

1862. This is also the common teaching of canonists.[3]

---

[1] Natural justice itself requires that the good servant should be rewarded for his fidelity and labor, and therefore receive a just and ample support for his labors, and that, on the other hand, the unworthy servant should be punished and lose the emoluments of his office. The Church, therefore, acts in harmony with natural justice and equity, when she deprives unworthy Ecclesiastics of such an income as will supply them with the comforts of life, and leaves them merely what is necessary to keep them from begging or doing secular work.

[2] Conc. Pl. Balt. III., n. 72.

[3] Cf. Schmalzg., l. 5, t. 39, n. 305; München, l. c., vol. ii., p. 234; Droste, § 122, pp. 156, 157.

Thus Stremler[1] writes: "For the rest, dismissal from benefice always leaves to the Ecclesiastic who is dismissed the right to the means of subsistence. The ecclesiastical judge is bound in conscience to provide for the support of the person condemned, and if he refuses to comply with this duty of justice, he can be compelled to do it by his Superior. He should assign to the cleric who is deprived of his benefice and who has no other means of subsistence an alimentary pension, or keep him in a monastery, according to the gravity of his offence, and not allow him to tramp about, deprived of all means of living. For, say the Sacred Canons: "*Paupertas cogit ad turpia.*"

1863. This whole teaching is based on the general principle, frequently laid down in the Sacred Canons, that an Ecclesiastic, even though he is guilty of crime, nevertheless remains an Ecclesiastic, and should therefore not be placed in such a position as to be obliged to go begging, or to engage in secular pursuits. In fact, what is the dignity and power of the priesthood? St. Augustine exclaims: "O veneranda sacerdotum dignitas, in quorum manibus, velut in utero virginis, Filius Dei incarnatur; O venerabilis sanctitudo manuum! O felix exercitium! Qui creavit me (si fas est dicere) dedit mihi creare se: et qui creavit me, sine me, Ipse creabit se, mediante me."[2] St. Ephrem calls the priesthood "magna, immensa, infinita dignitas."

1864. The Church has been at all times most anxious to preserve and to increase the respect due to the priestly dignity and character, and to remove and forbid whatever may tend to lessen it. Hence she has, from the earliest days down to the present, forbidden priests to enter upon secular pursuits or to beg for a living.[3] The reason is thus given by the S. C. de Prop. Fide, in its Instruction "de titulo ordinationis" issued for the United States, Apr. 27,

---

[1] Des Peines eccl., pp. 31, 32, 33. [2] Hom. 2 in Ps. 37.
[3] Can. 26, Dist. 86; Can. 1, 2, 3, 9, Dist. 87; Can. 23, Dist. 93.

1871: "Cum indecorum omnino sit, atque a clericorum, qui in sacris ordinibus constituuntur, dignitate prorsus alienum, ut ipsi aut emendicatis subsidiis aut ex sordido quæstu ea quæ ad vitam necessaria sunt sibi comparare cogantur." The Council of Trent[1] also says: " It beseems not those who are enrolled in the divine ministry, to beg, or to exercise any sordid trade, to the disgrace of their order."

1865. In order to remove Ecclesiastics from any necessity of begging or engaging in secular business, the Church strictly enjoins that those who are promoted to sacred orders should be provided with a competent and sufficient means of support.[2]

1866. Now, as we have seen, the motives which cause the Church to assign to priests a suitable living and to forbid them to beg or engage in sordid trade, apply also, in a measure, to priests and Ecclesiastics whose conduct has made them unworthy of their office. For, even though they are guilty of crime, they are nevertheless priests forever. The sacerdotal character and dignity remain in them for all eternity. Consequently the Church is solicitous to preserve even in them the dignity of the ecclesiastical state. Hence, even when she deprives such Ecclesiastics of their offices or parishes, she does not take away from them all means of subsistence; she does not reduce them to beggary or the necessity of engaging in sordid secular avocations.[3] She does not, it is true, supply them with the ample and honorable support which is due, as a matter of justice, to the worthy priest, who labors

---

[1] Sess. 21, cap. 2 de Ref.   [2] Conc Trid., sess. 21, cap. 2 de Ref.

[3] Where these Ecclesiastics, who are dismissed, or suspended *a beneficio*, have other sources of income besides those of the office from which they have been dismissed or suspended—*v.g.*, where they have means of their own—the Ordinary is not bound to give them even a moderate allowance. For, as was seen, the moderate support is to be given only to those *who need it*, and who would otherwise be obliged to beg or do secular work for a living.

Support of Dismissed Rectors.   99

faithfully in the ministry. But she nevertheless gives him such a support as will enable him to meet his actual wants. She does this, not so much as a matter of justice, or out of consideration for the offender, as out of regard for the ecclesiastical dignity.

1867. Of course, the Church gives this *moderate* or *scanty* allowance only to those who are willing to amend. For to those who persist in their evil course and give no sign of amendment nothing whatever need be given, unless they are in extreme need or in danger of starvation.

1868. This is apparent also from the following declaration of the S. C. de Prop. Fide, inserted in the Acts of the *Third Plenary Council of Baltimore*:[1] " Utrum et quomodo declarandum sit, sacerdotes titulo Missionis ordinatos, qui se indignos reddiderunt sacri ministerii exercendi, hoc titulo privari ; neque Ordinarium teneri ad sustentationem illis præbendam." To this question the Cardinals of the Propaganda, in their general meeting, held Febr. 4, 1873, replied: " In casu, prout exponitur, prævia declaratione ejusmodi sacerdoti ab Episcopo facienda, et quamdiu prædictus Sacerdos in sua prava vivendi consuetudine perseverat, nullum exhibens sinceræ resipiscentiæ signum, Episcopum non teneri ad sustentationem illi præbendam. Sejunctim autem a resolutione dubiorum per epistolam significetur Ordinario (eidem episcopo), ut ad dictam declarationem non deveniat, nisi postquam paternis ac repetitis monitis ejusmodi sacerdotem ad resipiscendum frustra invitaverit."

1869. It is in the light of this declaration that the following decree (n. 77) of the Second Plenary Council of Baltimore, as retained by the S. C. de Prop. Fide, in its Instructions *Quamvis* of July 20, 1878,[2] and *Cum Magnopere* of 1884,[3] is evi-

[1] P. 210.   [2] Ad Dubia, § I.
[3] Art. xlv. The words are: " Concilii Pl. Balt. II. decreta, n. 77. 108, quoad juridicos effectus remotionis missionariorum ab officio, nullatenus innovata seu infirmata intelliguntur."

dently to be understood : "Sacerdotes quibus per Ordinarii sententiam sacerdotii exercitium interdictum fuerit, *nullum jus habent ad sustentationem ab eo petendam* cum ipsi se sua culpa missionibus operam navandi incapaces reddiderint."

What has been said holds not merely of dismissal, but also of deposition, which is nothing else than dismissal joined with disqualification for any future appointment.

§. 2. *Support of suspended Ecclesiastics.*

1870. We here speak only of suspension *a beneficio*, which alone affects the income of the benefice or office. By suspension *a beneficio* is meant the prohibition to draw the income of the benefice. In the United States, the act of the Bishop forbidding a Rector or an assistant priest to draw his salary would be suspension *a beneficio*. This suspension may be total or partial. In other words, an Ecclesiastic may be forbidden to draw his salary, either wholly or only in part. In the following lines we speak of total suspension from benefice.

1871. *Q.* Is an Ecclesiastic who is suspended from receiving the income of his office to be left without any support whatever? In other words: Is a cleric who is suspended *a beneficio* deprived, during the time of his suspension, completely and absolutely, of the income of his benefice or office, in such a manner as not even to be allowed to receive as much as is necessary for his support?

A. When the suspension is inflicted, not as a censure proper or correctional punishment, but as a vindicatory punishment (which is the case when it is imposed for a determinate period of time, or for crimes altogether past), the ecclesiastical judge is bound to assign to the person thus suspended, out of the income of his benefice or office, as much as is required for his support.[1]

[1] Schmalzg., l. 5, t. 39. n. 305; Kober, The Suspension, p. 122; Glossa in Cap. 25, de elect., v. *admiserunt* (l. 6).

1872. This teaching is clearly laid down in the law of the Church. One or two examples from the Sacred Canons will place it in a clearer light. A certain deacon had knowingly and wilfully celebrated mass before he had been ordained a priest. Pope Urban III., (A. D. 1186.) to whom the case was referred, ordered that for this crime he should be suspended from his office and benefice for two or three years, as the Third Lateran Council directs; but that nevertheless he should be left the necessary means of support, lest he should be obliged to return to secular pursuits. His words are: " De beneficio autem misericorditer agatur cum eo, ne sustentatione privatus ad sæculi negotia revertatur."[1] The *Cap.* 25, *de electione* (i. 6) gives another instance. Certain Ecclesiastics had knowingly elected a person to an ecclesiastical office, who was disqualified by the Sacred Canons. For this offence, they had incurred suspension from their benefices for three years. Nevertheless the *Glossa*, commenting on the word *admiscrunt* of the above decretal, says: " Tamen modicam sustentationem debent tunc habere, ne ex toto egeant."

1873. In both these cases, there is question of suspension for a determinate time, and therefore of suspension inflicted as a punitive, and not as a correctional punishment. And reasoning from these canons, canonists assert it as a general principle, that an Ecclesiastic who is visited with a vindicatory punishment, whether it be dismissal or deposition, or a suspension which is punitive, shall always be provided with the necessary means of subsistence.

1874. Canonists, however, teach that an Ecclesiastic can be left temporarily without any support, where he is suspended *a beneficio*, not by way of pure punishment, but by way of censure proper or correctional punishment. In other words, an Ecclesiastic is not entitled to any support

[1] Cap. Ex litteris, de cleric. non ord. (V. 28.)

whatever, except he be in extreme or absolute want, when the suspension from his income (*suspensio a beneficio*) is inflicted upon him as a *medicinal punishment or as a censure*. The same applies to excommunication, which also deprives an Ecclesiastic of his income, is always a *correctional* punishment, and can never be inflicted as a vindicatory punishment.[1]

1875. The reason is, that, in this case, the Ecclesiastic has it in his power to regain, at any moment, his income or support, by returning to the path of duty. For it is the peculiar characteristic of censures, when imposed as correctional and not as vindicatory punishments, that they are to be withdrawn as soon as the offender amends. They are *spiritual medicines* intended to heal a spiritual malady. Hence they should be discontinued as soon as the spiritual disease is cured, that is, as soon as the offender becomes penitent and recedes from his obstinacy and incorrigibility. Consequently, as soon as a person who is thus under censure becomes repentant, he acquires at once, by his amendment, the strict right to absolution from the censure, and the Superior is strictly obliged to accord this absolution, as soon as he becomes aware of this amendment.[2] If the Superior refuses to grant the absolution, the higher Superior, when appealed to, is directed by the Sacred Canons to impart it.[3] Consequently, if an Ecclesiastic, thus suspended for contumacy, or excommunicated, chooses of his own free will to remain deprived of his income, by continuing in his perverse, obstinate, and contumacious course, he has nobody to blame but himself, since he has it in his power at any moment to regain his income, by repentance. But even in this case, if the cleric is in extreme want, he should be given what is absolutely neces-

---

[1] Cf. Kober, Excom. p. 354.
[2] Cap. 25 de appell. (2. 28); Cap. 11 de Const. (i. 2).
[3] Cf. Kober., Excom., p. 451; Kober, Susp., p. 121.

Support of Suspended Ecclesiastics.

sary for his support, in order to keep him from starvation.[1]

1876. The case is quite different with punishments which are punitive, namely, with punitive suspension, with dismissal, and deposition. The cessation or withdrawal of these punishments depends rather on the will of the Superior or of the law, than on the amendment of the delinquent. It does not, at least absolutely speaking, lie in the power of the person punished to have the punishment remitted by good conduct. Hence the law of the Church provides that, not so much for the sake of the Ecclesiastic himself, as for the honor and dignity of the ecclesiastical state, to which he belongs, a moderate allowance should be given him for his support.

1877. We have just said that the withdrawal of vindicative punishments does not necessarily follow upon the amendment of the delinquent. However, it should be borne in mind that the Church's mission or end is to save souls. Consequently, even when she inflicts vindicatory punishments, she aims not merely at vindicating her laws and upholding her social order, but also at reforming the delinquent. Hence it may be said that all her punishments partake more or less of a medicinal character. Therefore, if the delinquent repents, the Church or the ecclesiastical judge remits even vindicatory punishments, either wholly, or at least in great part, unless the enormity of the offence or the greatness of the scandal demands otherwise.[2]

1878. This is also very beautifully stated by the *Third Plenary Council of Baltimore:* " Semper enim sumus parati eosdem (aberrantes), dummodo de insipientia sua dolentes cordique patris confidentes in domum paternam redeant, brachiis apertis recipère, eisque jura fratris junioris restau-

---

[1] Cap. 53 de app. (ii. 2); Glossa, ib. v. *subtrahuntur;* Kober, Excom., pp. 350, 355.

[2] Sanguineti, Inst., pp. 459, 400; Schulte, K. K. R., vol. ii., p. 387.

rare, gaudentes quod filius qui mortuus erat revixerit et qui perierat inventus sit. (Luc. xv. 24)." [1]

1879. *Q.* From what source is the above support to be taken, also in the United States?

A. From the income of the benefice, parish, or office of the delinquent, in the case of one suspended from benefice, or excommunicated. In the case of one dismissed or deposed, it is taken from the revenues of the parish or office of the person dismissed, where these revenues are sufficient; otherwise from other diocesan resources. It may be asked, whether in the United States, where the income of the parish or office is not large enough to provide this support, it may be taken from the taxes and alms which are collected for dispensations from the banns and impediments of marriage, or from other sources of a similar kind? There is certainly nothing in the law of the Church which forbids it. By the Sacred Canons, these taxes and alms are to be applied exclusively to pious and charitable uses. Now, both by the letter and spirit of the law of the Church, the support of indigent erring Ecclesiastics is pre-eminently a charity and a pious use.

1880. Finally we observe, from the rule laid down by which delinquent Ecclesiastics are to be provided with a moderate support, the *Glossa* [2] excepts the case of an Ecclesiastic suspended from benefice (*a pari*, if he is excommunicated) who has an income of his own. Its words are: "Sed si tales suspensi a beneficio haberent partrimonium vel aliud unde vivere possent, tunc ex beneficio nihil habere debent."

---

[1] Conc. Pl. Balt. III., n. 72.   [2] In cap. 25 de elect. (i. 6.), v. *Admiserunt.*

CHAPTER II.

TRANSFERS AS PUNISHMENTS.

(*Translatio pœnalis, translocatio.*)

1881. Having in the preceding chapter explained *dismissals* (*privatio parochiæ*), we shall now dwell briefly on *transfers* in their capacity of punishments.

ART. I.

Nature and Division of Transfers.

1882. *Definition.*—By a *transfer* (*translatio*) is meant the change or removal of an Ecclesiastic from one church or position to another, made by authority of the Superior, for cause.[1] The main difference between a *transfer* and a *dismissal* is this: by the latter, an Ecclesiastic is deprived of his church or office without being at the same time appointed to another, while by the former, he loses indeed the old church or office, but yet is at the same time appointed to a new one.

1883. *Division.*—How many kinds of transfer are there? These: 1. *Administrative* and *penal.* A transfer is administrative, when it is made by the Ordinary for reasons of *utility* or *necessity*, and therefore not for *crimes.* It is penal when it is made in punishment of *offences.* 2. *Voluntary* and *compulsory*, according as it takes place *with* or *against the will* of the incumbent. A voluntary transfer is therefore equivalent, partly, to a resignation, since the incumbent *freely* gives up the old parish for the new, and partly to an appointment to a new church. A compulsory transfer,

---

[1] De Angelis, Præl. l. i., t. 7, n. 1.

however, partakes on the one hand of the nature of a *dismissal*, since by it the incumbent is deprived of his church *against his will*, just as by dismissal, and on the other, of the character of an appointment to a new church or office.

3. Finally the transfer is either to an *inferior* or to a *better* church or office.

1884. *Q.* How are transfers made?

A. 1. It is prescribed by the law of the Church that Ecclesiastics shall not be transferred, especially against their will, except for *grave and sufficient cause of necessity or utility*, that is, except where it is *really necessary* or *evidently useful*.[1] The particular causes which make a transfer necessary or evidently useful, and therefore render it lawful, are indicated above, Vol. I., No. 362. Again, the law of the Church allows of transfers, also for *crimes*, in cases where there are no other causes of necessity or utility.

2. These causes are to be *legitimately established*.[2] For, as Leurenius[3] teaches, when the law prescribes that an act shall be done for cause, the latter is not presumed, but must be proved or shown to exist.

3. The transfer should, as a rule, be from an *inferior* to a *better* church or office. For a transfer from a *better* to an *inferior* church or office would belittle and reflect discredit, not only on the person transferred, but also on the better or higher office itself.[4] We say, *as a rule;* for it is plain that a person can be transferred to a *worse* or *lower* office, when he is guilty of offences or neglect of official duties, and has thus made himself unworthy of the better or higher office.

---

[1] Can. 34 et 35. C. vii. Q. 1; Cap. *Quæsitum* 5 de rer. perm. (iii. 19). Hence Leurenius says that, when transfers are made without grave cause, they are made in direct violation of the law of the Church, and should therefore be annulled by the Superior *ad quem*. (Leur., For. Benef., P. 3, Q. 855.)

[2] De Angelis, l. c., n. 2; Leur., For. Benef., P. 3, Q. 855.   [3] L. c.

[4] Cap. 1 et 4 de transl. (i. 7.); Santi, l. c., l. i., t. 7, n. 9.

Art. II.

Transfer of Irremovable Rectors also in the United States.

1885. *Q.* Can the Bishop, also with us, transfer an irremovable Rector, against his will, from one parish to another of the same diocese, for reasons of utility and necessity, although the Rector is not guilty of crime?

A. We distinguish between the transfer to an *inferior*, and the transfer to a *better* or *equal* parish. Now, in the estimation of all mankind, the transfer to a worse parish or office is regarded as a *humiliation* and a *disgrace*. Hence it is looked upon by men as a *grave punishment*. Accordingly, it is the unanimous teaching of canonists that a transfer to a worse or minor place, inflicting, as it does, dishonor and also diminution of income, is placed on the same footing with dismissal proper or *privatio*, and can therefore be made only in punishment of delinquencies. See Vol. I., No. 394, *sixth edition.*

1886. Thus Permaneder teaches: "The transfer of an Ecclesiastic against his will from a better to an inferior benefice or office is to be regarded as a *privatio* or dismissal.'[1] Phillips also writes: "The transfer to a smaller benefice or office is strictly a vindicative punishment or *pœna vindicativa*."[2] The Holy See has also repeatedly declared that transfers to inferior parishes or offices are *punishments*, and consequently imposable only for crime and by trial.[3] Consequently the Holy See always commands the Bishop to give a Rector who is transferred against his will for causes which are not crimes a parish that is better than or at least equal to the former in all respects.

[1] Permaneder, l. c., pp. 442, 443. See also Walter, § 239, p. 469; Phillips, Comp., § 87. iii. and § 188.

[2] Phillips, Comp., § 188 and § 87 iii; cf. Permaneder, p. 442.

[3] S. C. C. 26. Apr. 1871; S. C. C. 22 Martii 1873; cf. Analecta J. P. anno 1875, p. 607 and p. 880.

1887. But can the Bishop, also with us, transfer an irremovable Rector, against his will, to a *better* parish, or to one *at least equally as good* as the former, for grave reasons of utility or necessity, even though the Rector is not guilty of crime? There are two opinions, one affirming, the other denying. Those canonists who hold the negative, contend chiefly that such transfer is totally repugnant to the privilege of irremovability which these Rectors possess, and by virtue of which their parish can be taken away from them, against their will, whether by dismissal or transfer, only for the specific crimes and by the form of trial laid down in law, and therefore not for reasons of utility or necessity which imply no crime on the part of the Rector.[1]

1888. Those who hold the affirmative—and their opinion seems the more common opinion—maintain that the right of irremovability is not to be stretched so far as to redound to the evident and grave detriment of the Church and souls, and therefore does not exclude compulsory transfers when they are required by *most urgent and grave reasons of necessity and utility*, even though the Rector to be transferred is not guilty of crime.[2]

1889. However, these canonists teach at the same time, 1. that not every grave reason of necessity or utility is sufficient for such transfer, but that it is necessary that the Rector should have become *useless* in his parish,—*v.g.*, because of the hatred or ill-will of the greater number of the parishioners—and that, therefore, the transfer is not simply useful, but *imperatively necessary*.[3]

1890.—2. That the existence of these urgent and grave causes must be *established* beyond a reasonable doubt, and that by a proper investigation put on record, so that it may appear *ex actis*, whether there is cause. For if the Bishop

---

[1] Cf. Walter, § 239, p. 479.

[2] De Brabandere, Jur. Can. Comp., vol. i., p. 349. Brugis, 1882.

[3] Ib., arg. can. 6, Dist. 74; Cf. Pierantonelli, l. c., p. 208.

is unable to *prove* the existence of these reasons before the Holy See, to whom the person removed has recourse, the transfer will be revoked and the Rector reinstated in his parish. The reason is, that, unless the Bishop can show clearly that he acted from sufficient motives, the presumption will be that he was animated by unjustifiable motives, namely by ill-will, malice, or other personal feelings; or, as the canons say, that he was influenced, *non sanitate consilii, sed invidia et amentia*.[1] Pierantonelli holds that irremovable Rectors can be transferred against their will, even though it be to a *better parish*, only by a formal canonical trial, or by a canonical summary trial, where the solemn one cannot be given.[2]

1891.—3. That the incumbent should be induced, if possible, to consent freely to the proposed transfer: for to a person willing all is easy; to one unwilling, everything is impossible. It is not likely that an Ecclesiastic, transferred against his consent, will labor with fruit or alacrity in his new field. Hence such transfer would benefit neither the new church, nor the person transferred. And yet it is only for the purpose of benefiting either the Church or the incumbent that a transfer is allowed.[3]

1892.—4. That it shall clearly appear that the church to which the incumbent is transferred is really better than or at least as good as the former, both in honor and income, so that the Rector transferred will not suffer in his honor or revenues.

1893.—5. Finally, that, even where strong and urgent reasons of necessity demand a change, *v. g.*, where a Rector has alienated the good will of the majority (not merely of a few) of his parishioners, *v. g.*, by indiscreet zeal, by imprudence, and harsh temper, the transfer cannot

---

[1] Can. 7, 8, Dist. 74.   [2] Pierantonelli, Praxis fori eccl., p. 109.
[3] Pierantonelli, l. c., pp. 108-109.

take place,[1] where the evil calling for the transfer can be remedied by other means, *v. g.*, by the appointment of an assistant to aid the Rector.[2]

1894. From this it will be seen that, even in the opinion of those canonists who teach that irremovable Rectors can be transferred against their will to a better or equal parish, for reasons of necessity or utility, and not merely for crime, this compulsory transfer is hedged in with so many conditions and limitations that, practically speaking, it is not safe for a Bishop to make such a transfer, except for crime and by trial. Pierantonelli,[3] as we have seen, expressly teaches that the regular canonical trial (with us, the trial as outlined in the Instruction *Cum Magnopere*) must precede all involuntary transfers of irremovable Rectors.[4] We need not add that the principles here laid down respecting the transfer of parish priests who are canonically irremovable apply fully to our irremovable Rectors. For they enjoy the right of irremovability in the same manner as canonical parish priests proper. See above, Vol. I., Nos. 394 sq.; Nos. 643 sq., *sixth edition*.

Art. III.

Transfer of Removable Rectors, also in the United States.

1895. *Q*. How can Rectors with us, who are *amovibiles*, be transferred by the Ordinary, against their will, even to an inferior mission or office.

A. The Sacred Congregation de Propaganda Fide, in a recent important decision for the United States given March 18, 1887, answers thus:[5] "Cum vero agatur de translatione Rectoris (qui est amovibilis) ab una Missione ad aliam aut ad aliud officium etiam inferius, Ordinarii non

---

[1] Leur., For. Benef., Q. 867; De Brabandere, l. c, vol. i., p. 350.
[2] Arg. Conc. Trid., sess. 21, c. 6 de Ref.   [3] L. c., p. 109.
[4] Cf. Walter, l. c., p. 469.   [5] See the text of the entire decision in the Appendix.

Transfers as Punishments.

tenentur ad canonici processus instructionem; opus est autem ut hoc fiat graves ob causas, et habita meritorum ratione juxta dispositionem Concilii Plenarii Baltimorensis III. Tit. II., Cap. V., § 32. Si in casu translationis fiat recursus ad S. Congregationem, S. Congregatio remittet recursum ad Metropolitam, vel si agatur de Metropolita, ad Metropolitam viciniorem."

1896. Accordingly, 1. a *grave cause* is required. This is in harmony with the entire legislation of the Church. For, as we have seen, the Sacred Canons enact that Ecclesiastics who hold offices in the Church, even though they are *amovibiles*, and even though they are not Rectors of souls, shall not be transferred, especially against their will, without grave and sufficient cause. While this applies to *all* Ecclesiastics who hold offices, it applies with peculiar force to a *Rector of souls*, who should *know* his people, be a *father* to them, and who should therefore be *changed* or *transferred* as little as possible. See our *New Procedure*, Nos. 594, 595.

1897.—2. When Rectors who are *amovibiles* are transferred for causes of necessity or utility, *which are not crimes*, the transfer is to be made in such a manner as not to inflict dishonor, humiliation, disgrace, pecuniary loss, or other grave injury upon the person transferred. Now, in the estimation of all mankind, a transfer to a *worse* or *inferior* place is regarded as a *humiliation* and a *disgrace*, just as the transfer to a *better* place is looked upon by all as a *promotion* and an *honor*. Moreover, the transfer to a *worse* place naturally brings with it also a *decrease of income ;* for the smaller the place is, the smaller will be the salary or perquisites of its incumbent. Now, to inflict *disgrace* and *pecuniary loss* is a *punishment*, and should, as a rule, be imposed only for *offences* which make a person unworthy of his reputation, and of the esteem of others. Consequently a removable Rector, also with us, should, as a rule, be transferred to an inferior mission or place only in punishment of delinquencies. See our *New Procedure*, No. 596.

1898. Again, as a transfer to a *better* place is considered by all an *honor* and a *promotion*, and is therefore coveted by them, it should naturally be made *as a reward for merit*, namely as a reward for virtue, learning, valuable and long services rendered, fidelity and ability in the discharge of duties. In like manner, the transfer to a minor place, whether as to *honor or income*, is looked upon by all men as a *humiliation*, and is therefore greatly dreaded by them. Hence it should naturally be made *as a just desert or punishment for demerit*, that is, for offences, or grave negligence, or culpable inability in the discharge of duties. This is implied by the words *habita meritorum ratione* in the above decision of the Holy See. See above Vol. I., Nos. 395 sq., *sixth edition*.

1899. It is also in accord with God's own way of acting, as expressed in this beautiful passage of our Saviour: "Euge serve bone et fidelis: quia *in pauca fuisti fidelis, supra multa te constituam*."[1] It is also in harmony with the natural feelings and inborn sense of justice of all mankind. Everybody feels instinctively that promotion or transfer to a higher or better office is a deserved reward for merit; and that a transfer to an inferior place is a just punishment for demerit, or crime.

1900.—3. The above causes, whether of utility or necessity, or of crime or demerit, calling for the transfer of a removable Rector against his will, must be *legitimately established*.[2] This is plainly indicated by the above decision, when it allows of recourse to the Holy See against the transfer. This follows also from the principle laid down by all canonists, that, where the law requires a cause, the latter is

---

[1] Matt., xxv., 23.

[2] De Angelis, l. i.. t. 7, n. 2; id., l. i., t. 28, n. 7; See also a very important case decided by the Holy See, in the *Acta S. S.*, vol. iii., p. 512.

not presumed but must be proved. Consequently, as Leurenius teaches, it is necessary that the Ordinary, before making the transfer, should make a *causæ cognitio*, that is, a careful investigation, and thus obtain *proof*, in order that it may appear *ex actis* that there are really good and sufficient reasons for the transfer. For, continues Leurenius,[1] the mere *assertion* of the Superior that there are such causes is not to be believed by the Superior to whom the person transferred has recourse. In fact, canonists say that, unless the Ordinary clearly proves the existence of grave and sufficient causes for the compulsory transfer, also of removable Rectors, the presumption will be that he acted from personal motives, in which case the transfer will always be annulled by the Holy See.[2] However, the existence of the cause need not be established by a canonical trial, as the above decision of the Propaganda expressly states.

1901. It may perhaps be objected, here, that the above teaching appears to be in direct contradiction with the power of the Ordinary to remove or transfer, *at will—ad nutum*—a Rector who is *amovibilis*. The objection, however, does not hold. For the Holy See has frequently decided that the clause *ad nutum* means, not an *arbitrary* or *despotic* power, that is, not a power to remove or transfer without sufficient cause, but the *arbitrium boni viri*.[3] Now the will of a good man is that which is directed by reason, justice, and equity.[4] The power to transfer or dismiss removable Rectors is a *limited* and not an *absolute* power.[5]

[1] L. c., q. 855. [2] Ib.
[3] Pallotti, Coll. v., appellatio, Art. I., n. 240; Acta S. S., vol. 18, p. 74.
[4] De Angelis, l. i., t. 28, n. 7.   [5] Acta S. S., vol. iii., p. 506 sq.

CHAPTER III.

DISMISSAL COMBINED WITH DISQUALIFICATION FOR OFFICES.

(*Depositio.*)

ART. I.

Character of this Punishment.

1902. Deposition is a canonical punishment by which an Ecclesiastic is forever deprived of his office or benefice and of the right to exercise the functions or power of his *ordo*. We say, *forever:* for, as we have seen,[1] deposition not only deprives one of the benefices or offices which he actually holds, but, moreover, disqualifies him to obtain other offices, benefices, or dignities in future. It has, moreover, infamy or public disgrace annexed. This punishment, which, as is manifest, can be inflicted only on Ecclesiastics, is frequently mentioned by the older canons of the Church, in these or similar terms: " Deponatur ab ordine, ab officio, a presbyteratu."[2] In former times it was imposed more frequently than now; in fact, at the present day, it is but very rarely inflicted, simple dismissal coupled with perpetual suspension usually taking its place.[3]

ART. II.

Formalities.—Duration.

1903. The punishment of deposition is perpetual and irremissible in the sense that the Ecclesiastic so punished, has

---

[1] Supra, vol, i., n. 401, *sixth edition*.   [2] Can. Eum qui 40, c. 7, q. 1.
[3] Stremler, l. c., p. 35.

Dismissal Combined with Disqualification for Offices. 115

no right, even after he has done full penance, and amended, to be pardoned or released from it. The Superior, however, or Bishop may reinstate him, provided he be truly penitent, and provided the crime was not an atrocious one, such as wilful murder,[1] or the consecration of a person as Bishop who was not appointed.[2] We say, *the Bishop may;* for he is never obliged to do it. During the vacancy of the Bishopric, the chapter or its vicar may also grant the pardon or re-instatement. Deposition does not deprive a person of the privileges of the Ecclesiastical state.

1904. As deposition is at present scarcely ever imposed, we shall not expatiate on the crimes for which alone it can be inflicted and on the canonical trial which is required. Suffice it to say that deposition is, after degradation, the greatest punishment of the Church. Hence what we have said above, in speaking of dismissal, regarding the necessity of crime and previous trial, applies with much greater force to deposition. It can be imposed only for crimes which are enormous, give great scandal, and are expressly stated in law, such as wilful murder, public concubinage, etc.[3]

[1] Can. Minor 4, Dist. 5.   [2] Can. 7, c. 2, q. 3; München, l. c., p. 146.
[3] Stremler, l. c., p. 36.

CHAPTER IV.

DEGRADATION OF ECCLESIASTICS.

(*Degradatio.*)

ART. I.

Nature and Effects of this Punishment.

1905. Degradation is a canonical punishment by which an Ecclesiastic is wholly and forever deprived of the exercise of the power of the *ordo* (the indelible character of order remaining, of course), and also of all office, dignity, and benefice, by a solemn sentence of the judge, and is reduced to the state of a layman, losing all ecclesiastical privileges, namely *fori* and *canonis*, and given over to the secular arm. In a few words, therefore, as we have said,[1] degradation is not only a deposition, but also the expulsion from the ecclesiastical state and the putting back into the lay state, and therefore the loss of all ecclesiastical privileges.

1906. This punishment is justly and appropriately called *degradation*. For, what can be more *degrading* or *disgraceful* than to be reduced from the high rank of the priesthood to the level of the laity. It is not indeed to be imagined for a moment that the state of the laity is a degraded state; on the contrary, it is in itself a state of the highest honor. But when a Christian has been raised from the lay to the ecclesiastical state, and is afterward expelled from it and put back among the laity, for gross crimes, every body will see that such a fall is an extreme degradation.

---

[1] Supra, vol. i., n. 401, *sixth edition*, 1887.

1907. Degradation is twofold: *verbal*, which consists in the sentence itself of degradation; *real* or actual, which is, so to say, the execution of the verbal degradation. They differ therefore from each other simply as the commencement and completion of one and the same thing.[1]

1908. The verbal degradation does not *ipso facto* deprive one of the privileges of the ecclesiastical state; the real or actual does. Again, one who is verbally degraded may be re-instated by the Bishop; one who is actually or really, only by the Holy See. A person who is degraded remains bound by the vow of chastity, if he is in sacred orders, and consequently cannot contract marriage validly. He can validly absolve in case of necessity.

1909. Degradation can be inflicted only for enormous crimes, and even then only when they are expressly and clearly designated as punishable with degradation. Moreover, as this punishment is the greatest and severest inflicted by the Church on Ecclesiastics, it can be resorted to only as the very last means, and after all the other milder punishments have been applied in vain. Thus Pope Celestin III. says: "Quod si clericus... in homicidio fuerit deprehensus legitime, atque convictus, ab ecclesiastico judice deponendus est. Qui si depositus incorrigibilis fuerit, excommunicari debet; deinde, contumacia crescente, anathematis mucrone feriri; postmodum vero, si in profundum malorum veniens (hæc omnia) contempserit, cum ecclesia non habeat ultra quid faciat, ne possit esse ultra perditio plurimorum, per sæcularem comprimendus est potestatem."[2] As degradation is at present rarely, if ever, inflicted, we deem it unnecessary to enumerate the various crimes for which the law decrees it.

[1] Stremler, l. c., p. 37. [2] Cap. 10. (II. 1.)

Art. II.

Manner of inflicting it.

1910. *Q.* By whom and how can degradation be inflicted at present?

A. Formerly, degradation, even though but verbal, could not be imposed upon a Bishop save by twelve Bishops, nor upon a priest except by six Bishops; nor upon a deacon save by three Bishops. At present, however, the Bishop can alone, either personally or through his Vicar General, deputed to that effect, impose verbal degradation; and, *sede vacante*, the Vicar-Capitular can do it. As to real degradation, the old law has been changed somewhat, so that now, according to the Council of Trent, Sess. 13., C. 4 de Ref., the Bishop, instead of being bound to have six or three other Bishops, as above specified, can inflict it with a like number of mitred abbots, or, if they cannot be had, of other persons constituted in ecclesiastical dignity, who are of weight by their age, and recommended by their knowledge of canon law.[1]

1911. These priests or mitred abbots are not merely to give their advice; they are associate judges, and consequently have both a deliberative and a decisive vote in the trial and sentence. According to many canonists, moreover, their unanimous, not merely majority vote is required for degradation.[2]

1912. Finally we must observe that, at the present day, degradation, verbal or real, like deposition, is scarcely ever resorted to, dismissal or privation taking its place. In fact, real degradation is no longer practicable. For it consists chiefly in handing the offender over to the secular power for punishment. Now, at present, secular governments act, in these matters, altogether independently of the Church, and do not await her action, but proceed at once to punish Ecclesiastics, when they offend against the law of the land.

---

[1] Conc. Trid., sess. 13, c. 4 de Ref.   [2] Arg. cap. 3 de sent. et re jud.

CHAPTER V.

INFAMY AS A CANONICAL PUNISHMENT.

(*Infamia.*)

ART. I.

True Idea of Canonical Infamy.

1913. Infamy (*infamia*), in general, means public disgrace or the total loss of good name. Here it means not any and every loss of good name, but only that bad reputation which is accompanied *with public scorn, contempt, and shame.* A person may become infamous in two ways: *first,* by *the disposition of the law*—in our case, of the Sacred Canons—namely where the law or the sacred canons declare that a person committing certain heinous, base, and shameful crimes shall be regarded as infamous in the eyes of the law, and as such excluded from ecclesiastical offices and dignities.[1] *Second, by his very actions,* that is, by his low, vile, and disgraceful life and conduct, which bring upon him the *loathing and contempt* of others, so that he is looked upon by others, not only as bad, but moreover as base, mean, and contemptible, and that without any enactment of the law to that effect.[2]

1914. The first is called infamy of law (*infamia juris*); the second, infamy of fact (*infamia facti*). In both kinds of infamy, the crime or action that produces them is one that is not only bad, morally speaking, but moreover *base* and *shameful,* so as to produce in others, who are right-minded —for there is evidently no question of the opinion of people

---

[1] Schmalzg., l. 5, t. 37, n. 165. [2] München, l. c. vol. ii., p. 119.

who are themselves bad and infamous—not only dislike, but moreover loathing, contempt, and abhorrence.

1915. The infamy of fact, as Stremler[1] remarks, depends somewhat on the ideas, customs, and manners of the people and times. Thus an action may be looked upon as infamous by the people at one time and not so at another. Again, it may be contracted even by one innocent of the crime imputed to him; *v. g*, where a person, though innocently calumniated, is nevertheless unable to show his innocence.

1916. The infamy of the law, as we have seen, is that which is decreed by the law or Sacred Canons for vile and base crimes. We say, *vile and base crimes*; for the law does not impose infamy for every crime, but only for those which are of a shameful kind.[2] Now the law of the Church enacts that some crimes shall produce infamy *ipso facto*, that is, by the very fact of their commission; others, only upon juridical conviction and sentence. Now, what are the crimes, for which the law of the Church inflicts infamy *ipso facto*? All those crimes for which the civil, that is, the Roman law imposed infamy *ipso facto*, except where the canon law expressly ordains the contrary. Thus the canon *Omnes*, 6, q. 1, says: "Omnes vero infames dicimus, quos sæculi leges infames appellant." Now the Roman law imposed infamy *ipso jure* for such crimes as keeping bad houses, usury, and others which are given by Reiffenstuel.[3]

1917. We say, the *Roman law*; for, as Stremler[4] well observes, this rule cannot be applied, at least generally speaking, to the civil or secular laws of the present day. For, by a deplorable derangement of modern ideas, some of the secular laws of our times designate as infamous certain actions which can never become even criminal in the eyes of the Church. Yet, in many cases, the infamy decreed by

[1] L. c., p. 42.
[2] L. 7 ff. de publ. jud. (48, 1).
[3] L. 5, t. 37, n. 55.
[4] L. c., p. 43.

Infamy as a Canonical Punishment. 121

our civil legislation is based upon just motives, and therefore would seem to obtain also in the eyes of the Church.

1918. The Sacred Canons, besides enacting that the above infamy of the civil law shall also hold in the Church, have also directly decreed that infamy shall be contracted *ipso facto* for certain crimes. The latter are thus enumerated in the canon *cum Infames* 17, C. 6, Q. 1 : " Infames esse eas personas dicimus, quæ pro aliqua culpa notantur infamia, id est, omnes qui christianæ legis normam abjiciunt, et statuta ecclesiastica contemnunt, similiter fures et sacrilegos et omnes capitalibus criminibus irretitos; similiter et incestuosos, homicidas, perjuros, raptores, maleficos, veneficos, adulteros: qui fratres calumniantur aut accusant et non probant," etc.

We observe here that the infamy which the Church annexes *ipso facto* to the above crimes is not contracted unless the crime is *notorious*. According to Stremler, this notoriety must be established either by a declarative judicial sentence, or by a juridical confession of the guilty person, or by juridical proof of the crime.[1] That the crime must be notorious is plain. For infamy is the bad opinion, mingled with scorn and contempt, entertained by a number of persons, and consequently cannot, by its nature, exist where the crime is occult.[2]

1919. What are the crimes that produce infamy only *per sententiam judicis*, that is, not *ipso facto*, but only upon judicial conviction and sentence? Infamy is produced, not by every crime of which a person is convicted, but only by those crimes that are styled public (*crimen publicum*), such as forgery, adultery, robbery, theft, etc.[3] Thus the Roman law, as adopted by the Church, says: "Infamem non ex omni crimine sententia facit, sed ex eo quod judicii publici causa habuit; itaque ex eo crimine, quod judicii publici non

---

[1] Stremler, l. c., p. 42. [2] Schmalzg, l. 5, t. 37, n. 166.
[3] Reiff., l. 5, t. 37, n. 38.

fuit, damnatum infamia non sequetur."[1] To contract this infamy, therefore, two things are requisite: 1. a public crime, as explained; 2. juridical conviction thereof, and condemnation. The infamy in the case is not annexed to the juridical proceedings, but to the crime.[2]

ART. II.

Effects of Infamy of Law or Fact.

1920. *Q.* What are the effects of infamy, whether of law or of fact?

A. 1. Both the *infamia juris* and the *infamia facti* are a canonical disqualification (*inhabilitas*) for ecclesiastical offices, dignities, and benefices. The law of the Church says: "Infamibus portæ non pateant dignitatum."[3] Hence persons who are infamous are canonically incapable of being appointed to the above offices. The reason is, that offices and dignities are the reward of merit, and therefore should not be conferred on criminals. If a person, infamous by law, were nevertheless appointed to an ecclesiastical office, the appointment would be *ipso jure* null and void, at least *in foro externo*. Nay, those who have contracted the *infamia juris* are even to be deprived of the offices and benefices which they actually possess;[4] a judicial sentence, however, is required for this deprivation. We say, *infamia juris*; for those who are under *infamia facti* cannot indeed be appointed to offices, but they do not lose those which they already hold.[5]

1921.—2. Both those who are infamous by law, and those who are infamous by fact, are deprived of certain rights and privileges; that is, they cannot act as judges, advocates,

[1] L. 7. ff. de publ. jud. (48. 1). [2] München, l. c., vol. ii., p. 123.
[3] Reg. 87 in 6º; l. 2, C. de dignit. (12. 1).
[4] L. 12, C. de dignit.; cap. 11 de excess. Prael.
[5] Reiff., de Reg. juris, reg. 87, n. 6.

Infamy as a Canonical Punishment.

assessors, witnesses, etc. 3. They become irregular. Hence those who are infamous by law cannot be promoted to orders, nor exercise those which they have already received.[1] We say, *infamous by law*; for those who are infamous by fact cannot, it is true, be promoted to orders, but they can exercise those which they have already received, although they should be suspended from office by the Superior, until they have either been absolved or condemned by a canonical trial.[2] From all this it will be seen that infamy is, properly speaking, a canonical punitive penalty, and as such always presupposes a grievous crime.

[1] Can. final. dist. 51 ; Schmalzg., l. c., n. 173.   [2] Stremler, l. c., p. 45.

CHAPTER VI.

CANONICAL DISABILITY FOR ECCLESIASTICAL OFFICES AND BENEFICES.

(*Inhabilitas.*)

ART. I.
Character of this Punishment.

1922. Disqualification (*inhabilitas*) for ecclesiastical *offices, dignities and benefices*, is a canonical punishment by which a person becomes incapable and unfit to be validly appointed to any ecclesiastical office or benefice whatever, in such a manner that his appointment would be null and void *ipso jure*, and prior to any judicial sentence.[1] An instance of this canonical disability occurs in the cap. 2, and 15 *de hæret.* in 6° (v. 2), where Popes Alexander IV. and Boniface VIII. enact that heretics, their defenders, favorers, and believers, together with their children, even to the second generation, shall be excluded from all ecclesiastical offices and benefices. It is evident, therefore, that this incapacity is a very severe ecclesiastical punishment and therefore always presupposes a great crime.

1923. Though often the effect of irregularity, this punishment must nevertheless be carefully distinguished from it. *Irregularity* incapacitates a person directly for the reception and exercise *of orders;* *disability* disqualifies him directly for appointment to *ecclesiastical offices, benefices, and dignities.*[2]

[1] Reiff., l. c., l. 5, t, 37, n. 20.   [2] München, l. c., p. 163.

Art. II.

Effects of this Disability.

1924. This punishment disqualifies a person radically and absolutely for ecclesiastical offices. Still it affects only those offices which a person has not yet acquired. Hence an Ecclesiastic who incurs this punishment cannot, it is true, be appointed to any office in future, but he does not lose those which he already possesses. In conclusion, this punishment is frequently the consequence of other canonical punishments, such as infamy, deposition, and irregularity.[1]

[1] Stremler, l. c., p. 32.

CHAPTER VII.

CANONICAL UNFITNESS FOR ORDERS AND THE ECCLESIASTICAL STATE BY REASON OF CRIME.

(*Irregularitas ex delicto*).

ART. I.

Definition of and Difference between " Inhabilitas" and Irregularity.

1925. In the preceding article we have explained the punishment of canonical disqualification for *ecclesiastical offices and positions*. In the present, we shall discuss the canonical disqualifications for *orders and the ecclesiastical state*. The exalted dignity of the sacerdotal ministry and of the ecclesiastical state demands that all those should be excluded from it, who are in any way either unfit or unworthy, and who are calculated to bring disgrace upon it. Hence the Church, in order to provide for the honor, dignity, and éclat, which should, like a halo, surround the priesthood and render it respected and revered in the eyes of the whole world, has established certain rules, regulations, or qualifications, as a condition *sine qua non* of the licit admission to the ecclesiastical state, and to the reception of orders and the exercise of those already received.

1926. All those who lack these requirements are said to be irregular (*irregulares*), that is, outside or beyond the rule (*regula*) or conditions laid down by the general law of the Church for admission or membership among her ministers, and in consequence excluded from the list of Ecclesiastics.[1]

---

[1] Stremler, l. c., p. 45; München, vol. ii., p. 137.

The direct object, then, of this canonical incapacity is to maintain the respect due to the ecclesiastical state. We say, *the direct object;* for when the cause of the disqualification lies in the crime and bad life of the person disqualified, the Church inflicts the disqualification also for the purpose of punishing the guilty party, and bringing him back to a sense of duty. Hence the incapacity arising from crime is, properly speaking, a vindicatory punishment.

1927. To prevent confusion of ideas, let us clearly define the meaning and nature of this unfitness or irregularity as it is commonly called. The unfitness in question is a canonical hindrance or disability which disqualifies a person to receive orders and to perform the functions of the orders already received.[1] Let us explain this definition. We say, *a canonical hindrance;* because it is and can be inflicted only by the canon law, that is, by the common or general law of the Church, but not by a judicial sentence. Now the Pope alone or a general council approved by him can make laws for the entire Church. Hence, they alone can establish or impose this incapacity, and that only by an *act of legislation*, but not by way of a particular sentence.[2] The other terms of the definition will be set forth below, when we come to the effects of this incapacity.

1928. A person may bring dishonor and opprobrium on the ecclesiastical state, either by reason of *natural defects* or deformity, bodily or mental, which, though not in any sense culpable, nevertheless inspire horror and disgust, or aversion, in others; or by *crime or vicious conduct* calculated to bring the sacerdotal state and ministry into disesteem and contempt. Accordingly, canonists divide the disqualification in question into two kinds: one caused by natural defects; the other produced by crime. The latter alone, as we have seen, is a punishment; the former is simply a

[1] Reiff., l. 5, t. 37, n. 63.
[2] Cap. 18 de sent. excom. in 6°; Schmalzg., l. 5, t. 37, n. 67.

legal prohibition. We shall here confine ourselves chiefly to the incapacity by reason of crime, as we are treating of punishments. We say, *chiefly;* for incidentally we shall also speak of the disqualification which arises from natural defects, since both these incapacities are so closely interwoven as not to be completely separable.

1929. This canonical unfitness, whether by reason of crime or defect, may be partial or total. It is total when the incapacity extends to the reception of *any "ordo" whatever*, and also to all *exercise* whatever of the *ordines* already received. It is partial when it disqualifies, *v. g.*, only for the *reception* of orders, but not for the *exercise* of those already received.[1] When the disqualification proceeds from crime, it is always perpetual, that is, it can cease only by dispensation. But when it is caused by natural defects, it is temporary, that is, it lapses of itself, as soon as the defect passes away. When a person desires to be relieved of the disqualification by reason of defect, before the defect has really passed away, a dispensation is needed.

Art. II.

Effects of this Punishment.

1930. *Q.* What are the effects produced by the canonical disqualification which springs from crime?

A. Before answering directly we premise that this unfitness never incapacitates for actions which are common to Ecclesiastics and laics, such as receiving the sacraments (except the *ordo* of course), assisting at divine service, being buried in consecrated ground, or associating with the faithful. The reason is, that it excludes temporarily from the body or membership of Ecclesiastics only, and therefore merely from the privileges of the *ecclesiastical state*.[2]

---

[1] Schmalzg., l. c., n. 70. [2] Schmalzg., l. c., n. 89.

Ecclesiastical State by Reason of Crime.

1931. We now answer directly: The chief effects are incapacity for orders and for appointment to ecclesiastical offices; privation of ecclesiastical offices and benefices which a person already possesses, at the time he incurs the irregularity. We shall briefly explain each of these effects, under separate heads.

§ 1. *Incapacity for Orders.*

1932. Irregularity disqualifies a person to *receive orders or even the tonsure licitly.* Hence it is distinguished from the *inhabilitas*, which, as we have explained, excludes directly only from ecclesiastical *offices*. The unfitness in question, moreover, disqualifies a person to exercise the functions of *orders already received.* For it may be contracted by one who has already received orders; and then, if it proceeds from crime, it forbids the exercise of any function whatever of orders;[1] if from defect, only those functions of orders which cannot be decorously or properly performed because of the defect.

§ 2. *Incapacity to be appointed to Ecclesiastical Offices.*

1933. This is the second effect, though it is so only *indirectly.* For, as was seen, irregularity does not not fall directly on ecclesiastical *offices*, but only on the *ordo*. However, indirectly and consequentially, the unfitness in question, affects also ecclesiastical offices. Thus, by the very fact that it forbids or disqualifies a person to receive orders, it also, indirectly and as a necessary result, prohibits the acquiring of or appointment to an office which cannot be exercised without exercising the *ordo*. Hence a person who is irregular cannot be *licitly* (it is a probable opinion that he can be *validly* appointed) appointed to an ecclesiastical office, benefice, or dignity,[2] at least if the irregularity

---

[1] Cap. fin. de temp. ord.; Cap. 21 de accus.
[2] Conc. Trid., sess. 14, Cap. 7 de Ref.

is total; for such total unfitness thrusts him completely out of the ecclesiastical state. The case, however, is different when it is but partial and is contracted by one already in orders, not by reason of crime, but óf defect.[1] In this case, the irregular Ecclesiastic can be validly and licitly appointed to an ecclesiastical office, at least when its duties can be decorously discharged, notwithstanding the defect.[2]

§ 3. *Dismissal from Ecclesiastical Offices.*

1934. When and in what manner does the unfitness in question entail privation of the offices which a person has obtained before incurring the unfitness? If the unfitness is caused by defect, *v. g.*, arising from infirmity or accident, the Ecclesiastic thus disabled should not and cannot be deprived of his office or benefice, nor compelled to resign it by his Superior, lest, as Pope Innocent III., writing to the Archbishop of Arles, in 1210,—Cap. *Ex parte* 5, (III. 6)—says, affliction be added to affliction. But even where it is the result of crime, it does not *ipso facto* produce dismissal. The person who is thus irregular (*ex delicto*) should ask for a dispensation from the unfitness.[3] Meanwhile he can retain the office and receive its income; however, he cannot exercise those functions of his office which require the exercise of the *ordo*, but must discharge them through a third party. If he neglects to seek for a dispensation, he can and should be deprived of his office by the ecclesiastical Superior, upon due canonical trial.

1935. We have just said that an irregular Ecclesiastic cannot exercise those functions of his office which require the *ordo*;[4] for irregularity contracted by one who already holds an office does not forbid the exercise of those func-

---

[1] Arg cap. 2 de cleric. ægr.   [2] Schmalzg., l. c., n. 92.

[3] Arg. cap. 5 de cleric. vel monach.; Cap. 6, 7, de cleric. excom. ministr.; Cap. 10 de excess. præl.

[4] München, l. c., vol. ii., p. 138.

tions of an ecclesiastical office or benefice, which are not acts of the *ordo*, but purely acts of the *officium*, *v.g.*, acts of pure administration or of external jurisdiction.[1] Consequently an Ecclesiastic who is irregular may inflict censures, make appointments to ecclesiastical offices; parish-priests (with us, rectors) who are irregular may lawfully assist at marriages, and even lawfully give permission to others to administer certain sacraments, and perform ecclesiastical functions.[2] From what has been said, it will be seen that, while the canonical unfitness in question sometimes becomes the occasion of dismissal from office, and causes it indirectly, yet it does not fall directly upon ecclesiastical offices or benefices.

ART. III.

Causes of this disqualification.

§ 1. *Criminal causes.*

1936. For what causes is this canonical disqualification incurred when it is the result of crime? The unfitness *ex delicto* is one of the heaviest vindicatory punishments of the Church. Hence it can be incurred only for crime—and that for a crime which is very serious, external, consummated, and expressly stated in law as having irregularity annexed. Whether *occult* (not *internal*), though external, crimes produce irregularity is disputed. According to St. Alphonsus, the truer opinion is that which affirms that they do cause irregularity.[3] We say, *and expressly stated in law;* for both the irregularity which is caused by crime, and that which proceeds from natural effects, is incurred only in cases clearly and distinctly laid down in the Sacred Canons.

1937. Now what are the crimes for which the law of the Church decrees irregularity? These: 1. Wilful and

[1] München, l. c., pp. 153, 155. [2] Schmalzg., l. c., n. 102. [3] Craiss., n. 1766.

deliberate reiteration of baptism;[1] 2. Apostasy from the faith;[2] 3. Furtive or improper reception of sacred orders;[3] 4. The exercise of an *ordo* which a person has not yet received, *v.g.*, when a mere deacon says Mass.[4]

1938.—5. The violation of censures; in this case, however, a person incurs the disqualification only when he knowingly, and wilfully, and culpably receives an *ordo*, or performs a function of an *ordo* already received, while he is under censure, namely of excommunication, suspension, and interdict.[5] We say, an *ordo*; for a person who performs an act of *jurisdiction* while he is under censure does not contract the unfitness. This—the violation of censures—is one of the principal sources of the incapacity in question. Of course, where the censure is null and void, though considered valid in the external forum, its violation does not entail irregularity in the forum of conscience.[6] 6. Homicide and mutilation, provided the killing or maiming be voluntary and premeditated.[7] Here we observe that this unfitness for crime is always contracted *ipso facto*, though for the *forum externum* a declaratory sentence is generally required.

§ 2. *Natural causes.*

1939. What are the natural defects which produce the canonical unfitness in question? By reason of natural defects, the following persons chiefly are irregular: (*a*) Those who are insane; (*b*) those who are blind, lack the left eye, are dumb, epileptic, lame, leprous, cripples, hunchbacks; those who have no nose nor ears, and persons of a very small and stunted stature; (*c*) those who are illegitimate.

1940. (*d*) Those who are illiterate. Canonists, however, do not agree as to what degree of illiteracy induces the disa-

---

[1] Tit. de apost. et reit. bapt. (v. 9).   [2] Eod.   [3] Tit. de eo qui fuit. (v. 30).
[4] Tit. de cler. non ord. ministr.   [5] Tit. de cleric. excom. ministr. (v. 27).
[6] Stremler, p. 49.   [7] Tit. de homic. (v. 12); Conc. Trid., sess. 14, C. 7 de Ref.

bility in question. Here we may remark that, speaking in general, the degree or grade of knowledge, as prescribed by the Council of Trent is:[1] (a) Those who are to receive first tonsure should know the rudiments of faith, and how to read and write;[2] (b) those who are to be promoted to minor orders must at least understand the Latin language;[3] (c) those who are to be ordained priests, must by a careful previous examination have been proved to be capable of teaching the people those things which it is necessary for all to know unto salvation, as also fit to administer the sacraments.[4]

1941. Canonists here also call attention to the utility and necessity of the study of canon law. The *journal du droit canon.*, Apr. 1883, page 147, says: "The Church does not allow Ecclesiastics to be in ignorance of the Sacred Canons. Thus the *canon* Nulli 4, Dist. 38, decrees: 'Nulli Sacerdotum liceat ignorare canones.' Again the *can. Ignorantia* 1, Dist. 38, enacts: 'Sciant sacerdotes scripturas sacras *et canones.*'" But when the Church addresses herself to Bishops, continues the above *Monthly*, she recommends this study to them with a zeal and an earnestness that are equalled only by the unbounded ardor with which she invites them to apply themselves to this study.

1942. Another celebrated canonist writes that at the present day the knowledge of canon law is more than ever indispensable. For, he continues, it is only by a thorough knowledge of ecclesiastical law, that arbitrary action will be avoided both on the part of the Superior and of the inferior. It is only when the inferior as well as the Superior knows how far, where, when, and how he can proceed, that the authority of the one is respected, and the rights of the other are protected. Especially is this knowledge essential

---

[1] S. C. C. Burgi S. Sepulchri 27, Feb. 1875.
[2] Conc. Trid., sess. 23, cap. 4. de Ref.   [3] Ib. cap. 11 de Ref.
[4] Conc. Trid., sess. 23, cap. 14 de Ref.

in order that the right steps may be taken in criminal and disciplinary proceedings and investigations.[1]

ART. IV.
Does Ignorance excuse from this Disability?

1943. Is it necessary, in order to incur the canonical incapacity in question, that a person should have a knowledge both of the law forbidding the crime (we speak of *irregularitas ex delicto*, as the *irregularitas ex defectu* is certainly incurred by a person who is ignorant of the law or of the irregularity), and of the canonical disqualification annexed to the commission of the crime? For the answer, so far as the knowledge of the law is concerned, we refer to No. 1710, where the principles involved in the question are fully set forth. For the answer, so far as the knowledge of the incapacity is concerned, see No. 1707, where the principle is laid down that ignorance merely of the punishment, when there is question of purely vindicative punishments, does not exempt from them. Now irregularity is a punitive punishment. Hence also it is the common opinion of canonists that the disqualification in question is contracted by a person who is unaware that it is annexed to the crime he has committed, and only knows that his offence is forbidden by the law of the Church.

1944. We say, *common opinion;* for the contrary opinion, which holds that the incapacity is not incurred in the case, is probable according to Schmalzgruber,[2] Palao, Suarez, Sanchez, La Croix, and others. The chief reason upon which it is based is that the disqualification is a most severe punishment, which the delinquent is bound in conscience to execute himself, and before any declaratory sentence. Now it seems equitable that such a severe punishment should

---
[1] Schulte, K. K. R., vol. ii., p. 113.   [2] L. c., n. 108.

not be incurred, except when the offender is fully cognizant, not merely of the law, but also of the punishment.

1945. Here we remark, in passing, that all irregularities, whether they proceed *ex defectu* or *ex delicto* are incurred *ipso jure*, since they are always *latæ*, never *ferendæ sententiæ*. Consequently, when a person commits a crime which the law punishes with irregularity, he incurs, *in foro interno*, the irregularity *ipso facto*, and without any judicial sentence. We say, *in foro interno;* for *in foro externo* no person is, generally speaking, regarded as irregular, until a *declaratory* sentence has been given to that effect. In other words, no person is considered irregular in the external forum, until he has been juridically declared irregular.[1]

ART. V.

How this Disability is removed.

1946. *Q.* In how many ways is the unfitness for orders and the ecclesiastical state removed?

A. In four: 1. The unfitness resulting from a passing *defect* or deformity ceases of itself, as soon as the defect passes away. Thus, if it proceeds from want of the prescribed age for ordination, or of the requisite learning, or from want of good name (provided the want of reputation, that is, infamy, be only *facti*, not *juris;* for the infamy of law does not cease, save by dispensation)[2] it disappears of itself as soon as the proper age is reached, or the necessary learning attained, etc.

1947.—2. Craisson[3] holds that the unfitness which springs from *crime* and certain disqualifications arising from defects are taken away by baptism. But as Schmalzgruber well remarks, baptism does not, properly speaking, remove any irregularity or incapacity whatever, for the simple reason

---

[1] Stremler, l. c., p. 46.   [2] Can. 7, c. 2, q. 3.   [3] Man., n. 1771.

that, prior to being baptized, a person is not subject to the laws of the Church, and therefore cannot contract any disqualification. The infamy of fact, even though caused by murder, is the only irregularity blotted out by baptism.[1]

1948.—3. The unfitness arising from *illegitimacy* is removed, though only as to the reception of orders, by solemn profession in a religious order. We say, *though only* etc. ; as a matter of fact, however, all religious orders have the privilege by which their religious, though illegitimate by birth, can be chosen prelates.

1949—4. Finally, the disabilities of which we speak in this article are removed by dispensation or act of clemency of the Superior. Now, what Superior can remove disabilities? The rule is: " Omnis res, per quascunque causas nascitur, per easdem dissolvitur."[2] Now, only the Superior who is possessed of *universal* jurisdiction—namely the Pope and general councils—can establish an irregularity, and that only by a *general law*, not by a special command. Consequently the supreme Pontiff alone can remove or dispense from irregularities, whether caused by crime or defect.

1950. Bishops can do so only where this power is delegated to them, but not by their own inherent or ordinary authority. The reason is, that these disabilities can be established only by the supreme authority in the Church, as we have seen. But a Bishop cannot relax the law of his Superior—namely of the Pope or general council.

1951. We say, *only where this power is delegated to them;* now the Council of Trent[3] has authorized Bishops to dispense in all cases of irregularities arising from a *crime that is secret*—except that proceeding from voluntary homicide, and those crimes which have been already carried before the contentious forum. By secret or occult crimes, canonists here commonly understand those crimes which, though

---

[1] Schmalzg., l. c., n. 110.   [2] Reg. 1. de Reg. Jur. (v. 41).
[3] Sess. 24., c. 6 de Ref.

known to and provable by several witnesses, nevertheless have not yet become notorious, that is, known to the greater part of a place, neighborhood, or community, which should contain at least ten persons.[1]

1952. The power granted to Bishops, in this matter, by the Council of Trent, is possessed also by regular prelates, abbots, generals of orders, and provincials, and others having quasi-episcopal jurisdiction independently of the Bishop. The reason is that the power granted to Bishops in the Cap. 6 de Ref., sess. 24 of the Council of Trent is a *favor*, and hence should be extended to the prelates just mentioned; for favors should be always liberally construed.[2] But neither Bishops nor the other prelates can remove disabilities arising from defects, except in the case of disability from illegitimacy and similitudinary bigamy.[3]

1953. Our Bishops in the United States (as a rule all Bishops of missionary countries), by particular law, that is, by special Papal indult, have power "Dispensandi in quibuscumque irregularitatibus, exceptis illis, quæ vel ex bigamia vera, vel ex homicidio voluntario proveniunt; et in his etiam duobus casibus, si præcisa necessitas operariorum ibi fuerit, si tamen quoad homicidium voluntarium, ex hujusmodi dispensatione scandalum non oriatur."[4]

---

[1] Schmalzg., l. c., n. 115, 116.
[2] Grandeclaude, tom. iii., p. 526.
[3] Ib., n. 121.
[4] Facult. Form. I., n. 2.

SECTION II.

Temporal and Corporal Vindicatory Punishments.

CHAPTER I.

VARIOUS KINDS OF THESE PUNISHMENTS.

1954. Thus far, we have spoken of those vindicatory punishments which are of a spiritual nature. We shall briefly describe those of a temporal or corporal character. Of these, not a small number, that were formerly in vogue, have now gone completely out of use. Among these may be classed corporal punishments, *i. e.*, whipping and flogging, imprisonment, and exile in the strict sense of the term.[1] The chief punitive punishments of a temporal character which are still in use are pecuniary fines, assignment to a monastery or house of retreat, and exile in a broad sense or mild form.

ART. I.

Pecuniary Fines.

1955. By a pecuniary fine (*mulcta pecuniaria*) is here meant the payment of a sum of money which is imposed by the ecclesiastical judge, *in foro externo*, upon a person, in punishment of a crime committed by him.[2] From this definition it will be readily seen that we do not speak here of the payment of money imposed as a penance by the confessor, in the tribunal of penance, but only of those fines which are inflicted by the *ecclesiastical judge, as such*, and consequently only *in foro externo* and as canonical punitive punishments.

[1] Phillips, Lehrb., p. 396.   [2] Benedict XIV., de Syn., l. 10., c. 9., n. 3.

Various Kinds of Temporal Punishments. 139

1956. Of the Sacred Canons enacted prior to the Council of Trent, some enjoin, others forbid pecuniary fines in the ecclesiastical forum. Likewise the practice in the Church, prior to the Council of Trent, was not uniform on this head, some Bishops being in favor of, others opposed to the principle of imposing fines in punishment of crimes. However, the Council of Trent put an end to all uncertainty in this matter. For in session 25, c. 3 de Ref. it expressly gives Bishops power to impose fines in certain cases. Here are the words of the Council: "Liceat eis (episcopis) si expedire videbitur, in causis ... ad forum ecclesiasticum quomodo libet pertinentibus, contra quosdam, etiam laicos, *per mulctas pecuniarias*, quæ locis piis ibi existentibus, eo ipso quod exactæ fuerint, assignentur ... procedere et causas definire."

1957. This Council itself imposed pecuniary fines as punishments for crime both upon Bishops and inferior Ecclesiastics. Thus it decrees that Bishops who are absent from their see, without legitimate reason, shall incur the loss of a fourth part of one year's income;[1] that concubinary Ecclesiastics shall first be *ipso facto* deprived of the third part of the fruits, rents, and proceeds of all their benefices whatsoever, and finally, if they remain incorrigible, of the benefices themselves.[2]

1958. In what manner are these fines to be imposed? Fagnani remarks correctly that they can be inflicted only by judicial sentence pronounced after due trial of the case, but not extrajudicially, *i.e.*, not without trial. This applies to fines involving a considerable amount of money, but not to small fines.

1959. When can fines be imposed by the ecclesiastical judge? 1. As a matter of course, in all cases where the law of the Church authorizes it, *v. g.*, in the case of concubinary

---
[1] Conc. Trid., sess. 6, c. 1. de Ref.
[2] Ib., sess. 25, c. 14 de Ref.; cf. Bened. XIV., l. c., c. 9, n. 6.

Ecclesiastics, as we have seen. 2. The Bishop can, in making diocesan statutes, annex a pecuniary fine, as an ordinary punishment to their violation; he can also, as judge, inflict fines in cases where the law of the Church does not prescribe any particular or ordinary punishment, but leaves the penalty to the discretion of the judge.[1] But where the law of the Church prescribes a canonical punishment for a crime, the ecclesiastical judge is not allowed to commute it into a pecuniary fine. Such a commutation would be regarded as immunity granted for money.[2]

1960.—3. Finally, in cases where the offence is not so great as to deserve spiritual punishments, such as censures, a pecuniary fine may be imposed. The Council of Trent[3] enacts that censures should not be inflicted rashly or for slight causes, lest they become more despised than feared, and produce ruin rather than safety. Hence it enjoins on all ecclesiastical judges, of whatsoever dignity they may be, that in all causes, criminal and civil, both during the proceedings or trial and in giving judgment, they abstain from ecclesiastical censures, as often as pecuniary fines can be imposed and collected; and only when such fines cannot easily be imposed shall it be lawful for ecclesiastical judges to employ censures, provided, however, that the character of the crime so require, and that there be contumacy, and upon due trial.[4]

1961. What is to be especially avoided when these fines are imposed, is the desire of gain or making money by this means. Abuses of this kind seem to have occurred not unfrequently in former times. In order to cut off all temptation of perverting the ends of justice and of extorting money, the Church has enacted that the Bishop or ecclesiastical judge can never appropriate these fines to his own uses; nor can he employ them for the purpose of

---

[1] Conc. Trid., sess. 25, c. 3 de Ref.
[2] Sess. 25, c. 3 de Ref.
[3] Arg. cap. Licet 3, de pœnis (v. 37.)
[4] Stremler, p. 61; Craiss., n. 6355.

Various Kinds of Temporal Punishments. 141

paying the salary of his Vicar-General, or of the officials of his chancery or tribunal; nay, he cannot apply the least portion of them even to the fabric of the Cathedral or the repairs of the Bishop's house; nor can he allow any part of them to go to the treasurer of these funds; but he must apply them exclusively to pious and charitable purposes, that is, to the poor, to hospitals, orphan asylums, and the like.[1] These fines, moreover, should be deposited in the hands of a special treasurer, from whose accounts it shall clearly appear that they have all been applied to charitable uses.[2]

1962. *Custom in the United States.*—Direct pecuniary fines are not in use with us. It is, however, the opinion of not a few of our ablest divines, that moderate pecuniary fines might sometimes be advantageously imposed instead of other canonical punishments, such as *censures*. In fact, it is apparent that, where a fine will obtain the desired result, recourse to censures is not laudable.

ART. II.

Ecclesiastical Imprisonment.

1963. In former times there were ecclesiastical prisons, properly speaking, and the law of the Church authorized ecclesiastical judges to decree imprisonment, against Ecclesiastics and laics, for grave crimes, proven juridically, *i.e.*, by a formal trial.[3] At the present day, imprisonment proper is no longer, at least generally speaking, inflicted by ecclesiastical judges. Ecclesiastics who have been proved guilty of crime, instead of being imprisoned by the Bishop, are, also in the United States, sometimes sent to religious houses or other places of retreat, to do penance.[4]

---

[1] Conc. Trid., l. c. [2] Bened XIV., l. c., l. 10, C. 10, n. 5
[3] Arj. cap. 15, de sent. excom. in 6º (v. 11). [4] Cf. Stremler, p. 63.

1964. *Q.* What is the legislation of the Third Plenary Council of Baltimore on this head?

A. In harmony with the above teaching, the Council enacts: "Quo efficacius aberrantes in semitam rectam reducantur enixe commendamur, ex S. C. de Prop. Fide consulto, ut domus quædam a religiosis viris regendæ instituantur, ubi sacerdotes lapsi, qui spem fundatam conversionis exhibent, pro tempore ab episcopo statuendo, vitam degant." (Conc. Pl. Balt. III., No. 77).

ART. III.

Exile in a Mild Form.

1965. Exile, in the ecclesiastical sense of the term, consists in this, that an Ecclesiastic or laic who is guilty of crime is expelled from the diocese, and forbidden to return. Sometimes a person is banished merely from a particular city or locality, but not from the entire diocese. The Bishop or ecclesiastical judge may inflict this punishment, in order to cause scandals to cease, to oblige delinquents to break off their evil habits, to remove them from the occasion of sin, and, in general, to prevent a number of crimes, especially against morality. This punishment is still inflicted at times, though much more rarely than was the case formerly.

[1] Stremler, p. 63.

PART IV.

REPRESSIVE PUNISHMENTS WHICH ARE REFORMATIVE.

(Pœnæ medicinales, censuræ.)

1966. Having spoken of the repressive punishments which are *punitive*, it now remains to treat briefly of the *correctional* or, as they are commonly called, censures. We shall first explain those properties which are common to all censures; next the peculiar characteristics of each censure in particular.

SECTION I.

Reformative Punishments, in General.

1967. Under this heading we shall discuss, in separate articles, the nature and the various kinds of the punishments in question; by whom and upon whom, for what cause, and in what manner they are inflicted; what reasons exempt from them; when and how a person who has incurred them is released from them.

CHAPTER I.

NATURE OF THESE PUNISHMENTS.

1968. A reformative punishment (or censure, as it is commonly styled) is a spiritual and medicinal punishment, by which a person who is baptized, delinquent, and incorrigible, is deprived of the use of certain spiritual goods or benefits, by ecclesiastical authority, until he recedes from his incorrigibleness.[1] Let us briefly explain this definition. We say, *a punishment*; for a censure is a privation of spiritual benefits, and therefore inflicts pain and disgrace. Hence, like every punishment, it presupposes a crime; for, as we have seen, there can be no punishment, where there is no guilt.

1969. We say, secondly, *medicinal;* because, as has been shown, they are primarily and directly administered for the purpose of curing a person who is morally infirm, of bringing him back to a sense of duty, and causing him to break off his evil ways. They are spiritual *medicines* rather than *punishments* proper. Now medicines are given a sick person only as long as he is sick, and discontinued as soon as he is cured or on the fair way to recovery.[2] In like manner, these punishments, when inflicted upon a delinquent,[3] should be withdrawn as soon as he amends and becomes repentant.[4] Consequently, they should not be inflicted for a determinate period, *v.g.*, for three months, since it is always understood, by virtue of the law of the Church, that they can last only as long as the obstinacy in sin continues, and should be withdrawn as soon as the amendment has taken place.[5]

1970. We say, moreover, *incorrigible*, for it is, as was already shown, the peculiar feature of these punishments that they not only presuppose a crime, but also incorrigibility or *obstinate persistence* in crime. Hence a person, in order to become liable to these punishments, must be not only guilty of crime, but must, moreover, persist in his criminal course, *after having been duly warned and admonished*.

1971. This warning (*monitio canonica*), which must precede the punishment, can emanate either from the law itself or from the ecclesiastical judge or Superior. Hence a person

---

[1] Schmalzg., l. 5, t. 39, n. 1; Bened. XIV., de Syn., l. 10, C. 1, n. 1.
[2] Soglia, vol. ii., p. 561.   [3] Stremler, l. c., p. 173.
[4] Supra, n. 1796.   [5] Arg. cap. 1. de sent. excom. in 6º. (v, 11).

may become contumacious in two ways; first, when he does not heed the warning of his ecclesiastical Superior, addressed to him individually and personally; second, when he violates a law of the Church, with the full knowledge of the law and of the censure annexed. For, in this second case the law itself is a standing warning to all. Here it should be observed that these punishments should be imposed only on persons who, though incorrigible, yet give hopes of amendment, but not upon persons who are so absolutely incorrigible as to preclude all hope of their repentance. For medicines are not administered to patients who are beyond all hope of recovery.

1972. We say, *spiritual goods;* for, although the punishments in question sometimes take away temporal goods, as happens, *v.g.*, in suspension *a beneficio*, which strips a person of the salary or income of his office or benefice—yet they do so only secondarily and indirectly. Primarily and directly, they extend only to spiritual benefits. Nor do they dispossess a person of *all*, but merely of certain spiritual privileges, namely of those *which depend on the Church*, *v.g.*, the sacraments, public prayers, sacred functions. Hence they do not of themselves deprive a person of *sanctifying grace*. Thus it can happen that a person may be under censure, and yet be in the state of grace, *v.g.*, where the censure is imposed upon a person who is innocent.

CHAPTER II.

VARIOUS KINDS OF REFORM PUNISHMENTS.

1973. There are three kinds of reformative punishments, namely excommunication, suspension, and interdict.[1] Observe that excommunication is the severest of all correctional punishments, since it dispossesses a person, for the time being, of all spiritual benefits depending on the Church, and therefore contains or combines in itself the effects of both the other censures. Hence, in the decretals, the censures of suspension and interdict are grouped and discussed under the one title *de sententia excommunicationis*.

ART. I.

Reformative Punishments " a jure " and " ab homine."

1974. Reform punishments are inflicted in two ways: (*a*) *a jure*, that is, by law, and (*b*) *ab homine*, that is by the proper Superior. These are technical terms. Let us explain them. A reformative punishment termed *a jure* is that which the law itself attaches to a crime. We take the word *law* here in its proper sense, that is as an enactment which has of itself a *permanent and perpetual binding force*, as contradistinguished from a mere command or precept, which is essentially of a *temporary obligation* and lapses with the death of the Superior by whom it was given.[2] Hence by punishments *a jure* we mean not only those which are contained in the common law of the Church, namely the

[1] Cap. Quærenti, 20. de v. s. (v. 40.) [2] Konings, n. 98, 4°.

Various Kinds of Reform Punishments. 147

Sacred Canons, and the decrees of Popes and Œcumenical Councils, but also those which are enacted by Plenary and Provincial Councils, and by episcopal statutes made in diocesan synods.[1] The reason is, that the latter decrees, no less than the former, are real and true laws, though binding only in particular localities. For their binding force is not transitory, and does not cease with the death of the Superior by whom they were enacted, but is of itself perpetual, and they remain in force till lawfully abrogated.

1975. On the other hand, a correctional punishment *ab homine* is that which is annexed by the proper Superior (*ab homine*) *v. g.*, by the Bishop, to the violation of a *precept* or *command*, as contradistinguished from a *law*. Reformative punishments *ab homine*, like precepts, have no perpetual binding force. They cease to be of force, whenever the jurisdiction of the Bishop by whom they were made expires, that is, as soon as the Bishop dies, is removed, transferred, or resigns, though, if once incurred, they cease only by absolution. They are called forth only on occasion of peculiar and passing circumstances, and are intended to last as long as these peculiar circumstances exist.[2]

1976. Now reformatory punishments which are *ab homine* may be inflicted in two ways: (*a*) by way of a *general* precept, order, or command—*per sententiam generalem, v. g.*, when the Bishop, by reason of a certain crime which is very prevalent in his diocese, issues a circular letter, mandate or precept, imposing censure on any one who shall commit the offence; (*b*) by way of a *particular* command or injunction—*per sententiam specialem*—laid upon one or more *determinate* persons, *v. g.*, if the Bishop puts a person on trial for a crime, and upon conviction pronounces sentence inflicting censure upon him; or also when he threatens a certain person or persons with censure, in case they persist

[1] Ib., n. 1661, 2º. [2] Kober, der Kirchenbann, p. 51.

in their evil ways. The general precept, therefore, is addressed indiscriminately to all the subjects of the Bishop ; the particular, to certain individuals who are specified.[1] As will be seen, the reform punishments *a jure* bear a considerable resemblance to those *ab homine per sententiam generalem.* Both extend, not to a particular individual, but to all subjects in general ; both refer equally to *future* crimes committed after the enactment of the law or precept.[2]

ART. II.

Reform Punishments " ferendæ " and " latæ sententiæ."

1977. For a correct understanding of censures it is of great importance to distinguish between correctional punishments which are *latæ sententiæ* and those which are *ferendæ sententiæ.* Censures *latæ sententiæ* are those which are incurred *in foro interno,* by the very fact of the commission of the crime (*ipso facto*), that is, the very moment the crime is committed, and without any intervention whatever of the ecclesiastical Superior or judge, and therefore without any sentence, even declaratory.

1978. Correctional punishments *ferendæ sententiæ*—called also threatened censures--are those which are incurred only by a formal and special condemnatory sentence of the proper Superior, pronounced after due previous warning and the prescribed trial.

Now, by what marks can it be known whether these punishments are *ferendæ* or *latæ sententiæ ?* As a general rule, it may be said they are *latæ sententiæ,* when their wording is such as to show clearly that the law-giver wishes them to be incurred the very moment the crime is committed.[3] Such is the case (*a*) with phrases of the past or present tense, *v. g., excommunicamus; excommunicatus est* or

---

[1] Gury—Baller., n. 933 adn. b. [2] Kober, l. c., p. 50. [3] Kober, l. c., p. 61.

Various Kinds of Reform Punishments. 149

fuit; excommunico; suspendantur; volumus aut jubemus esse excommunicatum, suspensum, aut interdictum. (*b*) Where these phrases are used: *ipso facto, ipso jure, sine alia sententia.* (*c*) Where the language is imperative, *v. g., incidat in excommunicationem, maneat suspensus.*

1979. They are *ferendæ sententiæ*, as a rule, when the words, in which they are couched, refer to the future, and therefore merely threaten them. Such phrases are, *v. g., excommunicabitur, suspendetur;* or if they require the intervention of a third person, *v. g., excommunicetur per episcopum.*

1980. It has been objected by some canonists that punishments *latæ sententiæ* are opposed to the very law of nature. For it is repugnant, they say, to the natural feelings, that a person should be himself the executor of the punishments to which he has rendered himself liable. But it must be remembered that censures *latæ sententiæ* do not inflict any positive, corporal, or other external pain, but merely negative and spiritual; they simply deprive a person of certain spiritual benefits; the person incurring them is passive; the censure executes itself.[1] Moreover, it should be borne in mind that correctional punishments *latæ sententiæ* produce their effects *ipso facto, i. e.*, without any judicial sentence, *only in foro interno;* for *in foro externo* they do so only upon a declaratory sentence of the proper ecclesiastical judge, which must be preceded by a trial. We say, *declaratory* sentence, for no condemnatory sentence is needed, since the law itself, which inflicts the censure, *condemns* the offender.

Art. III.

General Remarks.

1981. As we have seen, correctional punishments, should

[1] Kober, l. c, p. 55.

not be imposed for any determinate time. For, as was shown, they are *medicinal* in their character, and should therefore last only as long as the spiritual sickness continues, that is, until the obstinate offender returns to better ways. They are consequently, by their very nature, indeterminate as to time. Their duration is commensurate with, and depends upon, the continuance of the offender in his incorrigibility. As soon as the latter ceases, the former should be withdrawn. Hence, in the definition of these punishments, we say that by them a person is deprived of certain spiritual benefits, *until he recedes from his contumacy.*

1982. We said above, *when inflicted as such;* for correctional punishments—namely suspension and interdict, but not excommunication—may sometimes be imposed, not as correctional, but also as vindicatory punishments—*per modum pœnæ vindicativæ*.[1] In the latter case, they follow the rules of other punitive punishments, and may be inflicted for a definite period, *v. g.*, for three months, and, absolutely speaking, without the previous canonical admonition, though not without a previous citation and trial.

1983. Again, we remark, when a censure is invalid, it takes no effect whatever in conscience—*in foro interno*—and need therefore not be observed in this forum, though sometimes it has to be conformed to *outwardly* or *in foro externo*, as we shall see, for the sake of shielding the authority of the Superior. Finally, we observe that suspension and interdict only can be inflicted also as vindicative punishments; excommunication never.

---

[1] Cap. 7 de elect; Cap. 48 (v. 39); Schmalzg., L 5, t. 39, n. 30; Reiff., l. 5, t. 39, n. 28.

CHAPTER III.

WHAT PERSONS CAN INFLICT THEM?

1984. Two questions are here proposed: first, who are competent, *i. e.*, have power, to inflict correctional punishments; next, what conditions are requisite, in order that those who have this power, may exercise it validly and licitly.[1] In regard to the competency the question is not: Has the Church the power to punish? For it has been already fully shown that she has. The question therefore is: Who are the organs, or ministers, or officials through whom the Church exercises this power? To inflict the punishments in question is an exercise of power or jurisdiction, not in the internal *forum*, or in the forum of conscience, but in the external or social forum of the Church. It is an exercise of *external* jurisdiction, of the power to govern and to rule, which the Church possesses as an external and perfect society.

1985. Now this power is twofold, as was seen, ordinary and delegated, according as a person possesses it by reason of his office, or only by authorization from one having ordinary jurisdiction. Hence all those, and only those, who are vested with jurisdiction in the external forum of the Church, whether ordinary or delegated, can inflict correctional punishments or censures.

We shall treat under separate heads, 1. of those who have *ordinary* power; 2. of those who are vested with *delegated* jurisdiction.

[1] Cf. München, l. c., vol. i., p. 33.

ART. I.

Who are vested with " Ordinary" Power?

1986. *Q.* What persons have ordinary jurisdiction or power to inflict correctional punishments?

A. 1. The Pope has ordinary jurisdiction, *in foro externo*, all over the world. Hence he can inflict these punishments upon all the faithful, and also upon all Ecclesiastics, from the highest to the lowest—from the cardinal to the cleric in minor orders. Œcumenical Councils have the same power. 2. The Sacred Congregations of Cardinals, being the organs of the Pope and forming one and the same tribunal with him,[1] can inflict these punishments all over the world, in matters coming within their respective spheres.[2] 3. Legates of the Holy See can do so, in their territory, with the restrictions, however, imposed on them by the Council of Trent, as explained above.[3]

1987.—4. Bishops have ordinary jurisdiction in their diocese, and therefore can impose these punishments upon all their subjects,[4] and that as soon as they have been appointed or confirmed by the Holy See, even though they have not yet received consecration. For to impose censures is an act of jurisdiction, not of order.

1988.—5. Archbishops or Metropolitans have a twofold ordinary jurisdiction in *foro externo*; one over their own diocese; the other over the dioceses of their province.[5] In their own diocese, their power in the matter of censures is the same as that of Bishops described. So far as concerns the dioceses of their province, the jurisdiction of Metropolitans extends, as was shown,[6] (*a*) over the suffragan Bishops, (*b*) the subjects of these suffragans. Prior to the Council of Trent,[7] Metropolitans had power to excommunicate,

---

[1] Supra, n. 514. [2] Stremler, p. 181. [3] Supra, n. 521. (3°)
[4] Supra, n. 897. [5] Supra, n. 530, 531. [6] Supra, n. 529. [7] Supra, n. 530.

suspend, or interdict the Bishops of their province.¹ At present, however, according to the Tridentine enactment, this power is no longer vested in them,² so far as the suffragan Bishops themselves are concerned; though it is still possessed by them in regard to the Vicars-General and officials of the suffragans.³

1989. In what cases can the Metropolitan, at present, inflict correctional punishments on the Vicars-General and officials of his suffragans?⁴ 1. In all cases, where these officials violate any right of the Metropolitan, v. g., where they place obstacles in the way of appeals to the Metropolitans, or disobey injunctions or admonitions of the latter, made in the exercise of their metropolitical authority;⁵ 2. in all matters where the Metropolitan is obliged to exercise a supervisory authority, v. g., when the Vicar-General does not respect the rights of the Holy See, or continues to exercise jurisdiction even after his Bishop has been excommunicated.⁶ 3. Upon the subjects of their suffragans, the Metropolitan can inflict these punishments only on appeal and during visitation,⁷ since only in these cases does he possess jurisdiction over them.⁸

1990. The Vicar-General, being the representative of the Bishop, also in contentious matters, and forming morally one and the same person and tribunal with him, has, indeed, the power to inflict these punishments,⁹ though he cannot exercise it unless he has a special commission from his Bishop to that effect.¹⁰ The Vicar-General of the Metropolitan has, like the Metropolitan himself, so far as concerns

---

¹ Cap. 52 de sent. excom. (v. 39'; Cap. 1, de off. ord. in 6° (i. 16.)
² Conc. Trid., sess. 13, c 8; sess. 24. c. 5 de Ref.
³ Cap. 1. de off. vic. in 6° i 13)   ⁴ Cf. supra. n. 630.
⁵ Glossa. in cap 1 i, v. ration bili.   ⁶ Kober, der Kirchenban, p. 71.
⁷ Ca. 7. de sent. excom. in 6° v. 11.)   ⁸ Supra, n. 531.
⁹ C p. 3 de appe'l. in 6° ii. 15.)
¹⁰ Cap. 2 de off. vic. in 6° ,i. 13'. Kober, l. c., p. 74.

the subjects of the suffragans, the right to impose the correctional punishments in question on them only where an appeal is made to him.[1] 7. Vicars-Capitular (with us administrators, *sede vacante*) have, generally speaking, the same power as Bishops, in regard to inflicting these punishments.[2]

1991.—7. Both by the common law of the Church[3] and the special rules and constitutions of religious orders, as approved by the Holy See, these punishments (that is censures) can be inflicted upon their religious subjects, not only by the general and provincial Superiors, such as abbots, generals, and provincials, but also by local Superiors, as priors, Rectors, or guardians; by the general chapters, for the whole order; by the provincial chapters of some orders, for the province.[4]

1992.—8. Furthermore, national and provincial Councils can enact or impose censures for the whole nation or province. 9. Moreover, some other persons, *v. g.*, rural deans, in some places, though not in the United States, have the power in question, by virtue of privilege, custom, or rather prescription.[5] For it is certain that persons who have no power whatever by virtue of their office,[6] or by delegation, to impose correctional punishments, may acquire this power by prescription.[7] 10. To all the above must be added those who, by common error, are considered as Superiors by a presumptive title. 11. Parish Priests have no longer ordinary power to inflict censures, as by custom the power granted them by the common law of the Church, in this matter, has been abrogated, and their power reduced to the *forum internum*.[8] Finally we observe that nobody except the Pope can introduce a new kind of censure;

---

[1] Kober, l. c., p. 75.   [2] Supra, n. 637.
[3] Cap. 10 de major. et ob. (i. 33) ; Cap. 8. de statu mon. (iii. 35.)
[4] Kober, l. c., p. 78.   [5] Cf. Supra, n. 85.
[6] Kober, l. c., p. 77.   [7] Cap. 18 de præscr. (ii. 26.)   [8] Craiss., n. 6376.

inferior Superiors can merely inflict those censures which are already properly established.

ART. II.

Who are vested with "delegated" Power?

1993. *Q.* What persons have delegated jurisdiction to inflict the punishments in question?

A. All those to whom this power is given by those who are vested with ordinary jurisdiction, namely by the persons enumerated under the previous question. Bishops and others vested with ordinary jurisdiction often find it difficult, nay impossible, to take cognizance personally of all causes falling under their jurisdiction, and of inflicting personally the proper correctional punishments. Hence they can and do authorize others to act for them, and to inflict punishments in their stead. They are, speaking in general, free to select as their delegates for the exercise of this power any worthy and competent person whatever, except a *woman* or a *layman*.[1]

1994. Hence also the Instructions *Sacra Hæc* of June 11, 1880, and *Cum Magnopere*, of 1884, enact in Article XII.: "Compilatio processus committi potest probo ac perito viro *ecclesiastico*, cui assistat actuarius." The Instruction *Causæ Matrimoniales* of 1884 likewise decrees: "Munus moderatoris actorum Episcopus vel ipse sibi assumet, vel suum Vicarium generalem, aut alium probum et expertum virum *e clero* ad illud delegabit."[2]

1995. Here it may be asked, whether the Pope can, by virtue of the fulness of his power, authorize a *woman* to exercise this power? There are two opinions. The affirmative is maintained by Schmalzgruber, on the ground that the prohibition to delegate women is merely *juris ecclesi-*

---
[1] Supra, vol. ii., n. 718. [2] Instr. S. C. de Prop. Fide, *Causæ matrimoniales*, § 6.

astici, not *juris divini*; others, with St. Alphonsus, hold the opposite opinion as more probable, chiefly because, as they say, women are by divine law incapacitated for this delegation, and the Pontiff cannot dispense from a divine law. Those who teach the affirmative point, in confirmation of their view, to the *Cap. Dilecta, de majorit. et ob.* (I. 33), where it is stated that an abbess imposed suspension *ab officio et beneficio* upon certain Ecclesiastics subject to her, which action was sustained by the Pope, to whom the matter had been referred. But those Canonists—and they form the great majority—who hold the negative, say with the *Glossa*[1] that the suspension in the case was not a suspension proper, or a censure whose violation would have produced irregularity, but merely a command, on the part of the abbess, forbidding those Ecclesiastics to say mass, until they had corrected themselves, and withdrawing meanwhile their salary. In fact, the above *decretal* clearly states that the abbess could inflict no excommunication, and consequently, by implication, no other censure. The *Glossa*[2] also says that women are incapable of exercising jurisdiction proper.

1996. We also say above, *except a layman*. The Pope (not an inferior prelate) can, however, delegate this power to a layman.[3] As a person who has the first tonsure is a cleric and not a layman, he may receive this delegation, though it is more becoming that only priests or persons in sacred orders be authorized to impose these punishments.[4]

1997. Those who exercise this power of inflicting reformative punishments by delegation, that is, by authorization from the *judex ordinarius*, exercise this jurisdiction *only in the name and by the order or authority* of the latter.[5] From this it follows that their power lapses as soon as it is properly and lawfully revoked by the principal or Superior

---

[1] In h. c. v. *Jurisdictioni*.   [2] Ib.   [3] Cap. 2 de Judic. (II. 1.)
[4] Kober, l. c., p. 84.   [5] Ib.

delegating,¹ and also when the latter himself loses jurisdiction, whether by death, removal, transfer, resignation, suspension or excommunication, for it is plain that the agent or delegate cannot continue to act for and in the name of a principal who is himself no longer capable of exercising the power in question.

1998. However, the agent or delegate in the case retains jurisdiction (*a*) until he is properly notified of the death, removal, transfer, resignation, etc., of the principal; (*b*) and also when the case or matter is no longer *res integra*; *v. g.*, when he has already cited the parties,¹ in which latter case he can finish the case which he has already begun, even though he has become aware of the fact that his principal has lost jurisdiction.

1999. As has been seen,² the rule is that delegates cannot in turn authorize others to act for them. We say, *the rule is;* for, as we have also shown,⁴ Papal Delegates can generally appoint others in their stead, to take cognizance of causes and inflict the punishments in question.⁵

ART III.

Conditions for the Exercise of this Power.

2000. We come now to the second question, namely, what are the requisite conditions in order that the above persons, who have the power, ordinary or delegated, to inflict reformative punishments, may also validly and lawfully exercise this power? 1. There must be no canonical obstacle or impediment in the way. Hence a Bishop who is excommunicated or suspended as *vitandus*, cannot, even validly, inflict these punishments.⁶ Nay, according to some, this holds also when he is *notoriously* under censure although

---

[1] Our Counter-Points, n. 37. sq.
[2] Cap. 20 de off. jud. del. (I. 29.)
[3] Supra, vol. i., n. 229.
[4] Supra, vol. i., n. 228.
[5] Cap. 3. de off. jud. del. (I. 29.)
[6] Cap. Exceptionem, de except.

he is not *denuntiatus*,[1] for the notoriety in the case is placed on the same footing with the formal publication of the censure. If, however, the suspension or excommunication which he has contracted is occult, he can impose the punishments under discussion validly, indeed, though not licitly. The Vicar-General of such Bishop incurs the same disability, though not the censure; for the Vicar-General forms one and the same person, morally, with the Bishop.[2]

2001.—2. Again, the Superior shall, as a rule, be in his own diocese or territory, and that on pain of nullity of the punishment, when he inflicts it. We say, *as a rule;*[3] for the exceptions, see *supra*, No. 1721.

2002.—3. He shall act *with freedom of will* and not from compulsion. According to the more common opinion, the punishment inflicted by a Superior, when under grave fear, is valid, though illicit. For such fear does not, generally speaking, destroy the free will of the Superior. But the absolution from the censure, extorted unjustly from the Superior, by violence or fear, as by threats and menaces, is null and void.[4]

2003.—4. In like manner, he shall not proceed from *personal motives*, that is, from hatred, dislike, or revenge. Hence no one can or should, as a rule, inflict correctional punishments (or punishments of any kind) in his own cause, that is, for *personal injuries*. For both natural and positive law dictate that no one shall be judge in his own cause, or at the same time judge and accuser. "Nullus unquam," says the law of the Church, "præsumat accusator simul esse et judex vel testis."[5] The reason is that a judge or Superior inflicting punishment should be wholly free from personal bias or feeling, and act solely from a sense and love of justice. Now, considering the frailty of human nature, it

---

[1] Stremler, l. c., p. 182
[2] Cap. 1. de off. vic., in 6°.
[3] Can episcopi 9, q. 2; Supra, n. 634, 635.
[4] Cap. unic. de his quæ metu, in 6° (1. 20)
[5] Can. 1., c. 4, q. 4.

is impossible to expect that a person who is directly concerned or interested in a matter, will act with perfect impartiality.[1] Hence, too, the law of the Church presumes that a Superior who imposes the punishments in question for personal injuries acts from motives of hatred and revenge, and is very reprehensible.[2]

2004. This principle is fully borne out and illustrated by the Sacred Canons. A certain Bishop Januarius had excommunicated a person named Isidore for *personal injuries*, namely, for having been contumeliously treated or insulted by Isidore. Pope Gregory the Great, to whom the matter was referred, reprimanded the Bishop, in the severest terms, for having thus avenged a personal insult. The Pope, moreover, threatened to punish him if he should ever presume to do so again. Here is the stinging reproach of the Pontiff to Bishop Januarius: "Nihil te ostendis de cœlestibus cogitare, sed terrenam te conversationem habere significas; dum *pro vindicta propriæ injuriæ (quod sacris regulis prohibetur) maledictionem anathematis invexisti.* Unde de cætero omnino esto circumspectus atque sollicitus, et talia cuiquam *pro defensione propriæ injuriæ tuæ* inferre denuo non præsumas. Nam si tale aliquid feceris, in te scias postea vindicandum."[3] St. Cyprian writes similarly that, for injuries inflicted upon his *own person*, he would never impose any punishment. His words are: "Contumeliam episcopatus nostri dissimulare et ferre possum, sicut et dissimulavi semper et pertuli."[4]

2005. However, what has been said has reference only to *purely personal injuries*, for the case is different when there is question *of the rights of the Church*. When these are violently attacked and their existence threatened, the respective Prelate is at all times authorized to inflict the

[1] Cf. Konings, n. 1662.   [2] Schmalzg., l. 5, t. 39, n. 25.
[3] Can. inter querelas 27, c. 23, q. 4.
[4] Epist. 9 ad clerum; Cf. Kober, l. c., p. 87.

punishments in question upon the unjust assailant, since here there is question, not of rights that concern him *personally*, but of rights of his See which he is bound to preserve and defend, by virtue of his office.[1] For further information on this head we refer to what we have said above, No. 721. Besides conforming to the conditions enumerated, the ecclesiastical Superior, when about to inflict reform punishments, is obliged also to observe certain formalities, such as giving the delinquent due warning and a fair trial. But these formalities will be discussed in a separate article, later on.

[1] Cap. 6, de sent. excom. in 6⁰ (v. 11); Bened. XIV., de syn. l. 9., c. 9, n. 12.

CHAPTER IV.

UPON WHOM CAN CORRECTIONAL PUNISHMENTS BE INFLICTED?

ART. I.

Adult Members of the Church.

2006. No person can become liable to the punishments of the Church, correctional or punitive, *unless he is a member of the Church by baptism.* For infidels, that is, all those who are unbaptized, do not fall under the power of the Church.[1] The case is different with heretics, schismatics, and apostates. For although they have fallen away from the Church, they nevertheless remain in a certain sense members of her pale, by reason of their baptism, and are subject to her laws and authority. Hence, *per se,* they also fall under her punishments, correctional or punitive.[2]

2007. Of those who are members of the Church, only *adults* are, generally speaking, punishable with correctional punishments. For by the law of the Church children under the age of fourteen are not presumed to have that use of reason which is required in order that a person can become guilty of obstinate persistence in crime,[3] which obstinacy is, as was seen, an essential condition of the punishments in question. For the same reason, adults who have permanently lost the use of reason, *v. g.,* the insane, are not capable of being punished.

[1] Conc. Trid., sess. 14, c. 2 de sacr. pœnit.
[2] Kober, der Kirchenbann, p. 95.   [3] Cap. 12 de pœnit. (v. 38.)

Art. II.

Entire Communities.

2008. *Q.* Can the punishments in question be inflicted, not only upon individuals, but also upon *a whole community as such*, v. g., upon a whole religious confraternity, or a Parish, or Chapter, or other corporate body, secular or religious?

A. It is certain that *excommunication* cannot be thus imposed. This is expressly laid down in the law of the Church, as still in force. "In universitatem vel collegium," says Pope Innocent IV. (1245), "proferri excommunicationis sententiam *penitus prohibemus* . . . sed in illos duntaxat de collegio vel universitate, quos culpabiles esse constiterit, promulgetur."[1] For, as was shown, it is a principle both of the natural law, and of the positive ecclesiastical law, that punishment shall fall only on the *guilty person himself* and not upon the innocent. Hence, when members of a community or moral body become guilty of crime punishable with excommunication, they alone should, upon due conviction of their crime, be excommunicated, and that not collectively, but individually.[2]

2009. The case is different with *suspension and interdict*, which, as was seen, may be imposed upon a whole community or chapter, as such, that is, in its capacity of moral or corporate body. But a suspension which is inflicted upon a whole community or moral body,—*v.g.*, a Chapter, Cathedral, or collegiate, a monastery,—temporarily withdraws only those rights which belong to, or are exercised by the community or moral body, *as such*, but not those rights which are possessed by the members of such body, *as individuals.* In other words, the suspension will extend only to *corporate acts.*

---

[1] Cap. Romana 5. de sent. excom. in 6º (v. 11.)   [2] Kober, l. c., p. 100.

2010. Thus a Cathedral chapter can be suspended *ab officio* or also *a beneficio*. But the suspension from the *officium* will be merely from the *capitular* functions or office, viz., the right of election. And the suspension from the *beneficium* will be merely from the income which the canons have *as canons*, but not from that which they may derive from other ecclesiastical offices held by them. Consequently suspension *ab ordine* cannot be inflicted upon a moral body, because the exercise of the *ordo*, or sacerdotal functions, is a *personal*, not a corporate, right or power, that is, a power belonging to persons as individuals and not as members of the community.[1] Examples of suspension from office or from benefice inflicted upon ecclesiastical corporate bodies may be seen in the Cap. unic. ne sede vac. in 6° (III. 8); Cap. 1 Extrav. Com. de Elect. (l. 3); Cap. 40 de Elect. in 6°—(I. 6).[2]

2011. From this reasoning it will also be seen why excommunication cannot be imposed upon corporate bodies as such. For this punishment, by its very nature, dispossesses a person, for a time, of certain spiritual benefits, such as membership of the Church, of the sacraments, etc. Now all these are privileges which members of a moral body possess, not as members of such body, *but as members of the Church and by virtue of baptism*.[3] Whether an excommunication inflicted upon a whole community would be not only illicit, but also invalid, is controverted.[4]

2012. Hitherto we have seen that all those who are members of the Church can be visited with correctional punishments. This, however, is not to be understood as though a particular member could be punished *by any and every ecclesiastical Superior;* for a person can be punished only by that particular Superior who possesses jurisdiction, ordinary or delegated, over him and to whom, therefore, he

---

[1] Kober, die Suspension, p. 32.
[3] Kober, l. c., p. 31.
[2] Cf. Stremler, l. c., p. 188.
[4] Cf. Konings, n. 1659, q. 6.

is subject.¹ Who these are and over whom their authority extends, has already been shown.²

Art. III.
The Pope and Bishops.

2013. From the principle just laid down it follows that the *Pope* cannot incur any reformative punishments whatever, not even those *latæ sententiæ* inflicted by the general law of the Church. For he has no Superior on earth, and hence there is no one who can exercise jurisdiction over him. Again the highest law-giver, is not, in the ordinary sense,³ bound by his own laws, since no one can be his own Superior.⁴ Now the Pontiff is the highest law-giver in the Church, and from him all the general laws of the Church emanate, either directly or indirectly.⁵

2014. *Bishops*, by an express provision of the Sacred Canons, do not incur any of the suspensions or interdicts, inflicted *ipso facto* or *latæ sententiæ* by ecclesiastical law, save when they are expressly mentioned.⁶ This privilege or exemption does not, however, extend to *excommunication*; for the Cap. 4 just quoted, which was enacted by Pope Innocent IV., in 1245, only exempts them from *suspensions* and *interdicts*, but not from excommunications. Now privileges or exemptions, which, like the present one, derogate from the common law of the Church, must be strictly construed.⁷

---

¹ Cap. 21 de sent. excom. (v. 34).   ² Supra, n. 1859 sq.
³ L. 31 ff. de leg. (l. 3).
⁴ Nemo *sibi* imperare neque se prohibere potest " (L. 51 ff. de recept. 4. 8.)
⁵ Kober, die Excom., p. 119.   ⁶ Cap. 4 de sent. excom. in 6º (V. 11.)
⁷ Schmalzg., l. c.; Kober, l. c., p. 120.

Art. IV.

Strangers and Travellers.

2015. The Bishop, as has been seen, possesses jurisdiction over all those who belong to his diocese, laics as well as Ecclesiastics. Here several questions present themselves. First, it may happen that a diocesan or subject of the Bishop, lay or ecclesiastical, is travelling outside of the diocese, and while so travelling transgresses a law of the diocese to which he belongs, but from which he is absent at the time. Now suppose the law thus transgressed has a censure annexed. Does he incur it? In other words, and to make the question more general and applicable to all cases, does a subject who, while out of the diocese to which he belongs, violates a diocesan law having a censure annexed, incur this punishment? Observe, we say, *diocesan law;* for if he violates a *general law of the Church,* he is amenable to his own Ordinary.[1] Again, we say, *while out of the diocese;* for such a person can certainly be punished by censures, even while he is out of the diocese, for crimes committed *in the diocese.*

2016. We now answer the question. It is certain that reformative punishments or censures, which are enacted by *synodal* statutes or by way of a *general* precept—*per sententiam generalem, v.g.*, by circular letters, are not incurred by subjects when out of their diocese. This is expressly enacted by the law of the Church. "Statuto episcopi," say the canons, "quo in omnes qui furtum commiserint, excommunicationis sententia promulgatur, subditi ejus, furtum extra ipsius diœcesim committentes, minime ligari noscuntur: cum extra territorium jus dicenti non pareatur impune."[2] For such statutes or commands are *territorial*

---

[1] Supra, vol. ii., n. 784.   [2] Cap. 2. de Const., in 6º (I. 2.)

and do not bind out of the territory of the Superior by whom they are made.

2017. As to the correctional punishments which are imposed by way of a *special precept or command—per sententiam specialem—v. g.*, if the Bishop lays a command or prohibition upon some *particular subject or subjects of his*, under pain of censure, it is controverted whether this subject, violating the command while out of the diocese, can be visited with censure by his Bishop. The affirmative—that is, the opinion which holds that the delinquent can be visited with the censure, is the more probable opinion.

2018. We shall now invert the case, and consider the liability of the above stranger or traveller in relation to the correctional punishments of the *strange diocese where he is for the time being*. In other words, if the traveller is not liable to the local reformative punishments of his own diocese, as explained above, is he also exempt from the local correctional punishments of the diocese where he is at the time? Or, to put the question in a more general way: Do strangers, and travellers, and all those who are out of their own diocese, and in a strange diocese, fall under the correctional punishments of the Bishop in whose diocese they are for the time being?

2019. Before answering, we observe that they incur all the censures established by the *common law of the Church*, unless they are in abeyance in the place where they are for the time being. The reason is that a person remains everywhere subject to the common law, and consequently also to the punishments decreed by it. The Bishop in the case becomes competent to inflict the punishments in question, *ratione delicti*, as was seen above.[1]

2020. We now answer: They incur those censures of the Ordinary of the place where they are for the time, which

---

[1] Supra, n. 791.

are annexed to local laws the violation of which would disturb the public peace or order of the place, or be injurious to the common good of such place. In this sense, they become subject to the Bishop of the place, *ratione delicti*. They do not fall under any of the other censures of the ordinary of the place where they are for the time being.[1]

[1] Craiss., n. 6389 sq. ; Stremler, l. c., p. 186.

CHAPTER V.

FOR WHAT CAUSE CAN REFORMATIVE PUNISHMENTS BE INFLICTED?

ART. I.
Crimes which are Grave.

2021. As has already been seen above, censures are *punishments*, and therefore can be inflicted *only for crime*.[1] Hence, whatever frees from sin, *v.g.*,—ignorance, fear, inadvertence, exempts also from the punishments in question. Canonists here ask, whether these punishments can sometimes be imposed for *venial sins*. There are two opinions. Some canonists hold the affirmative, in this sense: they distinguish between grave and light censures; grave correctional punishments, they say, cannot be inflicted for light offences, but light censures can.[2] By *light censures* they mean, *v.g.*,—a suspension or interdict, which is but partial and not total, and not of more than two days' duration.

2022. Others maintain the negative,[3] and say that all correctional punishments or censures, no matter how partial and brief in duration, are *always very severe punishments*, depriving a person, as they do, of spiritual benefits, which are essentially of greater value than temporal, and moreover entailing temporal disadvantages,[4] especially loss or diminu-

---

[1] Supra, n. 1668, 1847.

[2] However, those canonists who hold this opinion concede that a Bishop or Superior would act very imprudently, by inflicting even what they regard as very light censures for venial faults. (Craiss., n. 6397.)

[3] This seems, at least practically, the only safe opinion.

[4] Thus Kober (Susp., p. 54) says, nobody will deny that to forbid an Ecclesiastic to perform some function of his office, or to deprive him of his income, wholly or partly, is of itself, apart from the injury to his good name and honor, already a very grave punishment for an Ecclesiastic.

tion of good name; that, consequently, they should never be imposed for sins which are merely venial. Thus Schmalzgruber [1] teaches that censures—namely, excommunication, suspension, and interdict, as they are usually inflicted, cannot be imposed for a light or venial offence. This, he maintains, is the opinion of all canonists. The reason given by him is, that the censures are *most severe punishments*, and therefore out of proportion with a venial fault. Now, reason and equity demand that the punishment shall be in proportion with the offence. [2]

2023. The words of this great canonist, whom Benedict XIV. calls *facile Canonistarum princeps*, are: "Dubitatur an ob *culpam venialem* censura infligi possit? Dicendum, excommunicationem majorem, suspensionem, et interdictum, prout communiter feruntur, *ob culpam venialem injungi non posse*. Ita ex *omnium* sententia tradunt Navar.... Et colligitur ex can. *Nemo* 41; can. *Nullus* 42, Causa, 11, Q. 3; et ex Trid. sess. 24, c. 3, de Ref. Ratio est, quia sunt *pœnæ gravissimæ*, ac pœnæ improportionatæ ad culpam levem." [3]

2024. We have said, *merely venial;* for these canonists all admit that when a sin, which is venial in itself, becomes grievous on account of certain circumstances, it may be punished with censures.

2025. This second opinion, then, is based on the theory that all repressive correctional punishments are severe punishments. [4] In fact, it is not an easy matter to discover any censure whatever (we always use the word censure as synonymous with correctional punishments and *vice versa*), that can be considered as light. For every censure, no matter how light, besides inflicting a spiritual punishment, injures the good name of a person thus punished. Again, the Sacred Canons require so much circumspection,

[1] L. 5, t. 39, n. 56, 57, 60.
[2] Cap. 5 de poenis, in 6º; Bened. XIV., De Syn., l. 10, c. 1, n. 2.
[3] L. V., t. 39, n. 56, 57.   [4] Pierantonelli, Praxis etc., p. 176.

such great prudence and precaution, in the infliction of these punishments, as to treat them always as most serious punishments. Thus the Council of Trent commands that censures should be inflicted only *sobrie magnaque circumspectione*, lest they should otherwise produce *perniciem potius quam salutem*.[1]

Hence it is the unanimous opinion of canonists that censures, as they are commonly inflicted, cannot be even validly inflicted save for grave offences.

Art. II.

They should be preceded by the Milder Remedies.

2026. Nay, as the celebrated canonist Kober[2] well remarks, they cannot be imposed even for grievous offences, *except after all other milder punishments have been applied and failed to produce any effect*. A skilful physician does not forthwith amputate a limb because of a sore or wound; he first tries to cure it by milder remedies. So also should a Bishop not make use of the sword of censures, even for great crimes, save when he has vainly applied all the other milder punishments.

2027. Consequently the rule is that these punishments should be imposed only in extreme cases, that is, only for the gravest and more heinous crimes, and even then only as a last resort, after all the lesser forms of punishment have been tried in vain. Thus Pope Benedict XIV.[3] inveighs strongly against the infliction of censures for any but very grave and enormous crimes. In support of his view, he quotes Gerson, who compares a Prelate inflicting censures, against the above rule, to a person who, wishing to chase a fly from his neighbor's face, cuts off the latter's head, and

---

[1] Sess. 25, cap. 3 de Ref.   [2] Der Kirchenbann, p. 140 sq.
[3] De Syn., l. 10, c. 1, n. 2.

to a person who, desirous of curing a slight wound in his horse's foot, cuts off the foot itself, and thus kills the animal.

2028. Hence also, as Pope Benedict XIV.[1] teaches, Bishops should scarcely ever, in their statutes, synodal or extrasynodal, impose censures which are incurred *ipso facto* by those violating such statutes; only where the general law of the Church inflicts censures *latæ sententiæ* should Bishops re-enact such censures, but rarely otherwise. Stremler[2] therefore well remarks that Superiors should act with exceeding moderation, in inflicting censures, and should be thoroughly versed in the teaching of approved canonists on this head.

2029. From what has been said, it follows that, if something be commanded under censure which, everything considered, is not a grave matter, the precept or command does not oblige *sub gravi*, and therefore no censure can be incurred for its violation.[3] We say, *everything considered;* for, as was seen, offences, which are of themselves venial, may become grievous, on account of circumstances, *v. g.*, because of the scandal they cause. The great difficulty, however, consists in determining practically what circumstances do render such an offence grievous. Canonists agree that no fixed rule can be laid down, but that it must be left to the prudence and conscience of the Superior to decide, in a concrete case, whether the circumstances are such as to authorize him to impose censures. It is a matter that requires the greatest circumspection on the part of the Superior. However, in this case, as in all other cases, he must be guided by the rule that he should inflict censures only in extreme cases, and when he has vainly applied the milder punishments.[4]

---

[1] L. c., c. 2, n. 15 sq.   [2] L. c., p. 191.   [3] Craiss., n. 6398.
[4] Kober, l. c., p. 141; Kober, Susp., p. 55.

Art. III.

Incorrigibleness.

2030. Hitherto we have shown that the punishments in question should be inflicted only for crimes, and that only for the graver and more heinous crimes, and even then only with extreme caution and very rarely. We now proceed a step farther, and say that they are not to be inflicted even for the greatest crimes, *unless the delinquent has openly and incontestibly shown his incorrigible, obstinate, and stubborn persistence in his crime.*[1] Kober says, let the crime be ever so enormous, the injury it has done ever so great, and the scandal it has given ever so serious, no censure can be inflicted, if the delinquent enters into himself, is sorry for his crime, repairs the scandal, and makes satisfaction, as far as he can.[2]

2031. Hence the Superior, before inflicting censure, must repeatedly address warnings and admonitions (*monitio canonica*) to the delinquent—*i. e.*, call upon him to amend. And only when, notwithstanding these warnings, he insolently and contemptuously persists in his wicked course, or refuses to repair the scandal he has given, can censure be imposed upon him. In fact, before proceeding to inflict the censure, the Superior must have juridical proof of the real existence of the stubbornness of the delinquent. He obtains this proof when he addresses to the delinquent a formal warning and command to amend, in such a manner as to be provable, *v. g.*, in the presence of two witnesses; or by having the delinquent himself sign the warning, which should be in writing. For, as soon as it is shown that this warning has been disregarded, proof is had of contumacy.[3]

2032. We have thus far, in the present article, shown

---

[1] Fessler, der Kirchenbann, p. 17.   [2] Kober, der Kirchenbann, p. 145.
[3] Kober, Susp., p. 56.

that correctional punishments can be inflicted (*a*) only for crimes, (*b*) which are very grave (*c*) and accompanied by incorrigibleness, (*d*) and even then only after the milder forms of punishment have been inflicted without effect. Besides, the crime, in order to be deserving of these punishments, must be *external, complete*, and *juridically established*. As we have already explained these points above, under Nos. 1692 sq., it is not necessary to dwell upon them again at present.

ART. IV.

Crimes which are entirely of the Past.

2033. *Q*. Can a Bishop inflict correctional punishments or censures for crimes *altogether past?*

A. He cannot, if the offence is purely and *entirely past* or ended, that is, does not, in a measure or certain sense, continue. Now a crime, though past, is said to continue in a measure, when the offender, though he does not repeat the crime, yet evinces no signs of sorrow for it, or refuses to repair the scandal given by him, or to make due amends.[1] The reason why these punishments cannot be imposed for offences altogether of the past, is, that these punishments are established and inflicted chiefly and directly for the purpose of reforming the delinquent and inducing him to break off his evil ways and disobedience. But it is evident that they would lack this characteristic if they were imposed as pure punishments for crimes which are completely of the past, and for which the offender is sorry and ready to make due reparation.[1]

2034. We say, if *the offence is purely and entirely past;* for where the guilty party has indeed ceased to commit the crime, but yet refuses to make the proper satisfaction, or

[1] Schmalzgr., l. 5, t. 39, n. 67.

repair the scandal he has given, and consequently evinces no true sorrow for his offence, his crime, though past as to the criminal act itself, nevertheless continues, morally speaking; there is present disobedience and contumacy, and consequently such a person may be compelled by censures to make amends.[1]

2035. However, as has been shown, suspension and interdict may be inflicted, not merely as correctional punishments, but also as punitive. Hence, when they are imposed *as vindicatory punishments*, they may be inflicted for crimes which have completely ceased and are not accompanied by present contumacy or persistence in criminal ways. Excommunication alone can be inflicted only as a reformative punishment, and therefore never for crimes altogether past.

2036. Besides, even for a crime altogether over, a person may be temporarily forbidden to receive holy communion, attend divine service, associate with others, etc., as is done in religious communities. But these prohibitions, though also called, in law, excommunications or suspensions, are not censures proper, since their violation does not produce irregularity; hence they are purely vindicatory punishments, or necessary precautionary measures to prevent scandal.[2]

Art. V.

Future Crimes.

2037. *Q.* Can a Bishop inflict the punishments in question for *future crimes?* that is, can he forbid future criminal acts, under pain of censure?

A. He certainly can, by way of a synodal statute, or an extrasynodal general mandate. In other words, he can, both in synod and out of it, make a *general enactment* imposing a reformative punishment upon any one who may

[1] S. Alph., l. 7, n. 49. [2] Craiss., n. 6407.

violate the command. Whether he can also do so by *special sentence*, or in a particular case, is a more involved question. In order to arrive at a clear understanding of the matter, it is necessary to observe that, where the crime is *altogether future* and has not, in some sense, already begun to be perpetrated, the Bishop cannot, in any way, threaten to inflict a censure, whether by way of *ferendæ sententiæ* or by way of *latæ sententiæ*. For to threaten a particular person, who is wholly innocent, with punishment, would be a grave injustice to such a person, since it would injure his reputation, inflict upon him poignant mental suffering, and subject him to grievous humiliation and indignity without any cause whatever. This is forbidden by the very law of nature.

2038. We say, *altogether future;* for where a person has, so to say, already begun to commit the crime, and taken the preparatory steps, tnus rendering it morally certain that he will consummate the crime, he can justly be threatened with the punishments in question, if he commits the crime or *corpus delicti*. Evidently no injury is done him. He has already commenced a criminal course, and the Bishop has a right, nay, a duty, to endeavor, by the threat of punishment, to hinder him from going any farther in his evil course and consummating the crime.

2039. Next we must distinguish between these two cases: one, where the Bishop, in a particular case, imposes a censure *ferendæ sententiæ*, namely where he merely threatens a censure, *v. g.*, where he informs Titius that if he does so and so, he will proceed to inflict upon him suspension by way of *ferendæ sententiæ*: the other, where he inflicts a censure *latæ sententiæ*, that is, where, *v.g.*, he notifies Caius that, if he fails to do so and so, he will be *ipso facto* suspended.

2040. Having given these explanations, we shall now answer the question. It is certain that the Bishop can inflict or rather threaten to inflict, by special sentence, *i. e.*, in a particular case, a censure of the first kind, that is, one which is *ferendæ sententiæ*, for crimes which are future, as explained.[1]

· 2041. On the other hand, it is held by some canonists that the Bishop cannot, even validly, inflict by special sentence a correctional punishment or censure, to be incurred *ipso facto*, for future crimes. Thus the Sacred Canons expressly enact: "Caveant tamen (episcopi) ne tales sententias excommunicationis, sive specialiter sive generaliter, in aliquos *pro futuris culpis, videlicet, si tale quid fecerint* . . . proferre præsumant."[2] And the *Glossa*, commenting on this passage, explains: " Aliud est statutum (a *general* mandate, made in or out of synod), et aliud sententia. Statutum enim bene potest fieri pro futuris delictis, hoc modo: statuimus ut nullus hoc faciat, et qui fecerit, sit excommunicatus ipso facto. Aliud est sententia quæ sic profertur: Excommunico T. si furtum fecerit; *et hoc hic prohibetur.*[3] We say, *by some canonists;* for others maintain the contrary.

2042. The reason given by those who maintain the negative is, that to impose by special sentence a correctional punishment in such a manner as to be incurred *ipso facto* is to inflict it without any previous trial or judicial proceedings; now the law of the Church, as in force also with us, both according to the Instruction *Quamvis*, 1878, and the Instruction *Cum Magnopere* of 1884, enjoins that, save in the extraordinary and exceptional case where suspension can be imposed "ex informata conscientia," the ecclesiastical judge shall not inflict censure, except for crime which has been *juridically established*, that is, proved by due ecclesiastical trial. Thus also the S. C. de P. F. expressly declared in 1867: " Justitia non patitur, ut

---

[1] Lib. 7, n. 49.   [2] Cap. Romana 5, de sent. excom. in 6º (v. 11).

[3] *Glossa*, in cap. cit. v. *futuris; Glossa* in cap. 2, de const. in 6º, (I. 2). v *commiserunt*.

pœnæ infligantur adversus eos, de quorum crimine *judiciaria ratione* adhuc non constat."[1] In fact, the law of nature requires that no person shall, as a rule, be punished, unless he has been heard in his own defence. Now, to inflict a punishment by special sentence *ipso facto* would be directly to violate the right of self-defence, since a person would be punished without any trial whatever.

2043. Whatever opinion may be adopted, it is certain that all *ipso facto* correctional punishments whatever, whether imposed by special sentence or by way of a *law or general mandate*, are incurred *ipso facto* only *in conscience and in the internal forum*, and do not hold or bind in the external forum of the Church, except upon due trial and declaratory sentence. For in the external forum no one incurs a censure by the criminal act itself, that is, *ipso facto*, but only upon declaratory or condemnatory sentence, both of which must be preceded by a trial.

[1] Apud Rota, Enchir., p. 277.

CHAPTER VI.

FORMALITIES OBSERVED IN INFLICTING CORRECTIONAL PUNISHMENTS, ALSO IN THE UNITED STATES.

2044. The coercive power of the Bishop, by which he is authorized to impose correctional punishments, is, like the legislative, an ordinary power, being inherent in his office of Bishop. Hence he can exercise it either personally or through others. Now the Bishop should indeed chastise offenders, repress abuses, and break up scandals. But he should do so, as Stremler [1] remarks, *in the manner prescribed by the Sacred Canons, and not otherwise.* Thus also the Instructions *Sacra Hæc* of June 11th, 1880, and *Cum Magnopere,* of 1884, enact: "Ordinarius pro suo pastorali munere tenetur... curare, ut.. remedia *a canonibus* statuta .. provide adhibeat." [2] And again: "Conscientiæ Ordinarii remittitur cujusque remedii applicatio, *canonicis præscriptionibus servatis* pro casuum ac circumstantiarum gravitate." [3]

2045. The question, therefore, naturally presents itself: What is this manner, or what are the formalities which the Bishop is bound to observe, when he inflicts correctional punishments or censures? They are chiefly three: The canonical warning and the precept, the ecclesiastical trial, and the sentence. We shall now explain each of these separately.

ART. I.

The Canonical Admonitions and the Precept.

2046. We have already shown what is meant by the canonical warnings and the precept, and with what formalities

[1] L. c., p. 200.   [2] Art. i.   [3] Art. iii.

they are given.[1] Here we shall merely add a few remarks which will elucidate still better what we have already said above. The canonical warning is of two kinds: (*a*) *general* or virtual; (*b*) *special* or express. It is special, when it is addressed to a *particular* person; general or virtual, when made to *a number* of persons in a *general way*, but not to any one in particular,—*v.g.*, when the Bishop enacts a statute, and threatens that all who violate it shall be visited with excommunication.

§ 1. *Necessity of the Previous Admonitions.*

2047. *Q.* Are the canonical admonitions always to be given before a repressive correctional punishment can be imposed?

A. First, in the case of censures which are inflicted *a jure*, in such a manner as to be incurred *ipso facto*, no *special* previous warning, and therefore also no precept is required.[1] The reason is, that the law itself or statute in question is a constant and standing admonition and precept. Hence no special admonition, distinct from that already contained in the law or statute, need be addressed to the offender,[2] for these punishments are incurred in the internal forum, *ipso facto*, that is, without any formality whatever. In other words, no admonition or precept, no trial or sentence, no intervention whatever of the ecclesiastical judge, is needed in the case; for *in foro interno* the censure *executes itself*, so that, the very moment a person has committed the offence designated in law as punishable *ipso fcto* with censure, he incurs it, in the internal forum, without any formality whatever. Consequently, when there is question of a person having incurred a censure *latæ sententiæ*, it is a matter of conscience for such person to determine whether he has really incurred it or not. If he knows that

---

[1] Cf. Craiss., n. 6409; Kober, Susp., p. 59. [2] Cap. 26. de appell. (ii 28.)
[3] Kober, Excom., p. 149.

he has committed the crime to which the censure is annexed, he is bound in conscience or *in foro interno* to observe it.

2048. We say, "executes itself *in foro interno;*" for the external effects of the censure do not follow, save when the matter has been brought before the *external forum*, or before the judicial tribunal of the ecclesiastical judge, and the latter, after due trial, has declared that the censure was really incurred.[1] Hence, so far as the *forum externum* is concerned, the punishments in question are not incurred, save after an ecclesiastical trial and a declaratory sentence, as we shall see below, when we come to speak of the trial which must precede correctional punishments.

2049. *Secondly*, in the case of all the other censures, namely, those inflicted *ab homine, per sententiam specialem*, and also those *a jure* which are merely *ferendæ sententiæ* (and by censures *a jure* we here mean also those enacted by statutes or regulations of the Bishop when made in synod, or when enacted out of synod, but by a general mandate), the special canonical warning is absolutely required, also in the United States, and all countries similarly circumstanced. Here is the express law of the Church on this head: "Cum speciali sit prohibitione provisum ne quis in aliquem excommunicationis, (suspensionis et interdicti) sententiam, *nisi competenti commonitione præmissa*, promulgare præsumat."[2] And again: "Nec in specie, nec in genere ... excommunicationum, (suspensionum aut interdicti) sententias *absque competenti monitione præmissa* promulgent, et si contra præsumpserint, injustas noverint esse illas."[3]

2050. For, as we have seen, correctional punishments are *medicinal* and not merely punitive. Hence, by their very nature, they presuppose not simply a crime, but, as we have seen above,[4] *obstinate persistence* in crime. Therefore they

---

[1] Fessler, der Kirchenbann, p. 21., note.
[2] Cap. 5 de sent. excom. in 6º (v. 11.)
[3] Cap. 61 de appell. (ii. 28.)
[4] Supra, n. 1886.

can be inflicted, not whenever a person is guilty of crime, but only when, *after being duly admonished*, he stubbornly continues in his criminal course. It is repugnant to the very nature of a censure that it should be imposed upon one who has not been duly warned beforehand, and who consequently is not contumacious.

2051. It is true that, in regard to correctional punishments *a jure* which are *ferendæ sententiæ*, some canonists hold that no previous special warning is needed, on the ground that in this case, as in the case of censures *a jure* which are *latæ sententiæ*, the law itself is a perpetual warning. But the more common opinion (which is also the more probable and practically the only safe opinion) teaches that a special warning, distinct and separate from that contained in the law, is required in the case. This is also clearly indicated in the cap. 26, x., *de appell.*, which enacts that the special warning can be dispensed with only in the case of censures incurred *ipso facto*, as explained above.[1]

2052. But it will be asked whether there may be any exceptional cases or circumstances that can dispense the ecclesiastical judge or Superior who is about to inflict a censure (of course we speak not of those censures *a jure* which are incurred *ipso facto*, since, as we have seen, no special warning is essential in their case) from the obligation of giving the special warning as just explained. Before answering, we premise that, when censures are inflicted as purely vindicatory punishments, no previous admonition is required. Now only suspension and partial interdict can be imposed as vindicatory punishments.[2]

2053. We now answer: According to some of the older canonists, the Bishop can omit the warnings in a few cases, namely, (*a*) where there is *periculum in mora*; (*b*) when

[1] Supra, n. 2047.
[2] Cap. Tam literis, de test; Cap. Cum in cunctis 7, de elect; Clem. 1 de hæret.; Clem. 2 de pœnis.

he defends himself against violence, exercised either against his own person or the rights of his Church, on the principle that he proceeds in the case as a *private person* acting in self-defence and can therefore oppose force by force, that is, he is not bound to observe the forms of law, where the unjust aggressor disregards them; (*c*) where both the crime and also the incorrigibleness are *notorious*, *v. g.*, where the offender has publicly declared that he will not obey the warnings, if given; for, as the law of the Church enacts,[1] where an excess or crime is *notorious*, the ecclesiastical judge is not bound to grant a trial, *i. e.*, to hear the defence or collect proofs, apart from the notoriety itself, which is considered the best proof.[2]

2054. But modern canonists unanimously reject these exceptions, advanced by some of the older canonists, as (*a*) being in part contrary to the *express* letter of the law, (*b*) and wholly opposed to the present discipline of the Church.[3] Their answer to the first case is that the ecclesiastical judge, *acting as a private person*, has no jurisdiction whatever, and therefore can inflict censures only in his *official capacity*. In regard to the second exception, arising from *periculum in mora*, they answer that the Sacred Canons have sufficiently provided for the case, by allowing the judge, in just such emergencies, to contract the *three* warnings into *one peremptory*, and to make the interval as short as possible. Finally, concerning the third case, they reply that the present general discipline of the Church has altogether abolished the procedure or trial *ex notorio*, and made the usual juridical proceedings obligatory, as was seen, even in *notorious crimes;* that, besides, notoriety can never sufficiently establish the incorrigibleness of the notorious offender, since, even where a person has, *v. g.*, publicly said that he will not obey the Superior's warning, it is possible, nay,

[1] Can. Manifesta 15, C. 2, Q. 1; Cap 9, de acc.   [2] Schma'zg., l. c., n. 32.
[3] Kober, Excom., pp. 153 sq.

Correctional Punishments, also in the United States. 183

presumable, that he may have done so from bravado or want of consideration.[1]

2055. We observe here that, absolutely speaking, no previous canonical admonitions nor precept are required, when there is question of inflicting *vindicative* punishments proper, nor even in the case of suspension and interdict when imposed as vindicative penalties.[2] We say, *absolutely speaking*; for, as we have stated before, it is advisable to give the canonical warnings and the precept, even in these cases. This is apparent from Articles, II., VII., of the Instruction *Sacra Hæc*, June, 11, 1880, and *Cum Magnopere* of 1884. This view seems also to be the one adopted by the *Third Plenary Council of Baltimore*, No. 309. It accords also well with the aim of ecclesiastical punishments. For, in all her punishments, even in those which are vindicative, the Church always aims not only at the *punishment*, but also at the *amendment* of the offender. Hence the Council of Trent inculcates upon Bishops the importance of *reproving*, *entreating*, and *rebuking in all kindness*,[3] before proceeding to punishments, medicinal or punitive.[4]

2056. Some canonists go so far as to maintain that there is no real practical difference between medicinal and vindicative measures, so far as the manner of inflicting them is concerned; that, practically speaking and as a rule, the canonical warnings and the precept, as well as the trial, are to precede vindicative as well as medicinal punishments.[5]

2057. The obligation of giving the canonical warnings and the precept certainly bind under pain of mortal sin, or *sub gravi*. Does it, moreover, bind *on pain of the invalidity* of the censure or correctional punishment? It seems cer-

[1] Kober, der Kirchenbann, p. 155.
[2] Schmalzg. l. 5. t. 39, n. 30; Reiff. l. 5, t. 39, n. 28. *Excommunication* cannot be imposed as a vindicative punishment. Arg. cap. *Cum in cunctis*, 7, de elect; Cap. *Sacro*, de sent. excom.
[3] Tim. iv. 2.   [4] Conc. Trid , Sess. xiii., cap. 1. de Ref.
[5] Droste, l. c., pp. 71—73.

tain that in the United States, where the Instruction *Cum Magnopere* obtains, and in Italy, France, and other countries not missionary, where the Instruction *Sacra Hæc* of 1880 is published, both the canonical warnings and the precept are obligatory on pain of invalidity of correctional punishments. For, as has been observed, according to these Instructions, both the warnings and the precept are *substantial parts* of the procedure that must go before the inflicting of repressive correctional punishments.

2058. We say, *according to these Instructions;* the question therefore presents itself whether also, according to the general law of the Church, as laid down in the Sacred Canons, which, though enacted prior to the above Instructions, are nevertheless still in force, the canonical warnings are obligatory *sub pœna nullitatis?* The affirmative is the common, more probable, and, at the present day, the only safe and true opinion, at least practically speaking.[1] Thus Barbosa,[2] after having stated that, according to some canonists, the canonical admonition is required only for the *licitness* or lawfulness, but not for the *validity* of the censure, teaches that the opposite opinion is the *sententia verior, et procul dubio communis et receptissima*, as is admitted even by some of those who hold the contrary view.

2059. That this holds also with regard to all *missionary countries* seems evident from *the very nature* of correctional punishments. For these punishments can be inflicted only for *contumacious* persistence in crime. Now there is no contumacy, or stubborn disobedience, where no warning has been given.

2060. In order to understand this more fully, we must distinguish between the triple and the single peremptory admonition. The law of the Church prescribes that the ecclesiastical judge must, as a rule, repeat the warning *three*

---

[1] Kober, Exc., p. 156; Idem. Susp. p. 59; Reiff., l. v., t. 39, n. 37.
[2] Coll. Decr., l. 2, t. 28, cap. Reprehens. 26, n. 3—6.

times before he can proceed to impose censures.¹ We say, *as a rule;* for when there are urgent reasons, the three warnings may be contracted into one peremptory warning.² Now the latter, that is, the single peremptory warning, is always required on pain of nullity of the punishment.

2061. But the case is different with the *threefold* warning. For it is true that, if the ecclesiastical judge or Superior, without urgent reasons, gives but one warning, the correctional punishment inflicted by him will be illicit, and he will be guilty of mortal sin and incur various punishments, but the censure will, generally speaking, be valid. We say, generally speaking; for in two cases the triple admonition is required, not only on pain of the illicitness, but of the invalidity of the censure, namely: 1. where the ecclesiastical judge wishes to inflict censure upon a person for communicating with, or not avoiding, another person excommunicated by himself:³ 2. when a delegate receives the power to inflict censures only on condition that he shall give the legitimate prescribed warnings beforehand.⁴

2062. For the rest, it must be borne in mind that the three admonitions can never be condensed into one peremptory, except when there are *urgent reasons* for so doing. For if the ecclesiastical judge or Superior *arbitrarily* or even *maliciously* changes the three warnings into one, he commits a mortal sin, and, according to the Sacred Canons, becomes *ipso facto* interdicted *ab ingressu ecclesiæ* for a month,⁵ that is, he is forbidden to put his foot into a church, and cannot there exercise any function of his *ordo*, nor assist at divine worship.⁶ The Const. *Apostolicæ Sedis* of Pope Pius IX. is silent in regard to this penalty.

2063. As to the *manner* in which the canonical warnings

---

¹ Cap. 9 de sent. excom. in 6º (v. 11).   ² Ib; Kober. Excom., p. 156.
³ Cap. 3 et 13 de sent. excom. in 6º.   ⁴ Kober, Excom., p. 157.
⁵ Cap. 48 de sent. excom. (5, 39).   ⁶ Kober, l. c., p. 158.

are given, see above, n. 1774. See also our *New Procedure*, Nos. 70 sq.

2064. When the canonical admonitions do not produce the desired effect, the *precept* is to be given. When even the latter proves of no avail, the reformative punishment or censure may be imposed, after due trial and conviction. In regard to the *precept*, see above No. 1789 sq. See also our *New Procedure*, Nos. 72-83.

ART. ...

The Trial.

2065. When the canonical warnings and the precept remain unheeded, the obstinacy of the offender becomes undoubted. But the Bishop cannot even then proceed immediately to inflict the censure or correctional punishment. He is obliged to give the delinquent a canonical trial, and only when, upon such a trial, both the crime and the offender's persistence in it have been fully and juridically established, can the correctional punishment be imposed.

2066. We shall now proceed to prove this, in the following order. First, we shall show that a trial is prescribed by the law of the Church, as still in force, prior to the infliction of censures; second, that, down to the year 1880, this trial had to be a formal or ordinary, not merely a summary one; third, that at the present day, the Holy See, by the Instruction *Sacra Hæc*, of June 11, 1880, has authorized Ordinaries of countries not missionary to use a simpler form of trial, whenever it is impossible or inexpedient to observe all the formalities of solemn canonical trials; fourth, that in the United States, the trial, as outlined in the Instruction *Cum Magnopere*, must precede not only vindicatory punishments, but also censures; fifth, that in all other missionary countries censures must, like vindicatory punishments, be preceded by a trial, which, though not the canonical trial, must nevertheless have all the substantial formalities of judicial proceedings.

§ 1. *The Necessity of a Trial according to the General Law.*

2067. We shall now discuss the first of these questions. The law of the Church, as it existed formerly and exists still, prescribes that a trial shall precede the infliction of correctional punishments, *i. e.*, censures, no less than of vindicatory. This is expressly laid down in the Sacred Canons. Thus Pope Nicholas enacts: "Nemo episcopus ... *excommunicet* aliquem, *antequam causa probetur* propter quam ecclesiastici canones hoc fieri jubent."[1] St. Augustine, the great Bishop of Hippo, explaining the discipline of the Church prevalent in his day, says: "Nos vero a communione prohibere (*i. e.*, excommunicare) quemquam non possumus, nisi ... *in aliquo ecclesiastico judicio nominatum atque convictum.*"[2] In the same place, a little further on, he inculcates this principle with still greater emphasis, and teaches that, where offenders cannot be given the benefit of a trial, prior to their being excommunicated, it is better to tolerate them rather than to separate them from the Church without a trial. His words are: "Quibus verbis satis ostendit (Apostolus Paulus) non temere, aut quomodolibet, *sed per judicium* auferendos esse malos ab Ecclesiæ Communione ; *ut si per judicium auferri non possunt, tolerentur potius.*"[3] In like manner, Pope Alexander III., († 1181) decrees: "Si vero (clerici) coram episcopo de criminibus *in jure confessi sunt, seu legitima probatione convicti*, dummodo sint talia crimina propter quæ suspendi debeant vel deponi, non immerito suspendendi sunt a suis ordinibus."[4]

2068. Nay, the Sacred Canons not only forbid the infliction of censures without a previous trial, but, moreover, de-

[1] Can. 11, c. 2, q. 1.   [2] Can. 18, C. 2, q. 1.   [3] Ib.
[4] Cap. 4, de Jud. (ii. 1).

cree severe penalties against those Superiors who presume to inflict these punishments without a trial. Thus Pope Nicholas enacts: "Si quis autem adversus eam (normam, *i. e.*, sine judicio) excommunicaverit aliquem, ille quidem qui excommunicatus est, majoris sacerdotis (*i. e.*, judicis appellationis) auctoritate ad gratiam sanctæ communionis redeat : is autem, qui non legitime excommunicavit, in tantum abstineat tempus a sacrosancta communione, quantum majori sacerdoti (*i. e.*, judici ad quem) visum fuerit, ut quod injuste egit, ipse juste patiatur."[1]

2069. As will be observed, these canons speak expressly of censures, and enact that they shall not be inflicted without a trial. To these enactments which refer directly to correctional punishments, we might add others, namely those which enjoin that no punishment whatever, and consequently no censures—for the general term, punishments, includes correctional as well as vindicatory remedies —shall be inflicted, save upon a trial. Thus Pope Melchiades, writing to the Bishops of Spain, enacts, "Neminem condemnetis, *ante verum et justum judicium.*"[2] Again Pope Marcellus decrees: "Non oportet quemquam judicari vel damnari, *priusquam legitimos habeat præsentes accusatores, locumque defendendi accipiat ad abluenda crimina.*"[3] So also does Pope Damasus ordain: "Habetur in decretis sanctorum Patrum sancitum, *non fore canonicum, quemquam sacerdotum judicare, vel damnare, antequam accusatores canonice examinatos præsentes habeat, locumque defendendi accipiat.*"[4]

2070. In like manner, the celebrated *Cap. Qualiter et quando,* issued by Pope Innocent III. in 1216, enjoins that, before inflicting any punishment whatever upon his subjects, a Prelate must give the latter a full and fair trial. The words of this famous decretal are: "Qualiter et quando debeat Prælatus procedere ad inquirendum et puniendum subdi-

---
[1] Can. 11, C. 2, q. 1 ; Can. 6, C. 24, q. 3. [2] Can. 13, c. 2, q. 8.
[3] Can. 5, c. iii., q. 9. [4] Can. vi. C. 3, q. 9.

torum excessus, ex auctoritatibus Veteris et Novi Testamenti colligitur . . . Debet coram Ecclesiæ senioribus veritatem diligentius perscrutari . . . *Debet igitur esse præsens is, contra quem facienda est inquisitio, nisi se per contumaciam absentaverit ; et exponenda sunt ei illa capitula, de quibus fuerit inquirendum, ut facultatem habeat defendendi seipsum : et non solum dicta, sed etiam nomina ipsa testium sunt ei (ut quid et a quo sit dictum appareat) publicanda, necnon exceptiones et replicationes legitimæ admittendæ : ne per suppressionem nominum, infamandi, per exceptionum vero exclusionem, deponendi falsum audacia præbeatur.*" This great constitution still obtains, since, as was observed, the Council of Trent expressly re-enacted it. [1]

2071. Finally Pope Gregory IX., in the decretal *Quæsitum*, issued in 1229, enacts in the most positive manner that crimes which are not proven by a trial cannot be punished. His words are: "Quæsitum est de sacerdotibus vel aliis clericis, qui per reatum adulterii, perjurii, homicidii vel falsi testimonii, bonum conscientiæ rectæ perdiderunt. Respondemus, quod si proposita crimina *ordine judiciario comprobata*, vel alias notoria non fuerint, non debent hi (præter reos homicidii) . . . in jam susceptis vel suscipiendis ordinibus impediri." [2]

2072. However, it may perhaps be objected that these canons are no longer in force; that they were abrogated by the Council of Trent, which in sess. 14, C. 1. de Ref., authorizes Bishops to inflict suspension *ex informata conscientia, i. e.*, without any trial. We answer: it is true that, in the place quoted, the Council of Trent gives Bishops the above power. But it is also true that this power is to be used only in the case of occult crimes, and in exceptional and extraordinary cases, as explained by us above, Nos. 1279 sq. For ordinarily the suspension must be preceded, according

---

[1] Conc. Trid., sess. 24, C. 5 de Ref.   [2] Cap. 17 de temp. ord. (I. xi.)

to the same Council, by a trial, as appears from the fact that, while this Council, on the one hand, introduces the procedure *ex informata conscientia*, it re-enacts and confirms, on the other, as we have seen,[1] the decretal *Qualiter et quando*, 24 de acc. (v. 1) enacted by Pope Innocent III. († 1216), which prescribes that Bishops and Superiors shall not inflict any punishment, whether vindicative or correctional—except upon a canonical trial.

2073. Finally, the law of the Church requiring a trial before the infliction of censures, except in the case of suspension *ex informata conscientia*, was re-enacted in the Instructions *Sacra Hæc* of 1880, and *Cum Magnopere* of 1884, the former of which forms the present law for Catholic or non-missionary countries, the latter for the United States. For, according to these Instructions, all repressive punishments, *i. e.*, not only vindicatory, but also correctional, and consequently also censures, must be preceded, as we have already seen, not only by the warnings and the precept, but also by a trial, to be conducted in the manner outlined by these documents.

2074. It is, therefore, beyond doubt, that, except in the case where sentences *ex informata conscientia* are allowed, all repressive punishments, whether punitive or correctional, must at the present day, as in former times, be preceded by a trial. This is, in fact, based upon the very law of nature, which forbids any one to be condemned or punished, unless he has been heard in his own defence, *i. e.*, unless a trial has been granted him. For our natural sense of justice tells us that the Superior cannot justly inflict punishment, unless he has been rendered morally certain of the offence, *i. e.*, unless the offence has been proven before him. Consequently the defence as well as the prosecution must be heard by him.[2] Therefore not even the Pope himself

---

[1] Supra, n. 1305.   [2] Supra, n. 704, 705, 706.

can inflict punishment, without observing the substantial formalities of trials. "Nec Nos," says Pope Gregory IX., "contra *inauditam partem* aliquid diffinire possumus."[1] The previous trial is so indispensable that a censure (except suspension inflicted *ex informata conscientia*,) imposed without it is absolutely null and void, also in missionary countries, as we shall see.

2075. Nay, the censure or correctional punishment is invalid, not only when the trial itself is entirely omitted, but also when an essential formality prescribed for trials is not observed during the trial; *v. g.*, where the citation is not made; if the accused is not allowed full liberty to defend himself; if the canonical exceptions submitted by the accused are rejected. Thus Reiffenstul[2] teaches: "Redditur censura *invalida* ob neglectum substantialem ordinem; ut si judex eam ferat nulla nec unica quidem præmissa admonitione, vel si omittatur citatio rei, isque ad sui defensionem non admittatur."

2076. The same holds, if there are no *juridical* or *canonical* proofs of the crime,[3]—*v. g.*, if there are not, as a rule, two witnesses who are above all suspicion,—and that even though the Bishop or proper Superior, by facts which have come to his knowledge extrajudicially, *i. e.*, outside of the customary trial, is fully convinced, personally and privately, that the crime has been committed by the defendant;[4] for, according to the old canonical axiom, "quod non est in actis, non est in mundo," so far as the external forum is concerned. Suarez[5] says: "Judex humanus non potest de sibi occultis judicare; est autem occulta (causa) quoad effectum ferendi sententiam, quamdiu *juridice* probata non est, *etiamsi alioquin privatim nota sit illi homini qui judex est*."

---

[1] Cap. 1, de caus. poss. (ii. 12); *Glossa, ib.*, v. diffinire. [2] Lib. v., n. t. 39, 37.
[3] Cap. 10, de const. (i. 2); Cap. 5, de in integr. rest. (i. 41); Clem. 2 de V. S. (v. 11); Kober, Excom., p. 165.
[4] Can. 2, 3, c. 6, q. 2.   [5] Disp. 4, sect. 7, n. 4.

2077. The only case (besides that *ex informata conscientia*) where the trial is not required as an essential condition for inflicting a censure is when the crime is so *notorious*, both materially and formally, as to admit of no doubt or excuse ; though, as we have seen above,[1] even in this case, it is now the universal custom and practice of ecclesiastical courts to give the accused, as a rule, a trial. See our *New Procedure*, Nos. 85 sq.

§ 2. *The Formalities of a Trial, according to the Sacred Canons.*

2078. We now come to the second question, which relates to the *kind* of trial that precedes censures. Our proposition is that, down to the year 1880, this trial had to be a formal or ordinary canonical trial (*judicium ordinarium, plenum, solemne*) and not merely a summary one. To prove this assertion, we need but repeat here the common teaching of canonists, as stated above, Vol. II., No. 1275, "that, apart from a special mandate of the Pope, the formalities of solemn or ordinary canonical trials must always be observed in criminal causes—*i. e.*, in causes where a punishment, vindicatory or correctional, is to be imposed—the summary trial being applicable only to civil causes of minor importance." This, of course, applies to countries where canon law obtains. For the formalities of ordinary canonical trials, see Vol. II., Nos. 932, sq., second edition, 1888.

§ 3. *The Trial according to the Instruction of June* 11, 1880.

2079. Our third thesis is that, at the present day, the Holy See has authorized Ordinaries of non-missionary countries, where canon law is in force, to use a simpler form, whenever it is impossible or inexpedient to observe all the formalities of solemn trials. This is proved from the express words of the Instruction *Sacra Hæc*, June 11, 1880, of

---

[1] Supra, n. 1263.

the S. C. EE. et RR : " Sacra hæc EE. et RR. Congregatio
... constituit facultatem Ordinariis expresse concedere ut
formas magis œconomicas adhibere valeant in exercitio
suæ disciplinaris jurisdictionis super clericis " (Proœm.)
Again the same Instruction, Art. IX., says: " Quoad media
pœnalia, animadvertant Reverendissimi Ordinarii præsenti
instructione *haud derogatum esse judiciorum solemnitatibus, per
Sacros Canones, per Apostolicas Constitutiones, et alias eccle-
siasticas dispositiones imperatis,* quatenus eædem libere effica-
citerque applicari queant; sed œconomicæ formæ consulere
intendunt illis casibus curiisque, *in quibus solemnes processus
aut adhiberi nequeant, aut non expedire videantur.*"

2080. Hence the above Ordinaries are bound at present,
prior to inflicting a censure or a vindicatory punishment, to
give the accused a formal or regular canonical trial, unless
this is impossible or inexpedient. This also proves clearly
what we have asserted in the preceding proposition, to wit,
that down to 1880, when the Instruction *Sacra Hæc* was
issued, the trial which preceded censures as well as punitive remedies was of necessity a formal or solemn canonical trial, not merely a summary one. For it would have
been absurd otherwise for the S. C. EE. et RR., in the
above Instruction, to authorize Ordinaries to lay aside the
solemn trial, and to use a simpler one. What need was
there for empowering Bishops to omit the formal trial
and substitute in its stead a simpler one, if they were
under no obligation to give the formal or solemn trial?[1]
See Vol. II. Nos. 1277, 1278.

§ 4. *The Trial in the United States according to the Instructions
of 1878 and 1884.*

2081. Our fourth proposition is, that in the United States
the trial, as outlined in the Instruction *Cum Magnopere* of
1884, must precede not only vindicatory punishments,

[1] Supra, vol. ii., n. 1277–1278.

but also censures. This is clearly pointed out by the Instruction itself, as we have already shown. The very teaching of the Instruction leaves no doubt on the matter. It is: "Instructio S. C. de Prop. Fide, de modo servando in cognoscendis et definiendis causis criminalibus et disciplinaribus clericorum in Fœderatis Statibus Americæ Septentrionalis." The trial, therefore, prescribed in this Instruction, *is to be observed* " (de modo *servando*)" or given, throughout the United States, in all criminal and disciplinary causes of Ecclesiastics. Now, by criminal and disciplinary causes, as has been seen, are meant all causes whatever where a repressive punishment,—*i.e.*, not only a punitive, but also a censure, or correctional remedy—is to be inflicted. This is placed in a still clearer light by Article IX. of said Instruction, which provides that the power to proceed *ex informata conscientia* remains in full force. The plain inference, therefore, is, that in all other cases the trial must precede the punishment, be it correctional or vindicatory.

2082. It should be observed that this same Instruction *Cum Magnopere*, in Article XII., enacts that, in dioceses where the *curia* cannot as yet be established, the trial can be conducted in the manner laid down in the Instruction *Quamvis* of 1878. See our *New Procedure*, Art. XII., Nos. 177, 178 sq.

§ 5. *The Trial in other Missionary Countries.*

2083. Our last thesis relates to missionary countries, such as England, Ireland, Scotland, Canada, Australia, and India, where canon law does not fully obtain, and where, moreover, no special form of trial obtains. We assert that in all these countries censures must, like vindicatory punishments, be preceded by a trial, which, though not the canonical trial, must nevertheless have all the substantial formalities of judicial proceedings, or of a full and fair trial. This is apparent from the fact that, apart from all positive legislation of the Church, the law of nature, which obtains also in missionary countries, forbids, as has been noted, any one to be punished, either with a reformative or punitive punishment, save after a fair trial and a judicial hearing. This trial, however, need not necessarily be always a canonical trial, formal or summary, in the strict sense of the word. For missionary countries are not supposed to have a complete canonical organization. They are supposed to be in a state of transition—going through the process of attaining gradually to the full, regular organization prescribed by canon law. Hence the non-essential formalities of canon law in regard to trials do not fully obtain in these places.

2084. Yet the trial must be full and fair. Consequently, as we said above, censures must, in missionary countries, be preceded by a trial, which, though not the canonical trial, *must nevertheless have all the substantial formalities of a full and fair trial.* This is guaranteed to every accused by the law of nature itself, which forbids any one to be condemned or punished, unless he has first been heard in his own defence. Now, what are chiefly these substantial formalities, required by the very law of nature to constitute a trial? 1. The defendant must be cited for trial, in order that he may be able to defend himself. 2. He must be allowed full and unrestricted liberty to defend himself. 3. Consequently, the charges, the testimony of the witnesses, etc., as prescribed in the Cap. *Qualiter et quando,* must be communicated to him; otherwise he could not defend himself. 4. All reasonable exceptions made by him must be admitted. 5. Finally, the proofs of guilt must be as full and conclusive as in formal canonical trials.[1]

[1] Supra, vol. ii., n. 693, 1270.

§ 6. *The Trials in the case of Censures inflicted "ipso jure."*

2085. What has been thus far said concerning the obligation of the trial or judicial proceeding applies not to censures *a jure*, which are *latæ sententiæ*, but only to censures inflicted *ab homine per sententiam specialem*, and to censures *a jure*, (as to what we mean by censures *a jure*, see above, No. 1974), which are *ferendæ sententiæ*. For, as we have seen, correctional punishments *a jure*, when *latæ sententiæ*, are incurred *in foro interno*, without any previous special admonition, and without a trial.

2086. We say, *in foro interno*; for *in foro externo* the censure does not hold, except when a trial has preceded. In other words, in order that the censure in question may produce its effects *in foro externo*, the bishop must give the offender a trial, and prove the crime by canonical proofs, obtained at the trial, and then pronounce *declaratory* sentence,—*i.e.*, pass sentence *declaring* that he has committed the crime, and really incurred *ipso facto* the censure.

2087. Hence, so far as regards the *forum externum*, there is, practically speaking, but little difference between censures which are *latæ sententiæ*, and the other censures; for, in the case of censures *latæ sententiæ*, if they are to hold *in foro externo*, there must always be a juridical investigation or trial.[1] Moreover, an appeal *in suspensivo* lies against the above declaratory sentence.[2]

Art. III.

The Sentence.

2088. Hitherto we have shown that a correctional punishment cannot be inflicted, save (*a*) after the canonical warning, and the precept, and (*b*) after due trial. Having spoken of these two essential prerequisites, it but remains

---

[1] Clem. 2 de Poen. (v. 8); Walter, p. 274.   [2] Pierantonelli, l.c., p. 218.

to explain the formalities to be observed in the very act by which the censure is inflicted, that is, in the sentence by which the ecclesiastical judge imposes the censure. When the Bishop or ecclesiastical Superior, having given the canonical warning, the precept, and also a trial, finds the guilt and the stubborn, persistence in crime juridically proven, he can then, but not before, proceed to pronounce sentence inflicting censure. In pronouncing this sentence, he is, also in the United States, obliged to observe certain formalities, which are partly peculiar to censures and partly the same as those which must be observed in all final sentences, as described above.[1]

§ 1. *Weighing of the Evidence.*

2089. Before pronouncing this final sentence, the judge should carefully sift and weigh the evidence produced at the trial, in order that he may duly ascertain whether the guilt is *legally proven* or not. In other words, he is bound to ascertain whether there is, juridically speaking, full and complete proof (*probatio plena*) of the crime. Full proof is required for conviction and condemnation in criminal and disciplinary causes, no matter whether the trial or proceedings are ordinary or but summary. It is expressly enacted in the *Clem. Cap. Sæpe* 2 de V. S. (v. xi.) that, in summary trials, the proofs submitted by the prosecutor in support of his case must be as full and complete as in formal canonical trials.[2]

2090. This weighing of the evidence, by the ecclesiastical judge, is no easy task. He has usually a large mass of evidence before him, and that of the most conflicting kind—

---

[1] Vol. ii., n. 1174 sq.

[2] Supra, n. 1270. Hence also the Instr. *Sacra Hæc* and *Cum Magnopere*, art. xvi., enact: "*Ad admittendam vero rei culpabilitatem necessaria est probatio legalis.*" The trial prescribed by these Instructions partakes more of the summary than of the formal canonical trial.

the evidence of the prosecution and the defense being naturally diametrically opposed one to the other. He must examine and appreciate the force of this evidence, not according to his own feelings, inclinations, or likes and dislikes, but solely according to the rules laid down by the Church in regard to the force of evidence. He should weigh with equal impartiality the evidence which is *for* and that which is *against* the accused. For the object of the trial is not merely to discover the *guilt*, but also the *innocence* of the accused. Thus the S. C. de Prop. Fide, in the Instruction *Cum Magnopere*, beautifully says: " Processus ex officio instruitur ... et usque ad terminum perducitur eo consilio, ut omni studio ac prudentia, *veritas detegatur, ac tum de crimine, tum de reitate, vel innocentia accusati causa eliquetur.*" [1]

2091. If, upon due and serious examination of the evidence, the ecclesiastical judge finds that the proofs are *equally probable or strong on both sides*, namely on the side of innocence as well as guilt, so that it appears just as probable that the accused is innocent as that he is guilty, it is certain that he must be absolved or acquitted; nay, he must be absolved, even though the proofs of guilt are much more probable than those of innocence. For both the natural and the positive law forbid any one to be condemned unless his guilt has been established as *certain*, not merely as probable.[2] In fact, both in formal and summary trials, the accused must be acquitted wherever there is any *reasonable doubt* as to his guilt. This is thus stated by the Instructions *Sacra Hæc* and *Cum Magnopere:* " ad admittendam vero rei culpabilitatem necessaria est probatio legalis, *quæ iis momentis constare debet, quibus veritas vere demonstrata elucescat, vel saltem moralis convictio inducatur quocunque rationabili dubio oppositi remoto.*" [3]

2092. Here we remark, in passing, that the *probatio legalis*

---

[1] Art. xi.   [2] Bouix, de Jud., vol. ii, p. 228.   [3] Art. xvi.

means the proofs or evidence obtained at the trial '—*i.e.*, the *allegata et probata in judicio*, or, as St. Thomas says: "ea quæ in judicio proponuntur et probantur." The private information of the judge is of no account.[1]

2093. But even when the ecclesiastical judge finds the guilt fully and juridically proven, he should not proceed forthwith to pronounce sentence imposing the censure or punishment which the Sacred Canons, or the decrees of plenary, provincial, or diocesan synods have laid down for the offence. He should, first, consider the *merits and circumstances of the case*, and the degree of malice, in order that he may see whether there are any extenuating or aggravating circumstances;—*v.g.*, whether the accused acted from great provocation or sudden impulse; or whether he acted with cool premeditation or studied malice. For according as he finds *greater* or *less malice*, he should inflict a *severer* or *milder* degree of punishment. He should, however, as was seen above, always incline to mercy rather than to severity, and sin rather on the side of clemency than of rigor. He should adopt as his rule of action the golden mean of being neither too severe nor too mild.[2]

2094. Above all,[4] should the ecclesiastical judge, in weighing the evidence, determining the degree of punishment, and framing the sentence to be pronounced, be careful not to allow himself to be swayed by any *personal motives* whatever,[5]—*v.g.*, of hatred, ill-will, dislike, favoritism. His sole motives should be zeal, charity, love of

---

[1] Pellegrino, l. c., p. 179, n. 36, says: "Dico, quod debet ferri sententia per judicem *secundum allegata et probata in processu*, (in judicio), non secundum conscientiam privatam." Can. Judicet 4, c. 3, q. 7.

[2] Supra, n. 747, 728.   [3] Pellegr. l. c., n. 53, 54.

[4] St. Ambrose in the canon. *Judicet* 4, c. 3, q. 7, beautifully says: "Judicet ille, qui ad pronuntiandum *nullo odio, nulla offensione, nulla levitate* ducatur."

[5] Pope Gregory the Great says: "Quicumque *hostili odio, vel inimicitiis* in judicando ducitur pervertit judicium Christi." (Can. 79, c. 11, q. 3.)

justice, to bring back the offender to the path of duty, and to deter others from crime.[1]

2095. Here it seems also opportune to recall what we have said above,[2] that, by the law of the Church, an ecclesiastical judge, whether ordinary or delegated, who, knowingly, pronounces an unjust sentence,—*v.g.*, who condemns a person whose guilt is only *probably*, and not *certainly*, established—or commits some other act of injustice in the course of the trial, whether through fear, favoritism, hatred, or hope of gain, *is bound to pay the party whom he has injured all the expenses of the trial, and also all other losses occasioned by it*. This principle is also clearly retained and indicated in our Instruction *Cum Magnopere* of 1884: " Haud ita facile Curiæ Episcopales ad damna vel expensas resarciendas damnari poterunt ; quoties enim ex processu informativo indicia sufficientia ad agendum contra inquisitum appareant, judex appellationis a talibus damnationibus abstineat, cum ea indicia sufficiunt ut in judice, qui antea processit, ea vera et propria calumnia excludatur, quæ ad hujusmodi damnationem requiritur."[3] From what has been said, it is plain that, even after the trial is closed, the ecclesiastical judge should take sufficient time to frame the sentence with great care and prudence, before he pronounces it.

§ 2. *Formalities of the Sentence.*

2096. It is for the purpose of preventing the ecclesiastical judge from pronouncing final sentence, inflicting punishment or censure, without duly taking into consideration what has been said above, that the law has always commanded, and still commands him, to observe certain formalities when he pronounces such sentence. As in a number of other matters, so also in the trial and sentence by which correctional punishments, especially excommuni-

[1] Pellegr., l. c., n. 4. [2] Supra, n. 1205 ; Cf. Pellegr, l. c., n. 3. [3] Art. xliv.

cation, were inflicted, the Church adopted the judicial formalities of the Roman law. Thus St. Gregory the Great, in the Instructions which he gave his legate, whom he sent to Spain, in order to decide various judicial controversies that had arisen there, points to the formalities which must be observed, according to the Roman law, by secular judges, when they pronounce final sentence, and expressly commands him to observe them in passing juridical sentence as an ecclesiastical judge, in ecclesiastical causes.[1]

2097. It is, then, safe to assume that, from the time of Pope Gregory the Great, ecclesiastical judges were bound, in passing sentence of excommunication, or suspension, or interdict, to observe all the formalities which the Roman law, and, afterwards, the canon law, prescribed for the pronouncing of *all final judicial sentences whatever*.[2] These formalities are still obligatory, and form the present law of the Church. They differ slightly, according as the trial is formal or merely summary. We have already fully explained them above, under No. 1174 sq.

2098. Although these regulations were designed to prevent hasty and inconsiderate sentences, yet, as Kober[1] testifies, it came to pass that many censures were unjustly inflicted, for the reason that some Prelates pronounced sentence, inflicting these severe punishments, without taking duly into account the circumstances of the case, and without observing the laws of justice and equity. These abuses and injustices were brought before the General Council, held at Lyons, in 1245, by Pope Innocent IV. The Council was urged to remedy these evils. Accordingly, that body took the matter into serious consideration, and, in its celebrated decree, called *Cum Medicinalis* 1, de sent. exc. in 6° (v. xi.), issued strict regulations, enjoining upon Prelates, in passing sentence of *excommunication*,

---

[1] Can. 7, c. ii, q. 1; Kober, Excom., p. 169.   [2] Ib.   [3] Ib., p. 170.

suspension, or *interdict*, the obligation of observing most carefully the formalities already in force, and adding new ones.[1]

2099. This constitution still forms the law of the Church, and is, as we shall see, re-enacted in the Instructions *Sacra Hæc* and *Cum Magnopere*. It enacts, under severe penalties, that the sentence should not only be in writing, and that a copy of it should be given the accused, if he asks for it, but, moreover, that it shall state clearly and distinctly the particular crime or act for which the censure is imposed, in order that it may appear, from the sentence itself, whether the crime is sufficiently grave to deserve so severe a punishment as a censure.[2]

3000. This latter regulation was a new enactment;[3] for, prior to this law, ecclesiastical judges were not bound, even in criminal causes, to set forth, in their final sentence, the reasons or crimes for which they imposed punishment.[4] At the present day, ecclesiastical judges must state the offence in their sentence, not only when they inflict censures, but also in all other sentences by which they impose a vindicatory punishment.

3001. We have, thus far, given a brief and imperfect outline of the legislation of the Church on the question under discussion. It now remains to group together and briefly explain the various formalities which were enacted from time to time, and which are still to be observed at the present day, in the pronouncing of final penal sentence, not only in formal, but also in summary trials.[5] These formalities of the final sentence in question, are chiefly: 1. It

[1] Kober, Excom., p. 172.

[2] Quisquis igitur excommunicat . . . . *causam excommunicationis expresse conscribat, propter quam excommunicatio proferatur.*" Cap. *Cum Medicinalis*, 1, de sent. excom. in 6º (v. 11).

[3] Ib. [4] Cap. 16, de sent. (ii. 27).

[5] These formalities are the same, no matter whether the sentence inflicts a censure or a vindicatory punishment.

must be drawn up *in writing;* otherwise, it will be invalid.[1]

3002.—2. It should be *read*, not merely *handed* or sent, to the accused; otherwise, it is void.[2] For, as Cardinal de Luca says, it is not sufficient that it be in writing; it is, moreover, necessary that it shall be read from the paper written out beforehand.[3] Hence the sentence which, though in writing, is simply handed or sent to the defendant, without having been first read and thus published to him, is invalid.[4] In like manner, the sentence which is pronounced, indeed, in the presence of both parties, but which was not written out beforehand, is invalid.[5] For, as the Roman law adopted by the Church says: "Huic adjicimus sanctioni, ut sententia, quæ dicta fuerit, cum scripta non esset, nec nomen quidem sententiæ habere mereatur."[6]

3003.—3. It should be pronounced by the *judge himself*, 4. and that *in the presence* of the parties,—*i.e.*, of the prosecution and the defence, unless they are contumaciously absent. Therefore, if the sentence were pronounced in the absence of the accused, it would be invalid,[7] unless the latter were contumaciously absent. 5. Wherefore, also, the accused *must be cited* to hear the final sentence, as explained already;[8] otherwise the sentence would be invalid.[9] 6. It must be pronounced *on the day*, at the hour and place designated in the citation sent to the accused to hear the final sentence; otherwise it would be invalid, since it would be regarded as having been pronounced, *non citata parte*.[10] Where, however, the defendant, though properly cited, is contumaciously

---

[1] L. Statutis 3, C. de sent. ex per. (7, 44); Cap. *Cum Medicinalis* cit.
[2] L. Statutis cit.
[3] Card. de Luca, l. 15. de jud., disc. xxxvi, n. 7, 8, 10, Venetiis, 1734.
[4] Pellegr., Praxis Vicar., P. ii., S. iii., Subs. i., n. 65, Venetiis, 1706.
[5] Konig, Jus can., l. ii., t. 27, n. 48.   [6] L. 3, C. de sent. ex per. (vii. 44.)
[7] L. de unoquoque ff. de re jud.; Pellegr., l c., n. 27.   [8] Supra, vol. ii., n. 1174.
[9] Cap. *Dudum* 2. de elect.; Pellegr., l.c., n. 15, p. 174.
[10] L. aut qui aliter, ff. quod vi; Pellegr., l.c., 176, n. 27.

absent, the ecclesiastical judge can pronounce the sentence at any time, after the time fixed for the sentence in the citation has expired.

3004.—7. It must *state the crime* or act for which the punishment is inflicted. This has been sufficiently explained already.[1] 8. It should not be pronounced on *Sundays* or *holy-days of obligation;* otherwise it would be invalid.[2] 9. Finally, a copy of the sentence must be given to the person condemned, if the latter asks for it. This copy must be properly authenticated and correspond word for word, both as to date and contents, with the orignal. See above Vol. II., Nos. 1174-1184.

§ 3. *Formalities of Sentences in the United States.*

3005. *Q.* What formalities are to be observed in the United States, by Bishops or Vicars-General, when they pronounce a final sentence imposing a censure or correctional punishment?

A. We have said above that the formalities there described are to be complied with, not only in formal, but also in summary canonical trials. From this it would seem to follow, as a matter of course, that these formalities must also be observed by ecclesiastical judges in the United States, where the Instruction *Cum Magnopere* obtains. For the trial prescribed in this Instruction, though a canonical trial in the strict sense of the term, partakes more of the summary than of the formal canonical process. However, all doubt in the premises is removed by the Instruction itself. For, as we say above, it virtually re-enacts the formalities prescribed by the general law of the Church.

3006. In fact, the enactments contained in this Instruction regarding the pronouncing of final sentences are: 1. "Tum omnia (acta etc.) ad Ordinarium remittuntur qui, ubi in

[1] Supra, n. 1181, 1182.; Schmalzg., l. 2, t. 27, n. 61.
[2] Supra, n. 1180; Pellegr., l.c., n. 22.

plenam causæ cognitionem devenerit *diem constituet in qua sententia dicenda est.*"¹ 2. "Præstituta die ab Episcopo vel Vicario Generali, præsente procuratore fiscali et defensore sententia pronunciatur, ejusque pars dispositiva Cancellario dictatur, expressa mentione facta, si damnationi sit locus, sanctionis canonicæ quæ contra imputatum applicatur."² 3. "Sententia reo intimetur."³

3007. Now, from these dispositions, it is plain that the ecclesiastical judge in the United States is obliged to observe the following formalities, in pronouncing final sentence by which he inflicts a correctional punishment.⁴ 1. The sentence shall be drawn up in writing,⁵ 2. read in court and dictated to the chancellor or secretary,⁶ 3. in the presence of the diocesan prosecutor and the defendant's advocate.⁷ The defendant himself may or may not be present, as he chooses. 4. Hence both the prosecutor and the advocate of the accused are to be invited or cited to appear in court at the time and place specified, to hear the final sentence pronounced.

3008.—5. According to the instruction *Sacra Hæc* of 1880, of which our Instruction *Cum Magnopere* is, with but few exceptions, an exact copy, the prosecutor and the defendant's advocate, on appearing in court on the day fixed for the final sentence, can plead their respective cause orally before the court, prior to the pronouncing of final sentence. Thus the Instruction *Sacra Hæc* says : (*a*) " Qui (ordinarius) diem constituit *in qua disceptanda et resolvenda sit* (causa). "⁸ (*b*) "Die constituta proponitur causa coram Vicario Generali, interessentibus Procuratore fiscali, defensore et Cancellario."⁹ (*c*) "*Post votum Procuratoris Fisci et deductiones defensionis* profertur sententia, etc." ¹⁰

¹ Art. xxxiii.   ² Art. xxxiv.   ³ Art. xxxv.
⁴ The same formalities are to be observed in the sentence inflicting *vindicative* penalties.
⁵ Art. xxxiv.   ⁶ Ib.   ⁷ Ib.   ⁸ Art. xxxiii.   ⁹ Art. xxxiv.   ¹⁰ Art. xxxv.

3009. In our Instruction *Cum Magnopere*, this is not allowed, special provision being however made in Article XXXIII.,[1] whereby the aforesaid final arguments or pleadings shall be made beforehand, and that in writing. The Instruction *Cum Magnopere*, as originally drawn up for the United States, and shown to our Prelates assembled in Rome in November 1883, did not differ in regard to the matter under discussion from the enactments of the Instruction *Sacra Hæc*. It was changed to its present wording at the suggestion of some of our Prelates, who represented that the oral pleadings of the parties or of the advocates might give rise in the United States to an odious class of ecclesiastical advocates, whose interest it would be to multiply controversies, and draw them out to an indefinite length of time.

3010.—6. It shall expressly state the offence for which the punishment is inflicted. 7. It shall also expressly mention the particular law of the Church authorizing the infliction of punishment in the case. For, as has been shown,[2] no offence can be punished by the ecclesiastical judge, unless it is expressly designated by an ecclesiastical law as punishable. 8. It shall be pronounced at the time and place designated in the citation for sentence. 9. Finally, a copy of the sentence, properly authenticated, and corresponding word for word with the original, is to be sent to the person condemned, in the manner described in Article XIV. of the Instruction *Cum Magnopere*.

3011. As already remarked, these formalities are obligatory, not only in sentences by which censures are inflicted, but also in sentences by which vindicatory punishments are imposed. For the Instruction *Cum Magnopere* lays down

---

[1] The words are: "Postquam Procurator fiscalis suas conclusiones ediderit, eædem defensori rei communicandæ sunt ut ad easdem, si placuerit, *in scriptis* respondeat."

[2] Supra, n. 1699.

the mode of procedure which is to be observed in inflicting both correctional and vindicatory punishments.

§ 4. *Penalties incurred for violating these Formalities.*

3012. Here it may be objected that, in the opinion of a number of canonists, three of the above formalities,—namely, (*a*) that the sentence be in writing, (*b*) that the crime be set forth, (*c*) and that an authentic copy of the sentence be given to the person condemned—bind only on pain of mortal sin and illicitness, but not invalidity, of the sentence, when there is question merely of inflicting correctional punishments, *i.e.*, censures, and not vindicatory. Before answering this objection, we remark that all canonists agree that the Bishop or ecclesiastical judge who presumes to violate any of these formalities *commits a mortal sin*, nay, a very grievous mortal sin, being guilty of a violation of a grave and very important law of the Church. On this head there is no doubt, no controversy. In fact, Pope Innocent IV., by whom the formalities are prescribed, in the celebrated Constitution *Cum Medicinalis*, inculcates their observance in so strict and solemn a manner, and decrees such severe punishments against ecclesiastical judges who presume to violate them, as to leave no doubt whatever on the subject.

3013. We shall now answer the objection. It is true that a number of canonists hold the above opinion.[1] Their chief argument is, that Pope Innocent IV. states in the Cap. *Cum Medicinalis*, that a person who is visited with censure, without the above formalities, shall, upon having recourse to the judge of appeal, *v.g.*, to the Metropolitan, be immediately released from the sentence. Hence, they say, the sentence in the case, though grievously sinful and illicit, is not invalid, otherwise there would be no necessity for

[1] Cf. Craiss., n. 6417

authorizing the judge of appeal to revoke it. But it is also true that the opposite opinion, which is maintained by Kober and other eminent canonists, and which teaches that the formalities in question bind, on pain of nullity of the sentence and the punishment inflicted by it—seems based on much sounder arguments and, consequently, much more probable. In fact, the law, (*i.e.*, not only the Cap. *Cum Medicinalis*, but also the Instruction *Cum Magnopere*, of 1884), expressly prescribes these formalities, and that for good reasons, as we have shown. The ecclesiastical judge who disregards them oversteps the bounds of his legitimate authority. Hence the following principle of canon law applies: "Quæ contra jus fiunt, debent utique *pro infectis haberi*."[1]

3014. And in reality, as we have seen, both the Roman and the canon law expressly declare *that all judicial sentences whatever, (consequently, also those which impose censures,) which are pronounced without the prescribed formalities, as explained above, are null and void.* Why the sentence imposing excommunication, or suspension, or interdict, should form an exception to this rule, especially when one remembers that the law nowhere makes the exception, seems incomprehensible, particularly when we call to mind that these censures are most severe punishments, and that, consequently, it must be a matter of grave solicitude to the Church to see that these sentences are not pronounced without mature deliberation, and therefore, not without the prescribed formalities. In fact, how much importance the Church attaches to these formalities, and how anxious she is that they should be carefully observed, is manifest from the strict and peremptory manner in which she orders them to be observed, and from the severe punishments she

---

[1] Reg. 64, de Reg. jur. in 6° (v. xii.); Barbosa, coll. in l. 5, sexti Decr., Reg 64, explaining this rule, says: *Paria enim sunt invalide fieri, et non fieri ;* again: *actus enim corruit, omissa forma legis.*

inflicts on those ecclesiastical judges who dare to violate them.¹

3015. Besides, the argument of those who hold the opposite view is not conclusive. For the phrase of Pope Innocent IV., *Superior vero, ad quem recurritur, sententiam ipsam sine difficultate relaxans, etc.*,² means simply that, when a sentence imposing a censure is pronounced without the formalities in question, the person so sentenced cannot, as a rule, *of his own accord*, or *by his own private authority*, consider it invalid and disregard it, but that he should leave the decision to the Superior, that is, to the judge of appeal, to whom he should have recourse, with the request that the sentence be *declared null and void*. The interests of order and authority evidently require that a person who is punished should not, except for very grave reasons, take it upon himself to disregard a sentence, even though null, except where it is patent to everybody that it is invalid. He should, therefore, as a rule, apply to the judge of appeal, in order to have the nullity of the sentence officially declared by him.³

3016. *Q.* What are the chief punishments incurred by ecclesiastical judges, also in the United States, who presume to disregard all or any of the above formalities, prescribed by Pope Innocent IV. in the Constitution *Cum Medicinalis?*

A. The following: 1. The person censured should, *at once*,⁴ *i.e.*, without being required to make amends, or to give any assurance of amendment, and without any previous examination of the merits of the appeal, be absolved of the censure by the person to whom he appeals. Whether this enactment has been modified by the decree of Clement

¹ Cap. *Cum Medicinalis* cit.   ² Ib.
³ Kober Excom., p. 176; Id., Susp., p. 63.
⁴ The *Glossa*, v. *difficultate* in cap. *Cum Medic.* explains this as follows: "Id est, quod sine mora, sine satisdatione, sine causæ cognitione, et sine aliquo excommunicati gravamine, hoc (*i.e.*, relaxatio excommunicationis), fieret, cum evidenter appareat, contra hanc Constitutionem latam fuisse."

XIII., issued in 1600, we shall discuss further on. 2. The Bishop, or ecclesiastical judge, who is guilty of violating any of these formalities, is to be condemned by the judge of appeal, (*a*) to pay all the expenses, with interest, incurred by the accused, (*b*) and to undergo other punishments, as the judge of appeal may see fit to inflict. All this is expressly enacted by Pope Innocent IV., in the Cap. *Cum Medicinalis* already quoted: "Si quis autem judicum hujusmodi constitutionis temerarius extiterit violator .... Superior, ad quem recurritur, sententiam sine difficultate relaxans, latorem excommunicato ad expensas et omne interesse condemnet, et alias puniat animadversione condigna, ut, pœna docente, discant judices, *quam grave sit excommunicationum sententias sine maturitate debita fulminare.*"

3017. Pope Innocent IV. inflicts, moreover, *ipso facto*, the "interdictum ab ingressu ecclesiæ" and the suspension "a divinis officiis" for one month. But, according to Craisson,[1] these two latter punishments, not being mentioned in the *Const. Apostolicæ Sedis* of Pope Pius IX., are now abolished. They never fell upon Bishops, but only upon inferior judges, such as Vicars-General. The reason is that Bishops are not expressly mentioned in the Cap. *Cum Medicinalis*.[2]

3018. What formalities must be observed in missionary countries, where, for instance, neither the recent Instruction *Sacra Hæc* of 1880, nor the older general law of the Church in regard to trials has as yet been introduced? In these countries, the formalities which are dictated by the natural law must be complied with. Accordingly 1. a trial, in which all the substantial formalities of trials are observed, must precede the sentence or punishment; 2. the sentence itself or the infliction of the punishment is to be (*a*) in writing, at least, on pain of mortal sin, (*b*) state clearly and fully the

[1] Man., 6418.   [2] Cap. 4 de sent. exc. in 6º (V. 11).

offence for which the punishment is inflicted, (c) and specify clearly the particular punishment inflicted.

§ 5. *Wording of the Sentence.*

3019. *Wording of the sentence, also in the United States.*—No particular form or wording is prescribed for the sentence. The latter is valid, no matter what may be its form or wording, provided the conditions or formalities, already described be complied with. The Roman Pontifical (P. III.) gives a formula, which, however, need not be adopted. Pellegrino, in his *Praxis Vicariorum*, says that the wording should be such as to state not only, as was seen, the crime and the canonical sanction, etc., but also, (a) the name of the judge, and whether he is an Ordinary or delegated judge ; (b) the names of the litigants,—*i.e.*, of the diocesan Prosecutor and of the defendant, when there is question of criminal and disciplinary causes with us, (c) the fact that the prescribed canonical admonitions, the precept, and trial were duly given to the accused, so that it may appear on the very face of the sentence that the prescribed juridical formalities were all duly observed.

3020. Hence the sentence should, for instance, read thus: Considering the charges made against N., considering that the previous admonitions and precept were duly given the accused ; considering, moreover, that a full trial was granted to him as prescribed,—*v.g.*, in the Inst. *Cum Magnopere;* having maturely and fully weighed and taken into account the proofs and allegations of the prosecution and defence submitted during the trial; having considered all that is to be considered, we find the crime charged against the accused—to wit—repeated drunkenness—on such and such days, and at such and such places—fully and canonically proven, and we hereby condemn N. for this crime, to suspension, etc.[1]

[1] Pellegr. l. c., p. 175, n. 21; *Ib.*, p. 181, n. 72.

§ 6. *Publication of the Sentence.*

3021. By publication (*denuntiatio censuræ*) we here mean the act of the proper Superior, by which the censure incurred by a person *in foro externo* is made publicly known. We say, *in foro externo;* for censures which are incurred only *in foro interno* cannot be published. Now a repressive correctional punishment is not incurred, and therefore, does not hold *in foro externo*, except when it is inflicted by a trial and judicial sentence, condemnatory or declaratory. Consequently, censures cannot be published, save when they have been preceded by a trial and judicial sentence. The only exception to this rule is when the censure has been *notoriously* incurred. But, as we show elsewhere, the trial is, practically speaking, necessary at present, also in notorious crimes.

3022. Nowhere does the law of the Church prescribe that the sentence inflicting a correctional punishment, or the fact of a censure having been incurred by a person, must be generally published. On the contrary, the cases where the law of the Church directs such publication to be made—*v.g., Clem.* 2. *de pœnis*, (v. 8), are to be regarded as exceptions to the rule. However, there is no doubt that the Bishop or ecclesiastical judge can, nay, sometimes should make this publication, when the circumstances of the case, —*v.g.*, the enormity of the crime, the scandal given, the danger of others becoming corrupted, and the continued obstinacy of the delinquent, render this step useful or necessary.[1]

3023. The object of the publication is twofold: (*a*) to cause the offender to return more speedily to the path of duty by means of the confusion and disgrace brought upon him through the publication; (*b*) to oblige the others to shun him in matters in which the censure requires it.

---

[1] Arg. cap. Pastoralis 53, de appell. (ii. :8); Kober, Suspension, p. 65.

Hence, when the Superior knows that the person censured has already reformed and been absolved, *in foro interno*, he should not make the censure publicly known.[1] The publication, which is simply an annex or complement of the censure itself, can be repeated frequently. Thus, in the Cap. 1, *de pœnis in Clem.* (v. 8), it is ordained that a person guilty of a certain crime should be excommunicated, and the fact of his having been excommunicated should be announced in the churches and other public places, *every Sunday and holy-day*, till the offender had made satisfaction.

3024. The *mode* and *extent* of the publication are left to the discretion of the Bishop or judge, Thus, so far as the extent of the publication is concerned, the ecclesiastical judge may publish it either in the whole diocese, or simply in the parish of the person censured, or only in the cathedral. Likewise, as to the *manner*, the Bishop is free to have the publication made by public announcement in the church during divine service, or by having it posted at the doors of churches or other public places, or even published in newspapers.[2]

3025. By whom is the publication to be made? The publication is an *act of ecclesiastical jurisdiction*, no less than the infliction of the punishment itself. Consequently it can be ordered only by the competent judge or Bishop, and that even where it is *notorious* that a person has incurred a censure.[3] When a person has *ipso facto* incurred a censure *a jure*, the right to make the publication belongs to the Bishop of the place where it has been incurred, or to the Ordinary of the domicile of the offender.[4] But in this case, as in all other cases, it is always left to the conscience and prudence of the Bishop or judge, to publish the censure or not.

3026. In case the Bishop or judge does not wish to make

[1] Kober, Excom., p. 179.
[2] Ib.
[3] Ib. p. 180.
[4] Arg. Can. 5, c. 6, q. 3.

the publication *in person*, he can depute others to make it for him. Thus a Bishop may appoint the parish priest of the person censured to announce the censure from the altar or otherwise publish it. Here the question arises: Is an inferior, *v. g.*, a parish priest, whom the Bishop deputes to make the publication, bound to obey, and to make the publication? He certainly is, as a rule.[1] We say, *as a rule*; for where the inferior knows from the *allegata et probata, i. e., from juridical documents or acts*, and where consequently he can prove juridically, that the censure in the case is unjust or invalid, he need not, nay, he cannot make the publication.[2] But where he knows the censure to be unjust, only from *private* information, and cannot prove it juridically, he must execute the orders of the Bishop or judge and make the publication, unless he can induce the judge to excuse him from the task.[3]

3027. Finally it is asked: Does an appeal against the censure or its publication, made after the censure is inflicted, but before it is made public, hinder the Bishop or judge from proceeding to the publication. We shall give the answer when we come to treat of appeals against censures.

[1] Cap. 28 de off. del. (i. 29.)   [2] Craiss., Man., n. 6423.   [3] Kober, l. c., p. 181.

CHAPTER VII.

APPEALS AGAINST REPRESSIVE CORRECTIONAL PUNISHMENTS.

Art. I.

Is it allowed to appeal against these Punishments?

3028. It is superfluous to say that it is allowed to appeal against all censures or correctional punishments, whether of excommunication, suspension, or interdict, no less than against other punishments and grievances; upon this point, there is no dispute whatever.[1] This right of appeal is not only conceded by the express law of the Church, as in force at present, but is, moreover, based on the very law of nature. For it is part of a just self-defence. In fact, the object of an appeal is to prevent an innocent person from being visited with punishment, injustice, or wrong. Now it is unanimously admitted that repressive correctional punishments are severe punishments.

Art. II.

Effects of Appeals against Censures already inflicted.

3029. Ordinarily appeals against vindicatory punishments have not merely a devolutive, but also a *suspensive* effect; that is, they not only confer upon the judge *ad quem* the power to re-examine the case and to revoke, modify, or ratify the sentence of the first instance, but, moreover, cause the sentence to remain inoperative, *i. e.*, cause its execution to be stayed until the higher judge has given his decision

---

[1] Cf. Leur., for. eccl., l. 2, t. 28, q. 1089, n. 1.

on the appeal. The reason is, that the execution require a new order or decree on the part of the judge. Now he cannot issue such new decree, after the appeal has been interposed, since his jurisdiction is suspended by the appeal, in regard to the cause appealed.[1]

3030. The case is different with appeals from correctional punishments or censures, *when interposed after the censure has been already inflicted*. Such an appeal produces, as a rule, merely a devolutive, but no suspensive effect, as has been seen above,[2] since a censure *executes itself*, and consequently its execution does not require any new act or decree on the part of the judge by whom it was inflicted. Hence it produces all its effects the very moment it is validly and justly pronounced or inflicted.[3]

3031. We say, *as a rule*; for in certain cases the appeal has a *suspensive effect*, even when it is interposed *after* the infliction or fulmination of the censure. Thus, according to the common opinion of canonists, the suspension and interdict *a temporalibus*, and not merely *a spiritualibus*, admit of a *suspensive appeal*, even *after* they have been actually inflicted.[4] In other words, when the suspension or interdict produces effects which are not *purely spiritual*, but partake of a *temporal character*, the appeal, even when interposed *after* the suspension or interdict has been inflicted, *suspends* the effect of the latter.

3032. Consequently an appeal against a suspension *a beneficio* produces a suspensive effect, even when interposed after the suspension has been already imposed. Hence the person who is thus suspended and who has appealed can continue to receive his salary or the income of his office, parish, (or, with us, mission) and to administer its tempo-

---

[1] Kober, Excom., p. 224.   [2] Supra, vol. i., n. 446.
[3] Cap. 20, de sent. exc. in 6º (v. 11); Cap. 37, de app. cum *Glossa, ib.*, v. interdictum; Cap. 52 de app. (ii. 28).
[4] Leur., for. eccl., l 2, t. 28, q. 1089, n. 10.

ralities, until the higher Superior or judge of appeal has decided the case.¹ The same holds true of appeals against a suspension or interdict which forbids (*a*) the taking possession of an office or benefice; (*b*) the privilege of voting or being voted for, at ecclesiastical elections; (*c*) the exercise of Pontificals; (*d*) the use of the pallium; (*e*) and other acts or rights of a similar character.² In all these cases, the appeal is suspensive, though made *after* the infliction of the censure.³

3033. One of the reasons, as we have seen, is, that the effects of these correctional punishments are not of a *purely spiritual* character, but extend to *external, material, and temporal interests*. Now, as has been observed, punishments which are not of a purely spiritual nature in their effects do not execute themselves, but need a *new decree* (*decretum executionis*) apart from the final sentence by which the punishment is inflicted. But this new decree cannot be issued pending the appeal.⁴

3034. A second and perhaps more cogent reason is this: Whatever is contrary to the ordinary and general law of the Church must be strictly construed. Now, according to the general law of the Church, as still in force, an appeal lawfully made against a sentence that has been passed produces a suspensive effect. Hence the disposition of the Cap. 20 de sent. exc. in 6° (v. 11.),⁵ which enacts that an appeal against an excommunication, as also against a suspension *ab officio divino* or *ab ingressu ecclesiæ*, when made after the censure has been inflicted, has only a devolutive but not a suspensive effect, must be restricted to those specific censures which are *expressly mentioned* in this

---

[1] Schmalzg., l. 2, t 28. n. 24.   [2] Bouix, de jud., vol. ii. p. 255.
[3] Stremler, l. c.. p. 308.   [4] Kober, Susp., p. 84.
[5] The words of the decree are : "Sane sicut excommunicatio, sic ab officio vel ab ingressu ecclesiæ lata suspensio, aut ipsius effectus, per appellationem sequentem minime suspenduntur."

decretal—namely to excommunication and to that suspension which is *ab officiis divinis* or *ab ingressu ecclesiæ*, and cannot be extended to any other kind of suspension or interdict.[1]

3035. Consequently the *Glossa*,[2] commenting on this decretal, says: " Et intelligas proprie de suspensione ab ingressu ecclesiæ, vel divinorum : quia in *suspensione a temporalibus*, puta ab ingressu possessionis beneficii, non haberet hoc locum. Talium enim suspensionum vel interdictorum *effectus bene suspenditur* per appellationem sequentem. . . . Puto igitur solum *in his mere spiritualibus*, per quas ligatur anima decretalem hanc habere locum."

3036. Again, Kober[3] maintains that an appeal interposed *after* the censure has been inflicted, even where the censure has *purely spiritual effect*, *v.g.*, suspensio *a divinis*, produces a *suspensive*, not merely a devolutive effect, when the censure is inflicted, not as a *correctional punishment* or censure, but as a *vindicatory punishment*, since the censure thus inflicted is placed on the same footing with vindicatory punishments, and is governed by the same laws.[4] Of course, this principle can apply only to suspension and interdict, since they alone can be inflicted as vindicatory, and not merely as correctional punishments.

3037. Nay, an appeal against any censure, whether of excommunication, suspension, or interdict, made *after* the censure has been already inflicted, even though it has been inflicted as a *medicinal punishment*, and even though it produces spiritual, and not merely temporal effects, has a *suspensive effect*, when the appeal is interposed *ex capite nullitatis, i.e., on the ground that the censure is invalid* and not merely unjust. This is expressly declared by Pope Bene-

---

[1] Leur., l. c. ; Kober, l. c., p. 84. [2] V. Sequentem.
[3] Susp., p. 86. Kober here quotes Strejk and Pirhing, l. 2, t. 28, n. 48, as favoring this opinion.
[4] St. Liguori. l. 7, n. 314.

dict XIV., in his celebrated Const. *Ad Militantis* of 1742, § 36. Now, as was seen, this provision, as well as others of said Const. *Ad Militantis*, is laid down in the Instructions *Sacra Hæc* of 1880, and *Cum Magnopere*, of 1884, as the law or rule to be followed in appeals at the present day. Of course, an appeal which is made *ex capite nullitatis* takes it for granted that the nullity of the censure *is doubtful*. For, where it is *certain* that the censure has been invalidly inflicted, it is not necessary for the person censured to appeal in order to have the censure declared invalid, since he can, of his own accord, disregard it, and that even publicly, when the nullity is publicly known.[1]

3038. Finally, when the correctional punishment is inflicted *a jure* and is *latæ sententiæ*, it is incurred, as we have seen, in the internal forum, by the very commission of the crime itself,—*i.e.*, *ipso facto*, without any juridical formality whatever. But in the external forum a declaratory sentence is required. Against this declaratory sentence it is allowed to appeal, and that not only *in devolutivo*, but also *in suspensivo*,[2] so that the appeal in the case suspends the effect of the declaratory sentence, and hinders its publication.[3] This has reference to a declaratory sentence, *after it is pronounced*.

3039. Does it also apply to a declaratory sentence which is *merely threatened?* In other words, is it allowed to appeal against the *mere threat*, on the part of the ecclesiastical judge, that he will proceed to pass declaratory sentence? There are two opinions. Leurenius[4] holds the affirmative. He maintains that if, for instance, a person were cited by the ecclesiastical judge to hear sentence pronounced, by which he is declared as having, *e.g.*, incurred excommunication or suspension, and if this person meanwhile appeals

[1] Schmalzg., l. 5, t. 39, n. 115; Craiss., n. 6430, Arg. cap. 2 de sent. et re jud. (ii. 27).
[2] Leur., l. c., q. 1090, n. 1. [3] Stremler, l. c., p. 417. [4] L. c., n. 2.

against this threat, this appeal will produce a suspensive effect, and, consequently, prevent the judge from validly pronouncing the declaratory sentence or publishing it. Stremler,[1] on the contrary, teaches the opposite. According to him, no suspensive appeal lies against the declaratory sentence in the case, which is merely threatened, but not yet pronounced. The reason assigned by him is, that the declaratory sentence does not inflict an irreparable injury, considering that it admits of a suspensive appeal after it is pronounced, which rights all and hinders the publication.

ART. III.

Appeal against the Publication of Censures.

3040. We have just seen that it is allowed to appeal against the *publication* of a declaratory sentence, in the case of censures which are *a jure* and *latæ sententiæ*, and that such appeal has a suspensive effect, and therefore, hinders the publication, or annuls the effect of the publication if made notwithstanding the appeal. We now ask whether this applies to the publication of correctional punishments, inflicted *ab homine*, and that *per sententiam particularem?* In other words: Let us suppose that a Bishop or ecclesiastical judge inflicts a censure upon a subject. The latter appeals against the punishment, or, also, fearing lest the judge will officially publish it, appeals directly against the proposed or feared publication. Is it allowed to appeal directly against the proposed publication? And if so, what effect has the appeal? Again, what effect upon the publication has the appeal interposed, not directly against the publication, but simply against the censure?

3041. So far as regards appeals made against the censure itself, and not directly against its publication, we must dis-

---

[1] L. c., p. 417.

tinguish between appeals that have a *suspensive* effect, and those which have merely a *devolutive*. Where the appeal has a suspensive effect, it hinders the ecclesiastical judge, as has been shown, from validly inflicting and, consequently, also from validly publishing a censure. Hence an appeal interposed against a censure which is *merely threatened*, or against a censure which, though *already inflicted*, yet admits of a suspensive appeal, prevents the valid publication of the punishment. Consequently, it is not necessary, in this case, to appeal directly against the publication.

3042. Where, however, the appeal against the censure itself has but a devolutive effect, there are two opinions as to the bearing which such appeal has on the publication. Kober[1] and some other canonists affirm that, as this appeal does not prevent the censure from taking full effect, so neither does it hinder the publication of the censure. For, they say, the publication of a censure is merely an adjunct, a complement of the censure itself, and does not add anything to the censure, but simply makes its existence known. They confirm their view from the enactment made by Pope Innocent III., (1214) which enjoins expressly : " Consuluisti nos, utrum si quis excommunicationis sententia innodatus, ante denunciationem ipsius ab ea . . . . curaverit provocare . . . . ipse (judex) denunciare possit eumdem (appellantem)? . . . . Respondemus, quod cum executionem excommunicatio secum trahat, et excommunicatus per denunciationem amplius non ligetur, ipsum excommunicatum denunciare potes."[2]

3043. Leurenius,[3] however, Sanchez, and others hold the opposite view. They argue thus : It is the express law of the Church that no innovation whatever, or change detrimental to appellant, shall be made, during the time the

---

[1] Excom., p. 185.   [2] Cap. 53, de sent. et re jud. (ii. 27).
[3] For. eccl., l. 2, t. 28, q. 1090.

appeal is pending;[1] that the judge *ad quem* shall, before all else, *i. e.*, before even entering upon the examination of the appeal, forthwith revoke and annul anything done by the judge *a quo* after the appeal has been interposed. Now, they continue, it is true that, prior to the Const. *Ad Vitanda* of Pope Martin V., the publication of the censure did not add new force or consequence to the censure, and was no innovation pending the appeal. Hence they admit that, down to the time of the Const. *Ad Vitanda*, the above decretal of Pope Innocent was the law of the Church. But, they say, the case has become entirely changed since the Constitution of Pope Martin was issued. For, by this Constitution, the status of the appellant is materially changed, to his detriment, by the publication of the censure. Indeed, according to this Constitution, an excommunicate becomes, after the publication of the censure, a *vitandus*, his acts are null, whereas, before the publication, he was merely *toleratus*, and his acts were valid. Hence it is evident that, at the present day, the publication makes the censure much more burdensome and causes it to bind much more strictly and fully, and that, consequently, the saying of Pope Innocent III., "Excommunicatus per denuntiationem *amplius non ligatur*," is no longer verified in our altered circumstances, as introduced by the Const. *Ad Vitanda*. They conclude therefore that, at the present day, the appeal in the case hinders the judge from validly publishing the censure.

3044. Nay, they contend that it is allowed to appeal directly against the *proposed* or *future publication* of the censure after the latter has been already inflicted, and that, by this appeal, the publication is suspended, so that it cannot be made, or if made, is invalid.[2]

3045. Of these two opinions, that of Leurenius seems to us, at the present day, the true, and, in fact, the only safe one to follow. For, as we shall see later, when we come to speak

[1] L. 1 ff. *Nihil innovari* (49. 7); Cap. 7 de app. in 6º (7. 15). [2] Leur., l. c.

of the Const. *Ad Vitanda* of Pope Martin V., which forms the present law of the Church, prior to this Constitution, censures produced the same effect, whether they were published or not. The publication added no new or additional effects. But, after this Constitution, the effect of the censures was greatly strengthened and increased by their official publication. Consequently it may be said that the legislation of Pope Innocent III., as laid down in the Const. *Præterea* 53. *de app.* has been modified by the subsequent Extrav *Ad Vitanda*.

ART. IV.

Effect of Appeals against threatened Censures.

3046. Thus far we have spoken of appeals which are interposed *after* the censure has been already inflicted. We come now to those appeals which are made *before* the correctional punishment is imposed. There is no doubt whatever, that, as was seen above,[1] it is allowed, at the present day no less than formerly, to appeal against a censure which is not yet inflicted, but is *merely threatened* or *impending*, and that such appeal has not only a devolutive *but also a suspensive effect.* This is the express, clear, and distinct law of the Church, as fully in force at the present day, also with us, and as endorsed by the unanimous opinion of canonists. In fact, Pope Celestin III., (1195) enacted: "Præterea requisiti fuimus, si quis judex ita protulerit sententiam: Nisi Sempronio intra 20 dies satisfeceris, te excommunicatum, vel suspensum aut interdictum esse cognoscas: et ille in quem fertur sententia, medio tempore appellans, ad diem statutum minime satisfecerit, utrum ille sententia tali ligetur, aut interposita appellatione tutus existat? Videtur autem nobis, *quod*

[1] Supra, vol. i., n. 446.

hujusmodi sententiam appellationis obstaculum debeat impedire."[1]

3047. Moreover, the decree of the Sacred Congregation of Bishops issued by command of Pope Clement VIII., in 1600, expressly declares that it is allowed to appeal, *etiam quoad effectum suspensivum* against a *threatened* or impending censure (*a gravamine... excommunicationis comminatæ*).[2] Pope Benedict XIII. in a Council held at Rome, in 1725, confirmed and re-enacted this decree.[3] Finally Pope Benedict XIV., in his celebrated Constitution *Ad Militantis*,[4] 1742, enjoins the strict observance of these laws, in the following passage: " Ubi vero agatur de censuris jam prolatis, *vel de comminatione... censurarum*, observetur omnino dispositio dictorum Decretorum Congregationis Episcoporum sub rec. mem. Clemente VIII., juxta additiones et declarationes præmem. Benedicti XIII."

3048. Now the Instructions *Sacra Hæc* (Art. XXXVII.) of 1880 and *Cum Magnopere* of 1884 (Art. XXXVII.) command that, in appeals, the regulations contained in the above Const. *Ad Militantis* shall be accurately observed. The words of these Instructions are: " Pro appellatione serventur normæ statutæ a Const. *ad Militantis* S. M., Bened. XIV. 30 Martii, 1742."[5] It is therefore certain, beyond a shadow of doubt, that, at present, with us no less than elsewhere, an appeal against a future or threatened censure is allowed and has a suspensive effect; that, consequently, such appeal *suspends* the jurisdiction of the judge *a quo*, so that he cannot proceed to inflict the punishment. And if he nevertheless inflicts the censure, the latter is *ipso jure* void, and can be wholly disregarded with impunity,[6] both *in foro interno and in foro externo*, since it is imposed by an ecclesiastical judge

---

[1] Cap. 40 de app. (ii. 28.) The same principle is laid down in Cap. 55 de app. (ii. 28); Cap. 14, de sent. exc., in 6º.
[2] Art. viii., ix.　　[3] Declar. ad Decr. ix.　　[4] Art. xlv.
[5] Stremler, p. 418.　　[6] Leur., For. Eccl., l. 2, t. 28, q. 1089, n. 1.

or Superior, whose jurisdiction has been suspended by the appeal.[1]

3049. This is manifest from the following decision of Pope Alexander III., contained in a letter to the Archbishop of York: A priest named R. had appealed to the Holy See against the Archbishop. Nevertheless, after making the appeal, he was excommunicated by the Archbishop. He disregarded the excommunication, and said Mass, etc., as though he had not been excommunicated, on the ground that it was invalid, having been inflicted after he had appealed. The Pope fully sustained the Priest and decided that the censure, having been inflicted after the appeal had been interposed, was null and void, and that, consequently, the Priest R. should not be molested or disquieted because he had violated the censure by saying Mass, etc.[2] When we come to ask why the Church allows a suspensive appeal against a threatened censure, canonists answer that a censure, once imposed, causes an irreparable harm or injury, since it carries its execution with itself.[3]

3050. From what has been said, it follows that the appeal against a threatened censure produces a suspensive effect, even though it (the appeal) be rejected by the judge *a quo*.[4] It follows also that if, for instance, a person were cited to hear sentence (whether of excommunication, suspension, or interdict) pronounced against him, he can appeal, and the appeal will suspend the jurisdiction of the judge, so that he cannot validly pronounce sentence.[5]

---

[1] Leur., for. eccl., l. 2, t. 28, q. 1089, n. 1.

[2] Cap. Ad Praesentiam 16, de app. (ii. 28); arg. Cap. 37, eod. The words of the Pope are: " Ideoque mandamus quatenus praedictum presbyterum, *pro eo quod post excommunicationem contra appellationem factam divina cantavit, nullatenus inquietes, sed ad eum statum reducas omnia in quo erant tempore appellationis emissae.*"

[3] Leur. l.c.; Stremler, l.c.; Kober, Exc. p. 227; Supra, n. 1161.

[4] Leur., l. c.   [5] S. C. C. S. Marci, 13 Apr. 1726; Stremler, p. 419.

Art. V.

Procedure before the Judge " ad quem," in adjudicating Appeals against unjust Censures.

3051. We now come to the *mode of procedure* to be observed in appeals against censures. We have already seen that, by virtue of an appeal interposed against a censure, the Metropolitan obtains jurisdiction to try or re-examine the case appealed to him, and to revoke or confirm the censure or correctional punishment inflicted by the judge *a quo*. While the Metropolitan, not being the superior *pleni juris* of his suffragans, can revoke censures inflicted by them only when he is appealed to, the Sacred Congregations of Rome, having full, ordinary, concurrent, and immediate jurisdiction all over the world, can revoke censures, not only when appeal is made to them, but whenever they see fit to do so.

3052. *Q.* How should the Metropolitan or judge *ad quem* proceed in taking cognizance of and deciding appeals interposed against censures?

A. There is question of censures, which are claimed to be *either* unjust *or* invalid. When the appellant claims that the censure is *unjust*, the judge *ad quem* cannot revoke the censure, or declare it invalid, *at the sole assertion, or statements, or proofs of the appellant*. He must *first hear the parties*, that is, not only the appellant, but also the appellee —*i.e.*, judge *a quo* or his representative. In other words, he must first cite both parties for the trial of the cause appealed, and then proceed to hear or try the case in the presence of both parties, and afterwards pronounce sentence, either revoking the censure or confirming it. Thus Pope Innocent IV. decides: "Sententias quoque interdicti vel suspensionis seu excommunicationis in appellantem ab eo a quo appellatum proponitur promulgatas, nullatenus *nisi*

Repressive Correctional Punishments. 227

vocatis partibus et de appellatione legitime constito revocent aut denuntient esse nullas."[1]

3053. The decree of the S. C. EE. et RR. *Ad Tollendas* (1600),[2] which is confirmed by Pope Benedict XIV., in his *Const. Ad Militantis*, and therefore made obligatory in the Instructions *Sacra Hæc* of 1880, and *Cum Magnopere* of 1884, likewise enjoins: "Censura ecclesiastica in appellantem prolata relaxari aut nulla declarari per judicem appellationis non possit, *nisi auditis partibus*, et *causa cognita*."[3]

3054. The manner in which the trial is conducted is the same as that in which any other appeal is tried. In the United States, the trial or hearing of the cause appealed is conducted according to the provisions of the recent Instruction *Cum Magnopere*. In Catholic countries, not subject to the S. C. de Prop. Fide, the formalities prescribed in the Instruction *Sacra Hæc* of 1880 must be observed.

3055. But suppose that, after hearing both parties, *i.e.*, the appellant and the appellee, *i.e.*, the judge *a quo* or his representative, *v.g.*, the diocesan prosecutor, the Metropolitan or judge *ad quem* finds it certain that the censure has been justly inflicted; or he finds it clearly certain that it has been unjustly imposed; or, finally, he finds it doubtful whether it has been justly or unjustly inflicted: how is he to proceed in each of these three cases? In the first case, namely, *where it is certain that the censure is just*, the judge *ad quem* must remit the appellant to the suffragan Bishop who inflicted the censure. And if the suffragan then maliciously refuses to give the absolution from the censure, though properly requested to do so by the appellant, the Metropolitan should himself impart it.[4]

3056. In the *second* case, namely, where *it is certain that the*

---

[1] Cap. Romana Ecclesia 3, de app. in 6° (ii. 15); *Glossa* in cas.
[2] Art. xiii.   [3] Cf. Cap. venerabilis 7, in 6. (v. 11).
[4] Cap. venerabilis 7 de sent excom., in 6°.

censure is unjust, the judge *ad quem* can and should himself revoke it or declare it invalid.

3057. In the *third* case, namely, where it remains doubtful whether the censure has been justly inflicted or not, the judge *ad quem* has a perfect right, if he wishes, to grant the absolution himself, though it is more becoming that he should remit the appellant to the judge *a quo*, with the mandate that the latter grant the release from the censure within a brief space of time fixed by him, *i.e.*, by the judge *ad quem*.[1] This is at present the universal law of the Church, as in force also in this country. For it is expressly enacted in the above quoted decree of the S. C. EE. et RR. *Ad Tollendas*.[2] This latter decree was confirmed by Pope Benedict XIII. in the Roman Council of 1725,[3] and also enjoined anew by Pope Benedict XIV. in his *Const. Ad Militantis*.[4] Now, both the recent Instructions *Sacra Hæc* and *Cum Magnopere* expressly declare that in appeals the regulations contained in the above Const. *Ad Militantis* must be observed.

3058. Besides, the Metropolitan or judge *ad quem* should, if he finds the censure clearly unjust, condemn the judge *a quo* by whom it was inflicted to pay the cost of the whole proceedings and completely indemnify the appellant. He should, moreover, if he finds that the circumstances of the case warrant it, impose other suitable and proportionate punishments upon the judge *a quo*. The latter shall be free from punishment, only in case he can prove, that, in inflicting the censure, he acted from ˙error,—*v. g.*, if he shows that he excommunicated the appellant, *in contumaciam*, believing that the citation had duly reached him, although afterwards, it is shown that it did not reach him.[5] The

---

[1] Cap. Venerabilis 7 de sent. excom., in 6 (v. 11); Kober. Excom., p. 229; Idem, Susp., p. 137.
[2] Art. xii. [3] Ad Decr. xii. Clementis XIII. [4] § 45.
[5] Cap. 48, de sent. exc. (v. 39); *Glossa*, l. c., v. *ex causa probabili*.

wording of this law, which is in full force at present, is as follows:[1] "Cum adversus excommunicatorem de injusta excommunicatione constiterit, *excommunicator condemnetur ad interesse excommunicato,* alias nihilominus, si culpæ gravitas postulaverit *superioris arbitrio puniendus,* cum non levis sit culpa, tantam infligere pœnam insonti; nisi forsan erraverit ex probabili causa, maxime si laudabilis opinionis existat." [2]

ART. VI.

Procedure before the Metropolitan in Appeals against "Invalid" Censures.

3059. But how is the judge *ad quem* to proceed in case the appellant claims that the censure inflicted upon him is not merely unjust, but is *invalid?* We must distinguish between two cases; namely between the case where it is *certain* and *undoubted* that the censure is null and void, and the case where it is *doubtful* whether or not it is invalid.

§ 1. *Procedure when the Censure is certainly Invalid.*

3060. If it is *certain, clearly manifest, and publicly known* that the censure is invalid,—*v.g.*,that it has been inflicted after an appeal had been lawfully interposed, or that any other requirement, condition, or formality prescribed by the Church as a substantial condition, or expressly on pain of nullity, has been set aside by the ecclesiastical judge or Superior,—it may be completely disregarded, not only *in foro interno,* but also *in foro externo,* privately and publicly, by the party censured, and that on his own private authority.

3061. Thus Pope Gelasius, writing to the Bishops of the East, decrees: " Sed si injusta (invalida) est sententia, tanto eam curare non debet, quanto apud Deum et Ecclesiam ejus

---

[1] Cap. 48 cit. [2] Cf. Instr. *Cum Magnopere,* art. xliv; Cf. Kober, Excom., p. 230.

neminem potest iniqua gravare sententia. Ita ergo ea se non absolvi desideret, qua se nullatenus perspicit obligatum."[1] Here, then, the principle is established that a censure or sentence which is clearly null and void does not bind either before God or in the face of the Church, that is, in the external forum of the Church; that, consequently, the person upon whom such a censure has been inflicted may entirely disregard it, of his own accord and on his own responsibility, both *in foro interno* and *in foro externo*.

3062. The same principle is laid down by Pope Gregory, when he says: "Non debet is pœnam sustinere canonicam, in cujus damnatione non est canonica prolata sententia."[2] Hence, the *Glossa*,[3] commenting upon this decree, says: "Si ergo constet tibi, quod sententia judicis est iniqua (invalida) potes judici violenter resistere ... ergo si quis celebrat post excommunicationem injuste (invalide) latam, non debet sustinere aliquam pœnam." It must be observed however, (*a*) that these two decrees apply only where the censure or sentence is *invalid* and not merely unjust; (*b*) and where its nullity is *certain and undoubted*. For if it is doubtful whether the censure is invalid or not, the person visited with censure must, as we shall presently see, appeal his case to the judge *ad quem*, in order to have the nullity declared officially.

3063. When is a censure *ipso jure* null and void? For the answer, we refer the reader to what we shall say a little further on, where we show that censures are invalid, because (*a*) of want of *jurisdiction* in the Superior; (*b*) of the omission of a *substantial* formality in the proceedings; (*c*) of absence of *canonical proof* of crime sufficiently grave to warrant the infliction of censures, although in reality the crime has been committed.

[1] Can. Cui illata 46, c. xi., q. 3. [2] Can. Non debet 64, c. xi., q. 3.
[3] V. non debet.

§ 2. *Procedure when it is doubtful whether the Censure is Invalid.*

3064. Where, however, it is *doubtful* whether the censure is *invalid* or not,—*v.g.*, where the person who has been censured claims that the censure has been inflicted upon him after he had made an appeal, or that the offence was not fully proved *juxta allegata*, or that, if proved, it was insufficient—the Metropolitan or judge *ad quem* when appealed to, should before all else, that is, before he enters upon the hearing of the merits of the case—*antequam audire causam incipiat* [1]—give the absolution *ad cautelam*, though only (*a*) by way of a *provisional measure*, (*b*) and *citata parte*,—*i. e.*, the appellee or judge *a quo*, and *visis actis*. Then he should proceed to hear the appeal, and at the end of the trial or investigation he should pronounce final sentence, declaring the censure either valid or invalid. If he declares the censure valid, the absolution "ad cautelam" given in the beginning of the hearing lapses, and the censure revives. But if he declares it null, it ceases absolutely, and the provisional absolution "ad cautelam" passes into an absolute and permanent release from the punishment.

3065. These regulations are thus enjoined by the Decree of Pope Clement VIII. *Ad Tollendas*:[2] "Absolutio ad cautelam, nonnisi citata parte " (the party against whom the appeal is made) " et visis actis, cum dubitatur de nullitate excommunicationis ab homine prolatæ vel a jure,[3] si

---

[1] Cap. 7 de sent. exc. in 6º.   [2] Art. xiii.

[3] Although here, and in the following documents, excommunication alone is mentioned, yet it is a well-known maxim of canon law that what is affirmed of one censure, applies equally to all the others, except, of course, where there is question of the specific nature of the particular censure. Hence, Schmalzgrueber, l. 5, t. 39, n. 104, expressly applies the law enacted in the above documents to *all* censures without exception.

occurrat dubium facti vel probabile dubium juris, concedenda erit, tuncque ad tempus breve cum reincidentia et præstita per excommunicatum cautione de stando juri et parendo mandatis Ecclesiæ tantum ; at si juxta formam a jure præscriptam apparebit, aliquem ob manifestam offensam excommunicatum fuisse, debitam etiam satisfactionem præstare, et si ob contumaciam manifestam, expensis pariter satisfacere et cavere de judicio, sisti coram excommunicatore is tenebitur, priusquam ad cautelam absolvatur."

3066. Pope Benedict XIII., (1725) in his explanations of and additions to this decree, enjoins: " Verum quoad absolutiones cum reincidentia, quæ Partibus concedi solent a judicibus, ad quos appellatur, ad effectum audiendi, cum inoleverit usus tam in Tribunali A. C. quam forsan etiam in Metropolitanis aliisque Tribunalibus appellationum, quod committantur absolutiones cuicunque Confessario, ita ut rei absque ulla reverentia proprii Ordinarii pro absolutis se publice habeant: Sanctitas Sua statuit ut in futurum hujusmodi absolutiones cum reincidentia, tam in Tribunali A. C. quam in Curiis Metropolitanis aliorumque judicum appellationum, committantur ipsis Ordinariis excommunicantibus cum clausula ut infra tres dies absolvant censuratos juxta commissionem ; quibus elapsis, si requisitus Ordinarius absolvere recusaverit vel neglexerit, absolvantur a Confessario juxta commissionis formam, quæ in præsenti servatur in dictis commissionibus absolutionum. . . . . Declaravitque rursus Sanctitas Sua, quod hujusmodi Commissiones de absolvendo præsentari debeant Cancellario Ordinariorum, a qua præsentatione currere debeant tres dies, post quorum lapsum, et non data absolutione, possint ab aliis absolvi, ut supra, in commissione."

3067. These enactments are expressly confirmed in the Const. *Ad Militantis*, of Benedict XIV., § 45, and therefore made obligatory with us, by the Instruction *Cum Magno-*

pere, [1] and in Catholic countries, by the Instruction *Sacra Hæc*, of 1880. [2]

§ 3. *How the Metropolitan imparts the Absolutio ad Cautelam.*

3068. From the regulations just given, it follows: *First*, that the absolution *ad cautelam*, in the case, is given, not *permanently*, but only *cum reincidentia;* in other words, the person who appeals against the censure *ex capite nullitatis* is released from it only *temporarily*, that is, only so long as the investigation or trial of his case lasts in the court of the Metropolitan or judge *ad quem*, and until a final decision on the whole case is rendered by the latter. As we have seen, when a person who has been placed under censure, whether of excommunication, suspension, or interdict, appeals to the Metropolitan or judge *ad quem*, and asserts that the censure inflicted upon him is invalid, or, at least, probably invalid, and where, consequently, it becomes doubtful whether the censure is valid or not, he must be heard, *i.e.*, his appeal must be entertained, and the validity or nullity of the censure investigated.

3069. Now, it may, nay, not infrequently does, take a long time for the Metropolitan to fully examine, hear, try, and decide the case. Delays, both legal and conventional, may and will occur. [3] Hence, considering that it is doubtful whether the appellant in the case is guilty or not, or whether the censure is valid or invalid, and that, therefore, it is possible that one who is innocent, or not validly under censure should, during the whole time of the trial or investigation of his appeal, suffer such a severe punishment as a censure, the law of the Church enjoins that the appellant, not only may, but shall be absolved *ad cautelam* and that, forthwith, *i.e.*, in the very beginning, and before the

[1] Art. xxxvii.
[2] What is meant by the *absolutio ad cautelam* will be explained later on.
[3] Supra., vol. ii., n. 1079 sq.

judge *ad quem* enters upon the hearing of the appeal, and shall remain released from the censure *ad interim*, that is, until his case has been tried by the Metropolitan, and final decision given by him.[1]

3070. This absolution *ad cautelam* is therefore simply a *provisional* measure. For, if, at the end of the investigation or trial of the cause, the Metropolitan or judge *ad quem*, to whom the case has been appealed, decides, by a final sentence, that the censure has been validly inflicted, it revives at once; if he decides otherwise, the appellant is then absolutely and permanently released from the censure.[2] By granting the *absolutio ad cautelam* in the case, the Metropolitan, as is evident, does not give any definitive decision whatever in regard to the alleged invalidity of the censure, or the merits of the case appealed. For he must grant this absolution before he enters upon the hearing of the case. He simply declares, by implication, that it is doubtful whether the censure is valid or not. Here we observe that the Metropolitan not only *can*, but is *strictly bound* to authorize this absolution, and that, as we shall see, prior to hearing the cause itself.[3] If he refuses to grant it, an appeal *in suspensivo* lies against such refusal, since it would inflict a *damnum irreparabile*.

3071. Here it may be objected that this regulation seems superfluous, since the appeal *ex capite nullitatis* produces a suspensive effect, as we have seen, and, therefore, relieves a person from the obligation of observing the censure, pending the appeal.[4] We answer, the *absolutio ad cautelam*, proceeding, as it does, directly from the competent ecclesiastical judge, takes away all doubt as to whether the appeal is rightly and properly interposed *ex capite nulli-*

---

[1] Cap. 2, 7, de sent. excom. in 6º (v. 11).   [2] Kober, Excom., p. 543 sq.
[3] Cap. Solet 2 de sent. excom. in 6º.
[4] Const. *Ad Militantis*, § 37; Droste, pp. 135, 136; München, l. c., vol. i., p. 588.

tatis and, moreover, officially confirms the suspensive effect of the appeal. This absolution is, therefore, equivalent to an official declaration of the competent Superior that the appeal is legitimately interposed *ex capite nullitatis* and is, therefore, suspensive.

3072. *Second*, it follows, from what has been said, and is also expressly enacted in the Sacred Canons, as still in full force, that the absolution in question shall be given " ante litis ingressum," or " antequam audire causam incipiant," (Metropolitani), [1] or " priusquam incipiat de veritate causæ appellationis cognoscere," [2] that is, before he enters upon the hearing or trial of the cause itself, as appealed to him. The *Glossa* [3] thus puts the question: Should the Metropolitan to whom the appeal is made, before he grants the *absolutio ad cautelam*, inquire into the justice or injustice (validity or invalidity) of the censure, where, for instance, the judge *a quo*, who inflicted it, claims that it is just, (valid), so that the appellant remains under censure pending the trial or investigation in regard to the nullity or injustice of the censure? The *Glossa* replies—and its reply is correct and applicable at the present day—that, according to the decision of Pope Innocent IV., the Metropolitan should, in all these cases, *before proceeding to hear the case, and before the nullity or injustice of the censure has been established*, absolve the appellant *ad cautelam*, after having received from him a pledge or promise that if it is found that he was guilty, and therefore justly censured, he will for the future obey the laws of the Church.

3073. There are only two exceptions to this rule ; namely, where the Bishop or judge *a quo*, (or his representative, *v.g.*, the *procurator fiscalis*,) by whom the censure was inflicted in the first instance, offers to prove within eight days [4] that the censure was imposed by him (*a*) for a *manifest offence*

---

[1] Cap. 7. de sent. excom. in 6º.   [2] Ib.   [3] In cap. 7, eod. v. Porro iste.
[4] For just cause the *judex ad quem* may prolong this period. *Glossa* in Cap. 2 de sent. exc. in 6º v. octo.

(*offensa manifesta*); (*b*) or for *manifest contumacy* (*contumacia manifesta*.) For in those two cases, the absolution *ad cautelam* is deferred for eight days.[1] If, within that time, the objector (*i. e.*, the *judex a quo* who objects to the granting of the absolution) does not prove that the censure was inflicted for a crime which is manifest, or for evident contumacy, he is to be condemned to pay the costs, and the appellant must be forthwith absolved *ad cautelam*.[2]

3074. But if he does prove the above assertions, the *absolutio ad cautelam* can be given by the judge *ad quem* or his delegate, only on these conditions: *First*, that the appellant or person to be absolved shall, before he is absolved, make due satisfaction; *second*, that, where he has been clearly shown to be guilty of manifest contumacy, he shall, moreover, pay the costs of the proceedings; *third*, that he shall present himself to the Superior by whom he was censured, and that in token of submission;[3] *fourth*, that he shall give a proper guarantee or at least promise that should it appear from the proceedings before the judge *ad quem* that he was guilty, and therefore justly censured, he will in future obey the laws of the Church.

3075. We have said, for a *manifest offence*. The *Glossa* explains this to mean a *notorious* offence.[4] We have also said, and *for manifest contumacy*. Pope Innocent IV.[5] and the *Glossa*[6] explain what is meant by manifest contumacy, by the following case. Suppose an Ecclesiastic is cited by his Bishop to appear for trial. He fails to appear and is excommunicated on that account. He appeals to the Metropolitan, and alleges that he refused to appear because the place to which he was cited was not safe, or because he was detained by a lawful impediment, *v. g.*, by sickness. On the other hand, the Bishop offers to show,

---

[1] Cap. Solet 2, de sent. exc. in 6º (v. 11.)   [2] Schmalzg., l. 5, t. 39, n. 104.
[3] Decretum Clem. VIII. *Ad Tollendas*, art. xiii.
[4] *Glossa*, in Cap. 2 de sent. exc. in 6ᶜ, v. manifesta.   [5] Cap. *Venerabilibus* cit.
[6] In cap. *Venerabilibus* cit.

within eight days, that the alleged excuses are clearly and notoriously without any foundation whatever, and that consequently the contumacy is *manifestly* inexcusable.

3076. Excepting in these two cases, the absolution *ad cautelam* must be always given when it appears that there is a reasonable doubt as to the validity of the censure, and before the hearing or trial of the cause appealed is commenced, no matter what objections the *judex a quo* or appellee may interpose.[1] Lest, however, this absolution lead to abuse and be obtained even by those who are *clearly and without a shadow of doubt* under valid and just censure, but who nevertheless claim that it is doubtful whether the censure inflicted on them is valid or not, the law of the Church ordains, *first*, that the absolution *ad cautelam* shall not be given *on the sole assertion* or statement of the appellant,[2] but *citata parte et visis actis;* in other words, the judge *ad quem* must in a simple, informal, and summary manner, hear not only the appellant, but also the appellee or party by whom or at whose instance the censure was inflicted, and also inspect the papers (*acta*) submitted by them, and thus ascertain the existence of the doubt in the case. However, the appellant, at this stage, is not bound to prove the nullity of the censure. He must merely show that a doubt may be entertained in regard to the validity of the punishment.[3] For as soon as the Metropolitan or judge *ad quem* finds, in his informal inquiry,[4] that it is doubtful whether the censure is valid or not, he is obliged forthwith to grant the absolution, notwithstanding any objections that may be urged by the judge *a quo* or his *procurator fiscalis*.

3077. *Second*, that the appellant should, before being

---

[1] Cap. 2 de sent. exc. in 6º. [2] Schmalzg., 1 5, t. 39, n. 104.

[3] For instance, because the crime was not fully proved "juxta allegata," or, if proved, is insufficient to warrant the punishment.

[4] This inquiry is similar to the "Summaria facti cognitio" of the Instr. *Cum Magnopere* of 1884.

absolved, give a proper guarantee, or at least a sworn promise that in case the proceedings before the judge *ad quem* show that he was culpable,[1] and consequently justly censured, he will in future obey the laws of the Church.[2]

3078. *Third*, lest the authority of the Bishop or the ecclesiastical Superior, by whom the censure has been inflicted, should fall into contempt, the Metropolitan cannot at present, as he could formerly, empower any simple confessor to impart the absolution *ad cautelam*, but must remit the appellant to his Ordinary or the judge *a quo*, by whom he was censured, with the command that the absolution be given by him *within three days*. If, then, the Ordinary or judge *a quo* refuses or fails to impart the absolution, within three days, any ordinary confessor can give it.

3079. With all these precautions, it is plain that the absolution in the case is at once a just measure of defence against a punishment that is possibly unjust, and a reasonable safeguard to the exercise of legitimate authority. Hence the *Glossa*,[1] not without strong reasons, seems to hold that the absolution *ad cautelam* should be imparted *ante ingressum litis*, *i. e.*, before the judge *ad quem* enters into the merits of the case, not only when there is question of doubt as to the validity of a censure, but also when there is reason to believe the censure to be *unjust*, though not invalid.

3080. These regulations are expressly recognized and re-enacted in the Decree of Pope Clement VIII. *Ad Tollendas*, and in the amendments and additions to this Decree made by Pope Benedict XIII., and in the Const. *Ad Militantis* of Pope Benedict XIV. They are applied to this

---

[1] Cap. 52, (v. 39.)
[2] Decretum Clementis VIII., l. c.; Kober, Excom., p. 546.
[3] Addit. Bened. XIII. ad Decr. Clem. VIII. § xii., xiii.
[4] In Cap. 7 de sent. exc. in 6° v. Porro.

country by the Instruction *Cum Magnopere* of 1884. Hence they are strictly obligatory with us.

3081. It is plain therefore, that in the case under discussion, namely where *a reasonable doubt*, either of law or fact, exists as to whether the censure is really invalid or not, the person censured cannot take it upon himself to decide of his own accord, and in his own favor, the question of the invalidity of the punishment. He must, therefore, appeal, and thus submit the question at issue to the judge *ad quem*. But pending this appeal he is exempted from the obligation of observing the censure, either *in foro interno* or *in foro externo*, since, as has been said above, the appeal interposed on account of alleged nullity (*ex capite nullitatis*) against a censure, even though already inflicted, has a *suspensive*, not merely a devolutive effect, and because, moreover, the *absolutio ad cautelam* must be granted by the judge *ad quem*.

3082. Hence, also, Barbosa [1] maintains that an Ecclesiastic is not to be considered irregular who, having appealed *ex capite nullitatis,*— *v. g.*, on the ground that no previous warning was given, — against a sentence of excommunication (suspension or interdict) pronounced upon him, celebrates Mass, etc., pending the appeal. This holds even though it be afterwards decided that the appeal was not valid.

Art. VII.

Procedure before the Metropolitan in Appeals against Threatened Censures.

3083. Thus far, we have spoken of the mode of procedure in appeals against censures which are made *after the censure has been already inflicted.* We shall now say a few words

[1] Collect. in. l. 2, t. 28, cap. ad Præsentiam 16, n. 3.

concerning the manner of hearing appeals which are made *against censures* not yet inflicted, *but merely threatened*.

3084. How should the *Metropolitan or judge "ad quem" proceed in taking cognizance of and deciding appeals interposed against censures which are merely threatened, but not yet inflicted?* The decree of Pope Clement VIII. *Ad Tollendas* thus gives the answer:[1] "Cum a gravamine, quod per definitivam sententiam reparari nequit, ut indebitæ carcerationis vel torturæ *aut excommunicationis, etiam comminatæ, appellatur: nonnisi visis actis, ex quibus evidentur appareat de gravamine, appellatio admittatur, aut inhibitio vel provisio aliqua concedatur.*"

3085. This decree is thus further explained by Pope Benedict XIII. in the Roman Council held in 1725:[2] "In causis vero comminatæ injustæ carcerationis, torturæ *vel excommunicationis*, Sanctitas Sua declarat et mandat, ut non expediantur inhibitiones generales et indefinitæ, sed tantum compulsoriales pro transmissione copiæ Actorum ad effectum cognoscendi, an sit deferendum necne appellationi, adjuncta in dictis litteris compulsorialibus inhibitione, ut interim judex a quo ad ulteriora non procedat: et quatenus visis actis, resultet evidens gravamen, tunc admittatur appellatio cum inhibitione, et causa cognoscatur coram judice ad quem; si vero de hujusmodi gravamine non constet, remittatur causa ad judicem a quo, cognoscenda in prima instantia."

3086. Now Pope Benedict XIV., in his Const. *Ad Militantis*,[3] decrees that these regulations shall be strictly complied with. His words are: "Ubi vero agatur . . . *de comminatione censurarum*, observetur omnino dispositio dictorum decretorum Congregationis Episcoporum sub rec. mem. Clemente VIII., juxta additiones et declarationes piæ mem. Benedicti XIII." We note that, as

[1] Art. ix. [2] Addit. et Declar. Benedicti XIII. ad Decretum ix. Clementis VIII.
[3] Art. 45.

already shown, the decree of Pope Clement VIII.[1] expressly states that the appeal against a *threatened* censure has a suspensive effect. As the Const. *Ad Militantis* of Pope Benedict XIV. is expressly laid down in our Instruction *Cum Magnopere* as the rule and mode of procedure to be followed in appeals, it is apparent that the above regulations fully apply to this country. Cf. our *Elements*, Vol. I. No. 446.

3087. Finally, what has been said of the appeal lawfully interposed *before* the censure is inflicted, holds equally true of the challenge (*recusatio judicis*) made against the judge, when interposed *before* the infliction of the censure. In other words, a challenge interposed against the ecclesiastical judge *v.g.*, Bishop or Vicar-General, *before* the censure is inflicted by the latter, has a suspensive effect,[2] like the appeal interposed prior to the infliction of the punishment.[3] In regard to appeals against censures, see also our *New Procedure*, No. 474.

[1] Art. viii.   [2] Can. 16, C. 2, q. 6.   [3] Ferraris, v. censura, n. 21.

CHAPTER VIII.

UNJUST AND INVALID CORRECTIONAL PUNISHMENTS.

ART. I.

When are Correctional Punishments unjust and invalid?

3088. We have thus far spoken of the nature of correctional punishments, of those who can inflict them, and of those upon whom they can be inflicted; also of the cause or crime for which such punishments can be imposed, and of the manner in which they are to be inflicted. The laws or regulations made by the Church on these heads are of two kinds: Some prescribe conditions or formalities which are *essential*. Consequently, if they are omitted, the censure is regarded as not having been inflicted at all, and is therefore invalid. Others lay down regulations which are not considered by the law as essentially necessary; hence, if they are omitted, the punishment will be illicit or unjust, but not invalid.

3089. Therefore a censure is *just and valid*, when all the requirements of the law of the Church, both essential and non-essential, have been accurately complied with by the ecclesiastical judge. It is *invalid*, when a substantial or essential condition prescribed by the Church is disregarded.[1] Finally, it is *unjust*, when a non-essential condition or formality is omitted, or when there is either no cause or crime at all, or one not sufficiently grave to warrant the infliction of the punishments in question.[2] We shall now examine more closely the effects which these three kinds of cen-

[1] Schmalzg. l. 5, t. 39, n. 8.
[2] Kober, Excom., p. 202; Id., Susp., p. 76; Stremler, l. c., p. 212.

sures produce, and see how a person who is visited with an unjust or invalid censure should conduct himself, and what means the law of the Church places in his hands to protect himself against them.

Art. II.

Effects of Correctional Punishments which are Just and Valid.

3090. When all the prescribed formalities, both essential and non-essential, have been carefully observed by the Superior who inflicts the punishment, the censure is *valid and just*, produces its full effect both *in foro interno* and *in foro externo*, and must, as a rule, be observed by the person censured. We say, *as a rule*; for as (*a*) the fear of a great evil, (*b*) or urgent necessity, exempts a person from incurring a censure, even though he does the act forbidden under censure, so does it also excuse him from the *external observance* of a censure which he has really, justly, and fully incurred.

3091. Thus, where a person who has justly fallen under a censure would, by observing it,—*v.g.*, by not saying Mass,—give scandal or defame himself, namely where it would become known, or at least suspected, that he had incurred censure, he is not obliged to conform externally to it. Of course this supposes that the censure is occult. The same holds of the case of urgent necessity, *v.g.*, the necessity of saying Mass in order to administer the viaticum to the dying.[1]

3092. With these exceptions, the censure which is just and valid must be observed both *in foro interno*, *i.e.*, before God and in conscience, and also *in foro externo*, *i.e.*, in the eyes of the law, and the person thus censured must conform to the punishment publicly as well as in secret and privately.

---
[1] Stremler, l.c., p. 222.

Art. III.

What Effects are produced by "unjust" Censures?

3093. We have seen that a correctional punishment is *unjust* (*censura injusta*), though valid, when a non-essential formality has been neglected, or when there is either no crime at all, or one not sufficiently serious to justify the censure. Now the absence of a crime or sufficient cause may happen in three ways: 1. Where in reality the accused has neither committed the crime, nor been proved guilty of it according to the *allegata et probata* of the trial. In this case, the censure is not merely *unjust*, but *ipso jure*, *null and void*. For the sentence inflicting it would contain an intolerable error on its very face.[1]

3094.—2. Where the accused has indeed really committed the crime sufficiently grave to deserve a censure, but has neither legitimately confessed it, nor been juridically convicted of it. In this case, also, the censure inflicted is *null and void*, and that *ipso jure*, and produces no effect whatever, at least *in foro externo*.[2] For, although in this case there is a sufficient cause in itself, or *secundum se*, and although it is known privately to the ecclesiastical judge, yet it does not exist *judicially*, or *secundum judicium*, or *in foro externo*.

3095.—3. The third case of absence of sufficient cause or crime is where there is in reality no crime or cause, and where, nevertheless, one has been juridically established, *v.g.*, by false and perjured witnesses, by forged documents, or by false confession of the accused, extorted from him by grave fear. Thus a person may be perfectly innocent, that is, guilty of no crime, or at least, of no crime sufficiently

---

[1] Cap. Per tuas, et cap. Venerabilis § Potest, de sent. excom. in 6º.
[2] Reiff., l. 5, t. 39, n. 39.

Unjust and Invalid Correctional Punishments. 245

grave to justify the infliction of censure, and yet be *juridically convicted of crime sufficiently grave to deserve censure*.

3096. Here there is in reality no cause whatever. It is true that the crime has been juridically established; that all the prescribed formalities have been carefully observed by the Bishop; that the canonical admonition has been properly given; that the trial has been conducted in the most correct manner. But the evidence was false; the documents forged; the witnesses perjured. The Bishop was misled. Or again, the judge may be animated by *personal feelings*, by passion, ill-will, hatred, or feelings of revenge; and actuated by these motives, he may, under the guise of the strict and accurate observance of all the required formalities, impose censure upon a subject whom he knows to be innocent.[1]

3097. Now it is certain that the censure thus inflicted is wholly *unjust*, and produces no effect whatever *in foro interno*, that is, before God and in conscience, and, therefore, can be completely disregarded *in private*.[2] Nevertheless, it is *valid* and produces its effect *in foro externo*. Why? Because it has been inflicted *in accordance with all the forms of law*, and the cause or crime, though really not committed, has nevertheless been established and therefore exists *in foro externo*. Hence a person thus censured would indeed before God and his own conscience be free from the censure, and privately he could disregard it. But *in foro externo* he would be obliged to observe it, until it had been revoked by the judge *ad quem*, as enacted in the above law of Clement VIII., or until his innocence and the error committed by the ecclesiastical judge had become publicly known.[3] In this sense is to be understood the oft quoted

---
[1] Kober, Excom., p. 211.
[2] Cap. 28 de sent. excom. (v. 39); Cap. 1. de sent. et re jud. in 6º (ii. 14); Kober, Excom., p. 216.
[3] Cap. Inquisitioni tuae 44, de sent. excom. (v. 39); Reiff., l.c., n. 41-44.

and oft misunderstood sentence: "Sententia Pastoris, sive justa, sive injusta fuerit, timenda est."[1]

3098. In fact, if in this case, where all the forms of law have been fully observed, the censure could be violated also in the external forum, and publicly, the door would be left wide open for the violation of the most just censures by malicious persons. For these persons, though justly found guilty *secundum allegata et probata* in the external forum, could always claim that, in conscience and before God, they were wholly innocent.[2] Again, a person thus unjustly but validly censured is, like every body else, bound to avoid giving public scandal. Now it is plain that he would give such scandal, if he openly and publicly disobeyed the authority of the Superior, *exercised in a lawful manner, that is, according to all the forms of law*.[3]

3099. Moreover, the natural law itself demands that the good of a particular person should give way to the common welfare of all. Now it is evident that the common good of the faithful requires that obedience should be shown externally and publicly to the competent authority, when it is exercised in accordance with the forms of law, until the injustice of the sentence is either declared by the higher ecclesiastical authority, or becomes publicly known.

3100. From this, however, it also follows that the person thus censured can completely disregard the censure *privately*, and also *publicly*, provided it be before persons *who are aware* of the injustice of the censure, or in places where it is *not known* that the censure has been inflicted upon him. In a word, he need not, even *in foro externo*, or publicly, observe the censure, where he can do so without giving scandal, namely, where it has not been officially published or is not generally known; nor in places where the censure is indeed publicly known, but where the

---

[1] Can. I., c. xi., q. 3; Ferraris, v. censura, n. 33.   [2] Reiff., l.c., n. 43.
[3] Cf. Schmalzg., l. 5, t. 39, n. 83; Leur., l. 5, t. 39, q. 556, n. 3.

innocence of the person censured is also known. For a person can give no scandal by disregarding a censure before persons who do not know he is under censure, or who, if they do know, also know that the censure is unjust or void.[1]

3101. It must, however, be observed that, although a person thus unjustly censured does not *per se* incur irregularity *in foro externo* by violating the censure, yet, if it is found out that he has violated it, or if he is accused and juridically convicted of such violation, he can be officially declared irregular, since he is validly under censure *in foro externo*. Nay, if, upon being so declared, he refuses to cease violating the censure, after having been admonished, he can be visited with new censures on account of his disobedience and seeming contempt of ecclesiastical authority.[2]

ART. IV.

Effects and Observance of "Invalid" Correctional Punishments.

3102. It has been shown above that a correctional punishment or censure is *invalid*, and not merely unjust, when a substantial formality or condition prescribed by the law of the Church is clearly set aside by the ecclesiastical judge. An invalid censure, or an invalid sentence inflicting censure, produces no effect whatever, either *in foro interno* or *in foro externo*. For, like every other invalid punishment or sentence, it is regarded by the Sacred Canons, which are still fully in force, also in the United States, *as not pronounced or inflicted at all*. No appeal, therefore, is necessary against it, since it is needless to appeal against that which has no existence in law.

3103. Hence a person who is clearly under an invalid censure can disregard it, on his own authority, both *in*

---

[1] Kober, l. c., p. 218.   [2] Reiff., l. c., n. 43.

foro interno and *in foro externo*, as we shall explain more fully later on. In truth, the law of the Church, by the very fact that it renders a sentence or punishment null and void, when it is inflicted without the prescribed essential conditions or formalities, deprives it of all effect whatever. Besides, the Sacred Canons declare, as we shall see later on, that a person may, of his own accord, disregard censures which are undoubtedly invalid.

3104. Now, when are correctional punishments invalid? In these three cases: 1. *Because of want of jurisdiction* on the part of the Superior inflicting the punishment. This can happen (*a*) either because the Superior has exceeded his jurisdiction as limited by law ; (*b*) or because he is under censure himself ; for a Superior who is himself excommunicated or suspended cannot inflict censure upon others ;[1] (*c*) or because the defendant has made an appeal before the censure was actually inflicted ; for, as we have seen, an appeal interposed against a threatened censure has a suspensive effect ;[2] (*d*) or, finally, if the Superior imposes a censure upon a person who is not his subject.

3105.—2. Next, a censure is *ipso jure* invalid and produces no effect whatever, *when the Bishop or ecclesiastical judge neglects a substantial formality in the proceedings*, *v.g.*, if he fails to give the previous canonical admonitions or precept, as described above ;[3] or if he does not give the accused a trial, as noted above ;[4] or if he indeed gives the trial, but sets aside some substantial formality prescribed for trials, *v.g.*, the citation of the accused, or the right which the accused has of fully defending himself.

3106.—3. *Finally, censures are " ipso jure " invalid, and not merely unjust, when they are inflicted without a sufficient cause or crime*, AS CANONICALLY AND JURIDICALLY ESTABLISHED. For, as we have seen above,[5] correctional punishments can

---

[1] Can. 4, c. 24. q. 1.   [2] Supra, vol. i., n. 446.   [3] Supra, n. 1757 sq., 2704.
[4] Supra, n. 2065 sq.   [5] Supra, n. 2021 sq.

Unjust and Invalid Correctional Punishments.

be inflicted *only for mortal sins, nay, only for very grave crimes.* Now, *in foro externo*, or in the eyes of the Church and of the Sacred Canons, as in force also in the United States, England, Ireland, and other missionary countries, it is not sufficient, as was seen above, that the crime has been really committed; it must be, moreover, *juridically proved* by canonical or legal proof. Otherwise the censure is *ipso jure* null and void. Hence, a censure, like every other ecclesiastical punishment, is *invalid*, not merely unjust, when it is inflicted upon a person who has indeed committed the crime for which censure has been imposed upon him, but who yet has not been convicted of it *juridically*, that is, *by canonical proof, juridically obtained*. For, in the external forum, (and the infliction of censures is always and essentially an exercise of power *in foro externo*), every offence, no matter how enormous, which is not juridically and canonically proven, is considered as not committed.

3107. Hence the Bishop or ecclesiastical judge, also with us, cannot inflict censure for a crime of the commission of which he is perfectly certain simply *by private information*. For to inflict a correctional punishment or censure is always a public judicial act, an exercise of public jurisdiction or of power *in foro externo*, also in this country and everywhere.[1] Consequently, it can take place only *on public or juridical knowledge*, that is, on information obtained by the Bishop or judge, not privately, but by competent juridical documents or testimony produced at the trial.[2] For the nature and various kinds of canonical or juridical proofs, see above.[3]

3108. We say *competent juridical documents;*[4] in other words, the proofs shall be canonical or legal (*probatio canonica, legalis*), that is, they shall have those qualifications and conditions which are prescribed by the law of the Church.

[1] Schmalzg., l. 5, t. 29, n. 80.
[2] Schmalzg., l. 5, t. 39, n. 80.
[3] Supra, n. 813 sq.
[4] Kober, Susp., p. 61.

250 *Unjust and Invalid Correctional Punishments.*

Consequently the proofs must be (*a*) without any flaw or defect; (*b*) full and perfect; (*c*) produced during the trial or *citata parte*, that is, they are to be produced in the presence of, or at least communicated to the accused, and his defence or answer thereto is to be received.[1]

3109. Hence, if, for instance, the ecclesiastical judge should, except as stated in Art. XX. of the Instruction *Cum Magnopere*, admit the testimony of witnesses who are clearly not *omni exceptione majores*, and should condemn the accused on their testimony, the censure would be not merely unjust, but *ipso jure* invalid. For in this case the judge would openly violate an essential prescription of law, which requires *canonical proof (probatio legalis)* for conviction. In like manner, if the ecclesiastical judge should inflict a censure for an offence which, though legitimately proven *secundum allegata et probata*, is yet clearly insufficient to warrant the imposing of a censure, the latter would be invalid, and not merely unjust. For he would violate a substantial requirement of the law, which forbids the infliction of censure except for grave and sufficient crime.

3110. It will be seen, then, that, while a censure which is

---

[1] Thus Pope Eleutherius enacts: "Caveant judices ecclesiae, ne *absente eo*, cujus causa ventilatur, sententiam proferant, quia *irrita erit*." (Can. 2, c. 3, q. 9). Pope Cornelius ordains: "Omnia quae adversus *absentes* in omni loco aut negotio aguntur aut judicantur, omnino evacuentur." (Can. 4, c. 3, q. 9). Pope Felix, writing to the Bishops of France, decrees: "*Absente adversario*" (*reo*) "non audiatur accusator" (Promotor fiscalis); "nec sententia, *absente alia parte*, a judice dicta, ullam obtineat firmitatem." (Can. 11. c. 3. q. 9).

Hence it is a well recognized principle that all *ex parte* or one-sided proceedings are null and void. Consequently the inquiry which precedes the citation (*processus informativus*) has no legal effect whatever, so far as concerns the establishment of the crime, unless all that was done in the inquiry be fully communicated to the defendant, and his answer or defence, or objections received. Thus only does the processus informativus become legalized. This communication or legalization (*legitimatio processus*) has for its object to convince the accused that no error or malice has crept into the proceedings, and also to enable him to defend himself. (Todeschi, Man. du Droit Can., p. 508).

unjust, must be observed *in foro externo*, until it is revoked by the ecclesiastical Superior, or until its injustice becomes known, *a censure which is invalid need not per se be observed either " in foro interno " or " externo."* The reason of this difference of effect is that in the case of an unjust correctional punishment the ecclesiastical judge, though setting aside non-essential formalities, yet observes those which are essential. Consequently his action stands before the law until it is properly reversed. But in the case of invalid censures, as in the case of all other invalid punishments, the ecclesiastical judge acts in direct violation of substantial prescriptions of the law of the Church; he exceeds the limits of his authority; therefore he acts simply *as a private individual*, and his acts have no force whatever in the external forum.

3111. Nor can it be objected that scandal might sometimes be given by persons disregarding invalid censures, since in some cases it might happen to be generally known that the censure had been inflicted upon such or such a person, and on the other hand it might not be known that it was invalid. The objection does not seem to us well taken. For this case is no longer supposable at the present day, since nothing would be more easy than to make known the defect which renders the punishment null and void. Again, the scandal, if any, would be produced, not by any fault on the part of the person censured who disregards the censure, but by the illegal action of the ecclesiastical judge. Finally, no one is bound to avoid a pharisaical scandal.

3112. While, however, it is true that a person can, of his own accord, disregard an invalid censure, and that both in the internal and external forum, privately and even publicly, provided the nullity be known publicly, it is nevertheless equally true that the nullity in the case *must be certain, clear, and wholly beyond any reasonable doubt.* For where there is any *reasonable doubt,* either of law or fact, as to whether the censure is invalid or not, the action of the

252 Unjust and Invalid Correctional Punishments.

Superior holds good, until it is reversed by the higher ecclesiastical judge.[1] Hence, in the case of doubt, the person censured cannot of his own accord disregard the censure, but must appeal *ex capite nullitatis* to the judge *ad quem*, in order to have the punishment declared invalid. This appeal, however, has, as was seen, a suspensive effect. Now, practically speaking, such doubts may not unfrequently arise. Thus, sometimes, a *dubium juris* may present itself, *v.g.*, it may not be clear whether a certain formality or condition is prescribed by the law of the Church as substantial or merely as accidental; as entailing nullity or merely illicitness. At other times, a *dubium facti* may crop out; *v.g.*, it may be doubtful whether, as a matter of fact, the ecclesiastical Superior has really exceeded his jurisdiction or set aside some essential formality or requirement.

ART. V.

Effects of Censures which are "a jure" and "latæ sententiæ."

3113. What we have hitherto said applies to correctional punishments inflicted by the Bishop or Superior, in particular cases, *i.e.*, to *censuræ ab homine, per sententiam particularem*, and also to *censuræ a jure* which are *ferendæ sententiæ*. We come now to correctional punishments *which are inflicted by the law itself and are incurred "ipso facto."* By the law we here mean, not merely the general law of the Church, but also all particular or *local laws*, such as synodal statutes.

3114. Now, as we have seen, censures *a jure* which are *latæ sententiæ* are incurred, *in foro interno*, even though the crime is not juridically proved, provided it has been really committed. But *in foro externo* these punishments are not incurred, until the Bishop or ecclesiastical Superior has

---

[1] The rule of all Roman and canon law is: "In dubio standum est pro valore actus."

Unjust and Invalid Correctional Punishments. 253

given the accused a trial and pronounced declaratory sentence. In other words, the Bishop cannot pass declaratory sentence, or publish the censure in the case, unless the crime has been juridically proven, or is completely notorious.

3115. Now, a person who has incurred a censure *in foro interno* must indeed observe it *in foro interno, i.e.*, in conscience and before God. But he is not bound to defame himself. Hence, if he cannot observe the censure externally, and before others, without causing them to suspect that he is under censure, he is not bound to conform to the censure publicly. We say, *who has really incurred, etc.;* for if a person commits the deed or crime to which the censure is *ipso jure* annexed, but has acted *from ignorance*, as explained above,[1] or from fear or inadvertence, he does not incur the censure, even *in foro interno*, and hence need not observe it either privately or publicly.

3116. The same holds, when the law itself or statute commanding or prohibiting something under censure is null and void. For the censure is an accessory of the law or statute, and is therefore void, if the statute itself is invalid.

[1] Supra, n. 1702.

CHAPTER IX.

PUNISHMENTS INCURRED FOR DISREGARDING CENSURES.

3117. Persons upon whom a correctional punishment has been validly and justly inflicted and who are not excused from its observance by any of the reasons given in the preceding article, *v. g.*, by reason of an appeal interposed, must abstain completely from those acts which the censure incurred by them forbids. If such a person nevertheless, knowingly and maliciously, performs such acts, he is guilty of a wilful violation of the censure and commits a *mortal sin*.[1] For such conduct is evidently a grave disobedience to the Church, and implies contempt of the Church and her coercive power.[2]

ART. I.

Irregularity as a Punishment for violating Censures.

3118. The Church has, moreover, established *severe positive punishments* for such violation of censures. The first of these is *irregularity* or *canonical disqualification to receive orders or to perform the functions of orders, whether major or minor, which a person has already received.*[3] Canonists prove this from the Cap. *Cum Æterni* 1 *de sent. et re jud. in* 6° (ii. 14), where Pope Innocent IV. decrees that ecclesiastical judges, both ordinary and delegated, who shall allow themselves to be influenced in their acts by personal motives, such as

---

[1] Cap. ult. de cleric. exc. min. (v. 27).   [2] Kober, Susp., p. 95.
[3] Supra, n. 1925 sq.

Punishments incurred for disregarding Censures. 255

hatred, feelings of revenge, favoritism, fear, gain, or hope of gain, or other unworthy motives, shall be *ipso facto* suspended from their office—"ab executione officii"—for one year; and if during said year they presume to exercise an act of "ordo," *they shall become irregular.*[1] They prove the same also from the Cap. *Cum Medicinalis* 1 *de sent. excom. in* 6° (V. 11), where the same Pope Innocent IV. enacts that ecclesiastical judges who dare to inflict censures without the formalities prescribed in said "caput" and explained above[2] shall incur *ipso facto* suspension for one month "ab ingressu ecclesiæ et divinis officiis," and if, during this month, when they are suspended, they dare to perform "officia divina," *they shall incur irregularity.*[3]

3119. It is to be noted, however, that not every wilful violation of a correctional punishment produces irregularity; but only that which consists in the exercise of *orders*, major or minor.[4] Thus, if a person who is, for instance, suspended *ab ordine* nevertheless performs acts of the *ordo, v. g.*, says Mass or administers the sacraments, he incurs irregularity. But if a person who is, for instance, suspended merely from acts *of jurisdiction* nevertheless performs acts of jurisdiction and even of the *ordo*, he incurs no irregularity whatever. Why? Because by his acts of jurisdiction he violated the censure, it is true. But the law of the Church does not impose irregularity for the violation of such a censure. By performing acts of order, in the case, the person has not violated any censure, since he was suspended only from *jurisdiction*, not from *orders*. Hence a person incurs irregularity only when he is forbidden by his censure to exercise acts of order—*v. g.*, when he is suspended *ab ordine*—and when, notwithstanding, he does perform an act of the *ordo*.[5]

---

[1] "Quod si suspensione durante *damnabiliter ingesserit se divinis irregularitatis laqueo se involvet.*" (Cap. *Cum Æterni* cit.)
[2] Supra, n. 2044. sq.   [3] Kober, l. c.   [4] Supra, n. 1929.
[5] Schmalzg., l. 5, t. 39, n. 308.

3120. Irregularity is always incurred *ipso facto*, and absolution from it reserved to the Pope.[1] As to the special faculties granted our Bishops by the Holy See, of absolving from irregularities, see our *Notes*.[2] As we have already observed, no violation of a correctional punishment produces irregularity, unless it is *intentional, wilful,* and *malicious*, and therefore committed *knowingly* and *wilfully*. For irregularity, as was shown above, is a *very severe punishment*, and therefore cannot be contracted where there is no crime, that is, where the violation of the censure, though justly and validly incurred, is unintentional or excusable, *v. g.*, because of urgent necessity, or for the purpose of avoiding defamation or scandal, or other just motive.[3]

3121. Here we also remark that, when a censure is null and void, as we have seen in the preceding Article, it produces no effect whatever, and consequently its violation can never produce irregularity.[4] We also observe with Card. Petra, that, when a sentence or censure is *notoriously unjust*, such injustice is equivalent to *nullity* of censure and has the same effects.[5] Consequently also, even in those cases where, as was shown in the preceding Article, a person should sometimes externally and publicly observe an unjust or invalid censure, in order not to give scandal, yet if such a person chooses nevertheless to disregard the censure publicly and give public scandal, he would not incur irregularity, since irregularity is produced only by the violation of a censure which is just and valid.

---

[1] Cf. Conc. Trid., sess. xxiv., c. 6 de Ref.

[2] Here is the faculty: "Dispensandi in quibuscumque irregularitatibus..." (Fac. form. 1 apud our *Notes*, p. 463).

[3] Præl. S. Sulp., n. 821.   [4] Supra, n. 3109.

[5] Card. Petra, Com. in Const. Innocentii VI. *Cum onus*, t. iv., p. 126, Venetiis, 1741.

Art. II.

Dismissal as a Punishment for disregarding Censures.

3122. The next punishment is, that if, upon being duly and canonically admonished, these persons do not leave off violating censures, but continue obstinately to perform *acts of the* "*ordo*," in direct violation of the censure, they can be *dismissed* (*privatio*), nay, even *forever deposed* (*depositio*) from their offices and benefices.[1] This punishment is *ferendæ sententiæ*, and, as has just been intimated, must be preceded by a special canonical warning, since it can be imposed only upon those who *obstinately* and *contumaciously* disregard correctional punishments.[2] Kober[3] holds that, even where the censure has been inflicted *for a fixed period* or as a *vindicatory punishment*, its violation produces irregularity.[4] Others deny this.[5]

Art. III.

Other Punishments incurred for violating Censures.

3123. Hitherto we have spoken of the punishments decreed for such a violation of a censure as is caused by *an act of order, major or minor*.[6] Now, what are the punishments incurred by those who wilfully and maliciously disregard a censure by exercising *acts of jurisdiction? First*, they certainly commit a *mortal sin*. *Secondly*, all acts of jurisdiction performed by them are *ipso facto* null and void, and those persons who are subject to a Superior thus exercising jurisdiction, in violation of a censure incurred by

---

[1] Cap. 3, 4, 6 de cleric. excom. min. (v. 27.) [2] Stremler, l. c., p. 219.
[3] Sup., p. 95.
[4] Arg. cap. 1 de sent. et re jud. in 6º (ii. 14.) ; Cap. 1 de sent. excom. in 6º (v. 11).
[5] Cf. Craiss., n. 1796. [6] Reiff., l. 5, t. 27, n. 22; Ib., adnotatio xl.

him, need not, nay, *cannot* obey him.[1] *Thirdly*, besides, the higher Superior may impose such other punishments as, in his judgment, the circumstances of the case— namely the scandal given, the malice of the offence—will justify.[2] *Fourthly*, there are other specific punishments decreed by the Sacred Canons, which, however, we shall discuss in the various parts of this work, as occasion offers.

[1] Kober, l. c., p. 104.   [2] Ib., p. 103.

CHAPTER X.

WHO CAN RELEASE FROM REPRESSIVE CORRECTIONAL PUNISHMENTS.

ART. I.

Do these Punishments cease of themselves?

3124. The object of correctional punishments, as we have seen, is chiefly to cause the delinquent *to reform and make satisfaction for what he has done*. The culprit is, to use the words of the Apostle, delivered over to Satan, in order that his *spirit may be saved*.[1] To reclaim the erring and wayward sinner is the primary and great object of the Church when she inflicts correctional punishments. Hence she never leaves the offender out of sight when she has visited him with a censure. Thus, while, on the one hand, *v. g.*, an excommunicate who is to be shunned —*vitandus*— is excluded from assisting at Mass and the other functions of divine worship, he is allowed to be present at sermons, because the word of God may perhaps bring him back to repentance.[2] The Bishop who has inflicted the censure is expressly commanded to constantly admonish, encourage, and urge him to return to the path of duty. He should unceasingly and lovingly follow the wayward offender, as the Good Shepherd followed the lost sheep, and by his fatherly kindness, so to say, compel him to return to the path of virtue.

3125. From this it would seem that, as soon as the end of the correctional punishment has been attained, that is, *as soon as the delinquent has become penitent, made satisfaction*, and

---

[1] I Cor. v. 5.   [2] Kober, Excom., p. 448.

repaired the consequences of his guilt, the censure should also cease of itself. This, however, is not the case. For in order that a censure, inflicted upon a person *as a censure*, may cease, *the intervention of the ecclesiastical judge or Superior and a formal remission (absolutio) on his part are necessary*.[1] For, as the inflicting of the censure is an act of jurisdiction, so must also its withdrawal or removal be effected *by an act of jurisdiction*. And as the Church binds by the censure, so also must she loose from it, by a special act or exercise of her authority. "Omnis res," says the law of the Church, "per quascunque causas nascitur, per easdem dissolvitur."[2]

3126. In fact, it is manifestly in the interest of a proper and well regulated discipline that not the person under punishment, but the Church or proper Superior shall be the judge to decide whether the offender has really become penitent, made proper amends, and is therefore entitled to regain his former status and to re-enter upon the possession and enjoyment of the spiritual benefits of which he had been deprived by the censure.

3127. On the other hand, it is *not left to the nod or whim* of the ecclesiastical Superior to give or withhold the release from the censure as he pleases.[3] On the contrary, the law of the Church, as in force also with us, is that, once the delinquent has amended, he obtains, by that very fact, *the right to the absolution*, and the superior *is bound* to grant it.[4]

3128. We said above, "For, in order that a censure inflicted *as a censure*," since censures imposed *as vindicative punishments*, for a specified time, *v.g.*, for six months, lapse of themselves with the expiration of the term for which they were inflicted, without any intervention or remission on the part of the Superior. Of course, the Superior by whom the censure was imposed as a *vindicative punishment*,

[1] Cap. 15, 28, 38, 58 de sent. excom.   [2] Cap. 1 de reg. jur. (v. 41).
[3] Kober, l. c., p. 452.   [4] Cap. 25 de appell. (ii. 28); Cap. 11 de const. (i. 2).

Release from Repressive Correctional Punishments.

for a certain time may, if he thinks it expedient, shorten this term and remit the punishment before the term has expired.[1]

ART. II.

Who can release from these Punishments when they are inflicted "a jure" and incurred "ipso facto"?

3129. *Q.* Who has the power to relieve a person from a censure incurred by him?

A. It is necessary to distinguish between correctional punishments, (*a*) which are inflicted by the law and are *latæ sententiæ*, (*b*) and those which are imposed *ab homine, per sententiam particularem;* again, those *a jure* are either reserved or not reserved. 1. As to *censures inflicted by the law—a jure*[2]—in such a manner as to be incurred *ipso facto*, it would follow, strictly speaking, from what has been said, that only the lawgiver *from whom they have emanated*, or his successor, delegate, or Superior can absolve from them, even when they are not reserved. For the general rule is that correctional punishments can be remitted solely by the Superior by whom they were inflicted. A well regulated discipline requires this.

3130. Hence, strictly speaking and *per se*, only the Pope and an Œcumenical Council can absolve from a censure, even though not reserved, inflicted by the general law of the Church; and likewise, only the Bishop can free a subject from censures enacted by Synodal statute or general command. However, this would make it very difficult, nay, sometimes impossible for the person under censure

---

[1] Kober, Susp., p. 128.

[2] And by these censures we mean, not only those inflicted by the *general* law of the Church, *v. g.*, those contained in the Const. *Ap. Sedis* of Pius IX., but also those imposed by Bishops, either in diocesan Synod—*per modum statuti*—or out of Synod, by general mandate—*per sententiam generalem*.

to be released from his punishments, even after he has become penitent.[1] Consequently the general law of the Church, made by Pope Innocent III., as construed by the universal practice of the Church and the unanimous teaching of canonists, has authorized *every confessor* to absolve from censures, *latæ sententiæ, whenever the lawgiver has not reserved the absolution to himself*.[2] This law is still in full force, also with us and everywhere.

3131. It is true that the Pontiff speaks merely of minor excommunication, but by parity of reason and because favors must be liberally construed, canonists unanimously extend the Pontiff's disposition to all censures. Likewise it is again true that Innocent III. treats solely of censures inflicted by the *general law*. Yet canonists also apply his Constitution to censures enacted by *local laws*, such as synodal statutes or enactments of Bishops *per sententiam generalem*, since these censures are placed on the same footing with censures *a jure communi*.

3132. Hence, in the case, any confessor can absolve from correctional punishments, which are (*a*) inflicted by law, general or local, (*b*) incurred *ipso facto*, (*c*) and not reserved. The question here arises: Can a confessor, in the case, give the absolution also outside the confession or the tribunal of penance, and *pro foro externo*, or merely in the tribunal of penance and solely *pro foro interno?*[3] There are two opinions; one affirmative, the other negative. Those who hold the *negative*, such as Stremler,[4] base their opinion on

[1] Kober, Excom., p. 464.

[2] The words of the Pope are: " A suo episcopo vel a *proprio sacerdote* poterit absolutionis beneficium obtinere . . . quia conditor Canonis ejus absolutionem sibi specialiter non retinuit, *eo ipso concessisse videtur facultatem aliis relaxandi*." (Cap. Nuper 29, de sent. excom. (v. 39.)

[3] According to Stremler, (p. 242) the absolution from censures *in foro externo* is that which is given outside of confession or the tribunal of penance ; that *in foro interno* is the one which is imparted in the tribunal of penance.

[4] Ib., p. 240, 243.

Release from Repressive Correctional Punishments. 263

the argument that the granting of absolution *outside the tribunal of penance* is an act of jurisdiction *in foro externo;* Now ordinary confessors have no such jurisdiction; hence, etc.

3133. The *affirmative*, which is the opinion of St. Alphonsus,[1] Varceno,[2] and others, is that every confessor can give the absolution in question *outside the tribunal of penance and pro foro externo*. This seems to us the more probable opinion. For while it is true that simple or ordinary confessors have no jurisdiction *in foro externo*, by virtue of their office, yet it is also true that they possess this jurisdiction in the case under discussion by virtue of special and *express authorization* of the common law of the Church, as laid down in the decretal *Nuper* of Innocent III., above quoted. In fact, this decretal places the *sacerdos proprius*, by whom is meant not only the parish priest, but every confessor, as canonists agree, on a footing of perfect equality with the Bishop, in regard to the granting of the absolution in question.[3]

3134. *Q*. Who can release from correctional punishments which are inflicted by the law (*a jure*) and are incurred "ipso facto," *when the author of the law in question has expressly reserved the absolution to himself?*

A. (*a*). Only the law-giver himself, or the Superior who has made the law containing the censure, and who has reserved the absolution to himself; (*b*) his lawful successor in office, (*c*) or his delegate, (*d*) or his direct and higher Superior. We say, *his higher Superior;* consequently the Pope can release from all correctional punishments reserved by Bishops, throughout the whole world; Generals of religious orders, from those reserved by inferior religious Superiors. The Metropolitan cannot absolve from the censure reserved by his suffragans, save when he makes the vis-

---

[1] L. vii., 70. [2] Comp., p. 908. [3] Kober, Excom., p. 469.

itation of the province, and when a case is appealed to him.[1]

3135. Again we say, *his lawful successor in office;* for the successor is considered *as one and the same moral person* with his predecessor, and therefore possesses the same power. Hence, whenever the Bishop dies, or is removed or transferred, or resigns, or in any other way loses his office and jurisdiction, the Cathedral *Chapter*,[2] through its Vicar-Capitular,[3] (with us, administrator) can absolve from all censures reserved by the Bishop to himself.

3136. We say also, *his delegate or representative;* for the Bishop or other Ordinary judge can at any time authorize another person to act for him in this matter, in such a manner that the absolution given by this delegate will have the same effect as though it had been imparted by the Ordinary himself. In fact it has become customary for the Pope and Bishops to delegate this power to a number of inferior ecclesiastics, in order that the persons under censure might not be put to the hardship of being obliged to apply to the Pope or the Ordinary himself for the absolution.[4] The Bishop or other Ordinary is perfectly free to select as his delegate for the exercise of this power any worthy ecclesiastic. He is, moreover, at liberty to bestow upon such delegate or representative the power to absolve either only *in foro interno*, or also *in foro externo*.

3137. Besides the cases just mentioned, where the Bishop or other Superior, *in a special and personal manner*, delegates others, there are other cases, where the *law* itself authorizes inferiors to release from the punishments under discussion, namely from censures which are inflicted *a jure* and are incurred *ipso facto latæ sententiæ*, and are moreover reserved. For these cases we refer the reader to Vol. I., Nos. 682, 683. For the special powers of the Bishops of the United States, see above, Vol. I., No. 684.

[1] Cap. 5. 7 de sent. excom. in 6° (v. 11).
[2] C. 1. de major. in. 6° (1. 17.)
[3] Conc. Trid., sess. 24, c. 16 de Ref.
[4] Kober, Excom., p. 483.

Art. III.

What Superior can remit these Punishments, when they are "ab homine"?

3138. We come now to the *remission of correctional punishments, which are imposed " ab homine per sententiam specialem."* These punishments or censures being inflicted by a particular sentence of the ecclesiastical judge, and not by the law, are always, by that very fact, regarded as reserved, and therefore can, without being expressly reserved, be remitted *solely by that ecclesiastical Superior by whom they were inflicted, or by his successor in office, or by his representative or delegate, or by his higher Superior, and no one else.*[1] This follows from the principles already fully explained. This is, moreover, clearly required in the interests of proper discipline and order. For if the punishment inflicted by one Bishop or Superior could at will be remitted by another Bishop, all discipline, order, and respect for authority would cease.[2]

3139. We say, *or by his successor or representative;* this point needs no further explanation; since what we have said above on this matter applies here also.

3140. We say again, *or by his higher Superior.* The Metropolitan, being indeed, as we have seen, the Superior of his suffragan Bishops, though not *pleni juris*, can release from the censures of suffragans which are *ab homine per sententiam particularem* only an appeal and during visitation, but not otherwise. When a person upon whom a censure has been inflicted by his Bishop, *per sententiam specialem*, appeals to the Metropolitan against the censure, the latter can, nay, is *strictly bound* to admit and take cognizance of the appeal.

3141. In regard to the manner in which appeals against

---

[1] Arg. L. 3 ff. de re jud. (42. 1); Can. 51, dist. 1 de pœnit.
[2] Schmalz., l. 5, t. 39, n. 93; Kober, l.c., p. 452.

censures are to be made, prosecuted, and heard, the law of the Church is that the same rules are to be followed as in all other appeals.[1] These rules have been fully explained in this work, both in the first volume, pp. 193 sq., 425 sq., and in the second, pp. 286 sq., to which places we refer the reader, and also in this third volume, Nos. 3051 sq.

3142. From what has been said, it follows that, when a person who has incurred a censure *ab homine per sententiam specialem* leaves the diocese of his Ordinary who censured him, he nevertheless cannot be absolved by any other than the Bishop by whom the censure was inflicted. Likewise, when a person has committed a crime in a strange diocese and is placed under censure by the Bishop of the place, he cannot be absolved by his own Bishop, save with the consent of the Bishop who imposed the censure.

3143. Finally, what has been said concerning absolution from censures *ab homine per sententiam specialem* applies also to censures *a jure* when *ferendæ sententiæ*. For the latter, in order to be really contracted, must be inflicted by special sentence, and are therefore placed on the same footing with correctional punishments *ab homine per sententiam specialem*.

[1] Kober, l. c., p. 83.

CHAPTER XI.

FORMULA, CONDITIONS, AND MODES OF RELEASE FROM CORRECTIONAL PUNISHMENTS.

ART. I.

Formula of Absolution or Release.

3144. The law of the Church does not prescribe any particular form of absolution from censures or correctional punishments. It is sufficient that the *will to release or absolve be clearly manifested*. This may be done by word of mouth or in writing. Thus, when the Pope confers a benefice upon an excommunicate, he is regarded as *eo ipso* absolving him from the excommunication.[1]

3145. We say, *clearly manifested;* for the will alone does not suffice; it must be manifested by some *external sign, word, or action*. It is not absolutely necessary that the person to be absolved shall *be present;* for as a person who is absent can be put under censure, by letter, so can he be released from it in like manner.[2] Nay, a person can be absolved by proxy. Thus it will be seen that the release or absolution from censures differs in various ways from sacramental absolution from sin. It is not necessary to express in the absolution the cause, *i. e.*, crime, for which the censure was inflicted, though it is expedient to do so.

3146. While no particular form of absolution is prescribed, yet when the absolution is given *in foro interno* the general formula, which the confessor recites immediately before giving the sacramental absolution in confession, is generally used, namely : " Ego te absolvo ab omni vinculo

[1] S. C. C. 26 Apr. 1749.   [2] Schmalzg., l. 5, t. 39, n. 102.

excommunicationis, suspensionis, et interdicti, in quantum possum et tu indiges."

3147. Where the absolution is imparted *in foro externo*, it is advisable to employ the formula given in the Roman Ritual¹ and the Roman Pontifical² for absolution from censures *in foro externo*.³ The absolution must be given *externally* or *publicly* whenever the censure has been officially published.⁴ The same holds of the excommunication incurred for publicly striking an Ecclesiastic, even though no official publication of the censure has taken place.⁵ Stremler⁶ holds even that the same applies where a censure, though not officially published, is *notorious*.

ART. II.

Conditions of Release from these Punishments.

3148. Some conditions are required on the part of the person releasing, others on the part of the person released. I. *On the part of the Superior absolving* it is necessary (*a*) that he should have power to absolve; otherwise the absolution is invalid. (*b*) Next, the Superior, before giving the absolution, should obtain full and undoubted information that the person to be absolved is penitent and has receded from his obstinacy, and also demand from him a promise or guarantee that he will in future conduct himself properly.⁷ Nay, when the correctional punishment has been inflicted for atrocious and very grave crimes, such as scandalously violating churches, severely striking an Ecclesiastic, incendiarism, etc., the Superior must oblige him *to swear* that he will obey the commands of the Church, and not commit the offence again in future.⁸

---

[1] Tit. de sacramento pœnitentiæ.
[2] Tit. Ordo excommunicandi et absolvendi; Cf. cap. 28, de sent. excom. (v. 39).
[3] Varceno, p. 908.   [4] De Herdt, Praxis Rit., p. 50.   [5] Craiss., n. 6463.
[6] P. 243.   [7] Kober, Susp., p. 132; Id., Excom, p. 512.   [8] Cap. 10, 11 (v. 39).

Modes of Absolution or Release.

3149. (*c*) The Superior absolving must be free from *grave and unjust fear* (*metus*) and *violence* (*vis*). For it is plain that the competent judge or Superior must act with *free will*, that is, not be coerced, either by unjust fear or physical force, into giving the absolution. A release from censures extorted by grave and unjust fear or by violence is null and void.[1] (*d*) He must not be deceived as to the principal cause. Hence the absolution is void when it is obtained through false representations,[2] unless it is apparent that the Superior wishes to absolve, notwithstanding the deceit or misrepresentation.[3]

3150.—2. *On the part of the person to be absolved* it is necessary, though only on pain of the illicitness of the absolution, (*a*) that he should *personally ask* to be absolved. The reason is, that, as these punishments are imposed in order to bring the obstinate offender back to the path of virtue, they should not be remitted until he has receded from his criminal conduct. Now a person refusing to apply for absolution would certainly not show that he regrets his crimes. We say *though only on pain of illicitness;* hence, while a person may be absolved without his request and even against his will, it should not be done except for reasonable causes.[4]

3151. (*b*) He must also, as a rule, prior to being absolved, whether *in foro interno* or *in foro externo*, repair the scandal he has given, and make satisfaction for the injury or damage he has inflicted on a third party. We say, *as a rule;* for the following cases are excepted: *first*, where it is morally impossible to repair the scandal forthwith; *second*, where, in the case of injury to a third party, the latter condones the injury either expressly or tacitly; *third*, where the injured party refuses to accept a just satisfaction

---

[1] Cap. unic. de iis quæ metu in 6° (i. 20).
[2] Cap. 22 (v. 39); Kober, Susp., p. 134.
[3] Schmalzg., l. c., n. 99.   [4] Schmalzg., l. c., n. 100.

offered; *fourth*, where the person to be absolved is unable to make restitution, in which case, however, he must either give a proper guarantee or promise *on oath* to make restitution as soon as he can.[1]

ART. III.

Modes of Release from these Punishments.

3152. *Q.* In how many ways can a person be released from correctional punishments?

A. In these: 1. Generally speaking, and apart from special circumstances, the absolution or release from the censure is granted *absolutely and unconditionally*.

3153.—2. But there are cases where it is either inexpedient or impossible to grant the release in so perfect and complete a manner. The Superior may find himself obliged to make the absolution dependent *on certain conditions*, so that it will take effect only after these conditions are complied with, and not otherwise. Hence, if, for instance, the absolution is given thus: " Absolvo te si satisfeceris," the absolution will be valid from the moment it has been given. Yet its effects will be suspended until the condition is fulfilled. The moment this is done it takes effect of itself. But if the condition remains unfulfilled the absolution takes no effect whatever.[2]

3154. All agree that such absolution or release is valid and licit, where the condition is of the past or present. But some hold that when the condition relates to something *future*, the release is invalid. They argue chiefly that, as the *sacramental* absolution from sins cannot be imparted on a condition to be fulfilled in the future, so neither can the absolution from censures be given on a condition relating to the future. The opposite opinion, however, is to be

---

[1] Cap. Odoardus, de solut. ; Cap. 23 de V. S.   [2] Kober, Excom., p. 537.

Modes of Absolution or Release. 271

retained as the true one.[1] For it is true, indeed, that the sacramental absolution cannot be validly conferred as above. But it is also true that the release from censures is not a *sacramental act*, but a *judicial sentence, act, or decree*, and therefore depends on the will of the ecclesiastical judge giving it. Therefore the latter can suspend the effect or make it contingent on a future condition. A sacrament, on the other hand, by virtue of divine institution, produces its effect *ex opere operato, i.e.*, at once and immediately, as soon as the proper matter and form are present. Hence the effect of a sacrament cannot be suspended by a minister. Nevertheless, the *absolutio conditionata* from censures must always be considered as the *exception to the rule*, and should not be given by the ecclesiastical judge except for good and sufficient reasons of necessity or utility.[2]

3155.—3. The *absolutio ad cautelam* is the next mode of releasing from censures. It is given either as a *precautionary measure* in the exercise of *voluntary* jurisdiction, or as a *provisional and precautionary measure* in the course of the exercise of *contentious* jurisdiction. There are many ecclesiastical acts which, when performed by or in favor of a person who is under censure, are either invalid or at least entail certain disadvantages upon him. In order to prevent such invalidity or disadvantage, and to cut off all possible doubt and scruple of conscience, the absolution *ad cautelam* is given, so that, if the party has really incurred a censure of which he is supposed to be entirely ignorant, he may not suffer therefrom. Thus, in order to remove any possible doubt as to the validity of the sacramental absolution, the absolution *ad cautelam* is always imparted by the Confessor in the tribunal of penance, immediately prior to giving the sacramental absolution, in these words: " Dominus noster Jesus Christus te absolvat et ego auctoritate

---

[1] Schmalzg., l. 5, t. 39, n. 103.   [2] Kober, l. c., p. 540.

ipsius *te absolvo omni vinculo excommunicationis (suspensionis) et interdicti, in quantum possum et tu indiges.*"[1] In like manner it is also frequently imparted in advance of the conferring of orders, of appointments to ecclesiastical offices or benefices, and of the conferring of other favors and privileges, in order to remove any possible obstacle to the validity of these acts.[2] In all these cases it is evident that the absolution *ad cautelam* is imparted (*a*) in the course of the exercise of *voluntary* jurisdiction, (*b*) and either *in foro interno* or *externo*. It is also plain that the absolution *ad cautelam*, in the above cases, supposes that the censure is *unknown*.

3156. Besides, the absolution *ad cautelam* is granted also in *judicial proceedings* and in the exercise of *contentious jurisdiction*, where it is *doubtful* whether a particular censure, inflicted upon a person, is valid or not. For, as we have shown above,[3] when a person who is visited with censure by his Bishop appeals on the ground of nullity of the censure, he is to be first provisionally absolved *ad cautelam*, so that he is free from the censure during the hearing of the appeal. As will be seen, this sort of absolution is made use of only where there is doubt as to the existence of the censure, or its validity or justice, but never where it is certain that a person has been validly and justly put under censure.

3157.—4. *Ad reincidentiam.* This mode of absolving, which occurs quite frequently, takes place when the absolution or release is granted, not *permanently*, but merely for a *certain space of time*, and with the proviso that, under certain contingencies, the censure shall be *ipso facto* reincurred, in all its extent.[4] Thus a person under a reserved censure, who, either because he is *in articulo mortis* or because of some other legitimate reason, cannot present himself for

[1] Rit. Rom. de Sacr. pœnit.
[2] Cap. Super eo 51 (v. 39).
[3] Supra., n. 3037.
[4] Kober, Excom., p. 547.

Modes of Absolution or Release.

absolution to the Superior reserving, and who is, on that account, validly absolved for the time being by a priest or confessor having otherwise no power to grant the absolution, must, according to the express law of the Church, present himself to the Superior reserving and receive his commands, as soon as he becomes well or the obstacle ceases.[1] If he culpably fails to do so, he falls *ipso facto* again into the censure from which he was absolved.[2]

3158. This absolution differs, among other things, from the conditional absolution in this, that, while the latter does not produce its effect immediately, *but remains suspended* until the condition *is fulfilled, the former takes effect at once* and remains in force until it is *ipso facto* revoked by the culpable failure on the part of the person absolved, *v.g.*, to present himself to the proper Superior.

3159.—5. Finally, the release from the correctional punishment may be imparted *only as to a certain effect, v.g.*, in order that a person under excommunication may become qualified to act as witness, or also as appellant against his Bishop. In this case, however, he is not freed from the censure itself, but only from some of its effects.[3]

[1] Supra, n. 682. [2] Cap. 22, de sent. excom. in 6º (v. 11.)
[3] Reiff., l. 5, t. 39, n. 266.

SECTION II.

Repressive Reform Punishments in Particular.

CHAPTER I.

EXCOMMUNICATION.

3160. Having, in the preceding chapter, discussed correctional punishments in general, we shall now take up each one in particular. As we have seen, there are chiefly three correctional punishments, namely, excommunication, suspension, and interdict. In the present chapter we shall confine ourselves to excommunication, reserving suspension and interdict for the two succeeding chapters.

ART. I.

Correct Notion of Excommunication.

3161. *The right of expelling refractory members is lodged in every society.*—Every human society which has an external organization must possess the right to expel from its body or membership any refractory member who, by his own fault, has rendered himself unworthy of belonging to it and enjoying its benefits and advantages. For it is plain that the expulsion of stubborn and ungovernable members is not only necessary to protect the honor and good name of a society, but, moreover, the only means of preserving its very existence. Hence we see, as a matter of fact, that every society, association, club, or guild, no matter how small, has exercised and does exercise this power. Civil society or the State makes use of this power on a large scale. It cuts off bad and unruly citizens from communication with others, by imprisonment, exile, and even death.

3162. *This right of expulsion is vested more particularly in religious societies.*—If this right is justly vested in every society or association, even though it has but a material and secular end in view, with how much greater reason should it not be lodged in a *religious* society, that has for its object the *sanctification* of its members. Our natural sense of justice and propriety demands that such a society shall exclude from its community all those members who, though repeatedly warned, nevertheless continue persistently to give scandal and to bring religion itself into contempt by their wicked life.[1] Only by exercising the right in question and by ejecting from its pale obdurate offenders can such a society preserve its own dignity, honor, and usefulness among men.

3163. Hence we find that even the Pagan and heathen religions of old made use of this punishment.[2] Among the Jews the right of expulsion from the pale of the Hebrew synagogue was exercised on a large scale.[3] At the present day we see that all the Protestant sects exercise this right of expulsion even more rigidly at times than the Catholic Church.[4] There can be no doubt therefore that this power is also vested in the Catholic Church, the only true Church of God, and that for two reasons: *first*, because she is an eternal society, and as such she must of necessity possess the means to enforce her rules and regulations, and therefore, to expel refractory members; *second*, because our Lord expressly wills it. For as He expressly authorized his apostles and their successors to *receive* men into the Church, so He also expressly gave them power to *expel* from her bosom such as had proved unworthy members.[5]

[1] Kober, Excom., p. 2.
[2] Cf. Cæsar, de Bell. Gall. l. 6., c. 13; Taciti Germania, c. 6. [3] Cf. Esra, x. 8.
[4] Cf. Const. of Ref. Church in America, p. 47; Discipline of the Meth. Ep. Church, pp. 134 sq.
[5] Cf. Matth. xviii. 15 sq.

3164. *True idea of excommunication.*—It would be a mistake to suppose that excommunication is merely an *external* exclusion from the Church, or the privation of the society or company of the faithful; for it reaches farther and extends to the *soul itself*, and deprives it of spiritual and interior favors.[1] It is true that it can never of itself separate a man from God and divine grace. Mortal sin alone can do so. Consequently, if excommunication is inflicted, even though it be with the observance of all the legal formalities, upon an innocent person, that is, one who is not guilty of mortal sin, it produces no effect whatever, so far as concerns his relations with God.

3165. But when a person has separated himself from God by mortal sin, the excommunication certainly aggravates the unhappy state of such a person, adding misery to misery, by depriving the sinner, who has lost the grace of God, of the helps and graces which the Church communicates to her children by the sacraments, of the merits and intercession of the saints in heaven, and of the public prayers and merits of the faithful on earth. Hence excommunication is fitly termed *a spiritual death, a giving over to Satan, the beginning of eternal damnation.*[2] Only a person who can fully realize what an inestimable blessing it is to be a child of the true Church can form a correct estimate of the severity of this punishment. It is the *greatest*, the *severest* punishment the Church can inflict.

3166. Hence it should not be imposed save in the *most extreme cases*, as a last resort, and after all other milder punishments have been vainly applied. The chief object of excommunication, as we have seen, *is to bring the sinner back to repentance.* He is delivered over to Satan, *in order that his spirit may be saved.*[3] This, however, is not the only aim of this punishment. A second end is, *to preserve the honor*

---

[1] Kober, l. c., p. 17.   [2] Kober, l. c., pp. 20, 21.   [3] II. Cor. xiii. 10.

and dignity of the Church. For, as we have seen, it would redound to the disgrace of the Church, if she allowed members to remain in her pale whose lives are shameful and profligate.

3167. Finally, a third object is *the good of the other faithful.* The excommunication is to keep them from being infected by the excommunicate, and deter them from following his bad example.[1] Excommunication, as here understood, may therefore be defined as *the expulsion from the external and internal membership of the Church, the complete withdrawal of all the graces and privileges acquired by baptism, the separation from the living body of Christ, and a thrusting back into the helpless state of unredeemed man.*[2] Schmalzgruber thus briefly defines it "as a correctional punishment instituted by the Church, by which the excommunicate is separated from the communion or fellowship of the faithful."

3168. From this it will appear that excommunication is a total exclusion from all the rights and privileges which a member of the Church possesses, whether in his capacity of simple laic or of an Ecclesiastic. Consequently laics who are excommunicated as *vitandi* are debarred from the right to receive the sacraments, or assist at Mass and other ecclesiastical functions, or to receive Christian burial, or to associate with the faithful, even in purely human matters.

3169. If the excommunicate be an Ecclesiastic, he incurs, besides the above disabilities of lay excommunicates, the loss of all his privileges and rights *as an Ecclesiastic.* Therefore he becomes suspended *ab officio et beneficio.* Hence he cannot say Mass, nor administer the Sacraments, nor perform any other sacred function; neither can he exercise any ecclesiastical jurisdiction, nor be appointed to any ecclesiastical office, dignity, or benefice. It may, therefore, be said, speaking in general, that, as by *baptism*

---

[1] Kober, l. c., p. 29.   [2] Ib., p. 32.   [3] L. v., t. 39, n. 112.

a person becomes a member of the Church and acquires all the rights flowing from this membership, so by excommunication he forfeits, for the time being, all these rights. And as by *ordination* a baptized person becomes an officer of the Church and obtains certain powers, so by excommunication he is forbidden to exercise these powers.

ART. II.

How many Kinds of Excommunication are there?

3170. Excommunication is distinguished into *major*, which is a complete expulsion from the communion of the faithful, and deprives the excommunicate of all ecclesiastical benefits, and *minor*, which divests a person merely of the *communicatio passiva, v.g.*, of the right to be appointed to an ecclesiastical office or benefice. Prior to the Const. *Apostolicæ Sedis*, issued by Pope Pius IX., of blessed memory, in 1869, everybody communicating with an excommunicate *vitandus in crimine criminoso* incurred major excommunication, and those having intercourse with him *in divinis*, minor. At the present day, the minor excommunication, as inflicted by the common law of the Church, is entirely done away with, since no mention of it occurs in the Const. *Apostolicæ Sedis* of Pius IX.[1]

3171. But the major excommunication incurred for having intercourse with an excommunicate still exists, though it is only incurred in these two cases: 1. Where a person communicates *in crimine criminoso* with a person who is by name excommunicated *by the Pope*, not by any other Superior; in other words, where a person knowingly aids and abets (for that is the meaning of *communicare in crimine criminoso*) another in the very crime for which he has been nominally excommunicated by the Sovereign

---

[1] Com. Reat., p. 58; Varc., p. 914; Konings, n. 1673: Avanz., n. 111.

Excommunication.

Pontiff.[1]   2. Where Ecclesiastics knowingly and wilfully communicate *in divinis* with persons who are *by name* excommunicated by the Roman Pontiff, and allow them to perform *officia divina, i.e.*, those functions which ecclesiastics perform as such or as ministers of the Church,[2] *v.g.*, to say Mass, or assist at Mass.

3172. Major excommunication, which, as we have seen, excludes a person from the Church and the society and communion of the faithful,[3] is called *anathema*, when it is inflicted against heresy or with certain impressive ceremonies, namely, when the Bishop pronounces it surrounded by twelve priests in sacred vestments and holding in their hands lighted torches, which they then throw down and tread under foot, meanwhile uttering certain words of malediction.[4] By the word excommunication, used without any qualification, is always meant major excommunication.[5] Excommunication is divided, moreover, into that *a jure* and that *ab homine;* that which is *ferendæ* and that which is *latæ sententiæ;* that which is just and unjust, valid or invalid. All these phrases have been already explained by us.

[1] This is the 16th excommunication reserved simply to the Pope, in the Const. *Apostolicæ Sedis* of Pius IX. and is thus given in this *Const.* : " Communicantes cum excommunicato nominatim a Papa in crimine criminoso, ei scilicet impendendo auxilium vel favorem."

[2] The Const. *Apostolicæ Sedis* of Pius IX. thus expresses this excommunication : " Clerici scienter et sponte communicantes in divinis cum personis a Romano Pontifice nominatim excommunicatis et ipsos in officiis recipientes."—Cf. Com. in Const. *Apostolicæ Sedis,* Reate, :874, n. 112, p. 58.

[3] Devoti, l. 4, t. 18, n. 7.   [5] Can. Debent, 106, c. 11, q. 3; Stremler, p. 254.

[4] Cap. 59, de sent. excom.

Art. III.

What Excommunicates are to be shunned?

§ 1. *Former Discipline.*

3173. Prior to the Council of Constance (1414-1418), the faithful were bound to *shun*, both in a *social* and *religious* point of view, all persons who had contracted major excommunication, whether *a jure* and *ipso facto* or *ab homine*, and by special sentence, and that even though their excommunication was not officially published. When the crime was public the faithful had to shun the excommunicate *publicly;* when it was occult, *i.e.*, known to a few persons only, the latter were obliged to avoid him *in private*. Now in those days a great many crimes had excommunication *ipso facto* annexed. Hence large numbers of the faithful incurred excommunication and had to be shunned. Add the uncertainty of knowing for certain whether they were really excommunicated. For frequently no judicial sentence or publication preceded the punishment or censure. The faithful were consequently obliged, not unfrequently, to rely solely upon their *own private judgment* as to whether such a particular person had incurred excommunication or not.

§ 2. *Present Discipline.*

3174. Naturally enough, many grave doubts and harassing perplexities arose from such a state of things. Persons found it not unfrequently difficult to tell whether they could associate with others or not. Many, therefore, very properly demanded that the obligation of avoiding excommunicates should be restricted to those cases where a clear judicial sentence, made properly public, left no uncertainty whatever in the matter. In view of these circumstances Pope Martin V. issued his celebrated Bull *Ad Vitanda* in the

Council of Constance, by which he changed the law as it stood then, and enacted that in future the faithful were not bound to avoid excommunicates, except (*a*) when they had been excommunicated by name, (*b*) and when, moreover, their excommunication had been officially made public, and that not merely in general, but specially and expressly.

3175. Here are the words of the Pope: "Ad vitanda scandala et multa pericula, quæ conscientiis timoratis contingere possunt " (here then is pointed out the scope of the Bull, as explained above), "Christifidelibus tenore præsentium misericorditer indulgemus, quod nemo deinceps a communione alicujus, sacramentorum administratione vel receptione, aut aliis quibuscumque divinis, intus et extra, prætextu cujuscumque sententiæ aut censuræ ecclesiasticæ a jure vel ab homine generaliter promulgatæ teneatur abstinere, nisi sententia vel censura hujusmodi fuerit lata contra personam . . . . certam *a judice publicata vel denuntiata specialiter et expresse* . . . . salvo si quem pro sacrilega manuum injectione in clericum sententiam latam a canone adeo notorie constiterit incidisse, quod factum non possit aliqua tergiversatione celari, nec aliquo suffragio excusari, nam a communione illius, licet denuntiatus non fuerit, volumus abstineri juxta canonicas sanctiones."[1] This rule is a safe guide to the faithful in their conduct towards persons under excommunication, though it is, at the same time, a great protection to those excommunicates whose sentence is not published.[2]

3176. It is true that the Council of Basle (1435), Sess. XX., Cap. 2, and the Fifth Council of the Lateran (1512-1517), Sess. XI., partly repealed the above favorable legislation of the Council of Constance, by enacting that the faithful were bound to shun all excommunicates whose excommunication was *public*, or *notorious*, *even though their excommunication had*

---

[1] Ap. Kober, Excom., p. 248. [2] München, l. c., vol. ii., p. 193.

not been officially made public. But the Constitution of Pope Martin V. nevertheless remained and still remains in full force. Thus Pope Benedict XIV. writes: " In suo semper vigore permansit (Const. *Ad Vitanda*), non obstantibus contrariis Constitutionibus Conciliorum Basiliensis et Lateranensis." [1] It is true that Fagnani and some other canonists hold that the bull of Martin V. was abrogated by the subsequent decrees of Basle and the Lateran. But, as Pope Benedict XIV. says: [2] " Ejus (Fagnani) tamen doctrina fere communiter rejecta est, cum ubique sit recepta laudata Const. *Ad Vitanda*." [2]

3177. The law, then, of the Church, as it is in force at the present day, is that the faithful are not bound to shun the company or society of excommunicates, except when the latter are *publicly denounced by name as having incurred excommunication.* This rule has now, after the Const. *Apostolicæ Sedis* of Pius IX., no exceptions whatever. For while it is true that, by virtue of the Const. *Ad Vitanda* of Pope Martin V., persons who were *notoriously* guilty of laying violent hands on or of ill-treating Ecclesiastics [4] had to be shunned, both in religious and social intercourse, by the faithful, even though their excommunication had not been published officially, yet by general custom to the contrary, [5] and by the Const. *Apostolicæ Sedis* of Pius IX., [6] these *notorii percussores clericorum* need no longer be shunned, save when they are officially and by name published as excommunicates. [7]

3178. Hence it may be said that by the Const. *Ad Vitanda* and the Const. *Apostolicæ Sedis* of Pope Pius IX. all excommunications and other correctional punishments, namely

[1] De Syn., l. 6, c. 5, n. 2.   [2] Ib., l. 12, c. 5, n. 4.
[3] Cf. München, l.c., p. 192 ; Kober, l.c., pp. 250–255.
[4] Cf. Can. 29, C. 17, q. 4. This famous canon, *Si quis suadente diabolo*, was enacted by Pope Innocent III. and published by him in the Lateran Council, in 1139.
[5] Prael. S. Sulp., vol. iii., p. 272.
[6] Cf. Const. *Ap. Sedis*, excom. 2, R. P., res. simpl.
[7] Soglia—Vecchiotti, vol. ii., p. 329 ; Cf. Craiss., n. 6504.

suspension and interdict, which are imposed *a jure* and are *latæ sententiæ*, are, so long as the censure is not published, changed in the external forum into correctional punishments which are *ferendæ sententiæ*, so far as concerns the obligations incumbent on the faithful to shun the excommunicate, both in religious and social matters.[1]

3179. From what has been said it follows that no person excommunicated *a jure*, even though he be notoriously guilty of striking or ill-treating an Ecclesiastic or religious, and no matter how well-known it may be that he has fallen under excommunication, need be shunned by the faithful. The reason is that such a person has not been excommunicated *by name* (the law, whether general or particular, never excommunicates by name, as is plain) nor publicly denounced by the ecclesiastical judge.

3180. Whenever, therefore, a person has incurred excommunication, as decreed by law, *v.g.*, by the Const. *Apostolicæ Sedis* of Pope Pius IX., in order that the faithful may be obliged to avoid his company, whether in the religious or in the social and civil life, it is necessary that he be cited by his Superior for trial,[2] and that, upon conviction, the sentence be pronounced, declaring that he is guilty of the crime, and has consequently fallen under excommunication. Afterwards, this sentence must be officially promulgated or made public.[3] In like manner, when a person is visited with excommunication *ab homine*, and *per sententiam particularem*, namely when, having been placed on trial for crime and found guilty, he is by judicial sentence excommunicated, he need not be shunned by the faithful, except after this sentence has been officially made public by the judge.

[1] Prael. S. Sulp., l.c., p. 272.

[2] Except, of course, where the crime is altogether *notorious*, in which case, as we have seen, no trial is needed, at least *theoretically speaking*. For, practically speaking, a trial is required even where the crime is notorious.

[3] Craiss., n. 6496.

§ 3. *Publication of the Excommunication.*

3181. How is this *publication* to be made? It must be made (*a*) *officially*, *i.e.*, by the judge; (*b*) *publicly*, *i.e.*, in a *public place*, so that it can reach the whole community. Hence the sentence of the ecclesiastical judge pronounced after the trial in the presence of the parties is not a publication as here understood. Provided the publication be made in a public manner or place, *v.g.*, in the parochial church or public square of the city, it is immaterial whether it takes place (1) *viva voce*, *v.g.*, by public announcement in the parochial church during the time of divine service, when there is a concourse of people, (2) or *in writing*, *v.g.*, by placards posted in a public place or on the doors of a church, or published in newspapers.

§ 4. *Intercourse of the Faithful with " tolerati."*

3182. At present, therefore, all persons who are excommunicated, but whose excommunication *is not published* in the manner above set forth, need not be shunned by the faithful. Hence they are called *tolerati*, or *non vitandi*, in contradistinction to the *vitandi*, or those whose company and society the faithful are strictly bound to avoid. Observe, we say the faithful are *not obliged* to shun the society of an *excommunicatus toleratus*. For they *may*, if they choose, shun him, and that even publicly, when it is publicly known that he has incurred excommunication. In fact, not unfrequently it may be very praiseworthy to avoid the company of excommunicates who are *tolerated*, and thus to isolate them, both in order to bring them more speedily to a sense of their duty, and to guard against the danger arising from bad company.

3183. Observe, moreover, that the *Const.* of Pope Martin V., which, as above explained, is at present the law of the Church, was made *solely in favor of the faithful*, not of the excommunicate himself. The latter's status was not, *per se*, ameliorated. Thus the above *Const.* expressly says: " Per hoc tamen hujusmodi excommunicatos non intendimus relevare." Hence a person who is excommunicated as *toleratus* cannot, of his own accord, associate with the faithful. We say, *of his own accord;* for, as we shall see further on, he may administer the sacraments to the *faithful*, etc., *when he is asked* by them to do so.[1]

3184. Here the question arises, whether the faithful *can ask for and receive the sacraments* from an excommunicate who is tolerated (supposing him to be a priest) and otherwise associate with him in *religious matters.* Before answering we premise: 1. We say, *in religious matters;* for it is perfectly plain from what has been said that the faithful can keep up full intercourse with an excommunicate who is *toleratus, in social and civil matters—in humanis:* 2. The difficulty, in the case, arises from the fact that on the one hand, by the *Const.* of Pope Martin V., as still in force, the excommunicate *toleratus* is not allowed himself to have any intercourse, *in divinis,* with the rest of the faithful, while on the other the latter are allowed thus to associate with him.

3185. We now answer: There are two opinions. Some canonists hold the negative, on the ground that the excommunicate would thus be induced to perform an act which he is forbidden to perform, and thus to commit sin.[2] Others— whose opinion is the more probable —affirm that the faithful can without doubt ask and receive the sacraments in the case from one who is *toleratus,* even when they know him to be under excommunication. For the Const. *Ad Vitanda* clearly allows them to keep up full *religious intercourse* with these excommunicates. Accidentally, however, charity may oblige the faithful not to ask the sacraments from such an excommunicate, when they know him to be in the state of

[1] Stremler, l. c., p. 268.   [2] Ib.

mortal sin, lest they should thus become the occasion of the sacrilegious administration of the sacraments. But when there is a good cause, *v. g.*, when a person wishes to place himself in the state of grace, or make the Easter duty, he is not even bound by charity to refrain from asking for the sacraments from such excommunicates.

ART. IV.

Canonical effects produced by Excommunication, even at present.

3186. Before answering, we premise first, these effects may be considered (*a*) in reference to the person who is excommunicated: (*b*) to the other faithful who may come into contact with him. In relation to the *latter*, the effects are that they are bound, as we have seen, to shun and avoid the excommunicate (provided he is *vitandus*), like a leper spreading around him moral contagion and misfortune.[1] In regard to the *excommunicate himself* (whether he be *toleratus* or *vitandus*), the effect is a total expulsion from the Church, so that he is no longer considered a member of the Church, loses all the rights he has acquired by baptism, and is therefore completely stripped of all the rights and privileges attaching to membership of the Church, and which are common to and possessed by all the members of the Church, in their capacity of members.

3187. These effects show how pitiable is the state of an excommunicate. To be not only deprived of all those spiritual graces and benefits which the Church has at her disposal and which are accessible to all the other faithful and, so to say, their common heritage, but also to be cut off from all intercourse, both religious and social, political and civil, with them, is an awful punishment.[2]. It is plain that the law which prohibits the faithful from having any intercourse

[1] Cf. München, l. c., vol. ii., p. 167.   [2] München, l. c.

whatever, social or religious, with the excommunicate who is *vitandus*, is a natural consequence and outgrowth of excommunication. For in this manner alone will the faithful show their disapproval and abhorrence of the excommunicate's rebellious conduct and also be preserved from the sinful contagion, and the excommunicate himself be more easily brought back to a sense of duty, by his utter isolation.

3188. Hence also excommunication is very justly compared by canonists to the state of a citizen condemned to exile.[1] For, as a Roman citizen condemned to exile lost all his rights of citizenship, so also does an excommunicate become divested of all his rights as a citizen of the city of God on earth, *i.e.*, as a member of the true Church. Excommunication, however, is essentially, as to its duration, of a *temporary character.* It is, as we have seen, a spiritual *medicine*, a *reformatory* punishment. Consequently it must be revoked as soon as the delinquent has given proofs of amendment. Then must his spiritual exile cease, and the penitent culprit be reinstated in his rights as a member of the Church.[2]

3189. We premise *secondly*, excommunication (we always speak of *major* excommunication, as the *minor* no longer exists) cuts a person off from the communion of the Church, that is, expels him from the bosom of the Church, so far as concerns his *rights* and *privileges* as a member of the Church, but not so far as regards his *duties* and *obligations.* Hence a person excommunicated remains subject to the laws of the Church, just as a person deprived of his rights of citizenship is nevertheless bound by the laws of the land.[3]

3190. We premise *thirdly*. In order to understand better what benefits we are deprived of by excommunication, we

[1] St. Cyprian calls excommunication " an *exile* from the Church of Christ." Ep. 49. apud München, l. c., p. 167.
[2] München, l. c., p. 166.   [3] Stremler, l. c., p. 264.

must distinguish between the various kinds of spiritual benefits a Christian or member of the Church may possess. These benefits are of three kinds; 1. Those which are *purely interior*, namely faith, hope, and charity, divine grace. These constitute the supernatural bond, which unites the faithful to our Lord. 2. Those which are *purely exterior*, namely, which form that communion or fellowship that is simply external, namely the ordinary relations of social, civil, or secular life, such as conversing together, in a word, all the acts of daily social intercourse. 3. Finally those benefits which make up the *mixed communion*, namely certain ecclesiastical and exterior acts or ceremonies that produce spiritual favors and blessings, by virtue of their institution, as the sacraments, the public prayers or suffrages of the Church, the sacrifice of the Mass, benedictions, and other religious ceremonies and public acts of divine worship; the satisfactions and merits of our Lord and the Blessed Virgin and the Saints, as contained in the treasury of the Church and dispensed by her to the faithful by means of indulgences.

3191. Now it is certain, as has already been noted, that excommunication does not dispossess a person of the goods of the first class. For they do not depend on, and are not directly subject to the power of the Church. She is not the *exclusive* dispenser of them, since God often communicates them *directly* to the soul, without the Church's intermediary. Thus a person who has incurred excommunication for a crime may by contrition be reinstated in the grace of God, and yet continue to be excommunicated and to suffer all the effects of the excommunication.

3192. Therefore excommunication divests a person only of the benefits of the second and of the third class, namely of those privileges which we have called *purely external*, and also of those which are *mixed*. To understand this more fully, we must bear in mind that the Church is the *mystical body of Christ;* that the faithful are the members of this body. "We being many," says St. Paul,[1] "are *one body in Christ*, and every one, members one of another." Of this body, Christ is the head. Now, as in the natural body of man the various members are constantly influenced, acted upon, and directed by the head, so in the mystical body of our Lord—the Church—Christ unceasingly directs, assists, and illumines those who are members of this mystical body. Thus St. Paul writes: "We may in all things grow up in him who is the head; from whom the whole body, being compacted and fitly joined together, by what every joint supplieth, according to the operation in the measure of every part, maketh increase of the body, unto the edifying of itself in charity."[2]

3193. Of the gifts and benefits that accrue to us through this membership with Christ's mystical body some flow more directly from our Lord Himself, as the head; others more directly from the Church, to which our Lord communicated many gifts to be distributed by her among the faithful, through the sacraments, public prayers, etc. Now, as we have seen, excommunication deprives us of all those benefits which our Lord has committed to her as the sole dispenser, namely of the benefits of the *mixed* and *purely external* communion, but not, at least *per se*, of those which are *internal*.

3194. Having thus far spoken, in *general*, of the effects produced by the punishment under discussion, we now come to its *particular* consequences, both as regards the person under excommunication, and others. We shall briefly treat of each effect under a separate heading.

§ 1. *Exclusion from the Sacraments.*

3195. The first effect is exclusion from the sacraments. An excommunicate, whether he be *vitandus* or simply *tolera-*

---

[1] Rom. xii. 5.   [2] Ephes. iv. 15, 16.

tus, cannot lawfully receive any of the sacraments of the Church except (*a*) in *articulo mortis*, when he can be admitted to the Sacraments of penance, the Blessed Eucharist, and Extreme Unction,[1] and (*b*) unless he is excused by invincible ignorance, the fear of death, of mutilation, loss of property, or of any other grave harm or evil, bodily or spiritual, and then apart from any contempt of the censure.[2] The reason of this exclusion from the sacraments is plain. For evidently a person who has been expelled from the Church and the society of the faithful *cannot be allowed to receive her greatest spiritual favors*, to which her good and faithful children alone are entitled. Moreover, the very end and aim of the expulsion is to bring the person expelled back to a sense of duty, by withdrawing from him all his former ecclesiastical privileges, which attach to the membership of the Church.[3]

3196. We have said, *whether he be "vitandus" or simply "toleratus;"* for the prohibition applies not only to those whose excommunication has been officially made public, and who must therefore be *shunned* by the faithful (*denuntiati, vitandi*), but also to the *tolerati*. For the Const. *Ad Vitanda* of Pope Martin V. has made no change whatever *in favor of the excommunicate himself*. If a person who is under excommunication, out of the above cases of necessity, receives any of the sacraments, he commits indeed a mortal sin, nay, is guilty of sacrilege, but he does not incur any special ecclesiastical punishment. Yet, while the law of the Church has not laid down any specific punishment in the case, it is discretionary with the ecclesiastical judge or Superior to inflict such punishments in the case as he may deem proper. However, in the case of a person excommunicated who *knowingly*,—*i. e.*, who knows he is under excommunication and that the reception of orders is

---

[1] Præl. S. Sulp., l. c., n. 770.
[2] Craiss., n. 6509.
[3] Kober, l. c., p. 280.
[4] Kober, l. c., p. 282.

forbidden to excommunicates—receives *orders*, the law expressly provides that he shall be forever deposed by the ecclesiastical Superior.[1]

3197. From the fact that excommunicates are forbidden to receive, it follows as a logical and necessary consequence, that priests and other ministers of the Church are obliged to refuse to administer the sacraments to persons who are excommunicated, though only when the latter are *vitandi*.[2] For such administration would be a *communicatio in divinis* with such excommunicates as are to be *shunned*. A priest or other Ecclesiastic who nevertheless *knowingly* and *wilfully*, and therefore maliciously, administers the sacraments to them commits a mortal sin and, moreover, incurs at present, according to the Const. *Apostolicæ Sedis* of Pius IX., excommunication reserved *simpliciter* to the Pope, if the excommunicates in the case are such as have by name been excommunicated by the Pope himself and publicly denounced as such.[3]

3198. We say, *by the Pope himself;* for, when an Ecclesiastic administers the sacraments to persons excommunicated by name and denounced as such *by the Bishop or other lawful Superior*, he incurs *ipso facto* only the interdict *ab ingressu ecclesiæ*, as appears from the Const. *Apostolicæ Sedis* of Pope Pius IX., which reads: "Scienter celebrantes vel celebrari facientes divina in locis ab Ordinario, vel delegato judice, vel a jure interdictis, aut nominatim excommunicatos ad divina officia, *seu ecclesiastica sacramenta*, vel ecclesiasticam sepulturam admittentes, interdictum ab ingressu ecclesiæ ipso jure incurrunt, donec ad arbitrium ejus, cujus sententiam comtempserunt, competenter satisfecerint."[4]

3199. We have said, *though only when the latter are vitandi;* for at present it is allowed, as we have seen, to communicate

---
[1] Cap. 32 de sent. excom. (v. 39); Ib. *Glossa*, v. *ordinibus*.
[2] Cap. 18 de sent. excom. (v. 39).   [3] Cf. supra, n. 3043.
[4] Const. Ap. Sedis 1869, Interd. lat. sent., res. ii.

even *in divinis* with those excommunicates who are *tolerati*. Hence ecclesiastics who administer the sacraments to *tolerati* do not incur the above or any other ecclesiastical punishment. However, it must not be imagined that on this account a priest is *altogether free* to administer the sacraments to *tolerati*. For the general rule that unworthy persons are not to be admitted to the sacraments must be applied also to the excommunicates in question. Besides, a priest who without cause admits such persons to the sacraments might easily confirm them in their obstinate and perverse conduct, and moreover cause great scandal among the faithful. There can be no doubt, therefore, that a priest who, wilfully and without a reasonable excuse, administers the sacraments to *tolerati*, commits a mortal sin.[1]

§ 2. *Excommunicates cannot administer the Sacraments.*

3200. It is manifest that a person who is expelled from the bosom of the Church, and who is to be considered as a heathen and publican, cannot, with any propriety or decency, be allowed to dispense and administer her graces and means of salvation and her choicest gifts; nor to be her representative and authorized agent in the performance of holy functions.[2] Hence a person, or rather a priest or other Ecclesiastic under excommunication, *is strictly forbidden to administer the sacraments, or, to say Mass, or, in general, to perform any ecclesiastical or sacred function whatever.*[3] This is the general rule, which applies equally to the *vitandi* and the *tolerati*.

3201. Like all rules, however, this one also has its exceptions. Here a distinction should be drawn between an excommunicate *who is to be shunned*, and one *who need not be shunned*. The former—a *vitandus*—can administer the sacraments— only (*a*) in case of extreme necessity, namely, to

[1] Kober, L c., pp. 285, 286.   [2] Ib., p. 290.
[3] Arg. cap. ult. de cler. exc. min. (v. 27); Kober, l. c., p. 290.

persons who are *in articulo mortis*, and who cannot receive the sacraments from another priest. But what sacraments can the *vitandus* administer to the dying person in the case? It is admitted by canonists that he can administer Baptism and Penance, since these sacraments are of the greatest necessity. It is disputed whether he can confer the Sacraments of the Eucharist and Extreme Unction. With Kober[1] we hold that he can also administer the Blessed Eucharist, or rather Viaticum, in the case. For, if the law of the Church allows a person who is in need to receive bread and other food from the hands of a *vitandus*, why should this same law make it unlawful for a dying person to receive the Bread of Heaven from such a person?[2] It is generally conceded by canonists that the other sacraments —namely, Confirmation, Extreme Unction, Holy Orders, and Matrimony, cannot be administered by the *vitandus*, even to a person *in articulo mortis*. For these sacraments are in no sense absolutely necessary to salvation. However, in regard to Extreme Unction and Matrimony Kober[3] allows certain exceptions.

3202. (*b*) Secondly, the *vitandus* is authorized to administer the sacraments, (not only some, but all the sacraments) and also perform other sacred functions, whenever he is, so to say, *compelled* to do so, either by *force* (*vi*) or *grave fear* (*metu gravi*), *v. g.*, when he is threatened with death, mutilation, or loss of his property, and also when, being an *occult*[4] excommunicate, he would, by omitting those actions, manifest his crime and thus defame himself or incur other serious injury.[5] For the law of the Church does not bind under such grave disadvantages.

3203. The *toleratus*, on the other hand, can administer the sacraments and perform ecclesiastical functions, not only in

---

[1] l. c., p. 296.   [2] Cf. Schmalzg., l. 5, t. 39, n. 145.   [3] L. c., p. 267.
[4] The excommunication of a *vitandus* may be occult in some places.
[5] Supra n. 1716 sq.; Kober, l. c., p. 291.

the above cases, in which a *vitandus* can, *but also whenever he is asked expressly or tacitly by the faithful to do so.* For, as was seen, the Const. *Ad Vitanda* of Pope Martin V. allows the faithful to communicate, not only *in humanis* but also *in divinis*, with a *toleratus*; they have, consequently, speaking in general, *a right* to ask him for the sacraments; and he, on his part, when thus asked, has a right to comply with the request. We say, *when thus asked ;* for of his own accord the *toleratus* cannot exercise any of the above functions, since the Const. *Ad Vitanda* was enacted *only in favor of the faithful*, not of the excommunicate himself.

3204. When, out of the above cases, an excommunicate, whether *vitandus* or *toleratus*, *maliciously* or *intentionally*, *i.e.*, knowingly and wilfully, administers sacraments, or says Mass, or performs any other act of the *ordo*, he commits a mortal sin, and moreover incurs irregularity,[1] and that whether he be a *vitandus* or simply a *toleratus*.[2]

3205. It should be observed here that, except in the cases above given of necessity, etc., the sacraments conferred by a person excommunicated, even though he be a *vitandus*, are *illicit* indeed, but yet *valid*. The Sacrament of Penance alone is excepted, it being undoubtedly invalid, if administered, out of the case of necessity, by an excommunicate who is to be shunned. The reason is, that, besides the power of the *ordo*, the power of the *jurisdiction* is indispensable to the valid administration of this sacrament. Now a *vitandus* is deprived by the Church of all ecclesiastical jurisdiction. This, however, does not apply to a *toleratus*, since the Church does not divest him of jurisdiction with regard to those who apply to him for the sacrament.

3206. As the *vitandi* are, out of the cases given, absolutely forbidden to administer the sacraments, so are the faithful, on their part, strictly prohibited from *applying for* or

---

[1] Cf. supra, n. 3118 sq.   [2] Kober, l. c., p. 309.

Excommunication.

receiving the sacraments *from* them, except in the cases above stated. And if they nevertheless do so, they commit a mortal sin, but, at present, do not incur any positive canonical punishment, the excommunication, which was formerly incurred for the *communicatio in sacris*, in the case, being now abrogated.

3207. Only the reception of orders constitutes an exception. For those who knowingly receive orders from a Bishop who is excommunicated, suspended, or interdicted as *vitandus*, incur at present *ipso jure* suspension from the orders thus received. This is expressly enacted in the Const. *Apostolicæ Sedis* of Pope Pius IX., issued in 1869, which reads: "Suspensionem ab ordine suscepto ipso jure incurrunt, qui eundem ordinem recipere præsumpserint ab excommunicato, vel suspenso, vel interdicto nominatim denuntiatis, aut ab hæretico, vel schismatico notorio; eum vero qui bona fide a quopiam eorum est ordinatus, exercitium non habere ordinis sic suscepti, donec dispensetur, declaramus."[1]

§ 3. *Withdrawal of the "suffragia ecclesiæ."*

3208. Excommunicates, at least when they are *vitandi*, are excluded (*a*) from all share in the *public prayers* of the Church, recited by the faithful or the priest, in the name of the Church, (*b*) from the liturgical prayers said by the priest in the name of the Church, especially during the Sacrifice of the Mass, (*c*) and from all participation in the indulgences granted by the Church.[2] This privation is a great loss to the excommunicate. For in all the prayers which are found in the public liturgy, *v. g.*, in the missal, breviary, etc., and which the priest recites not unfrequently, together with the faithful, during the Mass, or when saying the breviary, or in public processions, or other liturgical functions, the

---
[1] Susp. 6ª Const. Ap. Sedis; Cf. Kober, l. c., p. 315.
[2] Arg. Cap. 28, 38, de sent. excom. (v. 39).

Church ever offers up supplications to God for the welfare of all her children. All the members of the Church participate in, and are benefited by these prayers. The excommunicate alone is excluded from them.[1] For him alone the Church offers up no prayers.

3209. We have said, *at least when they are "vitandi;"* for it is controverted whether the *tolerati* are also excluded from these prayers. Many canonists hold the negative. Kober[2] and other eminent canonists maintain the affirmative, chiefly on the ground that the Const. *Ad Vitanda* did not make any change whatever *in favor of the excommunicate himself.* We have said, secondly, *public prayers;* for neither the *tolerati* nor the *vitandi* are deprived of the *private* prayers of the faithful or the priest. Hence, while the faithful can offer their private prayers for an excommunicate, they are forbidden to include him or pray for him when they offer up the public prayers of the Church.

§ 4. *Excommunicates cannot assist at the Mass or other Ecclesiastical Functions.*

3210. In the first place, an excommunicate, whether he be *vitandus* or *toleratus*, is strictly forbidden to assist at the *sacrifice of the Mass.*[3] Hence, if, notwithstanding this prohibition, he assists at the Holy Sacrifice, he commits a mortal sin, unless he does so from ignorance, the necessity of avoiding scandal, or the loss of his good name, or from some other grave cause. We say, *whether he be vitandus or toleratus;* for to be present at the Holy Sacrifice is evidently a *communicatio in sacris* with the priest celebrating and the people hearing the Mass. Now, not only the *vitandi*, but also the *tolerati* are forbidden to communicate *in sacris* with others. For the Const. *Ad Vitanda* made no

---

[1] Kober, l. c., p. 241.   [2] Ib., p. 267-272 ; Cf. Schmalzg., l. 5, t. 30, n. 126.
[3] C. 1, dist. 25 ; Cap. 43 de sent. excom. (v. 39).

alteration whatever in the old legislation, *in favor of the excommunicate himself*.[1] As, on the one hand, the excommunicate is not permitted to be present at the Holy Mass, so, on the other, are the priest and the faithful prohibited, the one from saying, the other from assisting at Mass, in his presence.[2]

3211. *Q.* What is to be done, therefore, if an excommunicate is present, or assists at the Mass?

A. If he be a *toleratus*, the Mass should not be interrupted or intermitted. This follows from the principles already laid down. For, while the *toleratus himself* is forbidden to communicate *in divinis* with others, and therefore to assist at Mass, yet the celebrant in the case and the faithful are free to communicate thus with him, and consequently to celebrate, or assist at Mass, in his presence.

3212. If he is a *vitandus*, the celebrant, either personally or through another person, should call upon him, by name, to leave the church. If he refuses to obey, he should be ejected, and that even by force, if need be. If he cannot be put out without danger of greater evil or causing serious disturbance in the church, then (*a*) the others who are present must go out; otherwise they commit sin—according to some, a mortal sin, according to others only a venial—by associating or communicating in religious matters with a *vitandus*. (*b*) The priest should break off the Mass and leave the altar, in case he has not yet begun the "canon" of the Mass. If he has already commenced the canon, he should continue the Mass, though only with *one* server or altar-boy—(all the others being obliged to leave as above stated), as far as the communion inclusive. After consuming the Sacred Blood, he should forthwith leave the altar and finish the prayers that follow after Com-

---

[1] Kober, l. c , p. 323; Schmalzg., l. c, n. 130.
[2] Cap. 18 de sent. excom. in 6º (v. 11).

munion in the sacristy or some other proper place, or omit them altogether.¹

3213. If the celebrant does not observe this, but *knowingly* and *wilfully* celebrates Mass in the presence of a *vitandus*, he sins grievously, and, moreover, incurs at present, *ipso facto*, (*a*) the *interdictum ab ingressu ecclesiæ*, if the *vitandus* has been excommunicated and denounced as such by a Bishop or delegate judge;² (*b*) and *ipso facto* excommunication reserved simply to the Pope, if the *vitandus* in the case has been excommunicated by the Roman Pontiff.³

3214. *Observation.*—The *vitandus*, in the case, not only sins mortally by assisting at Mass, but, moreover, according to the Sacred Canons, as contained in the *Corpus Juris*, incurs a new excommunication reserved to the Pope.⁴ The same applies (*a*) to persons interdicted, when their interdict has been officially made public; (*b*) and to all those who prevent in any way the person excommunicated or interdicted from leaving the church.⁵ We say, *according to the Sacred Canons, etc.;* for the Const. *Apostolicæ Sedis* issued by Pope Pius IX. in 1869 is silent regarding this excommunication. Hence it would seem to be abolished.⁶

3215. As the excommunicate is excluded from the hearing of the Mass, so is he, moreover, forbidden to assist at the other divine services or functions of the Church—*officia divina*. By divine services (*officia divina*) are meant the saying of the breviary in choir, public processions and prayers, the blessing of the Holy Oils, of water, of candles, and other ecclesiastical functions of a similar kind.⁷ An excommunicate, even though *vitandus*, can, however, *assist at sermons*⁸ and enter the church, in order to pray privately,

---

¹ Clem. 2, de sent. excom. (v. 10); Cap. 16 de sent. excom. (v. 39); Kober, l. c., p. 324.
² Const. *Ap. Sedis* of Pope Pius IX., n. 17; Cf. cap. 8 in 6º (v. 7).
³ Const. Ap. Sedis Pii IX., *Interdicti*, n. 2.   ⁴ Clem. *Graves* 2, (v. 10).
⁵ Ib.   ⁶ Cf. Craiss., n. 6525; Varc. p. 919.
⁷ Kober, l. c, p. 326.   ⁸ Cap. 43 (v. 39).

provided the above divine offices are not being celebrated at the time. Again, though he is not allowed to recite the office *in choir*, he is nevertheless bound to say it *in private*, or by himself. The faithful, on their part, are bound not to assist at any *officia divina* at which the *vitandus* should presume to be present.

§ 5. *Disqualification for Appointment to Ecclesiastical Offices.*

3216. As even ordinary societies or associations would violate all rules of prudence, justice, and propriety, if they should appoint a person whom they had expelled from their membership for violation of their rules to any office or position in the society, so neither can so great and holy a society as the Church allow any one who has been excommunicated or expelled from her pale to *be appointed to any ecclesiastical office, position, or dignity*.[1] If she did otherwise, she would openly contradict herself. For by excommunication she would, on the one hand, forbid the excommunicate to hold any intercourse, especially religious, with the rest of her members; and on the other, by appointing such a one to an office, give him the fullest liberty to associate with them in religious and social matters.

3217. Hence the law of the Church, as still in force, expressly provides that an excommunicate *is absolutely incapable of being appointed to benefices or ecclesiastical offices of any kind*.[2] And if he is, nevertheless, appointed to such offices, the appointment is *ipso jure* null and void.[3] This disqualification must be understood *in the widest sense of the term*, both as regards the benefices and offices, and the person excommunicated. Hence it extends, 1. not only to excommunicates who are *vitandi*, but also to *tolerati*. For although at present, as we have seen, the faithful can communicate or associate with a *toleratus*, even in religious

---

[1] Kober, l. c. p. 340.   [2] Cap. *Postulasti*, 7 (v 27).
[3] Cap. 1, de rescr. in 6° (i. 3); Kober, l. c., p. 340.

matters, yet the *toleratus* himself must keep aloof from all association in religious matters with the faithful. Hence he cannot accept any appointment whatever. In fact, the appointment is evidently a favor to the appointee. Now, as was seen, the Const. *Ad Vitanda*, which is now the law on the matter under discussion, has made innovations only in favor of the faithful, *but not of the excommunicate himself*. Consequently every excommunicate, whether he be *vitandus* or *toleratus, notorious* or *occult*, is absolutely disqualified for an ecclesiastical appointment.[1]

3218.—2. The disqualification applies, moreover, to *all ecclesiastical appointments whatever*, and, therefore, not merely to *beneficia* proper, which are conferred for life, whether *majora* or *minora*, whether *curata* or *simplicia*, whether *sæcularia* or *regularia*,[2] but also to all ecclesiastical offices, positions, or dignities of whatever kind which are conferred but temporarily, *i. e.*, without any fixity of tenure, in other words, whose incumbents are removable, such as administrators of dioceses, delegated judges, and removable pastors.[3]

One of the reasons is that excommunicates are forbidden to exercise the functions of ecclesiastical offices, and consequently they are excluded from the offices themselves, since the *beneficium datur propter officium*.[4] Hence the appointment in the United States of an excommunicate to a parish or other ecclesiastical office, though we have no benefices proper, is null and void. All Superiors having the power of appointment are strictly forbidden to attempt to appoint an excommunicate to any ecclesiastical office or position.

3219.—3. The disqualification, however, does not comprise benefices or ecclesiastical offices to which the excommunicate *had already been appointed before he became excommunicated*. In other words, excommunication incapacitates a

[1] Kober, l. c., p. 344.   [2] Ib., p. 342.   [3] Schmalzg., l. c., n. 148.
[4] Cap. 15. de rescr. in 6° (i. 3).

person to be appointed to an office or benefice, but does not deprive him, at least *per se*, of the benefices and offices which he already possesses. The reason is, that the Church considers the state of a person under excommunication *only as a temporary state* and, therefore, does not *wish to* strip him *ipso facto* of his office or benefice.[1]

3220. We say, *at least "per se"*; for indirectly excommunication may cause the privation of ecclesiastical offices, namely, where the excommunicate remains for a year or longer in the excommunication. For the law of the Church is that persons who are suspended, excommunicated, or interdicted shall, if they obstinately remain a year or longer in their censure, and do not seek to be released from it, be deprived of their offices or benefices.[2]

3221. *Q.* Does excommunication deprive the excommunicate of the *fruits* or *income* (with us, salary of Rector, assistant, etc.), of his benefice or office?

A. We premise: We have already seen that, while excommunication suspends the excommunicate from his office, it does not deprive him of the office itself. We now answer: We must distinguish between benefices and offices legitimately and peacefully held by the excommunicate, and those to which he was appointed while under excommunication. In the latter case, he has no right whatever to the income, since the appointment itself was absolutely null and void, as we have seen.

3222. In regard to the former case, namely, in regard to the offices and benefices to which the excommunicate had been lawfully appointed, prior to his falling under censure, we refer the reader to what we have said above, Nos. 1874, 1875, where we fully discuss this whole matter, and show that the excommunicate forfeits his income, for the time being, except in case of extreme need, when he is entitled

---

[1] Kober, l. c., p. 350. [2] Cap. 8, de æt. et qual. (i. 14); Can. 36, c. 11, q. 3.

to what is necessary to preserve his life. But while it is certain that excommunication deprives the excommunicate of his ecclesiastical income,[1] it is debated among canonists whether it does so *ipso jure*, or only *post sententiam judicis*. Kober[2] and others maintain that the excommunicate is deprived of his income *ipso jure, i. e.*, by the very fact of his having fallen under excommunication, and without any judicial sentence. Schmalzgruber[3] holds it as the truer opinion that he forfeits it only upon judicial sentence.

§ 6. *Withdrawal of the " Communicatio Forensis."*

3223. The excommunicate is excluded from *all judicial proceedings* in ecclesiastical courts, and consequently from the functions of a judge, (with us, also members of Commissions of Investigation, where these bodies still exist), accuser or plaintiff, witness, notary, secretary, advocate, and procurator or attorney. This exclusion or disqualification is expressly decreed by the Sacred Canons, as still in force, also with us, and is, moreover, simply the result or consequence of the law of the Church, forbidding any intercourse whatever between the excommunicate and the faithful. For it is plain that in judicial proceedings the excommunicate necessarily comes into direct contact with the faithful, namely, with the parties interested, such as the judge, the opposing party, the witness, etc.[4] Besides, the Church, by depriving the excommunicate of all standing in her courts, and of all his judicial rights and advantages, wishes to make him realize his utterly helpless condition, and thus to cause him to return sooner to the path of duty.[5]

3224. We say, *in ecclesiastical courts;* for, although formerly the disqualification extended also to *secular courts*,[6]

---

[1] Cap. 53, de app. (ii. 28).
[2] L. c., n. 158.
[3] Kober, l. c., p. 416.
[4] Kober, l. c., p. 417.
[5] L. c., p. 351.
[6] Cap. 12, de except. (ii. 25).
[7] Cap. 1, de except. in 6° (ii. 12.)

yet, at the present day, it is confined to ecclesiastical courts. The reason is, that, at present, by general usage, association or communication between the excommunicate, even though *vitandus*, and the faithful, is allowed *in secular or worldly matters*.

3225. What has been said of the exclusion of the excommunicate from all share or participation in ecclesiastical juridical proceedings, applies, in its rigorous sense, *only to the " vitandi;"* that is, they alone are to be excluded *ex officio* and absolutely from these proceedings, and that whether the faithful, or the parties interested, demand it or not. The ecclesiastical judge is bound *ex officio* to repel them, even though he is not asked to do so.[1] But as regards the *tolerati*, it must be borne in mind, as we have repeatedly noted, that the faithful may keep up their intercourse with them *in all matters, religious or civil*, and therefore also in juridical proceedings. Hence the *toleratus* may, unless the faithful object, fulfil the office of judge, accuser, witness, notary, advocate, and procurator.

3226. We say, *unless the faithful object;* for, as we have seen, it is optional with them to associate with the *toleratus*, or not. They are at perfect liberty to object to his acting or being admitted either as a judge, or in any other capacity. Nay, they can make this objection *at any time* during the judicial proceedings.[2] And if the objection is proved, that is, as soon as the person objecting has shown that the person objected to is really under excommunication, the latter must be forthwith set aside. However, as it not unfrequently happened in ecclesiastical causes that the exception or objection of excommunication was made *maliciously and solely for the purpose of causing delay*, the Sacred Canons, as still in force, enact that the person who objects to another on the score

[1] Kober, l. c., p. 418.   [2] Cap. 12 de except.(ii. 25).

of excommunication must prove, *within eight days*, that his assertion is true, namely, that the person objected to is really under excommunication. Otherwise, the ecclesiastical judge should proceed with the case and condemn the person objecting to the expenses as taxed by the court, incurred by the person objected to.[1]

3227. While, however, an excommunicate cannot act as *accuser* or *plaintiff* before an ecclesiastical tribunal, yet he is obliged, if cited, to appear before it as *defendant* or *accused* in actions brought against him. Otherwise, as is plain, he would be able to elude justice, escape punishment, and thus be benefited instead of injured by his excommunication. As such defendant or accused he retains the *full right and liberty of defending himself*, just as though he were not excommunicated.[2] For the right of self-defense is a right guaranteed by the *very law of nature*, and therefore cannot be taken away by the law of the Church. In fact, the Sacred Canons expressly guarantee to the excommunicate the full right of defending himself.[3] Finally, such an excommunicate, when cited as an accused or defendant, can appear and defend himself either personally or through counsel.[4]

§ 7. *Loss of the Rights of Jurisdiction.*

3228. It is certain that an excommunicate is deprived of ecclesiastical jurisdiction, in such a manner that he cannot licitly exercise any act of jurisdiction, whether voluntary or contentious, whether of the internal or external forum.[5] The reason is, that it would be *very unbecoming* that a person expelled from the Church should nevertheless exercise jurisdiction over the other members of the Church.

[1] Cap. 1 de except. in 6º (ii. 12); Cf. Cap. 21, § 2, de off. del. (i. 29).
[2] Koher, l. c., p. 422.   [3] Cap. 5 de except. (ii. 25).
[4] Stremler, l. c., p. 274.
[5] Arg. cap. 24. (ii. 27); Cap. 1 in 6º (i. 13); Cap. 10 in 6º (i. 14).

3229. Again, ordinary jurisdiction is always annexed to and therefore lost or suspended with an ecclesiastical office. Now excommunication *always includes suspension ab officio* and therefore also the prohibition to exercise ecclesiastical jurisdiction. Besides, excommunication, as we have seen, forbids all intercourse between the excommunicate and the faithful. Now the exercise of jurisdiction by an excommunicate would certainly be a direct intercourse and communication between the former and the latter.[1] What we have said thus far holds not only of excommunicates who are to be *shunned* (*vitandi*) but also of the *tolerati*. For the latter commit a mortal sin by exercising any act of jurisdiction unless they are requested to do so by the faithful.

3230. We have said that the excommunicate cannot *licitly* exercise jurisdiction. The question now arises whether he can do so *validly*. Here we must distinguish between the *vitandi* and the *tolerati*. All canonists agree that a *vitandus is completely divested for the time being of all ecclesiastical jurisdiction*, whether of the internal or external forum, whether ordinary or delegated, contentious or voluntary, and that, consequently, all acts whatever of jurisdiction performed by him, while he is under excommunication, are *null and void*, and not merely *illicit*.[2]

3231. Hence such an excommunicate cannot *validly* (*a*) make any appointment whatever to an ecclesiastical office or benifice ; (*b*) act as judge or pass judicial sentence ; (*c*) hear confessions, except in case of extreme necessity ; (*d*) give faculties to administer the sacraments ; (*e*) act as elector or be elected or appointed to an ecclesiastical office. This, however, does not apply to the election of the Pope. For the law of the Church, as still in force, in order to cut off all occasion of schism, ordains that excommunication does

---

[1] Kober, l. c., p. 361.   [2] Schmalzg., l. c., n. 164.

not disqualify any one from the right of electing or being elected the Sovereign Pontiff.[1]

3232. Note that all acts whatever of jurisdiction, whether voluntary or contentious, performed by a *vitandus* are *ipso facto* null and void. Hence a person upon whom, for example, an ecclesiastical Superior—Bishop or Archbishop —who is *vitandus*, pronounces sentence, and inflicts, *v. g.*, suspension or some other punishment, need not, nay *should not* obey or comply with the sentence.[2]

3233. With the *tolerati*, the case is different. They are indeed forbidden, *of their own accord and without being requested, tacitly or expressly*, to have any intercourse with the faithful, as we have seen, and hence *cannot validly* exercise any jurisdiction, *whenever they are objected to by the faithful*. But when no objection is made to them by the faithful, then the law of the Church takes it for granted that they are requested, at least tacitly, to exercise jurisdiction. Hence the *tolerati*, even when it is publicly known that they are under excommunication, can validly exercise ecclesiastical jurisdiction, as long as no objection is made to them by the faithful or the parties interested, on account of the excommunication.

3234. We say, *as long as no objection is made to them;* for, as we have seen, the faithful or the parties interested are at liberty to object at any time to the *toleratus*, on the score of his excommunication. They are free to accept his acts of jurisdiction in any matter they please, *v.g.*, in matters when they are benefited, such as appointments to office; or to reject them in affairs which are disadvantageous to them, such as criminal proceedings against them. It is plain, therefore, that, if the faithful or the parties interested object to the *toleratus*, because of his excommunication, the latter *becomes forthwith,—i.e., as soon as the exception has been proved—*

---

[1] Clem., C. 2, § 4, de elect. (i. 3); Kober, l. c., p. 371.   [2] Can. 4, c. 24, q. 1.

incompetent to validly exercise any jurisdiction, and all acts of jurisdiction exercised by him, once he has been objected to, are invalid.[1] However, the objection, or as it is technically termed, *exceptio excommunicationis*, must be not merely *made* but also *clearly and fully proved*, and that, as we have seen, within eight days.[2]

3235. This legislation of the Church, by which the *tolerati* are not absolutely deprived of jurisdiction, is right and proper. For the good of the faithful and the tranquillity of their conscience require that they shall not be subject to constant doubts as to the validity of the jurisdictional acts of their Superiors. Now it is evident that, if the acts of jurisdiction of a *toleratus* were *eo ipso* invalid, continual perplexities would arise as to the validity of the acts of each and every Superior.[3]

§ 8. *Refusal of Christian Burial.*

3236. Excommunicates who are *vitandi*,[4] and who die while under excommunication, without any sign of contrition and without having received absolution, *are excluded from the honor and benefit of a Christian burial;*[5] in other words, their bodies must be buried in unconsecrated ground, and without any of the obsequies, rites, prayers, or solemnities with which the Church honors her faithful children who have died in the Lord. For the *sepultura ecclesiastica*, of which a *vitandus* is deprived, means three things: (*a*) to be buried in consecrated ground; (*b*) with the ecclesiastical rites, prayers, and ceremonies, usually performed at funerals in the church or at the grave; (*c*) the subsequent solemnities, such as the requiem of the month's mind.[6]

3237. In fact, it seems eminently proper and fitting, nay

[1] Cap. 12, de except. ii. 25\); Schmalzg, l.c., n. 1661.
[2] Cap. Pia, de except. in 6º (ii. 12\).
[3] Kober, l.c., p. 365.
[4] Ib., p. 337; Schmalzg., l,c., n. 127.
[5] Cap. 12, de sepult. (iii. 25).
[6] Kober, l.c., p. 331.

necessary to the maintenance of ecclesiastical discipline and order, that the Church shall not allow those who have been obstinately rebellious, and die thus, to be buried alongside of her true and obedient children, and be accorded those obsequies and funeral honors which she justly reserves for those who are in her communion.[1] Moreover, both the sacred ministers of the Church and the faithful would evidently become guilty of *communicatio in sacris* with an excommunicate *vitandus*, by performing the customary funeral rites of the Church, in the case, or assisting at them.

3238. Hence, also, all those who knowingly assist at the funeral of a *vitandus* and accompany the remains to the grave are guilty of forbidden intercourse with an excommunicate and commit sin. For intercourse with a *vitandus* is forbidden, not only when he is alive, but also when dead, until he has been absolved.

3239. Moreover, those who knowingly and wilfully and with contempt for the law of the Church, either by force, or threats, or other unlawful means, procure ecclesiastical burial for a *vitandus*, incur *ipso facto*, also at present, major excommunication. Thus the Const. *Apostolicæ Sedis* of Pope Pius IX., decrees: "Excommunicationi latæ sententiæ nemini reservatae subjacere declaramus, mandantes seu cogentes tradi ecclesiasticæ sepulturæ hæreticos notorios *aut nominatim excommunicatos* vel interdictos." Furthermore, those who knowingly permit (*v.g.*, parish priests or others in charge of Catholic cemeteries) the burial of a *vitandus*, incur at present, according to the Const. *Apostolicæ Sedis* of Pius IX.,[2] *ipso facto*, the *interdictum ab ingressu ecclesiæ*, and remain under it, until they shall have made condign satisfaction to the Superior whose sentence they have contemned by their action.[3]

3240. Nay, the Church goes farther and enacts that, where

[1] Kober, l c , p. 331. [2] *Interdicta*, ii. [3] Cf. Kober, l.c., p. 335.

Excommunication.

a *vitandus* has been buried in a Catholic cemetery, either by accident, error, or force, his body is to be exhumed and to be buried elsewhere, in unconsecrated ground, provided his grave can be distinguished from the graves of others. If it cannot be so distinguished the remains should not be exhumed, lest otherwise, by mistake, the body of a person not excommunicated be taken for that of a *vitandus* and exhumed in his stead.[1] But in both cases, the cemetery must be considered as *polluted*, and no burials can take place in it until it has been formally reconciled or consecrated anew.[2]

3241. This legislation may seem altogether too harsh to an age of mistaken sentimentalism like the present. But it is none the less founded on the justest reasons of propriety and discipline. For the Church owes it to those of her faithful children who lie buried in consecrated ground to watch over the sanctity of their last resting place, where they sleep till awakened by the mighty trumpet sound of the resurrection.

3242. With the *tolerati* the Church deals in a milder manner. As the faithful can, if they choose, associate with a *toleratus*, the Church does not deny them Christian burial.[3] If, however, a *toleratus* who is known to be an excommunicate dies without any signs of repentance, he may be deprived of Christian burial *as a notorious, or public sinner*.[4]

§ 9. *Exclusion from the Company or Society of the Faithful, in purely human affairs; that is, in the ordinary social Relations of Every-day Life.*

1. *Former Discipline of the Church.*

3243. Thus far we have seen that the excommunicate is excluded from the companionship of the faithful *in religious matters*. In other words, he is forbidden to receive or

---

[1] Cap. 12, de sep. (iii. 28); Clem. Eos 1, (iii. 7). [2] Cap. 7 de cons. eccl. (iii. 40).
[3] Kober, l.c., p. 337. [4] Prael. S. Sulp., t. iii., p. 269.

administer the sacraments; to assist at Mass and other divine functions and services of the Church, etc. The faithful,[1] on their part, are strictly bound to have no intercourse whatever with a *vitandus* in these *religious matters*, that is, they are forbidden to receive the sacraments from him, or to administer (if they be Ecclesiastics) them to him; to abstain from offering up the public prayers of the Church for him; to assist at the holy Mass or other divine functions with him; to appoint him to any ecclesiastical office, or to allow him to perform any function whatever of such office; to recognize him as an ecclesiastical judge; to allow or engage him to act as advocate, accuser, witness, or procurator or secretary before ecclesiastical courts; to submit to acts of jurisdiction performed by him; or to attend his funeral.

3244. But the Church goes still farther. In order to inspire the excommunicate with salutary feelings of repentance, and also to preserve the faithful from contagion by contact with him, the Church strictly commands the faithful to shun and avoid him or his society and company, *even in the ordinary social and civil relations and intercourse of daily life*.

3245. The end and aim of the Church in inflicting excommunication is to bring the refractory and obstinate offender back to repentance. Now it is plain that nothing is a more potent incentive for the sinner to return to obedience than the fact that he is, so to say, an outlaw from society, and that he is completely isolated and cut off from all association and external intercourse with others, even in purely human affairs, namely, in the social or civil relations of every-day life. The faithful are obliged, so to say, to completely disown him and withdraw from his company, as though he

---

[1] By faithful we here mean not only the laity, but also Ecclesiastics of whatever degree.

[2] Can. Excommunicatos 17, c. 11, q. 3; Can. 16, 18, 19 eod.

were afflicted with a contagious disease, and unworthy to be in the company of his fellowmen.[1] Moreover, the Church wishes to deter others from following the bad example of the excommunicate, by placing before their eyes the gravity of the punishment. Now, nothing could be better calculated to convince the faithful of the dread character of excommunication than the complete isolation of the excommunicate.[2]

3246. The obligation in question, incumbent on the faithful, of shunning the excommunicate *in humanis*, *i.e.*, of cutting off all *social intercourse* with him, dates back to the very time of the Apostles.[3] Numerous Councils inculcate and confirm this obligation. During the middle ages this exclusion of the excommunicate from all external social intercourse with the faithful was very vigorously enforced. Not only the faithful in general were strictly obliged to cut off all social and civil intercourse with the excommunicate, but also those who, owing to their state of life, *v.g.*, married people, children, servants, inferiors of every kind, could scarcely, even with the utmost good will, break off all intercourse with him.[4]

3247. This rigor was mitigated by Pope Gregory VII. (1073-1085), in a Council held at Rome, in 1078. In this Council it was enacted that the wives and children of excommunicates, their servants and employees, and all those who were in any way subject to them, should have the right to associate fully and freely with them in the relations of every-day life, *i.e.*, in all domestic, civil, and political matters.

2. *Present Discipline.*

3248. The rigor of the old law on this head was still further modified, as we have already explained, by the

[1] Stremler, p. 276.
[2] Kober, l. c., p. 379.
[3] Cf. I. Cor. v. 11.
[4] Kober, l. c., p. 387.

Const. *Ad Vitanda* of Pope Martin V. (1417-1431). For, prior to this Pope, the faithful were forbidden from having any intercourse in social matters with *any* excommunicate whatever, even though not *denuntiatus*. The Const. *Ad Vitanda*, as generally interpreted, restricted this prohibition to those who were excommunicated by name and published as such. These alone are called *vitandi*. By the letter of the law, therefore, as in force at present, the faithful, (excepting wives, children, etc., as stated above), are obliged to shun a *vitandus* in a social point of view.

3249. We say by the *letter of the law;* for, by general custom to the contrary, the law seems at present almost everywhere obsolete, so that now the faithful do not seem to be obliged to break off social intercourse with *vitandi*, except in so far as the law of nature itself commands it, namely, by reason of scandal, or danger to faith and morals.[1] Hence, even though it be said that the positive ecclesiastical law on this head no longer obtains, yet the natural and divine law, which commands us to cut off all occasions of sin, and therefore also to shun sinners and excommunicates if their society endangers our faith and morals or gives scandal, still holds.

3. *In what Social Matters are the Faithful obliged to Shun a "Vitandus."*

3250. *In what particular social or civil matters is it necessary for the faithful to shun the company of a vitandus?* Thus far we have stated, in general, that a *vitandus* must be shunned in social intercourse. Now we shall descend to the various particular cases or social actions in which, according to the letter of the law, intercourse must be broken off between the *vitandus* and the faithful. Canonists, following the *Glossa*,[2] generally sum up these cases or social

---

[1] Præl. S. Sulp., t. iii., p. 273, n. 772.
[2] In Cap. 3 de sent. excom. in 6° (v. 11), v. *aliis*.

Excommunication.

actions in the following verse: "Si pro delictis anathema quis efficiatur, os, orare, vale, communio, mensa negatur." Let us explain each of these words.

3251. *First*, by the word *os*, is meant all *speaking to* or *conversing* with persons, whether it be done publicly or privately, by word of mouth or in writing, by signs or words.[1] *Second*, the word *orare* refers to *private prayers*. The faithful are bound to shun the company of the *vitandus*, not only when they offer up the public prayers of the Church, or assist at other public ecclesiastical functions, but also when they pray *privately*. *Third*, by *vale* is meant *all external marks of respect, or friendship, or benevolence*, such as saluting, rising, etc., and that whether given privately or in public. *Fourth*, the word *communio* means *every kind of daily, civil intercourse*, all association in business matters, the making of contracts, the entering into partnership, and the like. *Finally*, by *mensa* is understood the *eating with a vitandus and living with him in the same house*, and therefore also the inviting or accepting an invitation to dinner,[2] etc.

3252. In all these relations of every-day life the faithful must shun the *vitandus*, at least, as was seen, in so far as the law of God and of nature commands us to shun and avoid public sinners. However, as was observed, the law of the Church has been greatly modified in this matter. Thus, at present, while, by this law, the faithful still commit sin if they keep up forbidden intercourse with a *vitandus*, yet they incur no ecclesiastical penalty, save as stated above under No. 3171. It must be observed also that the obligation of breaking off social intercourse *is mutual;* that is, the faithful are bound to avoid the company of the *vitandus*,[3] and the latter, on his part, is strictly forbidden to intrude himself into the society or companionship of the former.[4]

---

[1] Kober, l. c., p. 385.
[2] Ib., p. 385; Stremler, p. 281.
[3] Cap. 5, de cleric. excom. min. (v. 27).
[4] Kober, l. c., p. 386.

4. *When is Social Intercourse allowed with a "Vitandus?"*

3253. However, this prohibition of having any external social intercourse, though strict, is nevertheless not so rigorous as not to admit of any exceptions. We therefore ask: Is it allowed sometimes, even according to the letter of the law, for the faithful to associate with a *vitandus* in social matters? We say in our question, *in social matters;* for it is never allowed *in divinis, i. e.*, in *religious matters*, save out of grave fear, etc., as explained above, [1] and even then, apart from all contempt of the law of the Church or God. We now answer: canonists, following the *Glossa*, [2] usually sum up the various cases where the intercourse in question is allowed in the following verse " *Utile, lex, humile, res ignorata, necesse.* Hæc quinque solvunt anathema, ne possit obesse." We shall say a few words on each of these cases.

3254.—1. *Utile* means the *utility*, both spiritual and temporal, whether of the excommunicate or of the faithful. Thus it is allowed to speak or write to the *vitandus for the purpose of converting him.* [3] It is also permitted to give him alms or otherwise assist him if he is in great need, [4] lest by too great severity he might be driven to despair or become more hardened in sin. In a word, the faithful should not treat him as *an enemy*, but rather as an *erring brother*, and hence they should try, *in a spirit of Christian charity*, to bring him back to a sense of duty. For after all, the great end and aim of excommunication is to cause the offender to amend. [5] In like manner can the faithful associate with the excommunicate whenever it is to their temporal or spiritual advantage to do so.

3255.—2. *Lex*, by which is understood the law or state of

---
[1] Supra, n. 1700—1719.
[2] Ad Cap. 15 de sent. excom. (v. 39), v. Excommunicationis.
[3] Cap. 54, (v. 39).   [4] Can. 103, c. 11, q. 3.   [5] Kober, l. c., p. 390.

marriage—*lex matrimonii*. This concession was first made, as was seen above, under No. 1947, by Pope Gregory VII. Accordingly the wife may continue her conjugal relations with her excommunicated husband, not only so far as concerns the *debitum*, but also all other domestic relations.[1]

3256.—3. *Humile* means the subjection or obedience to and dependence upon the excommunicate. Hence, as was seen, according to the concession made by Gregory VII., *children* can associate freely in domestic and social matters of every-day life with their excommunicated parents; *pupils and wards* with their excommunicated teachers and guardians; *servants* and *employees* with their masters and employers; inferiors with their superiors; *subjects* with their sovereign or ruler. For the excommunication does not directly and *per se* deprive the excommunicate of *vested and properly acquired rights and privileges*. Hence it does not divest him of his paternal authority or of his civil power as a ruler, and consequently does not exempt subjects from the obedience due superiors.[2]

3257. We say, *subjects with their ruler or sovereign;* for, as in the case of parents and masters, excommunication did not divest them of their natural and vested rights, so neither does it deprive the ruler of his vested rights as sovereign. He retains, even though he is a *vitandus*, all his *political rights*, or all his rights as a sovereign. His subjects are bound to continue to obey him, pay their taxes, and fulfil all their other duties as subjects. It is true that, in the middle ages, excommunicated monarchs were sometimes deposed by the Pope, and their subjects freed from their oath of allegiance. But this was owing, not directly to excommunication, but rather to the *political position of supreme arbiter between princes and people which the Popes occupied in those days*, by virtue

---

[1] Schmalzg, l. c., p. 184.   [2] Kober, l. c., p. 393.

of the *jus publicum* then in force.[1] Of course, this intercourse is not allowed in *religious matters*.

3258.—4. *Res ignorata*, by which is meant ignorance, whether of law (*juris*) or of fact (*facti*). Hence persons do not commit sin, *qui ignoranter excommunicatis communicant*, *i.e.*, who are inculpably unaware of the law forbidding them to hold intercourse with a *vitandus* (*ignorantia juris*), or of the fact that the party with whom they associate are really *vitandi* (*ignorantia facti*).[2]

3259.—5. Finally *necessity*, by which is meant all cases of necessity, spiritual or temporal. Though it follows, as a matter of course, that cases of necessity must be excepted from the general rule, yet the Church, for the more complete tranquillity of the consciences of the faithful, has expressly enacted that it is allowed to associate in social or civil matters (*in humanis*) with a *vitandus*, whenever there is a *necessity*,[3] *temporal or spiritual*, for so doing, whether on the part of the faithful or of the excommunicate himself. Thus the faithful can keep up the social, every-day life intercourse with an excommunicate, whenever they need his assistance or good advice, or if they would otherwise incur a considerable loss.[4] Any of these causes or reasons, taken separately, suffices to enable the faithful to have social intercourse with a *vitandus*. And as a matter of course, it follows that the *vitandus* can, in these cases, also communicate with them.[5]

3260. All these reasons militate with much greater force *at the present day*. For there is no longer, at least practically

---

[1] Supra, vol. i., n. 483; Kober, p. 403.

[2] Can. 103, c. 11, q. 3; Schmalzg., l. c., n. 190.

[3] Can. 103, c. 11, q. 3. This canon gives the decree of Pope Gregory VII., by which the rigor of the old law was mitigated.

[4] Can. 110, c. 11, q. 3. This canon gives the decree of Pope Urban II., which sets forth the above mitigations.

[5] Reiff., l. 5, t. 39, n. 150.

speaking, any Catholic civil government; there is no public opinion in favor of observing this social ostracism. Hence modern canonists, as was seen, hold that the canonical law forbidding association with *vitandi*, in social or worldly affairs, is now generally obsolete; that the faithful are bound to shun such excommunicates only in as far as the law of nature and the necessity of avoiding scandal or moral contagion command it.

Art V.

What are the Excommunications inflicted by the Common Law of the Church and incurred " ipso facto" at the present day ?

3261. Hitherto we have spoken of excommunications in general. We now come to each one in particular. Space does not permit us to set forth the peculiar nature and characteristics of each one. We must content ourselves with merely giving a list of those which are still in existence. Of course, we here speak merely of those which are enacted by the general law of the Church, since it would evidently be impossible to give those which are contained in the statutes of dioceses, or are inflicted *ab homine per sententiam particularem.*

§ 1. *The Const. Apostolicæ Sedis of Pope Pius IX.*

3262. Formerly there were a great many excommunications, suspensions, and interdicts of the kind under discussion. Of these, some were reserved, either by the Bull *In Cœna Domini*, so called because, down to the year 1770, it was annually published on Holy Thursday (*in cœna domini*) or by other Pontifical Constitutions, to the Pope; others to Bishops; some to nobody. The Const. *Apostolicæ Sedis* of Pope Pius IX. of happy memory gave a new list of these correctional punishments and suppressed all that are not contained in this list, so that at present only those censures *a jure* and *la'æ sententiæ* are in force, which are given in the Const. *Apostolicæ Sedis*. It is therefore of the greatest practical importance that we should here briefly consider the nature, scope, etc., of this celebrated Papal document.

§ 2. *Scope and general Outline of the Constitution.*

3263. We observe, in the interpretation of a law the *scope* or *mind* of the lawgiver must always be examined and borne in mind. Now, in issuing the Const. *Apostolicæ Sedis*, it was the intention of Pope Pius IX., as is expressly stated in this Constitution, (*a*) to reduce to *as small a number as possible* the correctional punishments—namely excommunications, suspensions and interdicts—(inflicted *latæ sententiæ* and incurred *ipso jure*), which had been made from time to time by former Pontiffs and Councils and had gradually become very numerous; (*b*) to *modify* and *adapt* those that were to be retained *to the wants of our time*. For, many of them had been enacted under conditions and in circumstances which had become totally changed. Consequently they had *become inopportune*, and had come to give rise to numerous doubts, perplexities, and scruples of conscience, both in confessors and in penitents.

3264. For this purpose, Pope Pius IX. ordered that *a full and most careful revision* of all the correctional punishments *latæ sententiæ* which were then in existence should be made and laid before him, so that he might, upon due deliberation, determine which ones were to be *retained*, which *suppressed*, and which *modified* to suit the exigencies of the present day. When the revision had been submitted to him, he, with the advice of the Sacred Congregation of the Holy Office, and after mature deliberation, issued on the 12th of October, 1869, the celebrated *Constitutio Apostolicæ Sedis*, determining the number of correctional punishments *latæ sententiæ* to be in force in future, giving an accurate and complete list of them, and decreeing at the same time that only those were to be observed in future which were enumerated in said Constitution.

3265. The words of the preamble of the Const. are: "Decernimus, ut ex quibuscumque censuris sive excommunicationis, sive suspensionis, sive interdicti, quæ per modum latæ sententiæ, ipsoque facto incurrendæ hactenus impositæ sunt, *nonnisi illæ, quas in hac ipsa Constitutione inserimus, eoque modo, quo inserimus, robur exinde habeant.*" Hence, as we have already noted, all excommunications, suspensions, and interdicts *latæ sententiæ* which are not given in the Const. *Apostolicæ Sedis* are now abrogated. Consequently the Bull *In Cæna Domini* is no longer in force, but has been superseded by the Const. *Apostolicæ Sedis*.[1]

§ 3. *Reform Punishments decreed by the Council of Trent and retained in this Constitution.*

3266. However, after giving a specific list of the censures to remain in force, the Const. *Apostolicæ Sedis* also enacts: "Præter hos hactenus recensitos (casus excommunicationis) eos quoque, quos sacrosanctum Concilium Tridentinum excommunicavit, nos pariter excommunicatos esse declaramus."[2] As to suspensions and interdicts, this Const. enacts: "Denique quoscumque alios sacrosanctum Concilium Tridentinum suspensos aut interdictos ipso jure esse decrevit, nos pari modo supensioni vel interdicto eosdem obnoxios esse volumus et declaramus."[3] Here Pope Pius IX. expressly decrees that, besides the censures which are *specifically* given in the Const. *Apostolicæ Sedis*, those also which were made by the Council of Trent shall be in force.

3267. Now the Council of Trent enacts reform punishments in two ways, namely *directly* and *indirectly*. Those were enacted *directly* by it, which (*a*) either did not exist

---
[1] Cf Craiss., n. 1633, note 1.   [2] Our *Elements*, vol. i., p. 439.
[3] Ib. p. 440.

prior to said Council, but were made *first* or *originally* by it, and consequently were not merely *renewed* by, but had their *origin* in the Council of Trent; (*b*) or if they did exist previously and were renewed, their renewal or confirmation took place in such a manner, *as if they had been originally made by the Council.* Those, on the other hand, were made *indirectly* by it, which existed at the time of the Council, *v.g.*, in the *corpus juris*, and were merely *reaffirmed* or *confirmed* by it.

3268. Owing to this, the question is mooted by canonists, whether the Const. *Apostolicæ Sedis* decrees that not only those correctional punishments shall remain in force which the Council of Trent enacted *directly* or *originally*, but also those which it merely *reaffirmed*. The more common and probable opinion is, that those only are retained which were enacted *directly* and *originally* by the Council. For Pope Pius IX. distinctly says in the above *Constitutio* that those whom the Tridentine Council excommunicates—*excommunicavit*—or decrees suspended or interdicted—*suspensos aut interdictos decrevit*—he likewise declares excommunicated, suspended, or interdicted. These phrases can evidently be applied only to punishments which are not merely *renewed*, but *first* made by the Council.[1]

3269. The question, therefore, naturally presents itself: how are we to know which correctional punishments were *directly* inflicted by the Council of Trent, which *indirectly?* Canonists generally lay down the rule that the Council enacts them *indirectly, i.e.*, merely renews old censures, when it says, *v. g.*, " et qui secus fecerint ... *pœnas a jure inflictas* ipso facto incurrant;"[2] or "*antiquorum canonum* pœnas super his *innovando;*"[3] or when it mentions by name the particular old enactment which it renews, *v.g.*, "juxta Constitutionem Clementis V., etc." Where the Council does

[1] Soglia-Vecch., vol. ii., p. 353.   [2] Conc. Trid., sess. xi., can. 1 de Ref.
[3] Ib., cap. 22 de Ref.

Excommunication.

not use these or similar phrases, it imposes the punishments in question *directly* or *originally;* in other words, really *makes*, not merely *renews* them.

3270. *Q.* What are the excommunications *latæ sententiæ* directly enacted by the Council of Trent, and therefore still in force?

A. Before answering, we observe that even of those medicinal punishments which were enacted directly by the Council of Trent, only those remain in force, which had not fallen into disuse when the Const. *Apostolicæ Sedis* was issued. Hence, where a punishment, enacted directly by the Council of Trent, is no longer in force, either in general, or in a particular locality, the Const. *Apostolicæ Sedis* does not retain or revive it.[1]

3271. We now answer: There are nine excommunications. For the following persons incur excommunication *ipso facto*, reserved to no one:[2] 1. Those who publish, or cause to be published, books treating *de rebus sacris—i.e.*, Sacred Scriptures and annotations thereon, but not other books, even though they treat of sacred things, in the strict sense of the term,—without the permission of the Ordinary.[3] 2. Abducers of women, and their associates.[4] 3. Those who compel a woman to enter a religious order, or hinder her from doing so.[5] 4. Those who violate the liberty of contracting marriage.[6] 5. Secular magistrates who refuse to assist Bishops in preserving or restoring the enclosure of nuns.[7] 6. Those who usurp ecclesiastical property or goods.[8] 7. Those who deny that clandestine marriages, made with the free consent of the contracting parties, are true and valid, so long as the Church has not ren-

---

[1] Konings. n. 1700, q. 3.   [2] Cf. Konings, n. 1700, q. 2.
[3] Varceno. p. 455.   [4] Conc. Trid., sess. 4 de edit.; Cf. Sabetti, n. 1013.
[5] Conc. Trid, sess. xxiv., c. 6, de Ref. Matr.   [6] Ib., sess. xxv., cap. 18 de Regular.
[7] Ib., sess. xxiv., cap. 9 de Ref. Matr.   [8] Ib., sess. xxv., cap. 5 de Reg.
[9] Ib., sess. xxii., cap. 11 de Ref.

dered them invalid, or who assert that the marriage of children, without the consent of their parents, is null.[1] 8. Those who say that a person in the state of mortal sin, having contrition, need not, even when he can do so, go to confession before receiving holy Communion.[2] 9. Those who are guilty of duelling.[3]

3272. Of these nine excommunications, however, but the first four (n. 1, 2, 3, 4,) can be said to remain in force as Tridentine enactments. For, of the five remaining, one, namely that which refers to magistrates assisting Bishops to preserve enclosure, has fallen into disuse; the other four are contained in the Const. *Apostolicæ Sedis*. Thus, the excommunication against usurpers of ecclesiastical goods is comprised in Nos. 11, 12, of excommunications especially reserved to the Holy See, and partly in No. 3, of excommunications reserved to nobody. The excommunication against those who teach (*a*) that clandestine marriages are invalid, etc., (*b*) or that persons in mortal sin, etc., is included in No. 1 of excommunications reserved simply to the Holy See. Finally, the excommunication against duelling is comprised in No. 3 of excommunications reserved in a simple manner to the Holy See.[4] For full explanations of these punishments we refer the reader to moral theologies. The suspensions and interdicts directly inflicted by the Council of Trent and continued in force by the Const. *Apostolicæ Sedis* of Pius IX. will be given below.

§ 4. *Reform Punishments concerning the Election of the Pontiff, and the Regimen of Religious Orders.*

3273. Moreover, Pope Pius IX., in the Const. *Apostolicæ Sedis*, enacts: " Quæ vero censuræ, sive excommunicationis sive suspensionis, sive interdicti, Nostris aut Prædecessorum Nostrorum Constitutionibus, aut sacris canonibus præter

---

[1] Conc. Trid., sess. xxiv., cap. 1 de Ref. Matr. [2] Ib., sess. xxiii., can. 11, cap. 7.
[3] Ib., sess. xxv., cap. 19 de Ref. [4] Cf. Varceno, p. 955.

Excommunication.

eas quas recensuimus, latæ sunt, atque hactenus in suo vigore perstiterunt, sive pro *R. Pontificis electione*, sive pro *interno regimine* quorumcunque ordinum et institutorum regularium, necnon quorumcunque Collegiorum, Congregationum, Cœtuum, locorumque piorum cujuscunque nominis aut generis sint, eas omnes firmas esse, et in suo robore permanere volumus et declaramus."[1] Hence, besides the punishments enumerated by name in the Const. *Apostolicæ Sedis*, and those enacted directly by the Council of Trent, the above are also retained. The Const. *Apostolicæ Sedis* has therefore made no change as to the censures that had been previously enacted by Popes or Councils in regard to the *election of the Roman Pontiff* and the *internal regimen* of religious orders or pious communities with simple vows only or without any vows at all, or of pious places, *v.g.*, hospitals, asylums.

3274. Here it may be asked whether the reformative punishments *latæ sententiæ* concerning the *internal regimen* of religious communities, etc., as here continued in force, are the *particular* censures existing in a *particular* community, enacted indeed by the Roman Pontiff, (the Const. *Apostolicæ Sedis* intended to legislate only in regard to the censures made by the *general law* of the Church; and hence it is evident that we do not here speak of censures enacted by a *Superior* of a religious community), but only for a *particular* religious order, etc., or the general censures made by Popes and Councils *for all religious orders* or pious places all over the world. There are various opinions: One— that which is held by Avanzini,[2] Konings,[3] and others, *affirms* that they are the particular censures made by Popes for a *particular* order, etc. The other, supported by the author of the *Comm. Reat.*,[4] *denies* this, and maintains that they are the *general* correctional punishments made by

[1] Our *Elements*, vol. i., p. 440.   [2] Comm. in Const. *Ap. Sedis*, n. 57.
[3] N. 1700, q. 2.   [4] N. 164 (2).

Popes or Councils for the internal regimen of religious communities in general.

3275. The first or affirmative opinion is based chiefly on the argument that the Const. *Apostolicæ Sedis* expressly, *i.e.*, *by name*, confirms or re-enacts certain general medicinal punishments, relating to the internal regimen of these communities or places, *v.g.*, those which enforce enclosure.[1] Now it would be useless to expressly renew these punishments, if they were already declared to remain in force by the above clause of the Const. *Apostolicæ Sedis: Quæ vero censuræ . . . . latæ sunt, ... pro interno regimine quorumcunque ordinum regularium . . . .* eas firmas esse *. . . .* volumus. It certainly would appear superfluous to re-enact them *twice* in the same Constitution.[2]

3276. As will be seen from the clause of the Const. *Apostolicæ Sedis*—"quæ hactenus in vigore perstiterunt,"— the correctional punishments concerning the election of the Pope and the internal government of religious communities and pious places are continued in force *only in so far as they were actually in force at the time the Constitution was issued*. Consequently those which had fallen into disuse were not revived.

§ 5. *The Bearing of the Constitution of Pius IX. on Vindicatory Punishments.*

3277. Again it must be carefully borne in mind that the Const. *Apostolicæ Sedis* has reference only (*a*) to *correctional punishments, (censuræ), (b)* made by the *general law* of the Church, (*c*) and which are *latæ sententiæ*, *i.e.*, incurred *ipso facto*. We say *first, correctional punishments;* hence it has made no change whatever as to the ecclesiastical punishments which are *called vindicative, (pœnæ),* such as disabilities, dismissals, penal transfers. Yet, when the Const. *Apostolicæ Sedis* imposes correctional punishments, *v.g.*, excommunica-

---

[1] Excom. vi., vii., R. Pont. simpl. res.   [2] Konings, n. 1700, q. 2.

tion, for a certain crime which is already punishable by the old law with a punitive penalty, this very fact would seem to indicate that the *vindicative* punishment is abolished or rather absorbed in the one contained in said Constitution. For it is against the principle of sound law that one and the same act should be punished with *several* punishments, especially when one of them is as severe as excommunication.[1]

3278. We say, *secondly, latæ sententiæ;* for the Const. *Apostolicæ Sedis* has effected no change whatever in regard to correctional punishments which are *ferendæ sententiæ*. It did not legislate on the latter. We say, *thirdly, made by the general law of the Church;* for the Constitution did not pretend to make any legislation whatever in regard to *local punishments* inflicted by *local Superiors, v. g.,* diocesan or provincial Statutes.

3279. However, even where the Const. *Apostolicæ Sedis* abolishes a reformative punishment, it must not be imagined that it has also given permission to do the act to which the censure has been attached. The *prohibition* remains, only the *punishment* has been removed.[2]

§ 6. *How Correctional Punishments are reserved in this Constitution.*

3280. Of the correctional punishments contained in the Const. *Apostolicæ Sedis* some are reserved to the Holy See *in a special manner;* others only *in an ordinary manner;* others to Ordinaries; some, finally, to nobody. See Vol. I., No. 681. Of these four classes of punishments, some have been taken from the *old law* as it stood at the time, and inserted in the Constitution, *without any change, v. g.,* the *excom. spec.,* n. 10; the *simpl. excom.,* n. 12, 13; the *excom. nem. res,* n. 3. Others have indeed been taken from pre-existing laws, but have been somewhat *changed and adapted to*

---

[1] Comm. Reat. in Const. *Ap. Sedis.*   [2] Comm. Reat., § 17.

the altered condition of our times.[1] The former must be construed in the light of the old canons, as interpreted by approved canonists; the latter, *i.e.*, those which were *altered*, must be construed partly according to the old canons (namely, as far as they have not been changed), and partly according to the wording of the Constitution itself.

3281. Lastly, from what has been said, it follows that the Const. *Apostolicæ Sedis* of Pope Pius IX. is to be regarded at present as the *corpus juris* for correctional punishments *latæ sententiæ* enacted by the general law, so that none of these punishments are now in existence, except when it is (*a*) *expressly* given in this Constitution, (*b*) or has been enacted since the Constitution was issued, (*c*) or relates to the internal regimen of religious houses, (*d*) or was directly inflicted by the Council of Trent.

[1] Ib., § 15; Soglia-Vecch., l. c., p. 353.

CHAPTER III.

SUSPENSION.

ART. I.

True Idea of this Punishment.

3282. Every externally constituted society, in order to carry out its purpose and attain its ends, and to preserve its rights and guard its interests, *is obliged to appoint officers or organs of its own,* and assign to each a proper and distinct sphere of duties and rights. Still more is it necessary for such society to have the right *to remove, either permanently or at least temporarily, from office those officials who either neglect their duty or abuse their power.* No society or association, however small, whether religious or secular, could exist without this power.

3283. Again, every official enters upon his office with the express or tacit promise to fulfil its obligations punctually and faithfully. And if, instead of doing so, he but follows the dictates of his capricious whims, or even of self-interest, it is plainly he himself who challenges the Superior by whom he was appointed to take the office from him again, and to commit it to more faithful hands. Finally, every official who discharges the duties of his office in an improper manner *causes others to look with contempt upon the office and the society of which he is an officer.* And in case he is allowed to remain in office he will likewise *bring dishonor upon his fellow officials.*

3284. Guided by these principles and motives, all societies or associations, no matter how small, reserve in their constitution and by-laws *the right of removing or suspending officials for sufficient cause.* But especially has the state or civil government, both in ancient and modern times, always made an extensive use of the power to remove its officials, either temporarily or permanently, for good cause. Thus, in the United States, all officials whatever of the civil government, national or state, are subject to removal or suspension from office for cause and in the prescribed manner.

3285. These reasons apply with much greater cogency to a religious organization charged *with the sanctification of its members.* In fact, at all times has this power been exercised by religious denominations of every description, by the pagan no less than the Mosaic. At the present day, all Protestant sects exercise it, in the United States no less than elsewhere. It is, therefore, superfluous to show that the Catholic Church—the true spouse of Christ—has this power.[1] She possesses it both as a society, and by the express will of her divine Founder.[2]

3286. *Definition.*—We shall here speak merely of *relative or partial removal from office, i.e.,* of suspension, having already treated above of absolute or permanent removal or dismissal. What then is meant by suspension, in the canonical sense of the word? It is a canonical correctional punishment (*censura*) by which an Ecclesiastic, that is, an officer of the Church, who is guilty of crime, is temporarily deprived, in whole or in part, of the use or exercise of the power which he possesses, either by reason of his *ordo, or of his office, or of his benefice or income.*[3]

3287. We say, by which an *Ecclesiastic,* etc.; for a suspension can fall only on *Ecclesiastics, or officers of the Church,* since it is essentially, as appears from its definition, a punishment which forbids the exercise of the *ecclesiastical*

---

[1] Kober, Susp., p. 4.   [2] Cf. I. Tim. v. 19, 20.
[3] Schmalzg., l. 5, t. 39, n. 263; Prael. S. Sulp., t. iii., n. 781; Leur., For. eccl. l. 5, t. 39, q. 567.

ministry, that is, it forbids a person to exercise those rights and privileges which he possesses, *not in his capacity of layman*, but of Ecclesiastic.

This feature constitutes the characteristic and essential difference between suspension and the other correctional punishments. For both excommunication and interdict dispossess a person also of rights and privileges which he holds *as an ordinary member of the Church, and, therefore, by virtue of his baptism;* while suspension divests a person of the rights which he has *as an officer of the Church, and which he therefore possesses by reason of his ordination.* In other words, excommunication and interdict prohibit the enjoyments of rights and privileges which are the *common property, so to speak, of all the faithful;* suspension forbids the use of those rights *which are peculiar to the ecclesiastical or clerical state.*

3288. From this it will also be seen that an Ecclesiastic who is suspended, even though the suspension be complete and absolute, not merely partial, may nevertheless assist at Mass and other sacred functions, receive the Blessed Eucharist, and, in a word, enjoy all the other spiritual privileges which are common to all the faithful as such. For he possesses these rights, *not as an officer, but as a lay-member of the Church.*[1]

3289. We say, moreover, *who is guilty of crime;* for, as we have shown at length, neither suspension nor any other correctional punishment can be inflicted *except for crime.*[2] Neither can it be imposed, as we have also fully proved, without a previous trial, except in those cases where it is allowed to proceed *ex informata conscientia.*[3]

3290. We say, finally, *of the use or exercise;* for suspension does never, at least *per se*, deprive a person of the office or benefice itself. It is essentially *but a temporary prohibition to exercise the functions* of such office or benefice.

---

[1] Stremler, l.c., p. 293.   [2] Supra, n. 2021.   [3] Supra, n. 1279 sq.

Art. II.

Various Kinds of Suspension.

3291. Suspension is divided into three kinds: (*a*) suspension from the office only—*suspensio a solo officio*—by which an Ecclesiastic is removed from the exercise of acts of the *ordo* and the *jurisdictio*; (*b*) suspension merely from benefice —*suspensio a solo beneficio*—by which an Ecclesiastic, retaining intact the use or exercise of the power of order and jurisdiction, is deprived of the income of his benefice or office; (*c*) suspension simultaneously from both the office and the benefice—*suspensio ab officio simul et beneficio*—by which he is forbidden, not only to exercise any act, whether of order or of jurisdiction, but also to receive the income or salary of his office.

3292. Some canonists divide suspension into (*a*) suspension *ab ordine*, (*b*) *ab officio*, (*c*) and *a beneficio*. Schmalzgrueber[1] however and others, whose example we follow, simply divide it into suspension *ab officio* and *a beneficio*, including in the suspension *ab officio* the suspension from acts both of the *ordo* and the *jurisdictio*.[2]

3293. When the suspension is *ab officio simul et beneficio*, it is *complete* and *total*, absolutely speaking. But when it is merely from *either* of them, or but from some individual act pertaining to either, it is *partial* or *incomplete*. Schmalzgrueber[3] says that, when the suspension is inflicted absolutely and without any restriction, so that from the context of the sentence it cannot be ascertained whether the suspension is merely *ab officio* or *a beneficio*, it is to be taken as imposed both from office and benefice.[4]

3294. Again, the suspension *merely from office* (*a solo officio*) may be in turn total or partial, so far as concerns the acts

---

[1] L.c., n. 267, 268; Stremler, l.c., p. 295.
[2] L. c., n. 266.
[3] Cf. Craiss., n. 6572.
[4] Prael. S. Sulp., n. 783.

Suspension. 331

of order and jurisdiction. Thus the suspension *a solo officio* is *total*, when it forbids the exercise of *all acts whatever* of order, jurisdiction, and ecclesiastical administration; it is *partial*, when it prohibits (*a*) merely the exercise of acts of the *ordo*, either in whole or only in part;[1] (*b*) or merely acts of the *jurisdictio*, whether in whole or in part.[2] In other words, a person may be forbidden to exercise *any act whatever*, whether of the *ordo* or of the *jurisdictio*, or only *this* or *that act* of either. When the suspension is merely from acts of the *ordo* and not of the *jurisdictio*, it is called *suspensio a divinis*, or *ab ordine*, or *ab officio sacerdotali*.[3]

3295. Likewise, the suspension *a solo beneficio* may be, so far as concerns the income, salary, or temporal emoluments, either *total* or *partial*. In other words, an Ecclesiastic may be temporarily deprived of the *entire income* or only of *part* of it. Here it is necessary to call to mind that the *suspensio a beneficio* is never included in the *suspensio ab officio*, although the latter be inflicted absolutely and without any restriction. Hence an Ecclesiastic who is suspended merely *ab officio* has the full right to receive the entire income of his place or office, and administer the temporalities of each office, though he cannot perform any of its functions.[4] Like excommunication and interdict, suspension may be either *ferendæ* or *latæ sententiæ*, *a jure* or *ab homine*, just or unjust, valid or invalid.

Art. III.

Effects of this Punishment.

3296. Suspension, like the other reformative punishments of the Church, when validly inflicted, that is, for sufficient cause proved *secundum allegata in judicio* and with the

---

[1] *V.g.*, the saving of Mass.
[2] *V.g.*, the hearing of confessions, or of the right to vote in ecclesiastical elections.
[3] S'rem'er, p. 295.　　　　[4] Prael. S. Sulp. l.c., n. 783.

prescribed formalities, as has been shown, produces its effects *forthwith* and without any further external agency or execution. It executes itself.[1] What then are these effects? They vary according to the kind of suspension inflicted. We shall here discuss separately the effects of the three kinds of suspension as above enumerated, namely (*a*) that from office; (*b*) from benefice; (*c*) from both at the same time.

3297. *Q.* What are the effects of suspension *from office?*

A. As we have seen, suspension from office can be either complete or partial. If it is *partial*, the principle applies that correctional punishments, being *penal laws*, must be strictly construed,[2] and therefore not extended beyond the clear and express wording of the sentence imposing them, or the strict letter of the law enacting them. Hence a person suspended from the *ordo* is not suspended from *jurisdictio*, and can therefore exercise any act of jurisdiction that does not require at the same time the actual exercise of the *ordo*. Thus a Bishop who is suspended from the *ordo* only can delegate to others the power to absolve, though he *himself* cannot hear confessions and grant absolution.

3298. Nay, a person who is suspended only from this or that act of orders, can exercise all the other powers of orders. Thus a Bishop who is suspended merely from the *ordo episcopalis* or *a pontificalibus*, can exercise the ordinary *sacerdotal* functions, as exercisible by any Priest, such as hearing confessions, saying Mass not in pontificals, etc.[3] Likewise, a person suspended from priestly functions is not suspended from the functions of a deacon or subdeacon. The same principles apply to suspension from *jurisdictio*. From this it is evident that there are as many grades of

---

[1] Cf. Kober, Susp., p. 88.

[2] Thus the *reg. jur.* 49 in 6º says: "In poenis benignior est interpretatio facienda." Again: "Odia restringi, et favores convenit ampliari." (Reg. 15 de Reg. Jur. in 6º.)

[3] Schmalzg., l. c., p. 290.

suspension as there are functions, degrees, or acts, whether of order or of jurisdiction.

3299. If, on the other hand, the suspension *from office* is *total*, its effect is to prohibit absolutely all acts whatever, whether of order or of jurisdiction. This principle is founded in the very meaning of the word *office—officium*, which, in the language of the Sacred Canons and according to the general usage of the Church, has always and everywhere been used to designate the ecclesiastical office *in its entirety*; that is, all the rights whatever, whether of order or of jurisdiction, attached to or connected with said office, [1] and if a person thus suspended is *officially denounced* as suspended, his acts of jurisdiction are, as was seen, *ipso jure void*.

3300. We say *if officially denounced;* for if he is *tolerated*, *i. e.*, not published as suspended, his acts of jurisdiction are valid, though illicit, unless performed at the request, tacit or express, of the faithful.[2] We say, moreover, of *jurisdiction;* for acts of the *ordo* in the case are perfectly valid, though, of course, sinful, since the power of the *ordo* cannot be taken away by the Church.[3]

3301. According to some canonists, a person who is suspended *ab officio* is, by that very fact, also suspended *a beneficio*, on the plea that the income or salary is merely an accessory of the office, and that the accessory follows the condition or status of its *principal*. Against these few, all other canonists hold it as certain, as was seen, that a person who is suspended from *office* is not *eo ipso* suspended from *benefice*,[4] on the well-known maxims that penal laws are to be *strictly construed*, and that the income of an office is not forfeited by the incumbent, simply because he has become

---

[1] Arg. cap. 1 de sent. in 6º (II. 14); Cf. Kober, Susp., p. 88; Schmalzg., l. c., n. 2, 4.
[2] Schmalzg., l. c., n. 309.   [3] Kober, l. c., p. 103.
[4] Schmalzg., l. c., n. 297; Reiff., l. 5, t. 39, n. 168.

temporarily disqualified, or even permanently unable to discharge the duties of such office.

3302. Thus the law of the Church expressly provides that an Ecclesiastic who, by reason of sickness, old age, or want of sufficient talent, is unable to attend to the duties of his office,[1] shall nevertheless receive the income thereof, less, however, the salary of the coadjutor or vicar who is to be assigned to him.[2] Hence an Ecclesiastic suspended *ab officio* can continue to receive the income of his office, minus the allowance which has to be given to the person who is appointed to act as his substitute and discharge the duties of the office, for the time of the suspension.[3]

3303. *Q.* What are the effects of suspension *from benefice?*

A. We premise: By *benefice* we here mean the revenue or income *of any ecclesiastical office whatever*, removable or irremovable, and not merely of a *benefice* in the strict canonical sense of the term.

3304. We now answer: 1. As suspension from office does not, as was seen, comprise suspension from benefice, so neither does suspension from benefice include suspension from office. For these two kinds of suspension are clearly and constantly distinguished from each other in the Sacred Canons.[4] Now this would be superfluous, if they both meant one and the same thing. Hence a person, as was seen, may be suspended from or forbidden to receive the income of his ecclesiastical office or charge, and at the same time allowed, nay, obliged to perform all the functions of such office. In other words, a person may be suspended solely from the income or salary, without being suspended from any act, whether of order or of jurisdiction.

3305.—2. Suspension from benefice deprives a person, not merely of the income or salary, but, moreover, of the admin-

---

[1] Cap. 1, 3, 4, de cleric. ægr. (iii. 6); Conc. Trid., sess. xxi., Cap. 6 de Ref.
[2] Schmalzg., l. c.   [3] München, l. c., vol. ii., p. 232.
[4] Cap. 10 de purg. can. (v. 34).

istration of the temporalities of his office or benefice.[1] In other words, a person suspended from benefice cannot lease any lands or houses belonging to his benefice, nor sell any of its property or fruits, nor plead in court, either personally or through others, as the representative of the office; in short, he cannot perform any act which relates to the administration of the temporalities of his benefice or office.[2] Hence, also, an administrator should be appointed to manage the temporalities, or the person suspended may himself be authorized to continue the administration.[3]

3306.—3. Suspension from benefice or income *does not deprive a person of the office or benefice itself*, as has been repeatedly said, but merely of its income or emoluments; consequently a person suspended merely from benefice must perform all the duties of the office without drawing any income or salary therefore. But is a person thus suspended to be left *without any means of support and thus, if poor, obliged to beg?* We have given a full and detailed answer to this question above, under Nos. 1859—1880, where we also apply the principles of canon law on this point to the United States and other missionary countries.

Art. IV.

Punishments incurred for violating Suspensions.

3307. Q. What sin does a person commit, and what punishment does he incur by disregarding suspension?

A. We have already answered this question at considerable length above, under Nos. 3117 and 3123. According to the principles there laid down, a suspended person contracts unfitness for orders, that is irregularity, only when he

---

[1] Schmalzg., l. c., n. 303.
[2] Arg. Cap 8 de dol. et cont. (ii. 14); Cap. 1. 26 de Elect. in 6º.
[3] München, l. c., p 235.

violates the suspension *ab ordine*, that is, when he solemnly exercises an act or function of the *ordo*. For the law of the Church nowhere enacts that a person shall incur the disqualification in question by setting at nought the suspension from *benefice* or *jurisdiction*.

3308. However, a person, as was noted above No. 3123, who violates the suspension from benefice or from jurisdiction, *v. g.*, by drawing his salary or exercising an act of jurisdiction, is otherwise punishable, according to the discretion of the ecclesiastical judge or Superior, and may even be wholly deprived of his office or benefice according to the nature of the offence.

3309. Here it may be asked: Does a person incur unfitness for orders (*irregularitas*) for violating a suspension *ab ordine*, when the suspension is inflicted, not as a *correctional* (*censura*), but as a vindicatory punishment (*pœna*)? We premise, as has been already explained, suspension (and also partial interdict, but not excommunication) may be inflicted not merely as a *reformative* punishment, but also as a purely *punitive*, for crimes altogether past.[1]

3310. We now answer: the question is controverted. Kober,[2] Stremler, the author of the Prael. S. Sulpitii,[3] and others maintain the affirmative, namely, that he does incur the unfitness. They prove this assertion chiefly from the Cap. *Cum æterni* 1, *de sent. et re jud.*, which decrees that ecclesiastical judges guilty of injustice shall be suspended from office *for one year*, and that, if they disregard this suspension, they shall incur irregularity. Here, then, say the above authors, is a *penal*, not a *correctional* suspension, since it is inflicted for a specific period, namely one year, and yet its violation produces irregularity. Again, continue these canonists, the S. C. C. has repeatedly decided that the violation of the suspension inflicted *ex informata*

---

[1] Supra n. 2035. [2] Susp., p. 95. [3] N. 782.

conscientia entails irregularity. Now this suspension is usually inflicted as a *pure punishment*, and not as a censure, since it is imposed without any previous canonical warning.[1] S. C. de Prop. Fide, Instr. 20 Oct. 1884, § 11.

3311. St. Alphonsus,[2] however, holds the opposite or negative opinion as absolutely more probable, chiefly on the ground that the law decrees or inflicts irregularity only for *censure* and not for *pure punishments*. St Alphonsus, however, confines his conclusion to suspensions which are *penal*, *i. e.*, punitive, in the strict sense of the word, namely those imposed *ab homine* by sentence and for a crime completely past, and does not apply it to suspensions, which are inflicted, indeed, for a fixed period, but *per modum statuti aut præcepti* for a future crime, since such suspensions are in his opinion not purely penal.

3312. *Q*. How can it be known when a suspension is inflicted not as a *correctional* (*censure*) but as a *vindicatory* punishment (*poena*)?

A. We premise: suspension assumes the nature of a *purely punitive punishment*, when it is inflicted (*a*) for a crime which has no present continuance—*nullum habens tractum successivum*—but is *altogether past*, (*b*) and not so much for the sake of *reforming the delinquent*, as of *punishing* him.

3313. We now answer: It may be laid down as a rule that a *penal* suspension differs from a *correctional* as follows:
1. The *medicinal* suspension must always be preceded by a canonical warning, general or special;[3] while no canonical admonition or precept is required, at least absolutely speaking, for the *punitive* suspension, though, as was seen, it is necessary that the accused shall be given a canonical trial and that he be juridically convicted of crime. 2. The correc-

---

[1] Bened. XIV. De Syn., l. 12, c. 8, n. 5; Craiss., n. 1796.
[2] L. 7, n. 314.   [3] Supra, n. 1780.

tional suspension is not inflicted for a *specified time*, while the punitive is. 3. The reformative suspension ceases by absolution; the punitive by dispensation, by pardon, or by the lapse of the time for which it was imposed.[1] Hence it may be taken for granted that the suspension is a *mera poena* and not a *censura*, when it is inflicted without a previous canonical warning and for a fixed time, *v. g.*, three months, or *ad beneplacitum superioris*.[2]

ART. V.
Formalities in inflicting Suspensions.

3314. *Q.* What are the formalities which the Bishop or ecclesiastical Superior is bound to observe, also in the United States, when he is about to inflict suspension?

A. We have already given a full and comprehensive answer to this question above, under Nos. 2044 sq. The sum and substance of what we have said there is, that the Bishop, prior to imposing suspension, is to give the accused (*a*) the canonical warning, (*b*) the precept, (*c*) the trial. When the suspension is inflicted, not as a *reform* measure, but as a *vindicative* punishment, the trial alone is sufficient. The admonitions and the precept are not, absolutely speaking, required.

3315. The only exception to this rule is where suspension is inflicted *ex informata conscientia*, which, as was seen, can be imposed as well with as without any previous canonical warnings or juridical proceedings. It should be observed here that the only kind of suspension which is imposable *ex informata conscientia*, or without trial, is the suspension from *orders*, and from ecclesiastical degrees or offices, and dignities or honors. Hence Bishops, also in the United States, cannot, at least directly, suspend Ecclesiastics, *ex informata*

---
[1] Prael. S. Sulp., n. 782.   [2] Craiss., n. 6573, 6589.

conscientia, a beneficio, that is, from *administering* or *receiving the income* of their parish or office. *A fortiori*, they cannot impose *dismissal* (*privatio*) or absolute removal from office or parish, *ex informata conscientia*.

3316. While, however, the suspension which is imposed *ex informata conscientia* does not fall directly upon the *benefice* or *income*, it may, nevertheless, do so indirectly. Thus, if a Rector of a mission or parish is suspended from the *cura animarum*, and it becomes necessary to have the duties pertaining to the *cura* performed by a substitute during the time of the suspension, this substitute will receive a suitable income or salary, the amount of which is determined by the Bishop, and deducted, at least in part, from the income of the suspended incumbent. If the latter considers the amount too large, he can appeal to the Metropolitan or also to the Holy See.

3317. This is expressly decreed by the Propaganda, in its latest Instruction *Supra suspensionibus ex informata conscientia*, issued Oct. 20, 1884, and embodied in the *Third Plenary Council of Baltimore*. The words of the Sacred Congregation are: "Debent insuper exprimi partes exercitii ordinis vel officii, ad quas extenditur suspensio; quod si suspensus interdictus sit ab officio, cui alter in locum ipsius substituendus est, ut puta œconomus in cura animarum, tunc substitutus mercedem percipiet ex fructibus beneficii in ea portione, quæ juxta prudens Ordinarii arbitrium taxabitur. At si suspensus *in hac taxatione* se gravatum senserit, moderationem provocare poterit apud curiam Archiepiscopalem, aut etiam apud *Sedem Apostolicam*."[1] See above, Vol. II., Nos. 1286 sq.; Our *New Procedure*, No. 85 sq.

[1] Instr. S. C. de Prop. Fide *supra Susp. ex informata consc.*, § 4.

Art. VI.

Release from Suspensions.

3318. *Q.* How is suspension taken away, or how does it cease?

A. We have already answered this question above under Nos. 3124 sq. Here we merely add that, when suspension is inflicted *ad beneplacitum*, it lapses of itself by the death, resignation, or removal of the Superior by whom it was inflicted; if it is inflicted *ad beneplacitum Sedis*, it ceases only by dispensation of the Superior or his successor, not by his death or removal.[1] *Observation.* When the suspension has been really incurred by a person, it binds him *wherever he may be*, and consequently also outside of the diocese of the Bishop by whom it was imposed. For it *adheres to his person*, and consequently accompanies him *everywhere*. Hence canonists aptly say of suspension, or of excommunication, *afficit personam eamque sequitur sicut lepra leprosum*.[2] Therefore he remains under it until he is properly relieved from it, as shown above.

3319. *Q.* Can suspension be inflicted for *venial sins?*

A. The answer has been already given above, under Nos. 2021 sq.

Art. VII.

Suspensions a jure com. and latæ sent. in Force at present.

3320. *Q.* What suspensions *a jure com.* and *latæ sententiæ* are now in force?

A. Only those, as was seen, (*a*) which are expressly enumerated in the Const. *Apostolicæ Sedis* of Pope Pius IX., (*b*) and those inflicted originally or directly by the Council of Trent, (*c*) and finally those which regard the election of

[1] Craiss., n. 6588.   [2] Kober, Susp., p. 89.

the Supreme Pontiff, and the internal regimen of religious houses and pious places. We have already, in the first volume, pages 513 sq., *sixth edition*, given the suspensions contained expressly in the Const. *Apostolicæ Sedis* of Pius IX. It but remains, therefore, here to add those inflicted by the Council of Trent, which continue in force.

3321. They are as follows: 1. Bishops ordaining persons *not subject to them* without the permission of their own Bishop, are *ipso facto* suspended for one year from conferring orders, 2. and the person thus ordained is *ipso facto* suspended from the orders thus received, for as long a period as shall seem expedient to his own Ordinary.[1] 3. Bishops performing pontifical functions, *v. g.*, conferring orders, even though it be upon their own subjects, *out of their own diocese*, without the express leave of the Ordinary of the place, are *ipso jure* suspended from the exercise of episcopal functions, *i. e.*, of those functions which are acts of *the ordo episcopalis*, and not merely of the *priestly* order; 4. and those so ordained shall be similarly suspended from the exercise of their orders.[2]

3322.—5. *Titular* Bishops, *i. e.*, Bishops having no sees,[1] conferring orders, major or minor, or even first tonsure, on a person who is the subject of another Bishop, even though he be their own domestic, without the express consent of or without letters dimissory from that individual's own Bishop, are *ipso jure* suspended for one year from the exercise of pontifical functions; 6. and the person so promoted (provided he is in bad faith) shall in like manner

---

[1] Conc. Trid., sess. xxiii., cap. 8 de Ref. The person ordained, in order to incur the suspension, must be ordained *knowingly, i. e.*, he must *be in bad faith*. Kober, Susp. p. 151. Observe that, according to Const. *Apostolicæ Sedis* of Pius IX., a person, even in good faith, who is ordained by a Bishop who is excommunicated, suspended, or interdicted by name, and denounced as such, does not incur suspension, but yet is prohibited from exercising the order thus received, till dispensed by the Holy See.

[2] Conc. Trid., sess. vi., cap. 5 de Ref.   [3] Supra, vol. i., p. 513, *sixth edition*.

be suspended from the exercise of the orders thus received for as long as to his own Prelate shall seem fit.[1]

3323.—7. A person promoted to orders *per saltum*, that is, by leaping over or omitting an intermediate order, is *ipso facto* suspended from the order thus received, and can be promoted to a higher order only by dispensation, which can be granted by the Bishop, provided such person has not exercised the ministry of the order received *per saltum*.[2] We say, *provided*, etc.; for if he exercise the ministry in the case, he incurs irregularity, and then the dispensation or permission to be promoted to higher orders can be given only by the Holy See.[3] The Church has at all times ordained that persons should be promoted to orders only *step by step—gradatim*, receiving first the lowest, then the next highest, and so on, without omitting any intermediate grade.

3324.—8. Persons who, without being constrained to receive sacred orders, by reason of some Ecclesiastical office received or about to be received, are promoted to major orders through letters dimissory of Chapters or Vicars-Capitular or their agents, given during *the first year of the vacancy of the Episcopal see*, are *ipso facto* suspended from the exercise of the orders thus received, during the pleasure of the next appointed Bishop;[4] 9. and if the Chapter, Vicar-Capitular (with us, administrator), or any other persons whatsoever, who, during the vacancy of the See, succeed to the jurisdiction of the Bishop, in lieu of the Chapter, shall presume to give letters dimissory within *the first year* of the vacancy, they shall also be *ipso jure* suspended during a year from their office and benefice.[5]

3325.—10. Abbots conferring tonsure or minor orders, save upon regulars who are their own subjects; in like

---

[1] Ib., sess. xiv., Cap. 20 de Ref.   [2] Ib., sess. xxiii., c. 14 de Ref.
[3] Kober, Susp., p. 211.   [4] Conc. Trid., sess. vii., C. 10 de Ref; sess.
[5] Ib., sess. xxiii., c. 10 de Ref. ; Supra, vol. i., n. 637.

Suspension.

manner, other exempted persons not sending the letters dimissory for the ordination of their subjects to the Bishop in whose diocese they are, are *ipso jure* suspended for one year from their office and benefice.[1]   11. Finally, at least, where the Tridentine decree *Tametsi* is published or obtains,[2] all priests, secular and regular, who shall presume to unite in marriage persons belonging to another parish, or to bless them when married, without the permission of their parish priest, shall remain *ipso jure* suspended, until absolved by the Ordinary of that parish priest who ought to have been present at the marriage, or from whom the benediction ought to have been received.[3]

3326. *Note I.* As will be seen, the above suspensions, under Nos. 1-10, refer exclusively to, or are incurred solely by those Bishops and inferior Ecclesiastics who violate the Sacred Canons *concerning ordinations.* The 11th regards priests *solemnizing or blessing marriages* contrary to the decree *Tametsi.*

3327. *Note II.* Again observe, that of the suspensions under 1-10 three are incurred by Bishops and are reserved to the Pope; the others are incurred by others and are reserved simply to Ordinaries.[4]

3328. *Note III.* Of the three regular correctional punishments—namely excommunication, suspension, and interdict, *suspension is the one which is at the present day most commonly inflicted.*[5] Hence, also, it will be seen how important a correct idea of this punishment, in all its parts, is both to the superior and the inferior. To the former, that he may know when, for what cause, and in what manner he can inflict it; to the latter, that he may, when justly and validly visited with this punishment, acknowledge its justice and

---

[1] Conc. Trid., l. c.; Cf. Varceno, p. 969.
[2] Supra, vol. i., n. 660.
[3] Conc. Trid., sess. xxiv., cap. 1 de Ref. Matr.
[4] Va/ , p. 966.   [5] Stremler, l. c., p. 293.

bow to it, or, when unjustly and invalidly punished by it, seek and apply those remedies which the law of the Church places in his hands, and not look for redress in the secular courts.

CHAPTER III.

THE ECCLESIASTICAL INTERDICT.
(*Interdictum.*)

ART. I.
Correct Notion of the Interdict.

3329. The word *interdict* is synonymous with *prohibition* or *inhibition*. In general it means the act of a person forbidding something. As here understood, the interdict means a regular correctional punishment of the Church, by which, in punishment of crime, the public celebration of divine service (*officia divina*), the administration of certain sacraments, and ecclesiastical burial are forbidden in certain places or to certain persons.[1] The meaning of this definition will be rendered more clear, when we come to describe the effects of this punishment.

3330. *The origin* of the interdict dates back to the early days of the Church. Thus we read in the history of the Church that already in the fifth and sixth centuries persons guilty of certain crimes, *v.g.*, impurity, perjury, were forbidden to receive the Blessed Eucharist, or to enter the Church and assist at the divine service, either for a fixed time, *v.g.*, one year, or for an indefinite period, that is, until they amended.[2] Here we have a partial interdict. It was, however, only in the eleventh century that the canonical interdict received its full development. It consisted in the discontinuance of all public worship and all

---

[1] Arg. cap. *Alma* 24, de sent. excom. in 6º (v. 11); Leur., For. eccl., l. 5, t. 39, q. 573.

[2] Can. *Ad mensam* 24, C. xi., q. 3; München, l. c., vol. ii., p. 196.

solemn ecclesiastical functions, and was inflicted upon a whole kingdom or realm, or only on an individual city or church, or upon all or only some of the inhabitants of such places.

3331. Modern canonists generally remark, and not without truth, that interdicts, at least in the above comprehensive sense, *have now gone completely out of use.*[1] We say, *at least in the above comprehensive sense;* for *partial and particular* interdicts are still in vogue, as may be seen in the Const. *Apostolicæ Sedis* of Pope Pius IX.,[2] and in the Second Plenary Council of Baltimore.[3]

3332. *Specific characteristics of the interdict.*—While this punishment differs from excommunication and suspension, it nevertheless partakes of the nature of excommunication, and has some things in common with it. Thus, like excommunication, the interdict deprives members of the Church of spiritual benefits to which *all the faithful, without exception, are entitled.* But excommunication, as was seen, is far more comprehensive than the interdict. It is a *total*, though temporary *exclusion* from the Church and *all* its privileges; whereas the interdict does not exclude a person from the Church, but merely deprives him of *certain rights and privileges*, and is, so to say, a certain suspension of the laity.[4] Hence also, it is very properly said, that the interdict is a species of mild excommunication.[5]

3333. Another difference between excommunication and suspension on the one hand, and interdict on the other, is that the latter acts not merely on persons, but also on *places*, while the former can directly fall only on *persons*, not places. The interdict, however, has this in common with both excommunication and suspension, that it is, like them, a *correctional* punishment, and therefore aims at the reforma-

---

[1] Permaneder, l. c., p. 545.
[2] Interdicta, n. 1, 2.
[3] Can. 2, c. 36, q. 4.
[4] Fessler, Excom. and its Effects, p. iv.
[5] N. 186.
[6] München, l. c., p. 208.

tion of the offender rather than his punishment. It may, however, as has been said, be inflicted also as a *purely punitive* chastisement.

3334. Let us now see how the interdict differs from suspension. The latter, as was seen, deprives an Ecclesiastic of rights which he possesses *as an Ecclesiastic*, that is, of *official powers and privileges;* whereas the interdict divests a person only of those ecclesiastical benefits which he enjoys as a *lay member* of the Church. Hence, also, the interdict can fall directly only on *the laity* and not upon *Ecclesiastics, in their capacity of Ecclesiastics.* We say, *directly;* for indirectly or mediately, it acts also on clerics, namely in so far as they are not allowed to perform for others, or the laity who are under an interdict, certain ecclesiastical functions. In other words, the clergy are forbidden to celebrate divine service, etc., only because the laity, who are interdicted, cannot assist at them. It is true that Ecclesiastics can be directly *interdicted* from entering a church; but, as München[1] observes, this interdict is rather a species of suspension than a real interdict.

Art. II.
Various kinds of Interdicts.

3335. There are three kinds of interdict, namely local, personal, and mixed. The *local* (*interdictum locale*) is that which acts directly on a *place* or *locality*, forbidding *in such place* the celebration of divine worship, *i. e.*, Mass and other ecclesiastical functions, the administration of certain sacraments, and the giving of ecclesiastical burial. This interdict affects *persons* only indirectly, namely in as far and as long as they are in the place interdicted, so that, when they leave it and go to another not under an interdict, they can assist

---

[1] L. c., p. 214.

at Mass and receive the sacraments, together with Christian burial. This local interdict is either *general* or *particular*, according as it extends to an entire city, province, or realm, or only to an individual church.[1]

3336. The *personal* interdict (*interdictum personale*) is that which acts directly and immediately on *persons*, forbidding them (*a*) to hear Mass or assist at other divine services, (*b*) to receive certain sacraments, (*c*) and to be given ecclesiastical burial. As this interdict adheres to persons, it follows them wherever they may go, and binds them everywhere.

3337. Like the local interdict, the personal may be imposed (*a*) either on a number of persons forming a moral or political body, *v.g.*, upon all the inhabitants of a state, city, parish, religious community, or other body corporate, or confraternity, (*b*) or on some particular individual or individuals, *v.g.*, upon Peter or Paul.[2] In the latter case, it is called *particular;* in the former, *general*. Again, it may be inflicted either in (*a*) all its severity, *i.e.*, in such a manner as to produce all the effects of the personal interdict, (*b*) or only some of them, *v.g.*, if a person is interdicted from the celebration of the Mass, or from the reception of the sacraments, or from entering the church.[3] In the first case, the personal interdict is called *total;* in the second, *partial*.

3338. We observe that the *interdict* of entering a church (*interdictum ab ingressu ecclesiæ*) which we have just mentioned must not be confounded with the *suspension* from entrance into the church (*suspensio ab ingressu ecclesiæ*). The former, the interdict or prohibition to enter a church,[4] forbids a person to enter a church in order to celebrate or assist at Mass or other divine service there, or to perform any other act of the *ordo* in a church. Now, by church is

---

[1] Leur., l. c., q. 573.   [2] Schmalzg., l. v., t. 39, n. 324.   [3] Ib., n. 325.

[4] This species of prohibition or interdict is not comprised in the ordinary interdict, but is a kind of special or separate interdict. Hence it is incurred only when it is *expressly* and *specially* imposed. (Schmalzg., l. c., n. 383.)

The Ecclesiastical Interdict. 349

here meant any temple or other place set apart by the Bishop for *public* worship. Hence a person thus interdicted can go into and celebrate Mass and other divine functions, or assist at them, in a *private oratory* or in a cemetery chapel. Nay, such person may even enter a church, as above defined, in order to pray there, provided it be not during the time when divine service is going on there.[1] On the other hand, the suspension *ab ingressu ecclesiæ* is the same as the suspension *a divinis*, which has been already explained above, under the heading of suspension.

3339. We have above stated in general what places are interdicted when the interdict is a *general local one*. We shall now explain this a little farther. What places, then, are comprised under a general local interdict? 1. If a city is interdicted, all its suburbs together with their buildings are also interdicted. All the churches in such city also fall under the interdict, the cathedral not excepted. 2. If a diocese is laid under an interdict, all the cities, towns, and localities of such diocese with its churches fall under it. 3. When a church is interdicted, all its chapels and the adjoining cemetery are also interdicted. The reason in each of these cases is that, when something is interdicted as a whole, all its parts and places contiguous to it are included.

3340. Furthermore, a local interdict, as we have seen, acts only indirectly on persons. In other words, Ecclesiastics cannot publicly celebrate divine worship, and the faithful cannot assist at it, in the place interdicted, not because *they themselves* are forbidden to celebrate or assist at it, but solely because the *place* or *locality* is declared to be one where the above actions *shall* not take place.

3341. From this it is plain that *no one* can celebrate or assist at divine service in the place interdicted. Hence the local prohibition or interdict must be observed, so far as concerns the *public* celebration of divine worship, etc., by

[1] Schmalzg., l. c., n. 383; Stremler, l. c., p. 346.

all persons whatsoever who may be in the place, and consequently also by strangers, by the laity and the clergy, by the regulars, *i.e.*, exempted persons no less than by the secular Ecclesiastics, nay, even by the Bishop himself by whom the interdict was fulminated.

3342. We say, "so far as concerns the *public* celebration," etc.; for, as we shall see below, Ecclesiastics, both secular and regular, may every day *privately*,—*i.e.*, with closed doors, in a low voice, without the sound of bells and without admitting those who are interdicted by name, or gave cause to the interdict—say Mass, recite the office, etc., in churches and monasteries.[1] Before the time of Pope Boniface VIII. this was not allowed. The rigor of the old law was relaxed by this great Pope in his decretal *Alma*, which now forms the law on this head. Of course, it is clear that Ecclesiastics, secular or regular, cannot celebrate as above, if they are themselves under a personal interdict, nor can they do so in the case of a *special* local interdict, *v.g.*, in a church specially interdicted, nor in the case of a general *personal* interdict; they can do so only in a *general* local interdict.[2] Moreover, those who are the cause of the interdict (we speak here of a general local interdict), *i.e.*, those on account of whose crimes and wicked conduct the interdict has been inflicted, are expressly excluded by Pope Boniface VIII. (1294-1303), in his celebrated decretal *Alma*, which forms at present the law of the Church on this matter, from the above privilege of celebrating or assisting at divine service. For they incur *ipso facto* also a personal interdict,[3] and consequently cannot take part in divine worship anywhere, even out of the place interdicted.[4]

3343. Having shown what places fall under a local interdict when it is a general one, also what persons and how persons

---

[1] Cap. *Alma* 24 de sent. excom. in 6° (v. 11.)
[2] Schmalzg., l. c., n. 366; Stremler, p. 355.
[3] Cap. Si sent. 16 de sent. excom. in 6°.   [4] Schmalzg., l. c., n. 333.

are indirectly affected by it, we now proceed to the personal interdict. What persons then are comprised under a *personal* interdict, when the latter is *general, i. e.*, when a nation, community, or other moral or corporate body is interdicted? Each and every member of such nation, or community, or body corporate, and consequently (*a*) also those who are innocent, for they fall under the interdict because they are members of a guilty community; (*b*) Ecclesiastics and religious, unless they are declared exempt from it.

3344. The following persons, however, are exempted from a general personal interdict: 1. Strangers, *v.g.*, merchants, students, government officers,—even though they have lived for a considerable time among the interdicted citizens; 2. Bishops, unless they are expressly mentioned;[1] 3. Infants not yet arrived at the use of reason—*nondum doli capaces*,—and insane persons. They cannot, however, receive ecclesiastical burial, since Ecclesiastics cannot officiate at or give such burial. 4. Those who leave the community or people interdicted, in order to establish a domicile elsewhere; for by that very fact they cease to belong to the community or people interdicted.[2]

3345.—5. If the *laity* is interdicted, the *clergy* is not considered as interdicted; and *vice versa*, if the clergy is interdicted, the laity is not included. 6. If the secular clergy is interdicted, even though by the Pontiff or other Superiors vested with jurisdiction over seculars and regulars, the religious are, at least according to the more probable opinion, excluded, except (*a*) when they have a secular benefice; for then they constitute one body with the secular clergy; (*b*) where all *ecclesiastical* persons are interdicted; for all religious whatever, whether male or female, are regarded as *ecclesiastical persons*.[3]

---
[1] Cap. 4 de sent. excom. in 6º (v. 11).   [2] Schmalzg., l. 6, t. 39, n. 336.
[3] Ib., l. c., n. 339.

Art. III.

By Whom and for what Cause can they be imposed?

3346. *Q.* Who can inflict an interdict?

A. Only those who have jurisdiction in the contentious forum. Hence the rule is that an ecclesiastical Superior who can impose excommunication and suspension can also inflict an interdict. The following persons, therefore, can fulminate an interdict: 1. The Pope and his legates, nuncios, and delegates and subdelegates; 2. Bishops and others having quasi-episcopal jurisdiction over their subjects; 3. Vicars-Capitular, pending the vacancy of the see.[1] 4. Regular prelates can inflict a personal interdict upon their subjects, but not a local one.[2]

3347. *Q.* For what causes can an interdict be imposed?

A. Only for crimes, and not for any other cause. The reason is that it is a grave punishment. Now reason itself dictates that, where there is no offence, there shall be no punishment. Moreover, the interdict is one of the *severest ecclesiastical punishments*. In some respects, it is even severer than excommunication itself. Now the Church, following the rules of natural and positive law, inflicts the most rigorous penalties only for the most heinous crimes,[3] and even then only with great circumspection and but seldom, namely, only when the delinquent has become entirely incorrigible and there is no other means of bringing him back to the path of duty. Hence an interdict (as has already been said of excommunication and suspension) can be inflicted only for offences which, besides being external and complete, are mortal.

3348. Nay, as reason and equity and natural justice demand that there shall be a due proportion between the crime and its punishment,[4] it follows that, when the interdict

[1] Conc. Trid., sess. xxiv., c. 16 de Ref.
[2] Fessler, Excom., p. 17.
[3] Schmalzg., L. 5, t. 39, n. 340, 341.
[4] Stremler, p. 348.

is general, whether local or personal, and therefore affects a whole community, it cannot be inflicted save for crimes which are, at least in a measure, *public* and *common*, or imputable to the *entire community* affected; *v.g.*, (*a*) when the crime is committed by the *head* of the community or of the civil government, and approved of by the community; (*b*) if the community itself, such as a Chapter, in its capacity of community, breaks a law; (*c*) where the offence, without being committed by the community as such, is, nevertheless, perpetrated by a majority of its members taken in their individual capacity.[1] Hence such an interdict can never be inflicted for crimes, no matter how enormous, of private individuals.[2]

3349. *Q.* Can one or more individuals (not a community) be put under a partial and brief interdict for a *venial sin?*

A. We have already given the answer above, Nos. 2021, 2022, to which place we refer the reader. We here but add with Stremler [3] that, at the present day, the affirmative opinion is but little sustained in theory, and entirely abandoned in practice. Hence it would at present be rash and imprudent, as Stremler says, to follow in practice the opinion which affirms that the interdict or other censure may be imposed for venial offences. This becomes truer still, when we consider, as the same author continues, that the spirit of the Church in our day is to use the censures more sparingly than ever, and only in matters of great importance to the welfare of the Church.[4]

Art. IV.

Formalities to be observed in inflicting the Interdict.

3350. They are, generally speaking, the same as those required for excommunication and suspension, and therefore

---

[1] Stremler, p. 345. [2] Arg. cap. *Non est*, 11 de Spons.; Schmalzg., l. c., n. 345.
[3] P. 349. [4] Ib.

regard either the canonical admonition and the precept, or the trial, or the manner of pronouncing sentence.[1] As they have been already explained, we deem it unnecessary to repeat them here.

ART. V.

Effects of Interdicts.

3351. Q. What are the effects of an interdict?

A. An interdict forbids the following acts: 1. To celebrate Mass, or to assist at it, or to perform any other ecclesiastical function or assist thereat;[2] 2. To administer or receive certain sacraments;[3] 3. To give or receive ecclesiastical burial.[4] The interdict produces all these effects, if it is inflicted unrestrictedly; but if it is imposed in a restricted manner, it will, of course, produce only such effects as the Superior interdicting may wish.[5] We shall now briefly discuss each of these three effects.

§ 1. *Prohibition to celebrate or assist at Divine Service.*

3352. By *divine service or ecclesiastical functions* are here meant those functions which are usually performed only by Ecclesiastics, as the Mass, blessing of the baptismal font, of palms on Palm Sunday, of candles on the Feast of the Purification; also the blessing of a church, of sacred vestments, of holy water; also the saying of the office in choir.[6] According to the old law of the Church, as it existed down to the thirteenth century, it was absolutely forbidden, at any time during an interdict, to celebrate or assist at any of these functions.[7]

3353. But the rigor of this law was relaxed by Pope

---

[1] Cf. Schmalzg., l. c., n. 49; Stremler, p. 353. [2] Cap. *Permittimus* 57 (v. 39).
[3] Cap. *Responso* 43 (v. 39); Cap 16 de sent. excom. in 6º.
[4] Cap. *Quod in te* 11 de pœnis et pœnit.   [5] Schmalzg., l. c., n. 350.
[6] Ib., n. 361.   [7] Cap. 57 (v. 39); Cap. 16 in 6º (v. 11).

Boniface VIII., in his celebrated decretal *Alma*, which now forms the law of the Church, on this head. According to this decretal, it is allowed, at present, for Ecclesiastics, secular or regular, unless they are personally interdicted, in time of a general local interdict (but not during a particular local interdict, nor during a *personal* interdict, whether general or particular), daily to say Mass and to perform the other acts of divine service (*officia divina*) in all churches and monasteries, provided the following conditions prescribed in the Cap. *Alma* by Boniface VIII. be observed: (*a*) That it be done in a low voice; (*b*) with closed doors; (*c*) without the sound of bells, without singing, or without the use of the organ; (*d*) that those persons who are under excommunication, or a personal interdict, or have been the cause of the local interdict, be excluded.

3354. These excommunicates or interdicted persons are to be excluded only in case they are excommunicated and interdicted by name, and denounced publicly as such; for, as was seen, the faithful are bound to shun only those who are *denounced*.

3355. Moreover, at present, according to the decretal *Alma* and later concessions, it is permitted, during a general local interdict, to celebrate Mass and perform the other divine functions, *with all the customary solemnities and publicity*, on Christmas, Easter, Pentecost, the Assumption of the Blessed Virgin, the Immaculate Conception and its Octave, and on Corpus Christi and its Octave. On these festivals, only those who are excommunicated by name and publicly denounced as such, and those whose excesses have caused the interdict, are to be excluded.[1]

§ 2. *Privation of the active and passive Use of certain Sacraments.*

3356. This prohibition extends not to all, but merely to

[1] Cap. *Alma* 24 in 6º (v. 11).

some sacraments. Prior to the time of Boniface VIII. the sacraments of Penance and the Holy Eucharist could be administered, during a general interdict, only to such as were dangerously ill.[1] Baptism and Confirmation could be administered to all.[2] But this Pope relaxed the severity of the above law, and granted that the Sacrament of Penance could be administered to all, and not merely to those who were dangerously ill;[3] that the Holy Eucharist, however, could be given only to those who were dying, or dangerously sick, and that *per modum viatici*, and also to those who were in danger of death otherwise than by sickness, *v.g.*, to those *about to be engaged in battle*, or about to enter upon a dangerous sea voyage.[4]

3357. The law, therefore, as at present in force, is that the sacraments of Baptism, Penance, and Confirmation can, during a general interdict, local or personal, be administered to all persons whatever, except (*a*) to those who are the cause of the interdict, *i.e.*, those guilty of the crime for which the interdict was imposed, and their abettors, favorers, and counsellors in said crime;[5] (*b*) those who are under a special personal interdict. Holy Orders cannot be conferred upon, nor can Extreme Unction be administered to any one during the time of a general interdict, personal or local.[6] Marriage, according to the more probable opinion, can be contracted by parties, even according to the Tridentine prescription *Tametsi* (where this is in force), during a general interdict, even in the place interdicted.[7]

§ 3. *Prohibition to give or receive Ecclesiastical Burial.*

3358. By Christian or ecclesiastical burial (*sepultura*

---

[1] Cap. *Quod in te* 11. (v. 38).   [2] Arg. cap. *Quoniam* 19 (v. 11).
[3] Cap. *Alma* cit.   [4] Cap. *Quod in te* 11 (v. 38); Reiff., l. c., n. 202, 203.
[5] Cap *Alma* cit.
[6] Cap. *Quod in te* cit. This decretal was issued by Pope Innocent III. (1198-1216.)
[7] Schmalz:, l. c., n. 358.

The Ecclesiastical Interdict.

ecclesiastica) we here mean not only (*a*) the inhumation or interment in a sacred place, as the church or cemetery which is blessed, (*b*) but also the entire funeral obsequies or solemnities, namely, the tolling of bells, the bringing the remains to the church, all the prayers, religious rites, and ceremonies, such as chanting the office of the dead, celebrating Requiem Mass—which are said or performed by the ministers of the Church, either in the church or at the grave.[1]

3359. *Q.* How does an interdict deprive persons of ecclesiastical burial?

A. We must distinguish between the various kinds of interdict. 1. If the interdict is *a general local one*, all the faithful without exception, even though they be infants or insane, are forbidden to receive ecclesiastical burial, in the place interdicted.[2] We say, *in the place interdicted;* hence, any of the faithful who may die, unless he be under a special personal interdict, can be conveyed outside the interdicted place and there receive ecclesiastical burial.

3360. From the general rule just stated are exempted all ecclesiastical persons.[3] They can receive ecclesiastical burial, during a general local interdict, provided (*a*) they are not under a special personal interdict; (*b*) have not given cause to the interdict; (*c*) that the burial take place quietly, without the tolling of bells or any other religious or ecclesiastical solemnity.[4]

3361.—2. If the interdict be a *special local* one, there is no doubt that ecclesiastical burial is forbidden in the particular place, or church, or cemetery interdicted, except to

---

[1] Cap. *Quod in te* cit.; München, l. c., vol. 2, p. 212; Brabandere, Jur. Can. Comp., vol. 2, n. 774.
[2] Cap. *Quod in te* cit.; Cap. 8. in 6º (v. 7) ; Clem. *Eos* 1 (iii. 7).
[3] The words *ecclesiastical persons* are here used in their broadest sense, *i.e* , they signify not only the secular clergy, even those only in tonsure, but also religious male and female.
[4] Cap. *Quod in te* cit.

- Ecclesiastics, or at least to those Ecclesiastics who are attached to the church interdicted.

3362.—3. When the interdict is a *particular personal* one it is plain that all persons whatsoever, even though they be Ecclesiastics, who are under such an interdict, must be deprived of ecclesiastical burial, provided these persons be published by name as so interdicted, according to the Const. *Ad Vitanda* of Pope Martin V. The same holds of any person whose crime has been the cause of the interdict. For such a one is always personally interdicted, even when the interdict of which he is the cause is local only.

3363.—4. Where the interdict is personal, indeed, but *general*, *v.g.*, if all the inhabitants of a city are interdicted, Stremler [1] holds that no one is deprived of ecclesiastical burial, as, according to the Const. *Ad Vitanda* of Martin V., only those who are interdicted by name and published as such must be shunned *in divinis*, but not such as are under censure only in a general way, as is the case in a general personal interdict. Schmalzgrueber [2] and Reiffenstuel, [3] however, seem to dissent from this view, and to teach that, when the sentence of a general personal interdict is duly published, it brings all the inhabitants interdicted within the provisions of the bull of Martin V.

3364. *Note.* According to the Const. *Ad Vitanda* of Pope Martin V., which constitutes the present law of the Church on this head, in all interdicts, local or personal, the persons who are affected by the interdict are not *vitandi*, and consequently cannot be deprived of ecclesiastical burial, save when the interdict is officially made public, that is, when it is officially proclaimed by the competent ecclesiastical Superior that such a territory or place, such a people or such an individual, has been interdicted. [4]

---

[1] P. 359. [2] L.c., n. 377. [3] L. v., t. 39, n. 213.
[4] Craiss., n. 6626; Schmalzg. l.c., n. 389.

Art. VI.

Punishments incurred for violating Interdicts.

3365. *Q.* What sin do *lay persons* commit, and what punishments do they incur for violating an interdict?

A. If during the time they are under a personal interdict they presume to receive any of the *sacraments forbidden them by the interdict*, they commit a *mortal sin*, being guilty of disobedience in a grave matter. In like manner do the faithful sin grievously, if they receive the sacraments in a *place which is interdicted.* [1]

3366. By reason of *assisting at divine worship*, they commit a mortal sin in the following cases: [2] (*a*) If they compel an Ecclesiastic to celebrate publicly and solemnly in an interdicted place; (*b*) If they dare to convene the people by the sound of bells or other public announcement, in order to assist at divine worship in an interdicted place; (*c*) If they presume to hinder persons who are by name excommunicated or interdicted from leaving a church or sacred place, after being admonished by the clergy to leave; (*d*) If they themselves, being requested to leave, refuse to do so. [3] Formerly laics also incurred excommunication reserved to the Roman Pontiff, in the four cases just mentioned. [4] At present, this punishment is no longer incurred, being omitted in the Const. *Apostolicæ Sedis* of Pius IX.

3367. *Q.* What sin do *Ecclesiastics* commit, and what punishment do they incur, by violating an interdict?

A. 1. They commit a mortal sin, when they violate an interdict, local or personal, by administering or receiving the sacraments, and also by celebrating in an interdicted place. [5]

2. Moreover, Ecclesiastics who celebrate Mass or exercise any other act of a sacred *ordo* while they are under a special

---

[1] Schmalzg., l. 5. t. 39, n. 391. [2] Ib., n. 392. [3] Clem. *Gravis*, 2, de sent. excom.
[4] Clem. *Gravis* cit. [5] Schmalzg., l.c., n. 390.

personal interdict, incur *ipso facto* irregularity, on the general principle that Ecclesiastics who violate a censure become irregular. 3. But when they knowingly (*a*) celebrate divine worship or cause it to be celebrated in places which are interdicted, either by the ordinary, or the delegated judge, or by the law, (*b*) or admit persons who are excommunicated by name to divine functions (*officia divina*), or to the sacraments of the Church, or to ecclesiastical burial, they incur at the present day, according to the Const. *Apostolicæ Sedis* of Pope Pius IX. (1869), only the interdict *ab ingressu ecclesiæ*, but they do not incur irregularity,[1] as they do not violate any censure incurred by them personally.[2]

ART. VII.

What Interdicts may be imposed at the Present Day?

3368. *Q*. What interdicts are at present incurred *ipso facto*, according to the Common law of the Church?

A. We premise: As we have already explained, the Const. *Apostolicæ Sedis*, issued by the saintly Pope Pius IX., in 1869, now forms the common law of the Church in regard to correctional punishments which are inflicted by the general law of the Church and incurred *ipso facto*, and all preceding legislation contrary to it is abolished. We now answer: Two, by the Const. *Apostolicæ Sedis*, and two by the Council of Trent, as continued in force by the Const. *Apostolicæ Sedis*.[3]

3369. They are: I. "Interdictum Romano Pontifici speciali modo reservatum *ipso jure* incurrunt Universitates, Collegia, et Capitula, quocumque nomine nuncupentur, ab ordinationibus seu mandatis ejusdem Romani Pontificis pro tempore existentes ad universale futurum concilium appel-

---

[1] See Const. *Ap. Sedis* of Pius IX., Interdicta, § II.
[2] Cf. Schmalzg., l.c., n. 394.   [3] Const. *Ap. Sedis*, Interdicta, *Denique* § II.

lantia."[1] II. Scienter celebrantes vel celebrari facientes divina in locis ab ordinario, vel judice delegato, vel a jure interdictis, aut nominatim excommunicatos ad divina officia seu ecclesiasticam sepulturam admittentes, *interdictum ab ingressu ecclesiæ* ipso jure incurrunt, donec ad arbitrium ejus, cujus sententiam contempserunt, competenter satisfecerint."[2]

3370.—III. "Non liceat capitulis, sede vacante, infra annum a die vacationis, ordinandi licentiam aut litteras dimissorias ... alicui, qui beneficii ecclesiastici accepti, aut recipiendi occasione cretatus non fuerit, concedere. Si secus fiat, capitulum contraveniens subjaceat interdicto."[3] IV. "Metropolitanus, suffraganeos episcopos absentes," (ultra secundum semestre tempus), "Metropolitanum vero absentem," (ut supra) "Suffraganeus episcopus antiquior residens, *sub pœna interdicti ingressus ecclesiæ eo ipso incurrenda*, infra tres menses per litteras seu nuncium Romano Pontifici denunciare teneatur."[4] As will be seen, these four interdicts are *personal*, not local.

3371. Besides these four, the Const. *Apostolicæ Sedis* of Pius IX. retains the interdicts made in regard to the election of the Roman Pontiff and the internal regimen of religious communities, in the following manner: "Quæ vero censuræ ... *interdicti* nostris aut prædecessorum nostrorum constitutionibus, aut sacris canonibus, præter eas quas recensuimus, latæ sunt, atque hactenus in suo vigore perstiterunt, sive pro R. Pontificis electione, sive pro interno regimine quorumcumque ordinum et institutorum regularium, necnon quorumcumque collegiorum, congregationum, cœtuum, locorumque piorum, cujuscumque nominis aut generis sint, eas omnes firmas esse, et in suo robore per-

---

[1] Const. *Ap. Sedis*, Interdicta, *Denique*.§ 1.   [2] Ib.,§ 11.
[3] Conc. Trid., sess. vii., cap. 10 de Ref.
[4] Ib., sess. vi., c. 1 de Ref. ; Cf. Soglia-Vecch., vol. ii., p. 368; Avanzini, Com. in Const. *Ap. Sedis*, p. 58.

manere volumus et declaramus."[1] All other interdicts *latæ sententiæ* are therefore abolished at present.

ART. VIII.
How do Interdicts lapse?

3372. *Q.* How do interdicts lapse?

A. 1 Interdicts inflicted for a specified time or until a certain thing is done, lapse of themselves (as excommunication and suspension), when the time has expired, or the condition been fulfilled. Before the expiration of such time or the fulfilment of the condition in the case, the interdict ceases only by absolution or by pardon (*dispensatione*), which no one can give save the person who inflicted it, or his Superior.[2] 2. If it has been imposed *per modum censuræ*, and consequently without any fixed time, it lapses, as a rule, only by absolution, as suspension and excommunication would in a similar case.

3373. We say, *as a rule;* for there are some exceptions. Thus a general personal interdict lapses with regard to the entire community by the very dissolution or dismemberment of such community, and with regard to individuals, as soon as they cease to be members of this community. Thus again, a special local interdict ceases, not only by absolution but also by the destruction of the place (*v.g.*, of the church) interdicted. A general local interdict ceases only by absolution.

3374. Having shown when interdicts lapse by absolution or by pardon, it remains to be seen by whom

---

[1] Const. *Ap. Sedis* of Pius IX., Interdicta, § Quæ vero.

[2] Schmalzg., l. c., n. 398. However, Bishops are authorized by the Council of Trent (Sess. xxiv., c. 6 de Ref.) to absolve or dispense from all interdicts (also from all suspensions) arising from a crime that is secret, even though reserved to the Apostolic See, except however (*a*) that proceeding from wilful homicide (*b*) and those crimes which have already been carried before a legal tribunal.

The Ecclesiastical Interdict.

this power of pardoning or granting the absolution can be exercised. When the interdict is *local*, whether general or particular, and even though reserved, it cannot be raised or relaxed save by the ecclesiastical Superior who has episcopal jurisdiction over the place interdicted. The same holds with regard to a *general personal* interdict, since it can be raised only by a person having jurisdiction *in foro externo* over the community interdicted. Otherwise, if every Ecclesiastic could raise such an interdict, it would naturally follow that ecclesiastical discipline would be weakened, and the punishment in question might frequently be remitted against the will of the Superior by whom it was imposed.[1]

3375. But when the interdict is a *particular personal* one, and not reserved, any confessor, at least according to a probable opinion, can absolve from it in the same manner as excommunication, when not reserved, can be remitted by any confessor.[2] Of course, if the interdict in the case (a special personal one) is reserved, the absolution can be granted only by the person to whom it was reserved or by his Superior.[3]

---

[1] Schmalzg., l. 5, t. 39, n. 400.

[2] Of course, the interdict (specially personal) must be inflicted *a jure* (*i.e.*, by the general law of the Church, or by particular law); for an interdict imposed *ab homine per sent. spec.* is always reserved.

[3] Schmalzg., l. c., n. 401.

CHAPTER IV.

INTERMISSION OF DIVINE SERVICE.

(Cessatio a Divinis.)

3376. The *cessatio a divinis* is a suspension or discontinuance of divine service (*officia divina*) in a place where it can and may otherwise be held. It is not a punishment properly speaking, and consequently not a correctional punishment or censure. For while it is ordered only on occasion of most grievous offences, yet it is not inflicted precisely *in punishment* of such crime, but *as a sign of grief and pain* with which the Church is afflicted on account of a most grave injury inflicted upon her and the honor of Almighty God, and as a reparation for such injury,[1] and also in order that by this public manifestation of grief and horror the delinquent may be compelled to desist from his wicked course and make due satisfaction.[2] It is a simple prohibition upon Ecclesiastics, enjoining them not to hold divine service in a certain place or places.

3377. This discontinuance of divine service, though an imitation of the interdict, and bearing a marked resemblance to it, is yet distinct from it and differs from it in various respects. First of all, this interruption is not a censure or correctional punishment, as was seen, *but a simple prohibition.* Hence those who violate it commit, indeed, a grievous sin, but do not incur irregularity. Next, it is always *local*, never *personal*.

3378. Finally, the effects of the intermission under discus-

---

[1] Schmalzg., l. c., n 402.
[2] Ex can. *Irrefragabili* 13 de off. ord. (i. 31); Cap. 2 in 6º (i. 16); Cap. *Quamvis* 8 de off. ord. in 6º.

Intermission of Divine Service. 365

sion are more far-reaching than even those of the interdict.[1] For it is the exact observance of what was presented for the time of an interdict by the older law of the Church, as in force prior to the mitigation introduced by Pope Boniface VIII., in his famous decretal *Alma Mater*, as was seen.[2] Hence, during a *cessatio a divinis*, it is not allowed to celebrate divine service or Mass, except once a week for the renewal of the sacred species, and even then only in the most private manner possible. Nevertheless many canonists, while admitting this to be according to the letter of the law, yet think that the custom to the contrary has sufficiently authorized the application of the Cap. *Alma Mater* also to the *cessatio a divinis*[3]

3379. *Q.* What are the effects of the intermission of divine service in question?

A. Speaking in general, these three: the privation (*a*) of divine worship; (*b*) of certain sacraments; (*c*) of ecclesiastical burial.[4] Are all these effects annexed to every *cessatio a divinis*, or can the ecclesiastical judge inflict a *cessatio a divinis* in such a manner that it will produce but one or two of the above effects? The Pontiff certainly can. As to others, the question is controverted. Some affirm that every ecclesiastical judge can inflict a *partial* cessation. Others deny this, on the ground that the above effects are all annexed to a cessation by the general law of the Church,[5] which cannot be changed by the inferior.[6]

3380. We shall now briefly explain how the cessation produces each of the three above effects. We have already sufficiently set forth how divine services (*officia divina*) are to be discontinued. Next, the sacraments which, as we have seen, can be administered during an interdict, can be also given during a *cessatio*. Finally, as to the ecclesiastical

---

[1] Craiss., n. 6638.
[2] Schmalzg., l. c., n. 407.
[3] Stremler, l. c., p. 365.
[4] Cap. *Non est vobis* 11, de sponsal.
[5] Arg., cap. 11 cit.
[6] Schmalzg., l. c. n. 406.

burial, a distinction must be drawn between the solemnities or ceremonies, such as saying the office of the dead, Mass of requiem, or the other prayers usually said by the priest at the funeral—and the inhumation or interment in blessed or consecrated ground.[1] The latter is allowed during a *cessatio;* the former are forbidden, since they are *officia divina,* which are prohibited.[2]

3381. *Who can inflict a cessation?* We premise: a cessation is imposed (*a*) either by the law itself (*a jure*), and ensues *ipso facto* when a Church is polluted or execrated; (*b*) or by the proper Superior (*ab homine*). Observe, in the present article we speak only of cessation imposed *ab homine.* We now answer: It can be ordered only by one who has jurisdiction *in foro externo,* as we have seen in the case of excommunication, suspension, and interdict. Hence it can be inflicted only (*a*) by the Pope; (*b*) by Bishops and others possessed of quasi-episcopal jurisdiction; (*c*) by the Chapter, through its Vicar-Capitular *sede vacante,* (with us, by the administrator of the vacant diocese.[4])

3382. *For what kind of crimes and in what manner can the cessation be ordered?* 1. The crime must be of the *gravest character* and, as a rule, of such a nature as to inflict very serious injury upon the Church, *v. g.,* laws enacted against the liberties of the Church; taxes or contributions unjustly imposed on Ecclesiastics.[5] 2. This crime should be *notorious* by notoriety of fact, so that the scandal given by it may be remedied by the cessation. 3. The order for the cessation must be given *in writing,* setting forth the *cause* or *crime* for which it is imposed. 4. The delinquent must be first *canonically warned.*[6]

3383. *Observation.* At the present day, the intermission

---

[1] Schmalzg., l. c., n. 413.   [2] Stremler, l. c., p 365.
[3] For the acts which cause a church to be polluted, see Sabetti, Comp., n. 916, q. 2.
[4] Schmalzg., l. c., n. 414.   [5] *Glossa,* in ca. v. 2 de off. ord. in 6° (l. 16.)
[6] Schmalzg., l. c., n. 417.

of divine service or *cessatio a divinis* has almost completely fallen into disuse, as Stremler [1] says. Interdicts, in like manner, as was seen, are now inflicted much less frequently than in former times; in fact, they may be said to have gone out of use, [2] at least, so far as their former comprehensive effects are concerned. Their observance, considering the temper of our times, would be scarcely feasible, nay, would redound rather to the destruction than *the edification* of the members of the Church.

3384. Yet we flatter ourselves that our discussion of interdicts and *cessations* has not been altogether abortive and useless. For while the application of the principles underlying these measures has changed at present, yet the principles themselves are as true to-day as they were seven hundred years ago. Besides, both the interdict and the cessation may be and are sometimes inflicted at the present day, though only in a mild form.

[1] P. 366.
[2] Fessler, Excom., p. iv.; Schulte, K. K., vol. ii., p. 391; Walter, § 186, p. 371.

FINIS.

CONTENTS.

BOOK III.—ECCLESIASTICAL PUNISHMENTS,   PAGE 7

PART I.

ECCLESIASTICAL PUNISHMENTS IN GENERAL.

CHAPTER I.
True Idea of Ecclesiastical Punishment.

Art. I. Has the Church a Right to Inflict Punishments?	7
Art. II. What is a Punishment?	9
Art. III. What are Crimes?	10

CHAPTER II.
The Various Kinds of Ecclesiastical Punishments.

Art. I. Penances,	12
Art. II. Punishments,	12
§ 1. Preventive and Repressive Punishments,	13
§ 2. Reforming and Vindicative Punishments,	13
Art. III. Procedure for Inflicting Punishments,	17
Art. IV. Ordinary and Extraordinary Punishments,	21
Art. V. Punishments *ferendæ* and *latæ sententiæ*,	23
Art. VI. Temporal and Spiritual Punishments,	23

CHAPTER III.
When and by Whom Ecclesiastical Punishments can be Inflicted.

Art. I. For what Unlawful Acts can a Person be Punished?	25
Art. II. When are Persons Guilty of Unlawful Acts Freed from Punishment?	29
§ 1. Ignorance,	30

§ 2. Forgetfulness and Inadvertence, ... 35
§ 3. Violence and Fear, ... 36
Art. III. Who can Punish? 37
  § 1. Can the Bishop Exercise Contentious Jurisdiction Out of His own Diocese? 37
  § 2. Can a Bishop Exercise Voluntary Jurisdiction Outside His own Diocese? 38
  § 3. Rules which Guide the Judge, when he Inflicts Punishment, ... 41
Art. IV. Upon whom can Punishments be Inflicted? . . 44

PART II.

ECCLESIASTICAL PREVENTIVE PUNISHMENTS.

CHAPTER I.

Spiritual Exercises.

Art. I. How are Spiritual Exercises Preventive Remedies? . 47
Art. II. How are they Imposed? 49

CHAPTER II.

Canonical Admonitions.

Art. I. What are the Canonical Warnings? 55
Art. II. When can the Warnings be Given? 56
Art. III. Is it Necessary that they shall be Given in a Legal Manner? 57
Art. IV. How are they Given Paternally? 61
Art. V. How are they Given in a Legal Form? . . . 65

CHAPTER III.

The Precept.

Art. I. What is the Precept? 68
Art. II. When can it be Enjoined? 69
Art. III. How is it Given? 72

Contents. 371

PART III.

REPRESSIVE VINDICATORY PUNISHMENTS.

SECTION I.

Spiritual Vindicatory Punishments.

CHAPTER I.

Dismissal of Rectors also in the United States.

Art. I. Correct Idea of Dismissal,	77
Art. II. Dismissal of Irremovable Rectors,	79
§ 1. Dismissal of Irremovable Rectors where the General Law fully Obtains,	79
§ 2. Dismissal of Irremovable Rectors in the United States,	84
§ 3. Dismissal of Rectors who are not Irremovable,	89
§ 4. Dismissal of Rectors in English-Speaking Countries Outside of the United States,	91
I. Dismissal in England,	91
II. Dismissal in Ireland, etc.,	93
Art. III. Support of Dismissed and Suspended Ecclesiastics,	95
§ 1. Support of Dismissed Rectors,	95
§ 2. Support of Suspended Ecclesiastics,	101

CHAPTER II.

Transfers as Punishments.

Art. I. Nature and Division of Transfers,	105
Art. II. Transfer of Irremovable Rectors also in the United States,	107
Art. III. Transfer of Removable Rectors also in the United States,	110

CHAPTER III.

Dismissal Combined with Disqualification for Office.

Art. I. Character of this Punishment,	114
Art. II. Formalities—Duration,	114

CHAPTER IV.
Degradation of Ecclesiastics.
Art. I. Nature and Effects of this Punishment, . . . 116
Art. II. Manner of Inflicting It, ... 118

CHAPTER V.
Infamy as a Canonical Punishment.
Art. I. True Idea of Canonical Infamy, ... 119
Art. II. Effects of Infamy of Law or Fact, ... 122

CHAPTER VI.
Canonical Disability for Ecclesiastical Offices.
Art. I. Character of the Punishment, ... 124
Art. II. Effects of this Disability, ... 125

CHAPTER VII.
Canonical Criminal Unfitness for Orders and the Ecclesiastical State.
Art. I. Nature of this Unfitness, ... 126
Art. II. Effects of this Punishment, ... 128
   § 1. Incapacity for Orders, ... 129
   § 2. Incapacity to be appointed to Ecclesiastical Offices, . 129
   § 3. Dismissal from Ecclesiastical Offices, . . . 130
Art. III. Causes of this Disqualification, ... 131
   § 1. Criminal Causes, ... 131
   § 2. Natural Causes, ... 132
Art. IV. Does Ignorance Excuse from this Disability? . . 134
Art. V. How this Disability is Removed, ... 135

SECTION II.
Temporal and Corporal Vindicatory Punishments.
CHAPTER I.
Various Kinds of these Punishments.
Art. I. Pecuniary Fines, ... 138
Art. II. Ecclesiastical Imprisonment, ... 141
Art. III. Exile in a Mild Form, ... 142

Contents.

PART IV.

REPRESSIVE REFORMATIVE PUNISHMENTS.

SECTION I.

Reformative Punishments in General.

CHAPTER I.

Nature of these Punishments. 143

CHAPTER II.

Various Kinds of Reform Punishments.

Art. I. Reformative Punishments *a jure* and *ab homine*,	.	146
Art. II. Reform Punishments *ferendæ* and *latæ sententiæ*,	.	148
Art. III. General Remedies,	.	149

CHAPTER III.

What Persons can Inflict them?

Art. I. Who are Vested with Ordinary Power?	.	152
Art. II. Who are Vested with Delegated Power?	.	155
Art. III. Conditions of the Exercise of this Power,	.	157

CHAPTER IV.

Upon Whom can they be Imposed?

Art. I. Adult Members of the Church,	.	161
Art. II. Entire Communities,	.	162
Art. III. The Pope and Bishops,	.	164
Art. IV. Strangers and Travellers,	.	165

CHAPTER V.

For what Causes can they be Inflicted?

Art. I. Crimes which are Grave,	.	167
Art. II. They should be Preceded by the Milder Remedies,	.	170
Art. III. Incorrigibleness,	.	172
Art. IV. Crimes which are entirely of the Past,	.	173
Art. V. Future Crimes,	.	174

CHAPTER VI.

Formalities to be Observed in Inflicting them, also in the United States.

Art. I. The Canonical Admonitions and the Precept, . 178
 § 1. Necessity of the Previous Admonitions, . . 179
 § 2. The Warnings Repeated Three Times, . . . 185
Art. II. The Trial, ... 186
 § 1. The Necessity of a Trial according to the General Law, 178
 § 2. The Formalities of the Trial according to the Sacred Canons, ... 192
 § 3. The Trial according to the Instruction of June 11, 1880, 182
 § 4. The Trial in the United States according to the Instructions of 1878 and 1884, ... 193
 § 5. The Trial in other Missionary Countries, . . 194
Art. III. The Sentence, ... 196
 § 1. Weighing of the Evidence, ... 197
 § 2. Formalities of the Sentence, ... 200
 § 3. Formalities of the Sentence in the United States, . 204
 § 4. Penalties Incurred for Violating these Formalities, . 207
 § 5. Wording of the Sentence, ... 211
 § 6. Publication of the Sentence, ... 212

CHAPTER VII.

Appeals against Repressive Correctional Punishments.

Art. I. Is it Allowed to Appeal against these Punishments, . 215
Art. II. Effects of Appeals against Censures already Inflicted, 215
Art. III. Appeals against the Publication of Censures, . 220
Art. IV. Effect of Appeals against Threatened Censures, . 223
Art. V. Procedure before the Judge *ad quem in adjudicating* Appeals against Unjust Censures, . . . 226
Art. VI. Procedure before the Metropolitan in Appeals against Invalid Censures, ... 229
 § 1. Procedure when the Censure is Certainly Invalid, . 229
 § 2. Procedure when it is Doubtful whether the Censure is Invalid, ... 231

Contents. 375

§ 3. How the Metropolitan imparts the *Absolutio ad Cautelam*, ... 233
- Art. VII. Procedure before the Metropolitan in Appeals against Threatened Censures, ... 239

CHAPTER VIII.
Unjust and Invalid Correctional Punishments.

Art. I. When are Correctional Punishments Unjust and Invalid ? 242
Art. II. Effects of Correctional Punishments which are Just and Valid, ... 243
Art. III. What Effects are Produced by Unjust Censures ? . 244
Art. IV. Effects of Invalid Correctional Punishments, . 247
Art. V. Effects of Censures which are *a jure* and *latæ sententiæ*, 252

CHAPTER IX.
Punishments Incurred for Disregarding Censures.

Art. I. Irregularity as a Punishment for Violating Censures, 254
Art. II. Dismissal as a Punishment for Disregarding Censures, 257
Art. III. Other Punishments Incurred, ... 257

CHAPTER X.
Who can Release from Repressive Correctional Punishments ?

Art. I. Do these Punishments Cease of themselves ? . . 259
Art. II. Who can Release from them when they are Inflicted *a jure* and incurred *ipso facto*? 361
Art. III. Who can Remit them when they are *ab homine* ? . 265

CHAPTER XI.
Formula, Conditions, and Modes of Release from Correctional Punishments.

Art. I. Formula of Release, ... 267
Art. II. Conditions of Release, ... 268
Art. III. Modes of Release, ... 270

SECTION II.

Repressive Reform Punishments in Particular.

CHAPTER I.

Excommunication.

Art. I. Correct Notion of Excommunication, . . . 274
Art. II. How many Kinds of Excommunication are there? . 278
Art III. What Excommunicates are to be Shunned? . . 280
    § 1. Former Discipline, ... 280
    § 2. Present Discipline, ... 280
    § 3. Publication of the Excommunication, . . . 284
    § 4. Intercourse of the Faithful with *tolerati*, . . . 284
Art. IV. Canonical Effects produced by Excommunication even at Present, ... 286
    § 1. Exclusion from the Sacraments, ... 289
    § 2. Excommunicates cannot Administer the Sacraments, . 292
    § 3. Withdrawal of the *Suffragia Ecclesiæ*, . . . 295
    § 4. Excommunicates cannot Assist at the Mass or other Ecclesiastical Functions, ... 296
    § 5. Disqualification for Appointment to Ecclesiastical Offices, ... 299
    § 6. Withdrawal of the *Communicatio forensis*, . . 302
    § 7. Loss of the Rights of Jurisdiction, ... 304
    § 8. Refusal of Christian Burial. 307
    § 9. Exclusion from the Company of the Faithful in the Relations of Every-day Life, ... 309
        1. Former Discipline of the Church, . . . 309
        2. Present Discipline, ... 311
        3 In what Social Matters are the Faithful Bound to Shun a *Vitandus?* 312
        4. When is Social Intercourse Allowed with a *Vitandus?* 314
Art. V. Excommunications in force at the Present Day, . 317
    § 1. The Const. *Apostolicæ Sedis* of Pius IX., . . . 317
    § 2. Scope and General Outline of this Constitution, . 318
    § 3. Reform Punishments of the Council of Trent Retained by Pius IX., ... 319

Contents.

§ 4. Reform Punishments Regarding the Election of the Pope, and the Regimen of Religious Orders, . 322
§ 5. The Bearing of the Constitution of Pius IX. on Vindicatory Punishments, ... 324
§ 6. How Correctional Punishments are reserved in this Constitution, ... 325

CHAPTER III.

Suspension.

Art. I. True Idea of this Punishment, ... 327
Art. II. Various Kinds of Suspension, ... 330
Art. III. Effects of this Punishment, ... 331
Art. IV. Punishments Incurred for Violating Suspensions, . 335
Art. V. Formalities in Inflicting Suspensions, . . . 338
Art. VI. Release from Suspensions, ... 340
Art. VII. Suspensions *a jure* and *latæ sent.* in force at present, 340

CHAPTER III.

The Ecclesiastical Interdict.

Art. I. Correct Notion of the Interdict, ... 345
Art. II. Various Kinds of Interdicts, ... 347
Art. III. By Whom and for what Cause can they be Imposed, 352
Art. IV. Formalities in Inflicting the Interdict, . . . 353
Art. V. Effects of the Interdict, ... 354
§ 1. Prohibition to Celebrate or Assist at Divine Service, 354
§ 2. Privation of the Active and Passive use of Certain Sacraments, ... 355
§ 3. Prohibition to Give or Receive Ecclesiastical Burial, 356
Art. VI. Punishments Incurred for Violating Interdicts, . . 359
Art. VII. What Interdicts may be Imposed at the Present Day? 360
Art. VIII. How do Interdicts Lapse? 362

CHAPTER IV.

Intermission of Divine Service.

Art. I. Nature of this Punishment, ... 364
Art. II. Its Causes and Effects, ... 365

ALPHABETICAL INDEX.

(The figures indicate the marginal numbers, not the pages.)

A

Admonitions, paternal, 1754; legal, 1759, 1784; obligation, 2047.
Ad Nutum, 1901.
Ad Vitanda, Const., Martin V., 3175.
Appeals, 3028; against censures, 3029; before censure, 3046; after censure, 3030; in temporal effects of censures, 3031; procedure, 3051.
Appeal ex Capite Nullitatis, 3071.
Apostolicæ Sedis, Const., of Pius IX., aim 3263; outline, 3264; censures, 3265; Council of Trent, 3266; Election of Pope, 3273; religious orders, 3274; Vindicatory and reform punishments, 3277 sq.

B

Benedict XIV., Const. ad Militantis, 3037, 3048.
Bishop, power to punish, 1720, sq.
Burial, Christian, 3236.

C

Causæ Criminales, 1677.
Causæ Disciplinares, 1678.
Causæ Matrimoniales, 1994.
Canonical Proof, 2089.
Censures, just, 3055; unjust, 3056, 3089; doubtful, 3057.
Church, right to punish, 1658.
Christian Burial, 3236; refusal, 8237; excommunicates, 3238.
Coercive Power, 1984; of Pope, 1986; of Bishops, 1987; of Metropolitans, 1987; of Vicars-General, 1990; of Religious Superiors, 1991; of Plenary and Provincial Councils, 1992; of Rectors, 1992; of Delegates, 1993.
Correctional Punishments, 3088; just and unjust, 3089; valid and invalid, 3090.
Costs, of trial, 2095.
Crime, 1663; different from sin, 1664.
Cum Magnopere, Instr. S. C. de Prop. Fide, 1672, 1677, 1687, 1696, 1729, 1745, 1755, 1763 sq.

D

Degradation, 1905; verbal and real, 1907; causes, 1909; form, 1910.
Deposition, 1902; form, 1903; duration, 1903.
Disabilities for ecclesiastical offices, 1922, 3216.
Dismissal from office, 1807, 1808.
Dismissal of irremovable rectors, 1815; causes, 1816; form, 1825; ipso jure, 1825; in the United States, 1827; in England, 1853; in Ireland, 1856.

Alphabetical Index. 379

Dismissal of removable rectors, 1841; decision S. C. de Prop. Fide of March 28th, 1887, 1844; causes, 1843; form, 1842; in England, 1854.
Disqualification for Ecclesiastical Offices, 1923; nature, 1922; effects, 1924.
Disqualification for orders, 1925 sq.

E

Excommunication, 3160; true idea, 3167; kinds, 3170; effects, 3186; publication, 3181.
Excommunicates, to be shunned, 3173; tolerated, 3182; social intercourse, 3243 sq.
Excommunicatus vitandus, 3200.
Excommunicatus toleratus, 3201.
Ex capite nullitatis, 3068; appeal, 3071.
Ex Inf. Conscientia, 2042.
External forum, 2043.

F

Fear, exempts from punishment, 1716.
Fines, pecuniary, 1955.
Forgetfulness, 1715.
Forum externum, trial, 2086, 2087, 3038.
Forum internum, 2043; trial, 1085, 2085.
Formalities, of trials, 2078; of sentences, 3005; obligation, 3012; violation, 3016.

I

Ignorance, 1702, sq.
Imprisonment, ecclesiastical, 1963; in the United States, 1964.
Inadvertence, 1715.
Incorrigibleness, 2030.

Infamy, 1913; of law and fact, 1914; causes, 1916; per sententiam, 1919; ipso jure, 1916; effects, 1920 sq.
Inhabilitas, 1922.
Instruction of the S. C. de Prop. Fide of 1878, 1677, 1681.
Irregularity, 1925; causes, 1928; effects, 1931; crimes, 1936; natural defects, 1939; ignorance, 1943.
Irregularitas, release, 1946; in the United States, 1953.
Irregulares, 1926.

J

Judge ad quem, 3051; appeals, 3051, 3052.
Jurisdiction, 1719; contentious, 1720, 1724; voluntary, 1722; ordinary, 1726; delegated, 1726; loss, 3228.

L

Legal Admonitions, 1785.

M

Maynooth, synod of, 1856.
Metropolitan, 3022; in appeals, 3055, 3059.
Monitio Canonica, 1971, 2031.

O

Oath in England and Ireland, 1858.
Orders, 1925; disqualifications, 1926.

P

Pius IX., Const. Apostolicæ Sedis, 3262.
Penance, 1665.
Pecuniary Fines, 1955; in the United States, 1962.
Præceptum, 1771, 1789; extrinsic form, 1797.

Preventive Remedies, 1666, 1737.
Privatio Definitiva, 1808.
Punishments, repressive, 1656; preventive, 1666; vindicatory, 1656; ordinary, 1685; discretionary, 1688; ferendæ and latæ sententiæ, 1686; temporal and spiritual, 1689.
Publication, of sentence, 3021; of censure, 3022; aim, 3023; mode, 3024; appeal, 3027, 3040.

R

Reformative remedies, 1966; character, 1968; duration, 1981; gradation, 2026.
Release from censures, 3124; power, 3124; conditions, 3148; form, 3144; kinds, 3152.
Release ad Cautelam, 3069–3078.
Remedies, preventive, 1730; reformative, 1730.

S

Sentence, personal motives, 2094; form, 2096-3004; in the United States, 3005-3011; wording, 3019; publication, 3021.
Spiritual Exercises, 1742.
Strangers, punishable, 2018.
Suffrages of the Church, 3208.
Summaria facti Cognitio, 1747, 1750.
Support, of dismissed Ecclesiastics, 1859; suspended, 1874; source, 1879.

Suspension, 3282; nature, 3286; kinds, 3291; ab officio, 3294; a beneficio, 3295; effects, 3296; publication, 3300; violation, 3307.
Suspensive appeal, 3046, 3051.

T

Third Plenary Council of Baltimore, 1676, 1740, 1773, 1861, 1878, 2055 sq.
Transfers, 1882; kinds, 1883; causes, 1884; form, 1884.
Transfer of irremovable rectors, 1885; causes, 1887; form, 1890; trial, 1894 sq.
Transfer of removable rectors, 1895; decision S. C. de Prop. Fide, 1895; causes, 1896; to an inferior place, 1897; for merit or demerit, 1898.
Travellers, punishable, 2015 sq.
Trial, ecclesiastical, 1825, 2065; obligation, 2067; form, 2078–2080; in the United States, 2081; in Ireland and England, 2083.

U

Unjust Censures, 3093.

V

Vindicatory Punishments, 1805 sq.
Violation of censures, 3117; penalties, 3119 sq.
Violence, 1716.

W

Warnings, canonical, 1674, 1697; necessity, 2047; three, 2054, 2061.

www.ingramcontent.com/pod-product-compliance
Lightning Source LLC
Chambersburg PA
CBHW030403230426
43664CB00007BB/723